BUDDHISM IN FAR EAST ASIA

Buddhism in Far East Asia

Dr Arvind Kumar Singh

MD Publications Pvt Ltd
New Delhi
www.mdppl.com

Published by :

MD Publications Pvt Ltd
'MD House', 11, Darya Ganj
New Delhi - 110 002
Phone : +91-11-41563325 (Customer Service)
+91-11-41562846 (Editorial)
E-mail (orders): contact@mdppl.com
Website: www.mdppl.com

ISBN : 978-81-7533-165-5

Published and Printed by Mrs. Rajni Gupta on behalf of **MD Publications Pvt Ltd** at Times Press, New Delhi.

CONTENTS

PREFACE

Buddhism is one of the oldest religions in the world. It is a path of practice and spiritual development leading to insight into the true nature of life. Buddhist practices such as meditation are means of changing oneself in order to develop the qualities of awareness, kindness, and wisdom. The experience developed within the Buddhist tradition over thousands of years has created an incomparable resource for all those who wish to follow a path — a path which ultimately culminates in Enlightenment.

The basic tenets of Buddhist teaching are straightforward and practical: nothing is fixed or permanent; actions have consequences; change is possible. Thus Buddhism addresses itself to all people irrespective of race, nationality, or gender. It teaches practical methods (such as meditation) which enable people to realize and utilize its teachings in order to transform their experience, to be fully responsible for their lives and to develop the qualities of Wisdom and Compassion. There are millions of Buddhists in the world today and their numbers are growing with every passing day. Different people follow different paths, but all traditions are characterized by non-violence, lack of dogma, tolerance of differences, and, usually, by the practice of meditation.

Japan, China, Korea, Mongolia are some of the main Far East Asian countries where Buddhism is a main religion. Though Buddhism has very little presence in Russia and other neighbouring countries, but Japan, Korea and Mongolia have a large number of Buddhist population. This book tries to cover the various aspects of Buddhism in this part of the world which has a sizable population of Buddhists.

I am very grateful to Mr. Pranav Gupta, Director, MD Publications Pvt Ltd, New Delhi who readily expressed acceptance and supported me fully for completing this book.

Dr Arvind Kumar Singh

Chapter - 1

FAR EAST ASIA
AN INTRODUCTION

The Far East is a term often used by people in the Western world to refer to the countries of East Asia. The term is often expanded to also include Southeast Asia and South Asia, for cultural reasons, for example because Buddhism is common to East Asia, Southeast Asia and South Asia. It is often considered a Eurocentric term that nevertheless retains frequent popular usage. "Far East" came because from Europe the Eastern Asia is the "farthest" of the three "easts" (the others being Near East and Middle East) literally near the Pacific Ocean. For the same reason, ancient Chinese people called western country "Taixi" i.e. anything further west than India.

The term Far East was popularized in the English language during the period of the British Empire as a blanket term for lands to the east of British India. Prior to World War I, the Near East referred to relatively nearby lands of the Ottoman Empire, Middle East to northwestern South Asia and Central Asia, and Far East for countries along the western Pacific Ocean and countries along the eastern Indian Ocean. Many European languages have analogous terms, such as the French *Extrême-Orient*, Spanish *Extremo Oriente*, Portuguese *Extremo Oriente*, German *Ferner Osten*, Italian *Estremo Oriente*, Polish *Daleki Wschód*, and Dutch *Verre Oosten*.

Significantly, the term evokes cultural as well as geographic separation; the Far East is not just geographically distant, but also culturally exotic. It never refers, for instance, to the culturally Western nations of Australia and New Zealand, which lie even farther to the east of Europe than East Asia itself. This combination of cultural and geographic subjectivism was well illustrated in 1939 by the Prime Minister of Australia, R. G Menzies. Reflecting upon his country's geopolitical concerns with the onset of war, Menzies commented that:" The problems of the Pacific are different. What Great Britain calls the Far East is to us the near north."

Far East in its usual sense is comparable to terms such as the Orient *which* means East; the Eastern world; or simply the East. South East Asia and the Russian Far East might now be included in the Far East to some extent due to recent Chinese migration to Russia, and the Korean Diaspora in Russia.

East Asia is a sub region of Asia that can be defined in either geographical or cultural terms. Geographically, it covers about 12,000,000 km^2, or about 28 percent of the Asian continent, about 15 percent bigger than the area of Europe. More than 1.5 billion people, about 40 percent of the population of Asia or a quarter of all the people in the world, live in geographic East Asia, which is about twice the population of Europe. The region is one of the world's most populated places, with the population density of East Asia, 131 per km^2, being about three times the world average of 45 per km^2.

Historically, many societies in East Asia have been part of the Chinese cultural sphere, and East Asian vocabulary and scripts are often derived from Classical Chinese and Chinese script. Major religions include Buddhism (mostly Mahayana), Confucianism or Neo-Confucianism, Taoism, and Chinese folk religion, and Shinto in Japan. East Asian calendars are often derived from Chinese calendar.

This combination of language, political philosophy, and religion (as well as art, architecture, holidays and festivals, etc.) overlaps with the geographical designation of East Asia for the most part, with a few exceptions, such as the overseas Chinese (including those in Singapore, Malaysia, Vietnam, and the West).

East Asia and Eastern Asia (the latter form preferred by the United Nations) are both more modern terms for the traditional name the Far East which describes the region's geographical position in relation to Europe rather than its location within Asia. However, in contrast to the United Nations definition, East Asia commonly is used to refer to the eastern part of Asia, as the term implies.

In many circumstances, the term East Asia is purposefully used to include all countries in Southeast Asia, especially when used in dualism with the term West Asia, the latter of which is then used to include those regions commonly considered West Asia, Central Asia and Southwest Asia.

Recently, East Asia has increasingly and commonly been described as a wide geographical area covering ten countries in ASEAN, P.R.China, Japan, South Korea, and the Republic of China (Taiwan) as part of economic and political regionalism and integration. The tendency of this usage, perhaps, started especially since the publication of World Bank on The East Asian Miracle in 1993 explaining the economic success of the Asian Tiger and emerging Southeast Asian economies (Indonesia, Malaysia, and Thailand). In addition, this usage has also been driven by Asia-wide economic interconnectedness since the cooperation between ASEAN and its three dialogue partners was institutionalized under the ASEAN Plus Three Process (ASEAN+3 or APT) in 1997. The idea of East Asian Community arising from ASEAN+3 frameworks is also gradually shaping the term East Asia to cover more than greater China, Korea, and Japan. Therefore, the term Northeast Asia is generally used to avoid confusion if only the greater China area, the Korean Peninsula, and Japan are specifically referred to, while Southeast Asia covers ten ASEAN countries.

CHINA

Ancient China was one of the earliest centers of human civilization. Chinese Civilization was also one of the few to invent writing independently, the others being Mesopotamia, the Indus Valley Civilization, the Mayan Civilization the Minoan Civilization of ancient Greece, and Ancient Egypt.

Archaeological evidence suggests that the earliest humans in China date from 2.24 million to 250,000 years ago. A cave in Zhoukoudian (near present-day Beijing) has fossils dated at somewhere between 300,000 to 550,000 years. The fossils are of Peking man, an example of Homo erectus who used fire.

The earliest evidence of a fully modern human in China comes from Liujiang County, Guangxi, where a cranium has been found and dated to approximately 67,000 years ago. Although much controversy persists over the dating of the Liujiang remains, a partial skeleton from Minatogawa in Okinawa, Japan has been dated to 18,250 ± 650 to 16,600 ± 300 years ago, so modern humans must have reached China before that time.

On 1 January 1912, the Republic of China was established, heralding the end of the Qing Dynasty. Sun Yat sen of the Kuomintang (the KMT or Nationalist Party) was proclaimed provisional president of the republic. However, the presidency was later given to Yuan Shikai, a former Qing general, who had ensured the defection of the entire Beiyang Army from the Qing Empire to the revolution. In 1915, Yuan proclaimed himself Emperor of China but was forced to abdicate and return the state to a republic when he realized it was an unpopular move, not only with the population but also with his own Beiyang Army and its commanders.

The Sino-Japanese War of 1937–1945 (part of World War II) forced an uneasy alliance between the Nationalists and the Communists as well as causing around 10 million Chinese civilian deaths. With the surrender of Japan in 1945, China emerged victorious but financially drained. The continued distrust between the Nationalists and the Communists led to the resumption of the Chinese Civil War. In 1947, constitutional rule was established, but because of the ongoing Civil War many provisions of the ROC constitution were never implemented on the mainland.

Today, mainland China is administered by the People's Republic of China—a one-party state under the leadership of the Chinese Communist Party—while the island of Taiwan and surrounding islands are administered by the Republic of China—a democratic multi-party state. After the founding of the People's Republic in 1949, both states claimed to be the sole legitimate ruler of all of "China". After the Kuomintang retreat to Taiwan in 1949, the Republic of China had maintained official diplomatic relations with most states around the world, but by the 1970s, a shift had occurred in international diplomatic circles and the People's Republic of China gained the upper hand in international diplomatic relations and recognition count. In 1971, under resolution 2758, the representatives of Chiang Kai shek to the United Nations were expelled from the intergovernmental organization. With the expulsion of the Chiang Kai-shek's representatives, and effectively the Republic of China, the representatives of the People's Republic of China were invited to assume China's seat on the UN Security Council, the UN General Assembly and other United Nations councils and agencies. Later attempts by the Republic of China to rejoin the UN have either been blocked by the People's Republic of China, which has veto power on the UN Security Council, or rejected by the United Nations Secretariat or a United Nations General Assembly committee responsible for the General Assembly's agenda.

JAPAN

The English word *Japan* is an exonym. The Japanese names for Japan are *Nippon* and *Nihon*. They are both written in Japanese using the kanji. The Japanese name *Nippon* is used for most official purposes, including on Japanese money, postage stamps, and for many international sporting events. *Nihon* is a more casual term and the most frequently used in contemporary speech. Both *Nippon* and *Nihon* literally mean "the sun's origin" and are often translated as the *Land of the Rising Sun*. This nomenclature comes from Imperial correspondence with Chinese Sui Dynasty and refers to Japan's eastward position relative to China. Before Japan had relations with China, it was known as *Yamato* and *Hi no moto*, which means "source of the sun".

The English word for Japan came to the West from early trade routes. The early Mandarin or possibly Wu Chinese word for Japan was recorded by Marco Polo as *Cipangu*. In modern Shanghainese, a Wu dialect, the pronunciation of characters 'Japan' is *Zeppen*; in Wu, the character has two pronunciations, informal and formal. (In some southern Wu dialects is pronounced, similar to its pronunciation in Japanese.) The old Malay word for Japan, *Jepang* (now spelled *Jepun* in Malaysia, though still spelled *Jepang* in Indonesia), was borrowed from a Chinese language, and this Malay word was encountered by Portuguese traders in Malacca in the 16th century. It is thought the Portuguese traders were the first to bring the word to Europe. It was first recorded in English in a 1565 letter spelled *Giapan*; (further details).

Japan is an island country in East Asia. Located in the Pacific Ocean, it lies to the east of the Sea of Japan, People's Republic of China, North Korea, South Korea and Russia, stretching from the Sea of Okhotsk in the north to the East China Sea and Taiwan in the south. The characters which make up Japan's name mean "sun-origin country", which is why Japan is sometimes identified as the "Land of the Rising Sun".

Japan comprises over 3,000 islands making it an archipelago. The largest islands are Honshû, Hokkaidô, Kyûshû and Shikoku, together accounting for 97% of Japan's land area. Most of the islands are mountainous, many volcanic; for example, Japan's highest peak, Mount Fuji, is a volcano. Japan has the world's tenth largest population, with about 128 million people. The Greater Tokyo Area, which includes the *de facto* capital city of Tokyo and several surrounding prefectures, is the largest metropolitan area in the world, with over 30 million residents.

Archaeological research indicates that people were living on the islands of Japan as early as the Upper Paleolithic period. The first written mention of Japan begins with brief appearances in Chinese history texts from the first century A.D. Influence from the outside world followed by long periods of isolation has characterized Japan's history. Since adopting its constitution in 1947, Japan has maintained a unitary constitutional monarchy with an emperor and an elected parliament, the Diet.

Japan is a constitutional monarchy where the power of the Emperor is very limited. As a ceremonial figurehead, he is defined by the constitution as "the symbol of the state and of the unity of the people". Power is held chiefly by the Prime Minister of Japan and other elected members of the Diet, while sovereignty is vested in the Japanese people. The Emperor effectively acts as the Head of state on diplomatic occasions. Akihito is the current Emperor of Japan. Naruhito, Crown Prince of Japan, stands as next in line to the throne.

Japan's legislative organ is the National Diet, a bicameral parliament. The Diet consists of a House of Representatives, containing 480 seats, elected by popular vote every four years or when dissolved and a House of Councilors of 242 seats, whose popularly elected members serve six year terms. There is universal suffrage for adults over 20 years of age with a secret ballot for all elective offices. The liberal conservative Liberal Democratic Party (LDP) has been in power since 1955, except for a short-lived coalition government formed from opposition parties in 1993. The largest opposition party is the social liberal Democratic Party of Japan.

KOREA

The name "Korea" derives from the Goryeo period of Korean history, which in turn referred to the ancient kingdom of Goguryeo. Merchants of the Middle East called it *Cauli* (from the Chinese pronunciation), which then came to be spelled Corea and Korea. Korea is now commonly used in English contexts by both North and South Korea.

In the Korean language, Korea as a whole is referred to as *Han guk (abbreviation of Dae Han Min Guk)* in South Korea, and *ChosOn* in North Korea. "The Land of the Morning Calm" is an English language nickname loosely derived from the hanja characters for Joseon, the name derived from the Joseon Dynasty and the earlier Gojoseon. (Choson and Joseon are two Romanizations of the same name.)

According to *Samguk Yusa*, the history of Korea began with the founding of Gojoseon in 2333 BC by the legendary Dangun. Limited linguistic evidence suggests probable Altaic origins of these people, whose northern Mongolian steppe culture absorbed migration and trade with the peoples of Manchuria and China. The adoption of the

Chinese writing system ("Hanja" in Korean) in the 2nd century BC, and Buddhism in the 4th century AD had profound effects on the Three Kingdoms of Korea. Baekje later passed on a modified version of these cultural advances to Japan.

Korea is a geographic area composed of two sovereign countries, a civilization, and a former state situated on the Korean Peninsula in East Asia. It borders China to the north and west, and Russia to the east, with Mongolia situated farther to the northwest, and Japan to the east. The Korean Peninsula is divided into two separate states, North Korea and South Korea. Before the division of the two states, the country was called Chosun/Joseon. South Korea is now called Hanguk while officially called Dae Han Min Guk. North Korean is called Bukhan or Joseon literally means "North of Han (guk), as in North of S.Korea").

In 1945, the Soviet Union and the United States agreed on the surrender and disarming of Japanese troops in Korea; the Soviet Union accepting the surrender of Japanese weaponry north of the 38th parallel and the United States taking the surrender south of it. This minor decision by allied armies soon became the basis for the division of Korea by the two superpowers, exacerbated by their inability to agree on the terms of Korean independence. The two Cold War rivals then established governments sympathetic to their own ideologies, leading to Korea's current division into two political entities: North Korea and South Korea.

With the defeat of Japan in 1945 the United Nations developed plans for a trusteeship administration, the Soviet Union administering the peninsula north of the 38th parallel and the United States administering the south. The politics of the Cold War resulted in the 1948 establishment of two separate governments, North Korea and South Korea.

In June 1950 North Korea invaded the South, using Soviet tanks and weaponry. During the Korean War (1950-1953) millions of civilians died and the three years of fighting throughout the nation effectively destroyed most cities. Around 125,000 POWs were captured and held by the Americans and South Koreans on Geojedo (an island in the South). The war ended in a ceasefire agreement at approximately the Military Demarcation Line (Korea).

MONGOLIA

Mongolia literally (*Mongol country/nation*) is a landlocked country in East and Central Asia. It borders Russia to the north and People's Republic of China to the south, east and west. Although Mongolia does not share a border with Kazakhstan, its western-most point is only a few miles from Kazakhstan's eastern tip. Ulan Bator, the capital and largest city, is home to about 38% of the population. Mongolia's political system is a parliamentary republic.

With the fall of the Qing Dynasty, Mongolia declared independence in 1911. The new country's territory was approximately that of the former Outer Mongolia. The 49 hoshuns of Inner Mongolia as well as the Mongolians of the Alashan and Qinghai regions expressed their willingness to join the nascent state, to no avail. In 1919, after the October Revolution in Russia, Chinese troops led by Xu Shuzheng occupied the capital but their dominance was short-lived. The notorious Russian adventurer "Bloody" Baron Ungern who had fought with the "Whites" against the Red Army in Siberia, led his troops into Mongolia, triumphing over Chinese in Niislel Khüree. He ruled briefly, under the blessing of religious leader Boghda Khaan before he was captured and executed by the Red Army assisted by Mongolian units led by Damdin Sükhbaatar. These events led to abolition of the feudal system and ensured the country's political alignment with Bolshevik Russia.

Mongolia is a parliamentary republic. The parliament is elected by the people and in turn elects the government. The president is elected directly. Mongolia's constitution guarantees full freedom of expression, religion, and others. Mongolia has a number of political parties, the biggest ones being the Mongolian People's Revolutionary Party (MPRP) and the Democratic Party (DP).

Mongolia uses a unicameral parliamentary system in which the president has a symbolic role and the government chosen by the legislature exercises executive power. The legislative arm, the State Great Khural, has one chamber with 76 seats and is chaired by the speaker of the house. It elects its members every four years by general elections. The State Great Khural is powerful in the Mongolian government with the president being largely symbolic and the prime minister being confirmed from the parliament.

TAIWAN

Taiwan is an island in East Asia. "Taiwan" is also commonly used to refer to the territories governed by the Republic of China (ROC) and to ROC itself, which governs the island of Taiwan, Orchid Island and Green Island in the Pacific off the Taiwan coast, the Penghu islands in the Taiwan Strait, and Kinmen and the Matsu Islands off the coast of mainland Fujian Province. The Kuomintang (KMT) party lost its control of mainland China to Chinese Communist Party in the Chinese Civil war and moved its government to the island of Taiwan in 1949 which it had acquired control of from Japan in 1945. Taiwan has since been controlled by the Republic of China although the People's Republic of China (PRC) has maintained that the PRC is the legitimate government of Taiwan. The island groups of Taiwan and Penghu (except the municipalities of Taipei and Kaohsiung) are officially administered as Taiwan Province of the ROC. However, in practice, almost all government power is exercised at the national and local (city/county) levels.

Taiwan is claimed by the People's Republic of China (PRC) although the PRC has never controlled Taiwan or any of the current ROC territory commonly referred to as "Taiwan". The PRC claims that Taiwan has been a part of China for hundreds of years, and was returned by Japan to China in 1945 after fifty years of Japanese occupation of Taiwan since 1895. According to the PRC, the KMT was the *de facto* government of Republic of China and that the PRC is the successor of the ROC and is therefore entitled to all ROC holdings, including Taiwan.

HONG KONG

Hong Kong, officially the Hong Kong Special Administrative Region, is a territory located on China's south coast on the Pearl River Delta, bordering Guangdong province to the north and facing the South China Sea to the east, west and south. It has a population of 6.9 million people, and is one of the most densely populated areas in the world.

The English language name "Hong Kong" is an approximate phonetic rendering of the Cantonese or Hakka name meaning "fragrant harbour" or "incense harbour".

The original "fragrant harbour" was a small inlet between the island of Ap Lei Chau and the south side of Hong Kong Island, now known as Aberdeen Harbour in English, but still called "Heung Gong Tsai" (Little Hong Kong) in Cantonese. The fragrance came from incense grown to the north of Kowloon that was stored around Aberdeen Harbour for export, before the development of Victoria Harbour. The village of Heung Gong Tsuen on Ap Lei Chau is perhaps the earliest recorded use of the name.

Beginning as a trading port, Hong Kong became a dependent territory of the United Kingdom in 1842, and remained so until the transfer of its sovereignty to the People's Republic of China in 1997. Along with Macau, Hong Kong is one of two special administrative regions and is not considered part of mainland China. Under the "one country, two systems" policy, Hong Kong has a high degree of autonomy, is largely self-governing, and maintains a highly capitalist economy.

Renowned for its expansive skyline and natural setting, Hong Kong is one of the world's leading financial capitals and a major business and cultural hub. Its identity as a cosmopolitan centre where east meets west is reflected in its cuisine, cinema, music and traditions, and although the population is predominantly Chinese, residents and expatriates of other ethnicities form a small but significant segment of society.

RUSSIAN FEDERATION

Russia or the Russian Federation (Rossiyskaya Federatsiya) is a transcontinental country extending over much of northern Eurasia. It is a semi-presidential republic comprising 83 federal subjects. Russia shares land borders with the following countries (counterclockwise from northwest to southeast): Norway, Finland, Estonia, Latvia, Lithuania (via Kaliningrad Oblast), Poland (via Kaliningrad Oblast), Belarus, Ukraine, Georgia, Azerbaijan, Kazakhstan, China, Mongolia and North Korea, and is also close to the United States (Alaska) and Japan. It borders the Arctic Ocean, the Pacific Ocean, the Caspian Sea, the Baltic Sea, and the Black Sea.

The Russian Federation stretches across a large extent of the north of the super-continent of Eurasia. Because of its size, Russia displays both monotony and diversity. As with its topography, its climates, vegetation, and soils span vast distances. From north to south the East European Plain is clad sequentially in tundra, coniferous forest (taiga), mixed and broad-leaf forests, grassland (steppe), and semi-desert (fringing the Caspian

Sea) as the changes in vegetation reflect the changes in climate. Siberia supports a similar sequence but is taiga. The country contains 23 World Heritage Sites and 40 UNESCO Biosphere reserves.

Chapter - 2

Buddhism in Far East Asia

The history of Buddhism spans the 6th century BCE to the present, starting with the birth of the Buddha Siddhartha Gautama. This makes it one of the oldest religions practiced today. Starting in India, the religion evolved as it spread through Central Asia, East Asia, and Southeast Asia. At one time or another it affected most of the Asian continent. The history of Buddhism is also characterized by the development of numerous movements and schisms, foremost among them where the Theravada, Mahâyâna and Vajrayana traditions, with contrasting periods of expansion and retreat.

Buddhism is both a world religion and a philosophy with between 230 and 500 million adherents worldwide. It is based on the teachings of Buddha Shakyamuni, sometimes known simply as "the Buddha", (Siddhârtha Gautama) who lived c. 5th century BCE in ancient India, in parts of what is now Nepal and the Indian states of Uttar Pradesh and Bihar.

Buddhism has spread through two main traditions; Theravada which extended south and east and now has widespread following in Southeast Asia, and Mahayana, which diffused first west, then north and later east throughout East Asia. Both traditions have since spread throughout the world. There are considerable differences between the various existing traditions regarding their canon of authentic scriptures, their emphasis on specific parts of what they respectively consider the Buddha's teachings and their subsequent interpretations as well as in the practices they consider most beneficial.

THE GREAT DEPARTURE

According to the Buddhist tradition, the historical Buddha Siddhartha Gautama was born to the Shakya clan, at the beginning of the Magadha period (546–324 BCE), in the plains of Lumbini in Ancient India. He is also known as the *Shakyamuni* (literally "The sage of the Shakya clan"). After an early life of luxury under the protection of his father, Suddhodana, the ruler of Kapilavastu (later to be incorporated into the state of Magadha), Siddhartha entered into contact with the realities of the world and concluded that life was inescapably bound up with suffering and sorrow. Siddhartha renounced his meaningless life of luxury to become an ascetic. He ultimately decided that asceticism couldn't end suffering, and instead chose a middle way, a path of moderation away from the extremes of self-indulgence and self-mortification.

At the age of 29, Siddhartha left his palace in order to meet his subjects. Despite his father's effort to remove the sick, aged and suffering from the public view, Siddhartha was said to have seen an old man. Disturbed by this, when told that all people would eventually grow old by his charioteer Channa, the prince went on further trips where he encountered, variously, a diseased man, a decaying corpse, and an ascetic. Deeply depressed by these sights, he sought to overcome old age, illness, and death by living the life of an ascetic.

He became a wandering ascetic, practiced yogic disciplines and meditation, studied with various teachers, and attained high states of consciousness; but still he did not find the answer to his question. He practiced severe forms of asceticism, almost to the point of death by starvation, all without gain. Finally he sat under a bodhi tree, determined not to rise from meditation until he had gained the insight he sought. Not long after, he attained enlightenment; he became the Buddha — the Awakened One. He had ascended through various stages of meditative awareness, he had seen all of his past lives, and he had seen directly into reality, into the nature of existence and the causes of suffering and rebirth. He pondered whether to try to teach these insights, so subtle and difficult to grasp to others; perhaps it would be futile. But finally he decided that at least some of the people would be able to understand; perhaps more importantly, they could be shown the path to arrive at these insights themselves. He gave his first sermon to a few disciples in the Deer park at Benares, and then continued to wander and teach for the next forty-five years, until his death at the age of eighty.

He was born in the 6th century BCE, a time of great turmoil and political change in India; many were unsatisfied with the Vedic religion, and new teachings had emerged, among them the Upanishads. The Buddha stood largely outside the Vedic tradition, criticizing many of its central teachings. Nevertheless, he had been influenced by that tradition and his teachings in turn would have a profound effect on later teachers in the Hindu tradition, such as Shankara; even in such Hindu classics as the Bhagavad Gita, some reaction can be seen to Buddhist teachings. But later centuries would see the Buddha's influence wane in India and instead spread to other Asian countries. Today Buddhism has spread throughout the world. Various sects have arisen as later teachers have reinterpreted and expounded upon the Buddha's basic teachings. Buddhism may be considered a religion, a philosophy, a way of life, or all three; here we will deal mainly with Buddhism as a philosophical system.

For the remaining 45 years of his life, the Buddha is said to have traveled in the Gangetic Plain, in what is now Uttar Pradesh, Bihar and southern Nepal, teaching his doctrine and discipline to an extremely diverse range of people— from nobles to outcaste street sweepers, mass murderers such as Angulimala and cannibals such as Alavaka.

This extended to many adherents of rival philosophies and religions. The Buddha founded the community of Buddhist monks and nuns (the *Sangha*) to continue the dispensation after his Parinirvâna (Pâli: Parinibbâna) or "complete Nirvâna", and made thousands of converts. His religion was open to all races and classes and had no caste structure. He was also subject to attack from opposition religious groups, including attempted murders and framings.

The Buddha intended his philosophy to be a practical one, aimed at the happiness of all creatures. While he outlined his metaphysics, he did not expect anyone to accept this on faith but rather to verify the insights for themselves; his emphasis was always on seeing clearly and understanding. To achieve this, however, requires a disciplined life and a clear commitment to liberation; the Buddha laid out a clear path to the goal and also observations on how to live life wisely. The core of this teaching is contained in the Noble Eightfold Path, which covers the three essential areas of Buddhist practice: ethical conduct, mental discipline ('concentration; or 'meditation'), and wisdom. The goals are to cultivate both wisdom and compassion; then these qualities together will enable one ultimately to attain enlightenment.

The following points are the fundamentals of Buddha's teachings:

- The Four Noble Truths: that suffering is an inherent part of existence; that the origin of suffering is ignorance and the main symptoms of that ignorance are attachment and craving; that attachment and craving can be ceased; and that following the Noble Eightfold Path will lead to the cessation of attachment and craving and therefore suffering.
- The Noble Eightfold Path: right understanding, right thought, right speech, right action, right livelihood, right effort, right mindfulness, and right concentration.
- Dependent origination: that any phenomenon 'exists' only because of the 'existence' of other phenomena in a complex web of cause and effect covering time past, present and future. Because all things are thus conditioned and transient (anicca), they have no real independent identity (anatta).
- Rejection of the infallibility of accepted scripture: Teachings should not be accepted unless they are borne out by our experience and are praised by the wise.
- **Anicca** (Sanskrit: **anitya**): That all things are impermanent.
- **Anatta** (Sanskrit: **anâtman**): That the perception of a constant "self" is an illusion.
- **Dukkha** (Sanskrit: **dukkha**): That all beings suffer from all situations due to unclear mind.

However, in some Mahayana schools, these points have come to be regarded as more or less subsidiary. There is some disagreement amongst various schools of Buddhism over more esoteric aspects of Buddha's teachings, and also over some of the disciplinary rules for monks.

The Buddha's reluctance to name a successor or to formalise his doctrine led to the emergence of many movements during the next 400 years: first the schools of Nikaya Buddhism, of which only Theravada remains today, and then the formation of Mahayana and Vajrayana, pan-Buddhist sects based on the acceptance of new scriptures and the revision of older techniques.

Despite of the support and patronage by Harshavardhana and by Pala kings, who came later, by the end of twelfth century A.D, Buddhism declined as a major religious force in the sub-continent . The growing influence of Bhakti movement and the religious bigotry of the Muslim invaders sealed what ever opportunities it had for revival and renewal. However Buddhism continued to flourish in other parts of the world, especially in China, Korea, Japan, Cambodia, Thailand and other far eastern countries.

Today Buddhism is practised in various parts of the world. In India it has the dubious distinction of a separate religion as well as a movement with in Hinduism. The Hindus consider the Buddha as an incarnation of Lord Vishnu. But the Buddhists disagree. As a religion, except in certain parts like Sikkim, Ladakh, Buddhism is a minority religion in India.

But in neighboring Nepal, Bhutan and Ceylon it is still very popular religion. Though it greatly disappeared in main land China, it still survives in many far eastern countries and Japan. The west was introduced to Buddhism mainly in the last century. It is presently attracting many new followers from the western world. As a religion and as a way of life, Buddhism has a great religions appeal to the educated and liberal minded people of the west. It has an inherent strength, a certain dignified charm . It will continue to attract many new followers.

Southeast Asia

During the 1st century CE, the trade on the overland Silk Road tended to be restricted by the rise in the Middle East of the Parthian empire, an unvanquished enemy of Rome, just as Romans were becoming extremely wealthy and their demand for Asian luxury was rising. This demand revived the sea connections between the Mediterranean and China, with India as the intermediary of choice. From that time, through trade connection, commercial settlements, and even political interventions, India started to strongly influence Southeast Asian countries. Trade routes linked India with southern Burma, central and southern Siam, lower Cambodia and southern Vietnam, and numerous urbanized coastal settlements were established there.

For more than a thousand years, Indian influence was therefore the major factor that brought a certain level of cultural unity to the various countries of the region. The Pali and Sanskrit languages and the Indian script, together with Theravada and Mahayana Buddhism, Brahmanism, and Hinduism, were transmitted from direct contact and through sacred texts and Indian literature such as the Ramayana and the Mahabharata.

From the 5th to the 13th century, South-East Asia had very powerful empires and became extremely active in Buddhist architectural and artistic creation. The main Buddhist influence now came directly by sea from the Indian subcontinent, so that these empires essentially followed the Mahayana faith. The Sri Vijaya Empire to the south and the Khmer Empire to the north competed for influence, and their art expressed the rich Mahayana pantheon of the Bodhisattvas.

The Buddha's teachings on ethics and living a good life also extended to the realm of the social and political. He was ahead of his time in many ways; considering all people as equal, he rejected the caste system and openly encouraged women to become students and teachers. He taught that governments had a responsibility to lead by example, to teach people ethics and to eliminate poverty by providing opportunities for the people to become prosperous. He was clearly opposed to all forms of war, and taught that violence can never create security. In keeping with these teachings, Buddhism is rare among world religions in that its followers never attempted to spread their beliefs through the use of force. Unique among victorious leaders, the Buddhist emperor Asoka in the third century BCE renounced violence and war, and put Buddhist ethical virtues at the center of his government.

Regarding the Buddhist path as a philosophy, one may consider its epistemology: certain claims of knowledge have been made, but how can they be known to be true? As stated above, the Buddha himself never asked anyone to accept unproven claims on faith, and in fact discouraged them from doing so. He maintained that his teachings could be verified by direct insight and reasoning, by anyone willing to consider them and to follow the necessary path of self-discipline. Starting from a few basic assumptions, such as impermanence and dependent origination, he derived a complex and consistent system of philosophy which has stood for centuries. Later teachers have validated his claim that others could reach the same insights, and they have expanded upon his basic teachings with impressive intuitive depth and intellectual rigor.

In this way the Buddhist teaching has itself become a kind of interactive and self-evolving process, much like its idea of pratityasamutpada. However, the end goal is still Nirvana, which is an experience ultimately beyond all concepts and language, even beyond the Buddhist teachings. In the end even the attachment to the Dharma, the Buddhist teaching, must be dropped like all other attachments. The tradition compares the teaching to a raft upon which one crosses a swift river to get to the other side; once one is on the far shore, there is no longer any need to carry the raft. The far shore is Nirvana, and it is also said that when one arrives, one can see quite clearly that there was never any river at all.

East Asian Buddhism is a collective term for the schools of Buddhism that developed in the East Asian region, most of which are part of the Mahayana (which means "The Greater Vehicle") transmission. These include Chinese Buddhism, Korean Buddhism, Japanese Buddhism, and Vietnamese Buddhism.

The majority of Chinese people practice Confu-buddhism, and great many of Japanese people practice Shin-buddhism. Some think that Korean Buddhism preserves, or is one of the traditions closest to, the original Buddhism. However, others suggest that this claim can be made by Theravada and Zen Buddhism.

The school of Buddhism most prominent in Sri Lanka and the Southeast Asian countries is Theravada Buddhism. Mahayana thought had originated in Indian Buddhist philosophers, whose teachings would filter into East Asian Mahayana.

BUDDHISM IN FAR EAST

Buddhism in China

The first contacts between China and Central Asia occurred with the opening of the Silk Road in the 2nd century BCE. The 1st century BCE "Records of the Great Historian" tells of the travels of the Chinese explorer Zhang Qian to Central Asia around 130 BCE, who reports about a country named Shendu (India), whose peaceful Buddhist ways are mentioned in writing in the 1st century CE Han history, the Hanshu.

The Silk Road transmission of Buddhism to China started in the 1st century CE with a semi-legendary or quasi-historical account of an embassy sent to the West by the Chinese Emperor Ming (58 – 75 CE). Extensive contacts however started in the 2nd century CE, probably as a consequence of the expansion of the Kushan Empire into the Chinese territory of the Tarim Basin, with the missionary efforts of a great number of Central Asian Buddhist monks to Chinese lands. The first missionaries and translators of Buddhist scriptures into Chinese were Parthian, Kushan, Sogdian or Kuchean.

From the 4th century onward, Chinese pilgrims also started to travel to India, the origin of Buddhism, by themselves in order to get improved access to the original scriptures, with Fa-hsien's pilgrimage to India (395-414), and later Xuan Zang (629-644). The Silk Road transmission of Buddhism essentially ended around the 7th century with the rise of Islam in Central Asia.

After 130 BCE, numerous embassies to the West followed Zhang Qian's travels, and there may have been some contacts with Buddhism around that time. Chinese murals in the Tarim Basin city of Dunhuang describe the Emperor Han Wudi (156-87 BCE) worshipping Buddhist statues, "golden men brought in 120 BCE by a great Han general in his campaigns against the nomads". However, there is no such mention of Han Wudi worshipping the Buddha in Chinese historical literature. The Hou Hanshu also records the visit of Yuezhi envoys to the Chinese capital in 2 BCE, who gave oral teachings on Buddhist sutras to a student, suggesting that some Yuezhi had already started to disseminate the Buddhist faith in eastern Asia during the 1st century BCE (Baldev Kumar (1973)).

The first documented transmission of Buddhist scriptures to China occurs in 148 CE, with the arrival of the Parthian missionary An Shih Kao in China, probably on the heels of the Kushan expansion into the Tarim Basin. An Shi Kao established Buddhist temples in Loyang and organized the translation of Buddhist scriptures into Chinese, testifying to the beginning of a wave of Central Asian Buddhist proselitism that was to last several centuries.

Buddhism in Japan

The arrival of Buddhism in Japan is ultimately a consequence of the first contacts between China and Central Asia which occurred with the opening of the Silk Road in the 2nd century BCE, following the travels of Zhang Qian between 138 and 126 BCE, which culminated with the official introduction of Buddhism in China in 67 CE. Historians generally agree that by the middle of the 1st century, the religion had penetrated to areas north of the Huai River.

In 467 CE, according to the Chinese historic treatise Liang Shu, five monks from Gandhara traveled to the country of Fusang: "The country of the extreme East" beyond the sea, probably eastern Japan, where they introduced Buddhism:

Fusang is located to the east of China, 20,000 *li* (1,500 kilometers) east of the state of *Da Han* (itself east of the state of *Wa* in modern Kyûshû, Japan). (...) In former times, the people of Fusang knew nothing of the Buddhist religion, but in the second year of Da Ming of the Song Dynasty (467 CE), five monks from Kipin [Kabul region of Gandhara] travelled by ship to Fusang. They propagated Buddhist doctrine, circulated scriptures and drawings, and advised the people to relinquish worldly attachments. As a result the customs of Fusang changed.

The initial period saw the introduction onto Japanese soil of the six great Chinese schools, including the *Huayan* and *Lü* that became respectively the *Kegon* and *Ritsu* in Japanese. In terms of geography, the six sects were centered on the capital city of Nara, where great temples such as the Tôdai-ji and Hokki-ji were erected. However, the Buddhism of this early period – later known as the Nara period – was not a practical religion, being more the domain of learned priests whose official function was to pray for the peace and prosperity of the state and imperial house. This kind of Buddhism had little to offer the illiterate and uneducated masses, and led to the growth of "people's priests" who were not ordained and had no formal Buddhist training. Their practice was a combination of Buddhist and Taoist elements, and the incorporation of shamanistic features of the indigenous religion. These figures became immensely popular, and were a source of criticism towards the sophisticated academic and bureaucratic Buddhism of the capital.

As noted above, much of Zen history is combined with mythology. The historical records required for a complete, accurate account of early Zen history no longer exist. Chan, as it is generally called when referencing Zen Buddhism in early China, developed from the interaction between Mahâyâna Buddhism and Taoism. Some scholars also argue that Chan has roots in yogic practices, specifically *kammammhâna*, the consideration of objects, and *kasina*, total fixation of the mind.

The entry of Buddhism into China was marked by interaction and syncretism with Taoic faiths, Taoism in particular. Buddhist scriptures were translated into Chinese with

Taoist vocabulary, because it was originally seen as a kind of foreign Taoism. In the Tang period, Taoism incorporated such Buddhist elements as monasteries, vegetarianism, prohibition of alcohol, the doctrine of emptiness, and collecting scripture into tripartite organisation. During the same time, Chan Buddhism grew to become the largest sect in Chinese Buddhism.

The establishment of Chan is traditionally credited to the Indian prince turned monk Bodhidharma (formerly dated ca 500 CE, but now ca early fifth century ,who is recorded as having come to China to teach a "special transmission outside scriptures" which "did not stand upon words". Bodhidharma settled in the kingdom of Wei where he took among his disciples Daoyu and Huike. Early on in China Bodhidharma's teaching was referred to as the "One Vehicle sect of India". The One Vehicle (Sanskrit Ekayâna), also known as the Supreme Vehicle or the Buddha Vehicle, was taught in the Lankavatara Sutra which was closely associated with Bodhidharma. However, the label "One Vehicle sect" did not become widely used, and Bodhidharma's teaching became known as the Chan sect for its primary focus on chan training and practice. Shortly before his death, Bodhidharma appointed Huike to succeed him, making Huike the first Chinese born patriarch and the second patriarch of Chan in China. Bodhidharma is said to have passed three items to Huike as a sign of transmission of the Dharma: a robe, a bowl, and a copy of the Lankavatara Sutra. The transmission then passed to the second patriarch (Huike), the third (Sengcan), the fourth patriarch (Dao Xin) and the fifth patriarch (Hongren).

The sixth and last patriarch, Huineng (638–713), was one of the giants of Chan history, and all surviving schools regard him as their ancestor. However, the dramatic story of Huineng's life tells that there was a controversy over his claim to the title of patriarch. After being chosen by Hongren, the fifth patriarch, Huineng had to flee by night to Nanhua Temple in the south to avoid the wrath of Hongren's jealous senior disciples. Later, in the middle of the 8th century, monks claiming to be among the successors to Huineng, calling themselves the Southern school, cast themselves in opposition to those claiming to succeed Hongren's then publicly recognized student Shenxiu. It is commonly held that it is at this point—the debates between these rival factions—that Chan enters the realm of fully documented history. Aside from disagreements over the valid lineage, doctrinally the Southern school is associated with the teaching that enlightenment is sudden, while the Northern School is associated with the teaching that enlightenment is gradual. The Southern school eventually became predominant and their Northern school rivals died out. Modern scholarship, however, has questioned this narrative, since the only surviving records of this account were authored by members of the Southern school.

Buddhism in Korea

In the 4th century A.D., at the time when Buddhism was first introduced to Korea, the Korean peninsula was divided into three separate kingdoms: Koguryo, Paekje and Shilla. Buddhism arrived first in the northern kingdom of Koguryo and gradually spread to Paekje, in the southwest, finally reaching southeastern Shilla in the 5th century A.D.

During the Three Kingdoms period, Buddhism slowly developed. After the unification of the peninsula in 668 by Shilla, the golden age of the unified Shilla Period (668-935) was followed by ritualistic Koryo (935-1392). Persecution ran high in the Choson Period as Neo Confucianism gained the favour of the ruling families. In 1945, after thirty-six years, the Japanese colonization of Korea came to an end: Korean Buddhism underwent a renewal.

When Buddhism was first introduced to Korea from China in 372 A.D., Shamanism was the indigenous religion. Shamanism is the ancient religion of animism and nature-spirit worship. The origin of Shamanism in Korea is unknown. It is based on the belief that human beings as well as natural forces and inanimate objects al possess spirits.

Since Buddhism was not seen to be in conflict with the rites of nature worship, it was able to naturally blend in with Shamanism. And so many of the special mountains believed to be the residence of spirits in pre-Buddhist times soon became the sites of Buddhist temples.

Korean Shamanism regarded three spirits with special reverence and importance: the Mountain Spirit, *Sanshin* (who is usually depicted as an old man with a tiger at his feet), *Toksong*, or the *Recluse*, and *Ch'ilsong* (the spirit of the seven stars, the Big Dipper). Buddhism accepted and absorbed these three spirits and, even today, special shrines are set aside for them in most temples. The Mountain Spirit, in particular, receives due veneration following the ceremonies honoring the Buddha in the main hall. This is in case the local mountain spirits, on whose land the temple stands, should become angry.

And thus Chinese Buddhism blended with Korean Shamanism to produce a unique form: Korean Buddhism. As in other Buddhist countries, the fundamental teachings of the Buddha remained the same, even though the form was uniquely Korean.

Buddhism in Mongolia

The indigenous religion of Mongolia prior to Buddhism was shamanism, which focused specifically on rituals and nature deities. There are still elements of modern Mongolian Buddhism that display the early amalgam between Buddhism and local shamanistic practices, such as the Mongolian Buddhist dance, the tsam. In addition to this dimension, Tibetan Buddhist monasticism made an important impact on the early development of Mongolian Buddhism. The Buddhist monk hood always has played significant political roles in Central and Southeast Asia, and the Buddhist sangha in Mongolia was no exception. Church and state supported each other, and the doctrine of reincarnation made it possible for the reincarnations of living Buddhas to be discovered conveniently in the families of powerful Mongol nobles, until this practice was outlawed by the Qianlong Emperor.

Although the emperors of the Yuan Dynasty in the 14th and 15th century had already converted to Tibetan buddhism, the Mongols returned to their old shamanist ways after the collapse of their empire. In 1578 Altan Khan, a Mongol military leader with ambitions to unite the Mongols and to emulate the career of Chinggis, invited the head of the rising Yellow Sect of Tibetan Buddhism to a summit. They formed an alliance that gave Altan Khan's legitimacy and religious sanction for his imperial pretensions and that provided the Buddhist school with protection and patronage. Altan khan gave the Tibetan leader the title of Dalai Lama (Ocean Lama), which his successors still hold. Altan Khan died soon after, but in the next century the Yellow Sect spread throughout Mongolia, aided in part by the efforts of contending Mongol aristocrats to win religious sanction and mass support for their ultimately unsuccessful efforts to unite all Mongols in a single state. Monasteries (momg.*datsa*n) were built across Mongolia, often sited at the juncture of trade and migration routes or at summer pastures, where large numbers of herders would congregate for shamanistic rituals and sacrifices. Buddhist monks carried out a protracted struggle with the indigenous shamans and succeeded, to some extent, in taking over their functions and fees as healers and diviners, and in pushing the shamans to the fringes of Mongolian culture and religion.

Buddhism in Taiwan

Buddhism was brought to Taiwan in the time of the Ming dynasty by settlers from Fukien and Kwangtung Provinces· It was discouraged by the Dutch colonial rulers who controlled Taiwan from 1624 until 1663, until Cheng Cheng-kung (Koxinga) drove the Dutch from Taiwan in 1663. His son Cheng Ching established the first Buddhist temple in Taiwan.

When the Qing dynasty took control of Taiwan by defeating of Cheng Ching's son, Ching Ning, in 1683, large numbers of monks came from Fukien and Kwangtung provinces to establish temples, and a number of different Buddhist sects flourished. Monastic Buddhism, however, would not arrive until the 19th century.

As a Japanese colony, Taiwan fell under the influence of Japanese Buddhism. Many temples experienced pressure to affiliate with Japanese lineages, including many whose status with respect to Buddhism or Taoism was unclear. (Emphasis on the Chinese folk religion was widely considered a form of protest against Japanese rule.) Attempts were made to introduce a married priesthood (as in Japan). These failed to take root, as emphasis on vegetarianism and/or clerical celibacy became another means of anti-Japanese protest.

Buddhism in Central Asia

When King Kanishka came to power in 78 AD in Central Asia a new system of chronology was adopted, replacing the chronology from the era of the Seleucids. During the Kushan period, various religious systems were widespread in Central Asia. These were the local cult of Mitra and Anahit, Zoroastrian pantheon (Ormuzd, Veretzanga, etc.) the Greek pantheon (Zeus, Helios, Helen, etc.) and the cult of local heroes (Siyavush in Khorezm and Sogd). The followers of Buddhism had been banished from Iran in the 2nd - 3rd centuries and found support in Central Asia, where Buddhism became widely practiced. According to Chinese chronicles Buddhism came to China in 147 from the country of the "big yue dzhi", and thanks to the Kushan missionaries Buddhism was adopted as the official religion of the court of the Chinese emperor, Huangdi (147-167).

During the archeological excavations in Khorezm (Bazaar-Kala, Gyaur-Kala, Gyaz-Kala) and Sogd (tali-barzu, Zohak-i-Maron castle, Er-Kurgan and others) it was found out that many settlements and castles dated back to the Kushan period. But the largest number of traces of Buddhist culture during the Kushan period was found in Tolharistan. Architectural fragments dating back to the Kushan period have been found in "Old Termez". Some Buddhist monuments date back to the period of the Great Kushans.

Chapter - 3

Buddhism in China

Chinese Buddhism refers collectively to the various schools of Buddhism that have flourished in China proper since ancient times. These schools integrated the ideas of Confucianism, Taoism and other indigenous philosophical systems so that what was initially a foreign religion (the buddhadharma) came to be a natural part of Chinese civilization albeit with its own unique character. Buddhism has played an enormous role in shaping the mindset of the Chinese people affecting as it has aesthetics, politics, literature, philosophy and medicine. During the Tang Dynasty while at its peak of vitality, Chinese Buddhism produced numerous spiritual masters.

Buddhism entered China a few centuries after the passing away of the Buddha, at a time when Confucianism and Taoism were the predominant religions in a country that was as big as a continent and rivaled India in historical antiquity and cultural pluralism. In the early phases of its entry, Buddhism did not find many adherents in China. But by the 2nd Century AD, aided to some extent by the simplicity of its approach and some similarities with Taoism, it managed to gain a firm foothold and acquired a sizeable following.

The arrival of many new Buddhist scholars from the Indian subcontinent and central Asia, like An Shih-Kao, a Parthinian monk, and Lokakshema, a Kushana monk from Central Asia gave an impetus to the new religion that had many attractive features besides an inbuilt organizational approach to the study and pursuit of religion. During the same period many Buddhist texts were translated from Pali and Sanskrit into Chinese.

The collapse of Han dynasty around 220 AD, was followed by a period of confusion which continued to trouble Chinese society for the next 350 years. During this period Confucianism and Taoism gradually yielded place to Buddhism. The new Mongolian rulers of China from the Northern Wei dynasty and some rulers in the south like Emperor Wu found in Buddhism a great opportunity to demolish the old order and establish a new one. As a result by 6th Century AD, China was teaming with millions of Buddhist monks and thousands of monasteries.

During this turbulent period in China, two major developments took place in Buddhism. One group consisting mostly of the sophisticated gentry dwelled on the philosophical and mystical aspects of Buddhism, while the other group dominated by rural folk followed Buddhism in their own superstitious and simple ways imparting to it in the process a peculiar Chinese Character.

During this period many Buddhist scholars came to China from the east and worked selflessly to make Buddhism a mass religion. Notable among them were scholars like Dharmaraksha (3rd Century AD) Kumarajiva (4th Century AD), who got a number of Buddhist texts translated into Chinese. By this time China produced its own eminent Buddhist scholars with extraordinary vision like Seng-Chao, Tao-Sheng and Fa-hsien who also contributed richly to the growth of Buddhism China through their translations.

Between the 6th Century AD and 10th Century AD China was ruled by Sui and T'ang dynasties who were also patrons of Buddhism. During this period Buddhism reached its glorious heights in China. At the same time the process of degeneration also began. Many Buddhist monasteries turned to serious business and indulged in farming, trade and money lending for their own benefit neglecting the spiritual side of their responsibilities. Strangely, in a very uncharacteristic way, the Buddhist monasteries cultivated the farm lands, ran mills and oil presses using slave labor and low ranking monks and hoarded vast amounts of precious stones and metals. They also indulged in pawn brokering and money lending.

Many new schools of Buddhism also emerged in China during this period. Each school derived its authority from some ancient Buddhist text or doctrine. Some of these schools spread to countries like Korea and Japan and contributed to the emergence of Buddhism as the predominant religion.

The fall of Buddhism began during the reign of a Chinese Emperor Wu-Tsung (841-847). Probably noticing the greed that characterized many monasteries, he ordered for the general destruction of all Buddhist establishments and return of all Buddhist monks and nuns to lay life. This shook the foundations of Buddhism though it did not destroy it. Emperor Wu dismantled the greedy monasteries probably to fill his own coffers, but not Buddhism. However his actions definitely reversed the fortunes of Buddhism in China and sowed the seeds of its decline .

From 11th Century onwards, China witnessed the reemergence of Confucianism and revival of people's interest in their traditional religions. By their own excesses and neglect of their primary duties, the Buddhist monasteries became the contributory factors to the declining popularity of Buddhism. During the same period the Buddhism faced tremendous challenges from the increasing popularity of Brahmanism and the aggressive policies of the Islamic rulers of the Indian subcontinent.

These new developments in the land of the Buddha had a direct impact on the fortunes of Buddhism in China since for a very long period the monks from the subcontinent provided a recurring source of inspiration and information to their brethren in China. This decline contributed greatly to the slackening of standards in the recruitment of monks and the emergence of some decadent schools of Buddhism. These schools deviated from the original rules prescribed by the Buddha for monastic discipline among the brethren and emphasized the need for exploring the lighter side of life in the practice of Buddhism instead of sorrow and suffering. One prominent example was the emergence of Pu-Tai, or the Laughing Buddha. He was but a decadent version of the exalted and highly revered Maitreyi Buddha.

The Yuan dynasty that came to power in 1280 adopted Lamaism as their state religion. It was the Tibetan version of Buddhism which gained ascendance in the mountainous country following the emergence of Vajrayana Buddhism in eastern India. During this period some secret schools of Buddhism also emerged in China. They believed in the future advent of Maitreya and the emergence of new world order. These schools practiced martial arts like Kungfu and sometimes indulged in the petty politics of the local warlords.

Although Buddhism lost most of its dynamism and vibrancy by the 20th century, it continued to flourish in China till the advent of the Communism. As is well known, the emergence of communism sounded the death knell of Buddhism. The Communist government of China did succeed officially in putting an end to the practice of religion by abolishing all forms of public worship and closing down all the monasteries.

The excesses of cultural revolution put an end to whatever hopes the followers of Buddhism had about its revival. Today Buddhism in China is a relic of the past, an ancient monument that has been ravaged and vandalized by the clash of classes and ideological notions. It is really difficult to say how long it would take for the cycle of Dhamma to regain its supremacy and whether it would ever happen at all.

CHINESE SCHOOLS OF BUDDHISM

The principal schools of Buddhism which flourished in China were:

1. The Vinaya School (Lu-tsung)
2. The Realistic School (Chu-she)
3. The Three Treatises School (San-lun)
4. The Idealist School (Fa-hsiang)
5. The Mantra or Tantric School (Mi-tsung or Chen-yen)
6. The Avatamsaka or Flower Adornment School (Hua-yen)
7. The T'ien-t'ai or White Lotus School (Fa-hua)
8. The Pure Land School (Ching t'u)
9. The Dhyana School (Ch'an)

1. THE VINAYA SCHOOL (LU-TSUNG)

As the name suggests, this school concentrated upon the monastic discipline (Vinaya) of the Buddhist monks and adhered strictly to do's and don'ts prescribed for them in the Vinaya Pitaka. This school was said to have been founded by Tao-hsuan in the 7th Century AD.

2. THE REALISTIC SCHOOL (CHU-SHE)

This school derived its inspiration from the Abhidhamma Kosha of Vasubhandu (316-396), a Peshawar based Indian monk who was originally a Sarvasthivadin and was faithful to the original teachings of the Buddha. In course of time it became a part of the latter day Idealist school.

3. THE THREE TREATISES SCHOOL (SAN-LUN)

This school followed the teachings of the Madhyamika sutras of the famous south Indian Buddhist monk, Nagarjuna who is remembered by history for his Sunyavada or the theory of Absolute emptiness. His approach to the notions of reality was akin to the Upanishadic idea of non-self and the doctrines of the Advaita or non dualistic schools of Hinduism. His ideas were brought to China by Kumarajiva (549-623) through the translation of the Sutras, which were later expounded in the form of commentaries by Chih-Tsang (549-623). Chih-Tsnag argued in one of his works that it would be possible to understand metaphysical truths only through negation of things in view of the limitations of the mind to understand transcendental reality. This school also derived its inspiration from the Shata Shastra (The treaties of Hundred Scriptures) of Aryadeva. With the emergence of the Idealistic school, this school suffered a decline. It was later revived in the 7th Century AD by an Indian monk called Suryaprbhasa.

4. THE IDEALIST SCHOOL (FA-HSIANG)

This school was founded on the ideals of Yogachara school of Vasubhandu as expounded in his Vimsatika- Karika or the Book of Twenty Verses. The school became popular because of Hsuan-Tsang (596-664) who traveled to India in the 7th Century AD to collect original Buddhist texts and bring them back to China. Hsuan Tsang was an adventurous monk who combined in himself the traits of a monk as well as inveterate traveler. Undaunted by the task ahead of him and driven by his goal to see the land of the Buddha, Hsuan-Tsang travelled to India by a circuitous route via the Silk Road through the perilious terrain of the north western frontires, and reached the University of Nalanda in eastern India after a great hardship. He spent considerable time there in the study of the Yogachara philosophy under the guidance of a teacher called Silabhadra. From there he went to the court of the famous Indian king by name Harshavardhana, who was a powerful but generous ruler of his times and ruled parts of northern and eastern India. He developed a great liking for the Chinese monk and insisted him to stay in his court for several years.

Hsuan-Tsang complied with the king's request and stayed in his court for a few years before resuming his journey. He returned to China after many hardships, and managed to carry with him a huge collection of about 650 Buddhist texts and some Buddha relics. He spent the rest of his life in the translation of the texts and in spreading the teachings of Vasubhandu. Despite of the fact that the translations he arranged were not superior in quality, Hsuan-Tsang earned a place for himself in the history of China by his unique contribution to the development of Chinese Buddhism. Through his familiarity with the teachings of Vasubhandu, he made the Idealist School one of the most popular schools of Buddhism in ancient China.

5. THE MANTRA OR TANTRIC SCHOOL (MI-TSUNG OR CHEN-YEN)

This is the Chinese version of Tantric Buddhism. It flourished in China for less than a hundred years, starting with the arrival of Subhakarasimha(637-735) from India during the reign of T'ang dynasty. Subhakarasimha translated the Mahavairochana Sutra which expounded the Tantric teachings. Two other monks who played a key role in the growth of Tantric Buddhism in China were Vajrabodhi (670-741) introduced the concept of Mandalas to the Chinese, while Amoghavajra said to have initiated three T'ang emperors into Tantricism. the Tantric school of Buddhism believed in magic, incantations, drawing of mandalas, casting of spells and elaborate and often secret rituals. The school was later replaced by Lamaism, which was a more popular version of Tantricism.

6. THE AVATAMSAKA OR FLOWER ADORNMENT SCHOOL (HUA-YEN)

This school flourished in China for about 200 years, starting from the 7th Century AD and attracted the attention of the famous Empress Wu (690-705). It was based upon the teachings of the Buddha as contained in the Avatamsaka Sutra. The followers of this school believed that the sutra contained the most complex teachings of the Buddha, not comprehensible to ordinary followers. The Avatamsaka school expounded a cosmic view of the universe containing the two principal aspects of the reality, namely li and shih, an approach which is in some ways resembles the concept of Purusha (spiritual) and Prakriti (physical) of Hinduism, adopted later on by the Tantric schools. It also believed that in each and every aspect the cosmic reality reflected the same relationships and balance of forces, signifying the ultimate truth of one in all and all in one. The school was founded by Tu-shun, whose commentary of Avatamsaka, known as Ha-chieh Kuan, (Contemplating the Dharmadhatu) provided the necessary background for the emergence of this school in the Buddhist world. He was followed by four patriarchs, Chihyen(602-668), Fa-tsang (exact period unknown), Chiangling(738-838) and Tsung-mi(780-841).

7. THE T'IEN-T'AI OR WHITE LOTUS SCHOOL (FA-HUA)

Like the Avatamsaka school, the White Lotus School also was based upon the highest teachings of the Buddha, but compared to the former, provided a more an elaborate view of the cosmic reality. It was founded by a Chinese monk by name Chih-i (538-597) who lived in Chekiang province of China, and formed his doctrines on the basis of the Saddharma-pundarika sutra, an ancient Buddhist text, which he believed to be the vehicle of all other truths. According to this school, Truth operated from three levels or aspects. At one extreme was the void or emptiness, the unknown or the non self, about which nothing much could be speculated except talking in terms of negation and denial. At the other extreme was temporariness that was in reality nothingness but would manifest itself temporarily or momentarily because of the activity of the senses, as some kind of an illusion or as an image on the film screen. The third level is a middle state, 'middle' for our understanding, but not necessarily middle, 'different' for our understanding but not necessarily different, because it unites the two and presents them together as the one Highest Truth.

These three levels of truth are also not separate or different from each other. They are the aspects of the same reality, that is universal as well as ubiquitous. The school advocated the practice of concentration and insight (chih and kuan) to understand the transience of things and attain the Buddha Mind in which the above mentioned three aspects of Truth reside in perfect harmony. Chih-i said to have become very popular during his life time and caught the attention of the emperor who donated the revenues of a district for the maintenance of his monastery. The While Lotus School was introduced into Japan in the 9th century AD and became popular as Tendai.

8. THE PURE LAND SCHOOL (CHING T'U)

This school was founded by Hui-yuan (334-416), who was originally a Taoist. It was based upon the teachings of the Mahayana school and the belief in the Bodhisattvas, the highest beings, who were next to the Buddha in the order and just a step away from salvation, but would postpone their own salvation for the sake of others. This school worshipped Amitabha and sought his grace for deliverance from this world under the notion that salvation could not be gained on ones own efforts (jiriki) but with the help of the other power (tariki), the grace of Amitabha. The school practiced devotional forms of worship and regular chanting of O-mi-to-fo (the Chinese rendering of Amitabha) as the means to salvation. It followed the teachings contained in the Smaller and Larger Sukhavati-vyuha sutras. The school was subsequently introduced into Korea and Japan where it flourished under three different names.

9. THE DHYANA SCHOOL (CH'AN)

This was the most popular of the Chinese schools of Buddhism, which became popular in Japan and later in the west as Zen Buddhism. Chan was a "way of seeing into the nature of ones own being" (D.T.Suzuki). Though it was introduced into China by an Indian monk by name Bodhidharma, around 520 AD, Chan was essentially a product of Chinese character, which unlike the Indian, evolved out of the practical and down to earth philosophy of life. Chan rejected book learning as the basis of enlightenment, set aside all notions and theories of suffering and salvation, and relied upon day to day events, simple thinking and ordinary living as the means to enlightenment. Enlightenment descended upon one as a sudden shift in awareness, not because of elaborate study of the Buddhist sutras, exposition of the philosophies, nor worship of the images of the Buddha but from a sudden shift in the paradigm, from an instantaneous chasm in the process of thought, from a kind of Eureka experience, characterized by a sudden opening of the mind and removal of a veil, after years of silent waiting and steady preparation. The Chan school discouraged the intellectual kind of pursuit of religion as it believed that any scholarly approach would tend to stiffen the mind and prevent it from experiencing the sudden flowering of Chan.

Although the Chan masters did not encourage preoccupation with scriptural studies, they encouraged the initiates to study the basic Chan scriptures like the Lankavatarasutra, the Vimalakritinirdesa, the Vajracchedika Sutras and some additional Chan texts as a part of their preparation for the subsequent stages of observing into the nature of things. By denigrating the scriptural knowledge, the Chan masters therefore were not promoting illiteracy, but were preparing the students to free themselves from opinionated intellectuality and scholarly affectations to emerge into a world of notionless observations.

The word 'chan' is a corrupt form of the Sanskrit word, 'dhyana' meaning concentrated meditation or contemplation. Dhyana was an essential aspect of Chan Buddhism aimed to develop inner stillness and accumulation of chi energy among the practitioners. But what Chan encouraged, more than the mechanical aspects of meditation, was the development of an unfettered and detached mind, that would not cling to anything and would not rest anywhere and would flow with the flow of life, gathering nothing and gaining nothing. Chan Buddhism did not place too much emphasis on meditation, unlike the Zen Buddhism of Japan, but on finding the Buddha mind in the most mundane tasks and conversations of day to day life. In short, Chan made living a deeply religious act aimed to break the encrusted layers of thought.

Chan Buddhism underwent a schism during the 7th century resulting in the formation of two rival school, a southern school led by Hui-neng and a northern school led by Shenhsiu. While the northern school disappeared over a period of time, the Southern school underwent further sub-divisions resulting in the formation of five Houses and seven sub sects of which two survived. One was Lin-chi and Tsao-tung.

Chan Buddhism influenced Chinese way of life profoundly. The Chan art became famous in ancient China for its spontaneity and simplicity of expression. But with the decline of Buddhism in China, Chan also gradually retreated into remote monasteries and gradually lost its appeal.

SILK ROAD TRANSMISSION OF BUDDHISM

The Silk Road transmission of Buddhism to China started in the 1st century CE with a semi-legendary or quasi-historical account of an embassy sent to the West by the

Chinese Emperor Ming (58 – 75 CE). Extensive contacts however started in the 2nd century CE, probably as a consequence of the expansion of the Kushan Empire into the Chinese territory of the Tarim Basin, with the missionary efforts of a great number of Central Asian Buddhist monks to Chinese lands. The first missionaries and translators of Buddhists scriptures into Chinese were either Parthian, Kushan, Sogdian or Kuchean.

From the 4th century onward, Chinese pilgrims also started to travel to India, the origin of Buddhism, by themselves in order to get improved access to the original scriptures, with Fa-hsien's pilgrimage to India (395-414), and later Xuan Zang (629-644). The Silk Road transmission of Buddhism essentially ended around the 7th century with the rise of Islam in Central Asia.

The first contacts between China and Central Asia occurred with the opening of the Silk Road in the 2nd century BCE. The 1st century BCE "Records of the Great Historian" tells of the travels of the Chinese explorer Zhang Qian to Central Asia around 130 BCE, who reports about a country named Shendu (India), whose peaceful Buddhist ways are mentioned in writing in the 1st century CE Han history, the Hanshu.

After 130 BCE, numerous embassies to the West followed Zhang Qian's travels, and there may have been some contacts with Buddhism around that time. Chinese murals in the Tarim Basin city of Dunhuang describe the Emperor Han Wudi (156-87 BCE) worshipping Buddhist statues, "golden men brought in 120 BCE by a great Han general in his campaigns against the nomads". However, there is no such mention of Han Wudi worshipping the Buddha in Chinese historical literature. The Hou Hanshu also records the visit of Yuezhi envoys to the Chinese capital in 2 BCE, who gave oral teachings on Buddhist sutras to a student, suggesting that some Yuezhi had already started to disseminate the Buddhist faith in eastern Asia during the 1st century BCE (Baldev Kumar (1973)).The Hou Hanshu then describes the enquiry about Buddhism made around 70 CE by the Emperor Ming (58-75 CE):

"There is a current tradition that Emperor Ming dreamed that he saw a tall golden man the top of whose head was glowing. He questioned his group of advisors and one of them said: "In the West there is a god called Buddha. His body is sixteen chi high (3.7 metres or 12 feet), and is the colour of true gold." The Emperor, to discover the true doctrine, sent an envoy to Tianzhu (Northwestern India) to inquire about the Buddha's doctrine, after which paintings and statues [of the Buddha] appeared in the Middle Kingdom."

This encounter is further described in a 6th century CE account by Yang Xuanzhi:

"The establishment of the Baima Temple (Temple of the White Horse) by Emperor Ming (58-75 CE) of the Han marked the introduction of Buddhism into China. The temple was located on the south side of the Imperial Drive, three leagues (li) outside the Xiyang Gate. The Emperor dreamt of the golden man sixteen Chinese feet tall, with the aureole of sun and moon radiating from his head and his neck. A "golden

god", he was known as Buddha. The emperor dispatched envoys to the Western Regions in search of the god, and, as a result, acquired Buddhist scriptures and images. At the time, because the scriptures were carried into China on the backs of white horses, White Horse was adopted as the name of the temple."

The military expansion of China into Central Asia under the rule of Emperor Ming at that time was very real, in particular with the campaign of the general Ban Chao, who managed to repel the Xiongnu from the Tarim Basin and control most of the area by around 75 CE. These contacts necessarily prompted some level of cultural exchange, and may indeed correspond to the first time Buddhist ideas were transmitted to China.

The first documented transmission of Buddhist scriptures to China occurs in 148 CE, with the arrival of the Parthian missionary An Shih Kao in China, probably on the heels of the Kushan expansion into the Tarim Basin. An Shi Kao established Buddhist temples in Loyang and organized the translation of Buddhist scriptures into Chinese, testifying to the beginning of a wave of Central Asian Buddhist proselitism that was to last several centuries.

CENTRAL ASIAN MISSIONARIES

In the middle of the 2nd century CE, the Kushan empire under king Kanishka expanded into Central Asia and went as far as taking control of Kashgar, Khotan and Yarkand, which were Chinese dependencies in the Tarim Basin, modern Xinjiang. As a consequence, cultural exhanges greatly increased, and Central-Asian Buddhist missionaries became active shortly after in the Chinese capital cities of Loyang and sometimes Nanjing, where they particularly distinguished themselves by their translation work. They promoted both Hinayana and Mahayana scriptures. Thirty-seven of these early translators of Buddhist texts are known.

- An Shih Kao, a Parthian prince who made the first known translations of Hinayana Buddhist texts into Chinese (148-170).
- Lokaksema, a Kushan and the first to translate Mahayana scriptures into Chinese (167-186).
- An Hsuan, a Parthian merchant who became a monk in China 181.
- Zhi Yao (c. 185), a Kushan monk, second generation of translators after Lokaksema.
- Kang Meng-hsiang (194-207), first translator from Kangju.
- Zhi Qian (220-252), a Kushan monk whose grandfather had settled in China during 168-190.
- Zhi Yueh (c.230), a Kushan monk who worked at Nanjing.
- Kang Sengkai (247-280), born in Chiao-chih in the extreme south of the Chinese

empire, and son of Sogdian merchant.

- Tan-ti (c.254), a Parthian monk.
- Po Yen (c.259), a Kuchean prince.
- Dharmaraksa (265-313), a Kushan whose family had lived for generations at Dunhuang.
- An Fachiin (281-306), a monk of Parthian origins.
- Po Srimitra (317-322), a Kuchean prince.
- Kumarajiva (c. 401), a Kuchean monk, and one of the most important translators.
- Fo T'u-teng (4th century), Central Asian monk who became a counselor to the Chinese court.
- Bodhidharma (440-528), was, according to Yang Xuanzhi, a monk of Central Asian origin whom he met around 520 at Loyang. Bodhidharma was the founder of the Chan (Zen) school of Buddhism.
- Five monks from Gandhara traveled in 485 CE to the country of Fusang ("The country of the extreme East" beyond the sea, probably Japan, although some historians suggest the American continent), where they introduced Buddhism:

"In former times, the people of Fusang knew nothing of the Buddhist religion, but in the second year of Da Ming of the Song dynasty (485 CE), five monks from Kipin (Kabul region of Gandhara) travelled by ship to that country. They propagated Buddhist doctrine, circulated scriptures and drawings, and advised the people to relinquish worldly attachments. As a results the customs of Fusang changed".

- Jnanagupta (561-592), a monk and translator from Gandhara.
- Shikshananda (652-710 CE), a monk and translator from Udyana, Gandhara.
- Prajna (c. 810), a monk and translator from Kabul, who educated the Japanese Kûkai in Sanskrit texts.

ARTISTIC INFLUENCES

Central Asian missionnary efforts along the Silk Road were accompanied by a flux of artistic influences, visible in the development of Serindian art from the 2nd through the 11th century CE in the Tarim Basin, modern Xinjiang.

Serindian art often derives from the art of the Greco-Buddhist art of the Gandhara district of what is now Pakistan, combining Indian, Greek and Roman influences. Highly sinicized forms of this syncretism can also be found on the eastern portions of the Tarim Basin, such as in Dunhuang.

Silk Road artistic influences can be found as far as Japan to this day, in architectural motifs or representations of Japanese gods.

CHINESE PILGRIMS TO INDIA

According to Chinese sources, the first Chinese to be ordained was Zhu Zixing, after he went to Central Asia in 260 to seek out Buddhism. It is only from the 4th century CE that Chinese Buddhist monks started to travel to India to discover Buddhism first-hand. Fa-hsien's pilgrimage to India (395-414) is said to have been the first significant one. He left along the Silk Road, stayed 6 years in India, and then returned by the sea route.

Tens of Chinese monks, possibly hundreds of them, visited India during that period.

The most famous of the Chinese pilgrims is Xuan Zang (629-644), whose large and precise translation work defines a "new translation period", in contrast with older Central Asian works. He also left a detailed account of his travels in Central Asia and India.

RELATION TO CONFUCIANISM AND TAOISM

Most of the Chinese gentry were indifferent to the Central Asian travelers and their religion. Not only was their religion unknown, but much of it seemed alien and amoral to Chinese sensibilities. Concepts such as monasticism and individual spiritual enlightenment directly contradicted the core Confucian principles of family and emperor. Confucianism promoted social stability, order, strong families, and practical living. Chinese officials questioned how a monk's personal attainment of nirvana (total state of peace and happiness) benefited the empire. Buddhism was less antithetical to Taoism, the other major religion of China. Indeed, upon first encountering Buddhism, many Chinese scholars regarded it as merely a foreign branch of Taoism.

Kang-nam Oh frames the mutual influential dialogue of Buddhism and Taoism within China and mentions Kumarajiva:

It is a well-known fact that since its introduction into China, Buddhism has had a close relationship with Taoism, more specifically with Neo-Taoism. As a result of this there developed the method of "matching the concepts" of Buddhism and Taoism, which was known as ko-i. By this method of analogy Buddhists adopted many Taoist terms and ideas to explain their concepts. Although this somewhat superficial and arbitrary method of matching was discarded as useless and misleading after the great translator and scholar Kumârajiiva arrived in 401 C.E., Taoist influence on Buddhism in general was not, and could not be, totally eliminated.

LOCAL INTERPRETATION OF INDIAN TEXTS

To thrive in China, Buddhism had to transform itself into a system that could exist within the Chinese way of life. Thus highly regarded Indian sutras that advocated filial piety became core texts in China. Buddhism was made compatible with ancestor worship and participation in China's hierarchical system. Works were written arguing that the salvation of an individual was a benefit to that individual's society and family and monks thus contributed to the greater good.

It is conjectured that the shocking collapse of the Han Dynasty in 220 and the resulting period of social upheaval and political unrest known as the Three Kingdoms period may have helped the spread of Buddhism. Buddhism was a minor force, however, compared with Daoism which was directly associated with efforts to defy the emperor (cf. Yellow Turban Rebellion). The Daoist Zhang family self-governed the Hanzhong Commandry for nearly 20 years until invasion by the renowned Chinese warlord Cao Cao.

A reason for the lack of interest mostly stemmed from the ruling entity and gentry. All the rulers were Han Chinese and had simply never heard of or knew too little of the religion. The Nine-grade controller system, by which prominent individuals in each local administrative area were given the authority to rank local families and individuals in nine grades according to their potential for government service, further consolidated the importance of Confucianism. Daoism too remained a strong force among the population and philosophers.

BUDDHISM GAINS POLITICAL TRACTION IN THE NORTH

Subsequent chaotic periods of Sixteen Kingdoms and Southern and Northern Dynasties changed the situation, resulting in state support of Buddhism. Most rulers of the Wu, Hu, and the Northern dynasties originated from more than ten distinct ethnic groups including either non-Han Chinese "barbarians", or Han Chinese after generations of "barbarian" influence. They did not propagate nor trust the combined philosophical concept of Confucianism and Daoism as zealously as their rivals in the south. Official support of Buddhism would eventually mould a new Chinese populace with a common ideology out of the diversely ethnic population, which would in turn consolidate these dynasties.

It is instructive that Buddhism propagated faster in northern China than in the south. Social upheaval in northern China worked to break down cultural barriers between the elite ruling families and the general populace, in contrast to the south where elite clans and royal families firmly monopolized politics. Daoist and Confucian political ideology had long consolidated the political status of elite clans in the south. Support of another religion would have unknown and possibly adverse effects, for which these clans would not risk their privileges. Furthermore pro-Buddhist policy would not be backed by the bureaucracy, which had been staffed by members of the clans. Southern rulers were in weaker positions to strive for their legitimacy - some were even installed by the clans. It was not until the reign of Emperor Wu of the Liang Dynasty that saw the official support of Buddhism. Rebellion of Hou Jing near the end of Emperor Wu's reign wreaked havoc on the political and social privileges of the elite clans, which indirectly assisted the spread of Buddhism. But Buddhism spread pretty well in the peasant populace, both in the north and the south.

MONKS AND RULERS JOIN FORCES

Arrivals of several prestigious monks in the early 5th century also contributed to the propagation of the religion and were welcomed by rulers of the Sixteen Kingdoms and Northern Dynasties. Fo Tu Cheng was entrusted by the tyrant Shi Hu of Later Chao. Kumarajiva was invited by Lü Guang, the founder of Later Liang, and later by Yao Xing, second ruler of Later Qin. Biographies of these monks, among others, were the subject of the *Memoirs of Eminent Monks*.

The direct experiential impact of contact with practicing monks should not be underestimated. Confucianism had no equivalent to holy men — the archetypical best and brightest was a wise government minister, not a saint. Daoist priests were more immediate, but given to relativism. It is notable that when another "foreign " religion, Nestorianism, sought to extol the virtues of one of its main benefactors they claimed he was so moral that "...even among the most pure and self-denying of the Buddhists, such excellence was never heard of". Through the actions and example of monks, Buddhists successfully laid claim to the high moral ground in society.

In this way Buddhism grew to become a major religion in China. By the start of the 6th century, Buddhism had grown in popularity to rival Daoism. We know they were successful because the monks were soon accused of falling into extravagance and their lands and properties confiscated by Emperor Wu of the Northern Zhou dynasty and Wuzong of the Tang Dynasty.

During the early Tang dynasty the monk Xuanzang journeyed to Nalanda in India and other important sites to bring back scriptures. He sought to expand influence of Mahayana over Theravada, though the Yogacara school he preferred differs significantly from the later Chinese Mahayana schools that developed such as Pure Land. The Tang capital of Chang'an (today's Xi'an) became an important center for Buddhist thought. From there Buddhism spread to Korea, and Japanese embassies of Kentoshi helped gain footholds in Japan.

The popularization of Buddhism in this period is evident in the many scripture-filled caves and structures surviving today. The Mogao Caves near Dunhuang in Gansu province, the Longmen Grottoes near Luoyang in Henan and the Yungang Grottoes near Datong in Shanxi are the most renowned of the Northern, Sui and Tang Dynasties. The Leshan Giant Buddha, carved out of a hillside in the 8th century during Tang Dynasty and looking down on the confluence of three rivers, is still the largest stone Buddha statue in the world. As a side note, duplications of Buddhist texts were considered to bring meritorious karma. Printing from individually carved wooden blocks, from movable clay type and from movable metal type, proved much more efficient and eventually eclipsed hand copying. The *Diamond Sutra* of AD 868, a Buddhist scripture discovered in AD 1907 inside the Mogao Caves, was the first dated example of block printing.

OPPOSITION TO BUDDHISM DURING LATER TANG

Not all persons in the Chinese community were with Buddhism, although Buddhism had already attained many followers. Buddhist temples and monasteries grew rich from donations. Tang rulers at first accepted Buddhism. Other Tang rulers viewed Buddhism as a threat.

There were several components that lead to opposition of Buddhism. One factor is the foreign origins of Buddhism, unlike Taoism and Confucianism. Han Yu wrote, *"Buddha was a man of the barbarians who did not speak the language of China and wore clothes of a different fashion. His sayings did not concern the ways of our ancient kings, nor did his manner of dress conform to their laws. He understood neither the duties that bind sovereign and subject, nor the affections of father and son."*

Other components included the Buddhists' withdrawal from society, since the Chinese believed that Chinese people should be involved with family life. Wealth and power of the Buddhist temples and monasteries also annoyed many critics.

As mentioned earlier, persecution came during the reign of Emperor Wuzong in the Tang Dynasty. Wuzong was said to hate the sight of Buddhist monks. In 845, he ordered the destruction of 4,600 Buddhist monasteries and 40,000 temples. Another 250,000 Buddhist monks and nuns had to give up their Buddhist lives. Wuzong cited that Buddhism was an alien religion, which is the reason he also persecuted the Christians in China. Ancient Chinese Buddhism never fully recovered from the persecution.

BUDDHISM AFTER FORFEITURE OF 845

SONG DYNASTY

Buddhist ideology began to merge with Confucianism and Daoism, due in part to the use of existing Chinese philosophical terms in the translation of Buddhist scriptures. Various Confucian scholars of the Song dynasty, including Zhu Xi (wg: Chu Hsi), sought to redefine Confucianism as Neo-Confucianism.

MING DYNASTY

"By the Ming period (1368-1644) the preeminence of Chan had been so firmly established that almost the entire Buddhist clergy were affiliated with either its Lin-chi or Ts'ao-tung lineages, both of which claimed descent from Bodhidharma."

DECLINE

Buddhism in Central Asia began to decline in the 7th century following the incursion of the Muslim Caliphate. The vigorous Chinese culture progressively absorbed Buddhist teachings until a strongly Chinese particularism developed.

Central Asian Buddhist monks from the Tarim Basin and East Asian Buddhist monks appear to have maintained strong exchanges until around the 10th century, as shown by frescos from the Tarim Basin.

THE POSITION OF THE CHINESE TRIPITAKA IN WORLD BUDDHISM

We must first acknowledge that the various schools of thought in Buddhism are indeed facets of the Triple Gem that is Buddhism. There is no room for superficial and dogmatic claims that one school is true whereas others are not. For instance the Mahayana schools should not be lightly dismissed as illegitimate, nor should the Sravakavana school conversely be despised as moribund. Only when the study and practice of Buddhism is carried out in a friendly and accommodating atmosphere, with mutual trust and understanding, will co-ordination and co-operation be possible. With this attitude, the trash and trimmings now enshrouding Buddhism can be removed to reveal the essential splendor of the Triple Gem. Thus Buddhism, which is well-adapted to this modern world, can be redeemed and developed for the purpose of the enlightenment and salvation of the world in its dire present need.

Buddhism stems from one point of origin and is highly adaptable under many circumstances. For different races, time and environments it seems to develop into entirely different shapes and forms. But a close study of its trends and modes of development, its adaptations to new environments whilst preserving the integral identity of its core, brings one to the realisation that the different forms of Buddhism are interrelated and that cooperation amongst them is entirely feasible. Generally, each school has its own characteristics and shortcomings. Buddhists should honestly survey these various schools, exchanging the shortcomings in each for the strengths in others on the basis of equality, and for the sake of pursuing truth. In so doing, the ultimate truth as experienced by the Buddha may be realized and his original intention, as embodied in his teaching, may be fully understood.

When we trace the different schools of Buddhism in the world today from their origins in India we can see that the profile sprouting of sectarian Buddhism seems to have taken place as follows:

(1) The sacred texts embodying the Buddha-dharma developed over time. The sutras and Vinaya Pitaka were the earliest to be compiled and circulated. Round about the beginning of the first century A.D., the researchers of the Agama Sutra and those dedicated to Sravaka practice had compiled the Abhidharma, emphasising the existential aspect of Dependent Origination. On the other hand, the Mahayana scriptures had been compiled by those who stressed the virtues of the Buddha and the practice of the Bodhisattva, emphasizing the aspect of emptiness as central to the attainment of real understanding of Dependent Origination.

By the third century A.D., Nagarjuna had composed his famous Sastras on the Madhyamika doctrine interpreting the Agama and Abhidharma on the basis of the

Mahayana sutras of the Sunyata school. At about the same time, Mahayana scriptures tending towards 'eternal-reality' idealism, such as the Srimaladeve-Simhanada Sutra and the Mahaparinirvana Sutra, had begun to be found, followed by sutras such as the Lankavatara Sutra. Along with this development, the Asters and Yogacaryas of the Sravastivada school accepted the "mind-only" aspect of the Mahayana school. They compiled a number of Sastras of the Yogacara Vijnanavada and eventually flourished as a great Mahayana school in their own right.

Then, at about the fifth century there was a further development of esoteric Yoga from the school of eternal-reality idealism. If one tried to follow the course of development of Buddhism as outlined above, one would have no difficulty tracing the evolution of the vast diversity of scriptures and doctrines held sacred by the many schools.

(2) Doctrinally, Buddhism was just Buddhism at first and there was no sectarian difference. It did not divide into the Sravakayana and Bodhisattvayana until about the beginning of the Christian era. Then in the scriptures of the Bodhisattvayana we begin to see the division of Hinayana and Mahayana.

In the second and third centuries scriptures of eternal-reality idealism started to appear in the Bodhisattvayana. In such Sutras were first seen the terms "noumenon, Sunya and Madhya"; and "Hina-, Maha- and Eka-yana." These scriptures of later date laid special emphasis on the achievement of Buddhahood, and were thus also classified as Buddhayana.

At the beginning of the fifth century, another 'yana', the Dharaniyana, sprung into existence from the noumenal school of Buddhism. This school classified all Buddha Dharma into the Tripitaka, the Paramita Pitaka (including everything of the exoteric schools), and the Dharani Pitaka. It also categorised the Dharma according to practice as: Catvri-satyani, Paramita, and greed-ingrained.

These classification are indicative of the diversification and development of Buddhism and are consistent with the schematic three periods of historical development proposed by the late Venerable Tai Hsu. The latter were as follows:

First 500 years after Buddha's demise — Hinayana in vogue with Mahayana in the background. The Pali Tripitaka are representative of the Buddhism of this period.

Second 500 years — Mahayana to the fore with Hinayana attendant. The Chinese Tripitaka reflects the development of Buddhism in this period.

Third 500 years — Tantric Buddhism took the lead, leaving the exoteric school in its wake. The Tibetan Tripitaka is the fruit of this period.

Chinese Buddhism — from which Japanese Buddhism derives is representative of the Buddhism of the second 500 years, i.e. it is founded mainly on Bodhisattvayana, which links the earlier Sravakayana and the later Buddhayana. It therefore effectively ties Buddhist history together.

As it plays such a pivotal role in the historical development of the Buddha-dharma, the Chinese Tripitaka deserves the special attention of all those concerned with the present development of world Buddhism. It is my humble opinion that only in the study of the Chinese Tripitaka can the contents of Buddhism be fully and totally understood. The Chinese Tripitaka offers the following:

(a) Agamas: All four Agamas belong to the Bhava division. The Madhyamagama and Samyuktagama were translated from the texts of the Sravastivada school while the Dirghagama and Ekottaragama were translated from those of the Mahasamghika or Vibbajyavada schools. Though admittedly it does not contain a complete set of the sutras of any single school, (the Pali Tripitaka does present a more complete set), a textual conglomeration of many schools does have its merits (The Tibetan Tripitaka contains no Agama at all).

(b) Vinayas: The Tibetan Tripitaka contains only the new rules of the Tamrasatiya sect, while the Chinese Vinaya contains all the following:

(i) The Mahasamghika Vinaya of the Mahasamghika school.

(ii) The five divisions of the Mahisasaka Vinaya, the four divisions of the Dharmagupta Vinaya, the pratimoksa of Mahadasyapiyah, and the Sudarsana Vinaya of Tamrasatiya. All these are rules of the Vibbajyavada school.

(iii) The old Sravastivada Vinaya and the new Mulasarvasti vadanikaya Vinaya, both of the Sarvastivada school.

(iv) The Twenty-Two-Points-Of-Elucidation Sastras of the Sammatiya sect of the Vatsiputriyas school.

This rich collection of materials from different sources greatly facilitates comparative studies of sectarian Buddhism.

(c) Abhidharmas: This body of scripture is common to the three main schools of Theravada Buddhism, namely, the Vibhajyavadins, the Sarvastivadins, and the Vatsiputriyas. In the Tibetan Tripitaka there are only the Prajnapti of the Jnanaaprasthanasatpadabhidharma and the later Abhidarmakosa.

The Pali Tripitaka contains seven Sastras. While the Chinese Tripitaka has an especially large collection of the work of the Sarvastivada school, it also possesses the Abhidharma work of practically all sects. The Chinese Tripitaka contains:

(i) The Samgitiparyaya, the Dharmskandha, the Prajnapti, the Vijnanakaya, the Dhatukaya, the Prakaranapada, the Jnanaprasthana, the Mahavibhasa, the Abhidharma-hrdaya -vyakhya, the Abhiraharmananyanyanusara and the Abhidharmasamayapradipika Sastras of the Sarvastivada school.

(ii) Of the works of Vibhajyavadins, it includes the Abhidharma Sastra of Sariputa, which is the only important work that links up the Southern and Northern Abhidharmas.

(iii) It also contains the Vimmuttimagga which is a different version of the Pali Visuddhimagga.

(iv) It further contains the Sammitiya Sastra of the Vatsiputriya School.

(v) The renowned Abhidharmakosa of the third to fourth century which combines the best teachings of the Sarvastivada and Sautrantika schools, and the Satyasiddi Sastra of Harivarman which greatly influenced Chinese Buddhism.

All these treasures of the Abhidharma may be found in the Chinese Tripitaka. It can thus be seen that although the works of earlier dates in the Tripitaka were not given the full respect due to them by the majority of Chinese Buddhists, the wealth of information they contain will be of great reference value to anyone interested in tracing the divisions of the Sravaka schools and the development of the Bodhisattva ideal from the Sravakayana. If these scriptures are ignored, I will say that it would definitely not be possible for anyone to fulfil the responsibility of co-ordinating and linking the many branches of world Buddhism.

(d) Mahayana scriptures of the Sunyavada

(e) Mahayana scriptures of the noumenon school, or the school of eternal-reality, are very complete in the Chinese Tripitaka. These scriptures are very similar to those found in the Tibetan Tripitaka. The four great Sutras, the Prajnaparamita, the Avatamsaka, the Mahasamghata, and the Mahaparinirvana (to which may be added the Maharatnakuta Sutra, making five great sutras), are all tremendously voluminous works. Here it may be pointed out that the Chinese scriptures are particularly notable for the following characteristics:

(i) The different translations of the same Sutra have been safely preserved in the Chinese Tripitaka in their respective original versions without their being constantly revised according to later translations, as was the case with Tibetan scriptures. From a study of the Chinese translations we can thus trace the changes in content which the majority of scriptures have undergone over time and reflect upon the changes in the original Indian texts at different points in time. Thus we have the benefit of more than one version for reference, recording the evolution of the scriptures.

(ii) The Chinese Mahayana scriptures that were translated before the Tsin Dynasties (beginning 265 A.D.) are particularly related to the Buddhism of Chinese Turkestan with its center in the mountain areas of Kashmir. These scriptures form a strong nucleus of Chinese Buddhist thinking. The translations of the Dasabhumika Sastra and Lankavatara Sutra all possess very special characteristics.

(f) Madhyamika: The Madhyamika texts of the Chinese Tripitaka are considerably different from the Tibetan renditions of the same system of thought. The Chinese collection consists mostly of earlier works, particularly those of Nagarjuna, such as the Mahaprajnaparamita Sastra and the Dasabhumika-vibhasa Sastra, which not only present Madhyamika philosophy of a very high order but also illustrate extensively the acts of a Bodhisattva.

Of the late Madhyamika works, i.e. works produced by the disciples of Nagarjuna after the rise of the Yogacara system, only the Prajnapradipa Sastra of Bhavaviveka has been rendered into Chinese. The Chinese Tripitaka dose not contain works or as many schools of this system as the Tibetan Tripitaka. The Mahayanavataraka Sastra of Saramati and the Madhyayata Sastra of Asanga clearly indicate the change of thinking from the Madhyamika to the Yogacara system.

(g) Yogacara-Vijnanavada: The Chinese Tripitaka contains a very complete collection of this system of thought. It includes important scriptures such as the Dasabhumika, Mahayanasamparigraha Sastra, and Vijnaptimatrasiddhi Sastra. While the Tibetan system was mainly founded on the teachings of Sthiramati which are more akin to the Mahayanasamparigraha school of Chinese work, the Chinese students of orthodox Vijnanavada follow the teachings of Dharmapala.

The Vinaptimatrasiddhi Sastra, which represents the consummation of the Dignaga-Dharmapala-Silabhadra school of thought, is a gem of the Chinese Tripitaka. The Hetuvidya which is closely connected with Vijnanavada, is not fully translated in the Chinese Tripitaka and cannot compare favourably with the works of Dignaga and Dharmakirti collected in the Tibetan Tripitaka.

This seems to indicate that the Chinese people were not logically inclined, and gives no weight to engagements in verbal gymnastics and debates. In times past this had relegated the position of Sastra masters in China to one of relative unimportance.

(h) The esoteric Yoga: The Chinese Tripitaka includes Chinese translations of both the Vairocana Śutra of the practical division, and the Diamond Crown Sutra of the Yoga division of the Tantric school of Buddhism. The only esoteric scriptures that are missing are those of the Supreme Yoga division which, as they arrived in China at a time of national chaos, did not have much chance to circulate widely. Its very nature of achieving enlightenment through carnal expressions also made Tantrism unacceptable to the Chinese intellectuals. However, the texts of esoteric Yoga are abundant in the Tibetan Tripitaka

From the above it can be seen that the Chinese Tripitaka is composed mainly of Mahayana scriptures of the second 500 years, yet translations were not restricted to scriptures of this middle period. The Chinese Tripitaka also possesses a wealth of works of early Buddhism as a good portion of the later productions.

Thus, if one could have a sufficient knowledge of the Chinese Tripitaka, and could extend his knowledge from there to include the Pali Tripitaka of the Sravakayana, and the Madhyamika and Supreme Yoga of the Tibetan system, then he would have little difficulty in gaining an accurate, complete and comprehensive panorama of the 1,700 years of development of Indian Buddhism, the record of which has been preserved in the three great extant schools of Buddhist thought.

The late Venerable Tai Hsu once said, "To mold a new, critical and comprehensive system, based on the Chinese Tripitaka, the Theravada teaching of Ceylon, and selected components of the Tibetan canon, should be the objective of the writing of a history of Indian Buddhism." Even more so, it should be the objective of co-ordinating and connecting the many tributaries of world Buddhism. It is our responsibility to discard the trimmings and to retain the very essence of the great Tripitakas, adapting Buddhism to the modern world so that it may fulfil its mission of leading the way, taking under its wings the miserable beings of the present era.

CHINESE BUDDHIST PHILOSOPHY

When Buddhism first entered China from India and Central Asia two thousand years ago, Chinese favourably disposed towards it tended to view it as a part or companion school of the native Chinese Huang–Lao Daoist tradition, a form of Daoism rooted in texts and practices attributed to Huangdi (the Yellow Emperor) and Laozi. Others, less accepting of this 'foreign' incursion from the 'barbarous' Western Countries, viewed Buddhism as an exotic and dangerous challenge to the social and ethical Chinese civil order. For several centuries, these two attitudes formed the crucible within which the Chinese understanding of Buddhism was fashioned, even as more and more missionaries arrived (predominantly from Central Asia) bringing additional texts, concepts, rituals, meditative disciplines and other practices. Buddhists and Daoists borrowed ideas, terminology, disciplines, cosmologies, institutional structures, literary genres and soteric models from each other, sometimes so profusely that today it can be difficult if not impossible at times to determine who was first to introduce a certain idea. Simultaneously, polemical and political attacks from hostile Chinese quarters forced Buddhists to respond with apologia and ultimately reshape Buddhism into something the Chinese would find not only inoffensive, but attractive.

In the fifth century AD, Buddhism began to extricate itself from its quasi-Daoist pigeonhole by clarifying definitive differences between Buddhist and Daoist thought, shedding Daoist vocabulary and literary styles while developing new distinctively Buddhist terminology and genres. Curiously, despite the fact that Mahâyâna Buddhism had few adherents in Central Asia and was outnumbered by other Buddhist schools in India as well, in China Mahâyâna became the dominant form of Buddhism, so much so that few pejoratives were as stinging to a fellow Buddhist as labelling him 'Hînayâna' (literally 'Little Vehicle,' a polemical term for non-Mahâyânic forms of Buddhism). By the sixth century, the Chinese had been introduced to a vast array of Buddhist theories and practices representing a wide range of Indian Buddhist schools. As the Chinese struggled to master these doctrines it became evident that, despite the fact that these schools were all supposed to express the One Dharma (Buddha's Teaching), their teachings were not homogenous, and were frequently incommensurate.

By the end of the sixth century, the most pressing issue facing Chinese Buddhists was how to harmonize the disparities between the various teachings. Responses to this issue produced the Sinitic Mahâyâna schools, that is, Buddhist schools that originated in China rather than India. The four Sinitic schools are Tiantai, Huayan, Chan and Pure Land (Jingtu). Issues these schools share in common include Buddha-nature, mind, emptiness, *tathâgatagarbha*, expedient means (*upâya*), overcoming birth and death (*samsâra*), and enlightenment.

HISTORICAL OVERVIEW

The development of Chinese Buddhist philosophy can be divided roughly into four periods: (1) the early introduction of Indian and Central Asian Buddhism (first–fourth centuries AD); (2) the formative development of Chinese versions of Indian and Central Asian Schools (fifth–seventh centuries); (3) the emergence of distinctively Sinitic Buddhist schools (seventh–twelfth centuries); and (4) the continuance of Chinese Buddhism into the present day (thirteenth century onwards).

From the fourth through the seventh centuries, Buddhists periodically realized that the positions being engendered in China were at variance with their Indian antecedents, and attempted to correct the problem, either through the introduction of additional translations or by clarifying differences between Buddhist and native Chinese ideas. By the eighth century, the Chinese had apparently become satisfied with the types of Buddhism they had developed, since from then on they lost interest in Indian commentaries and treatises and instead turned their attention toward Chinese commentaries on the Buddhist scriptures – such as the *Lotus Sutra* and *Huayan Sutra* – that had assumed importance for Chinese Buddhist traditions. Moreover, even though missionaries continued to arrive in China and new translations continued to be produced through the thirteenth century, none of the significant developments in Indian Buddhism (such as Buddhist syllogistic logic) from the seventh century onwards had any lasting impact on Chinese Buddhism, and many important texts and thinkers (for example, Dharmakîrti, Candrakîrti, Sântaraksita) remained virtually unknown in East Asia until modern times.

EARLIEST DEVELOPMENTS

The first undisputed reference to Buddhism in China is an edict by Emperor Ming to Liu Ying, king of Qu, in the year ad 65, which mentions sacrifices performed by the king to Buddha as well as favourable treatment for Buddhist monks and laymen; the edict also identifies King Liu Ying as a follower of Huang–Lao Daoism. For the next few centuries, the Chinese continued to view Buddhist texts and practices as a part of supplement to Daoism. Buddhism seemed to share important issues with the types of Daoism practised in this period, including the metaphysical primacy of emptiness, meditation techniques, dietary and behavioural disciplines, afterlife theories connected to moral and behavioural discipline, expansive pantheons and cosmologies, striving for the soteriological transformation of the ordinary human condition, rigorous and subtle intellectual traditions, and magical and yogic powers. These affinities, however, were more apparent than real, since the Buddhist approaches to these issues usually differed sharply from their Daoist counterparts, though Buddhists did not assert their distinctiveness until the fifth century.

Buddhist monks and businessmen representing a variety of Buddhist schools and disciplines continued to arrive in China, establishing Buddhist communities in Loyang and elsewhere. It took several centuries for the Chinese to notice how disparate the various forms of Buddhism really were. Initially the Chinese were most interested in Buddhist meditation techniques, including chanting and visualizations, which they adopted as supplements to Daoistic techniques. Daoism held out the promise that one could become a sage or perfected person, or even an immortal, but the exact details of how to accomplish this transformation remained elusive and vague. In comparison to many of the Daoist texts which were esoteric, hard to find, and frequently obscure in presentation, Buddhist texts seemed systematic and detailed, providing step-by-step procedures for practitioners.

Along with meditation manuals, the earliest Buddhist texts to become popular in China were Âvadana materials (legends of the Buddha and Buddhist heroes) and the Perfection of Wisdom Scriptures (*Prajñâpâramitâ Sutras*). About half a dozen schools formed around varying interpretations of the Perfection of Wisdom Scriptures, mixing ideas found in these and other Buddhist texts with concepts prominent among Chinese intelligentsia. One Prajñâschool, called the Original Nothingness school (*Benwu*), adopted a neo-Daoist cosmology: everything has emerged from a primordial, original emptiness, and everything returns to that void. This was a thorough misconstrual of Buddhist emptiness. Another school, called the Mind Empty school (*Xinwu*), equated the primordial Nothing with the nature of mind. Each of the Prajñâschools managed either to promote a metaphysical substantialized emptiness which they opposed to form, or smuggle an eternal self or spirit into their formulations, despite Buddhism's emphatic rejection of the notion of permanent selfhood.

Dao'an (ad 312–85) criticized the Prajñâschools, challenging their faithfulness to authentic Buddhist positions as well as the translation methodologies behind the texts they and other Chinese Buddhists had come to rely on. In particular, he criticized the practice of 'matching the meanings' (*geyi*), by which translators seeking Chinese equivalents for Indian Buddhist technical terms and concepts borrowed heavily from Daoist literature. This 'matching of meanings' was a mixed blessing. Packaging Buddhist ideas in familiar terms made them amenable and understandable, but the 'matches' were often less than perfect, distorting or misrepresenting Buddhism. For instance, early translators chose a well-known Daoist and Confucian term, *wuwei* (nondeliberative activity), to translate *nirvana*. Arguably, *wuwei* and *nirvâna* represent the teloi of Daoism and Buddhism, respectively, but it is not obvious that they denote the same telos.

Later, to emphasize the uniqueness of Buddhist *nirvana*, translators dropped *wuwei* in favour of a transliteration, *niepan*. *Wuwei* was retained to render another important Buddhist notion, *asamskkha* (unconditioned). The semantic connotations of Daoist *wuwei* and Buddhist *wuwei*, while possibly overlapping in some senses, were nonetheless quite distinct: for Daoists it meant a mode of interacting effortlessly and naturally with the world, while for Buddhists it denoted something unaffected by causes and conditions, that neither arose nor ceased. Chinese readers inevitably came to conflate the semantic ranges of such terms, which over the centuries led to some distinctively Chinese Buddhist concepts. After Dao'an, Chinese Buddhism asserted its distinctiveness from native Chinese traditions and Buddhists adopted increasingly critical hermeneutic approaches to translation.

THE AWAKENING OF FAITH IN MAHÂYÂNA

These debates and their ramifications dominated Chinese Buddhist thought in the sixth century. On one side was a substantialistic nondual metaphysic whose eternalistic ground was variously called Buddha-nature, mind, *tathâgatagarbha*, *Dharma-dhâtu* and suchness (*tathatâ*; in Chinese, *rulai*). On the other side was an anti-substantialist critique that eschewed any form of metaphysical reification, emphasizing emptiness as the absence of permanent selfhood or independent essence in anything. To the anti-substantialists the *tathâgatagarbha* position sounded dangerously close to the notion of eternalistic, reified selfhood that Buddha had rejected. Mahâyâna texts had declared that there were four conceptual perversions or reversals behind human delusion: (1) seeing a self in what lacks self; (2) seeing permanence in the impermanent; (3) seeing happiness in what is suffering; and (4) seeing purity in the impure. Yet starting with the earliest *tathâgatagarbha* texts – such as *The Lion's Roar of Queen Úrîmâla* – *tathâgatagarbha* was brazenly defined as 'self, eternal, happiness and pure'. In the face of these and other disparities, the Chinese asked how, if there is only one *dharma* (teaching), there can be such incommensurate variety.

The *Awakening of Faith in Mahâyâna*, a Chinese composition purporting to be a translation by Paramartha of an Indian text, became an instant classic by offering a masterly synthesis of Buddhist teachings that seemed to resolve many of the disparities. Its central tenet is that there is one Mind that has two aspects. One aspect is suchness and the other is *samsâra*, the cycle of birth and death, arising and ceasing. Suchness also has two aspects, emptiness and non-empty. Emptiness in this text means suchness is beyond predication, neither one nor many, neither the same nor different. Non-empty means it is endowed with all the marvellous qualities and merits of a Buddha, 'as numerous as the sands along the banks of the Ganges'. The link between suchness and the realm of arising and ceasing is *tathâgatagarbha* in association with the *âlaya-vijñâna*. Ignorance, enlightenment and pursuit of the Path are all on the arising and ceasing side.

In a pivotal passage that would become foundational for most forms of Chinese, Korean and Japanese Buddhism, the *Awakening of Faith in Mahâyâna* states that on the basis of Original Enlightenment there is non-enlightenment; on the basis of non-enlightenment there is initial enlightenment; and on the basis of initial enlightenment there is final enlightenment, which is the full realization of original enlightenment. Beyond the problem of theodicy that it raises (the text does not offer a clear explanation for why or how non-enlightenment arises), several issues emerge. First, suddenly there is no longer simply one enlightenment that is achieved at the culmination of a spiritual path, but instead several enlightenments, one of which (original enlightenment) precedes even entering the path. What the text calls initial enlightenment had been termed *bodhicitta* or *cittotpâda* (arousing the aspiration for enlightenment) in previous Buddhist literature.

Arousing this aspiration is what the title *Awakening of Faith in Mahâyâna* signifies. Now, rather than marking a singular, ultimate achievement, the term 'enlightenment' referred to several things: an atemporal originary ground upon which everything else plays out, including non-enlightenment; one's initial resolve or insight that leads one to begin pursuing the path; the final achievement at the end of the path, an achievement that is not only anticlimactic, but is little more than an unravelling of the intersection of original and initial enlightenment. This reinforced the conviction of Chinese Buddhists that the conflationist approach, with its emphasis on Buddha-nature or mind as ground, was the correct view.

One of the first to recognize the importance of the *Awakening of Faith in Mahâyâna* was a Korean monk named Wônhyo. He wrote a commentary on the text that reached China, where it influenced Fazang, a foundational thinker of the Huayan school, who used its ideas as a major cornerstone for his thinking. Since the *Dilun*, originally an independent text, had eventually been incorporated into the *Huayan Sutra* as one of its chapters, and that scripture became the basic text of the Huayan school, many of the issues that had emerged from the debates on the *Dilun* were absorbed and reconfigured by the Huayan thinkers. In a sense, it was ultimately Ratnamati's interpretation that prevailed after two centuries of debate. The *Awakening of Faith in Mahâyâna* became pivotal for Chinese Buddhism, is still one of the foundations of Korean Buddhism and, though it has been eclipsed in Japan by other texts such as the *Lotus Sutra*, many of its ideas, such as the idea of original enlightenment (*hongaku*), still exert a profound influence. This text set the stage for the development of distinctively East Asian forms of Buddhism.

THE CHINESE BUDDHIST SCHOOLS

Although the ideas and literature of many different forms of Buddhism reached China – including Sarvâstivâda, Mahîsâsika, Sammitîya, Dharmaguptaka, Sautrântika and others – only Madhyamaka and Yogâcâra developed Chinese schools and lineages. Madhyamaka disappeared as an independent school after Jizang, but its influence and the preeminence of Nâgârjuna never abated. The sixth century was basically a battleground of competing Yogâcâric theories.

In the seventh century the famous Chinese pilgrim Xuanzang (600–64) spent sixteen years travelling in Central Asia and India. He returned to China in 645 and translated seventy-four works. Due in part to his accomplishments as a traveller and translator, and in part to the eminent favour bestowed on him by the Chinese emperor upon his return, Xuanzang became the most prominent East Asian Buddhist of his generation. He promoted an orthodox form of Yogâcâra as it was then being practised in India, and students flocked to him from Japan and Korea as well as China. Not everyone was enamoured of the Buddhist ideology he had brought back. Zhiyan (602–68), who would later be considered one of the patriarchs of the Huayan school, was openly critical of Xuanzang's teachings, and Fazang had joined Xuanzang's translation committee late in Xuanzang's life, only to quit in disgust at Xuanzang's 'distorted' views.

While in India, Xuanzang had discovered how far Chinese Buddhism had deviated from its Indian source, and his translations and teachings were deliberate attempts to bring Chinese Buddhism back in line with Indian teachings. The ideas he opposed (primarily but not exclusively those that had been promoted by Paramârtha's school) were already deeply entrenched in Chinese Buddhist thinking. While he was alive his pre-eminence made him unassailable, but once he died his detractors attacked his successor, Kuiji (632–82), and successfully returned Chinese and East Asian Buddhism to the trajectory established by the conflationists. (Wônch'ûk, a Korean student of Xuanzang, was a rival of Kuiji who fared better with the revivalists since he attempted to harmonize the teachings of Paramârtha and Xuanzang).

The underlying ideology of this resurgence, which reached its intellectual apex over the course of the Tang and Song Dynasties (sixth–twelfth centuries), was neatly summarized by the label '*dharma*-nature' (*faxing*), that is, the metaphysical ground of Buddha-nature *qua dharma-dhâtu qua* mind-nature *qua tathâgatagarbha*. Fazang argued that orthodox Yogâcâra only understood *dharma* characteristics (*faxiang*), that is, phenomenal appearances, but not the deeper underlying metaphysical reality, '*dharma*-nature'. After Fazang, all the Sinitic Buddhist schools considered themselves *dharma*-nature schools; Yogâcâra and sometimes Sanlun were considered merely *dharma* characteristics schools.

Four *dharma*-nature schools emerged. Each school eventually compiled a list of its patriarchs through whom its teachings were believed to have been transmitted. Modern scholarship in Japan and the West has shown that these lineages were usually forged long after the fact, and frequently were erroneous or distorted the actual historical events. For instance, while Huiyuan was an active promoter of the Sarvâstivâdin teachings introduced during his time by Sanghadeva and Buddhabhadra, the later Pure Land schools dubbed him their initial Chinese patriarch on the basis of his alleged participation in Amitâbha rituals, allegations that were probably first concocted during the Tang Dynasty. Similarly, the lineage of six Chan patriarchs from Bodhidharma to Huineng is unlikely; the Huayan lineage (Du Shun to Zhiyan to Fazang to Chengguan) was largely an invention of the 'fourth' patriarch, Chengguan: his predecessors were unaware that they were starting a new lineage and rather thought that they were reviving the true old-time religion of Paramârtha. It was also during the Tang dynasty that Tantra briefly passed through China, from whence it was brought to Japan and became firmly established as the Shingon school.

THE CHINESE BUDDHIST SCHOOLS: TIANTAI

Though considered its third patriarch, the intellectual founder of the Tiantai school was Zhiyi (538–97). Responding to the proliferation of different Buddhist theories and practices, he proposed a masterly, detailed synthesis that definitively set Chinese Buddhism in its own direction. To the question of why there was an abundance of incommensurate teachings despite the fact that there could only be one *dharma,* Zhiyi replied that all the different vehicles of Buddhism were ultimately one vehicle (*eka-yâna*), an idea championed by the *Lotus Sutra*. More specifically, he offered a *panjiao,* or classificatory scheme of teachings, to explain the discrepancies. His *panjiao* was complex and brilliant (and further refined much later by Chegwan, a Korean Tiantai monk in China), but in simple form it can be summarized as follows:

Buddha offered different teachings to different audiences based on the differing capacities of audiences to comprehend what he preached. According to the basic narrative, which became the way all Chinese Buddhists thought of Buddha's teaching career, upon reaching enlightenment under the Bodhi Tree, Buddha, enraptured by his new vision, began to describe that vision in immediate and exuberant terms. This became the *Huayan Sutra*. (In reality, this 'sutra' is a collection of disparate texts – none probably composed earlier than the third century ad – that were gradually compiled together over several more centuries.) When he finished (it took two or three weeks) he realized that no one had understood the sublime meaning of his words, and immediately began to teach a simplified, preparatory teaching which became the Hînayâna teachings. After twenty years of preparatory teachings, he introduced the next level, beginners' Mahâyâna (basically Yogâcâra and Madhyamaka).

In the next period he introduced advanced Mahâyâna (the *Vaipûlya Sutras*), and finally in his last days, having now trained many advanced students, he preached the *Lotus Sutra* and the *Nirvâna Sutra*. In effect this *panjiao* asserts that the two highest sutras offered by Buddha were the *Huayan* and *Lotus;* but whereas the *Huayan* was too sublime to be understood by any save the most advanced or enlightened students, the *Lotus* represented Buddha's most comprehensive, cumulative, mature and accessible teaching, every bit as sublime as the *Huayan*, but now presented in a pedagogically effective manner. For that reason, Zhiyi made the *Lotus Sutra* the foundational text of Tiantai. As for the remaining teachings, as the *Lotus* itself explains, different 'truths' can be superseded once they have served their task of raising one to a higher level where a different 'truth' holds sway. Buddhism, according to the *Lotus* and Tiantai, is a system of expedient means (*upâya*) leading one with partial truths to ever greater, more comprehensive truths. Tiantai teachings are 'Round Teachings', meaning that they encircle or encompass everything and, lacking sharp edges, are therefore Perfect. Other forms of Buddhism are not 'wrong', but are only partial visions of the One Vehicle that Tiantai most perfectly and completely embodies.

Zhiyi, based on an exhaustive exposition of a verse from Nâgârjuna's *Madhyamaka-kârikâs* (24: 18), devised a theory of three truths: provisional, empty and middle. The first two are mirror images of each other, two ways of speaking about causes and conditions. A table can provisionally be called a table, since its perceptible form has arisen through causes and conditions, and it only exists provisionally on the basis of those temporary conditions. The table is empty because, being the product of causes and conditions, it lacks its own intrinsic, independent nature. It is 'middle' because neither the provisional nor the empty truth about the table fully captures its reality. It is both provisional and empty, and simultaneously neither provisional nor empty. As Zhiyi put it, 'wondrous being is identical to true emptiness'. Zhiyi sought many ways to express the nondual middle truth. For instance, rejecting the obvious dualism of the distinction most of his contemporaries made between pure mind (*xin*) and deluded thought-instants (*nian*), Zhiyi declared that every deluded thought-instant was identical to three thousand chilicosms.

The details of the formulas he used to arrive at the number three thousand is less important than fact that it is meant to encompass the full extent of Buddhist cosmological metaphysics. The whole universe in all its dimensions is entailed in every moment of thought. Rather than attempt to eliminate deluded thinking to reach a purified mind, Zhiyi claimed each moment of deluded thinking was already identical to enlightenment. One merely has to see the mind and its operations as they are. This idea was later taken over by the Chan (Zen) school, which expressed it in sayings such as 'Zen mind is everyday mind'.

The middle approach is also evident in the Tiantai notion of three gates, or three methods of access to enlightened vision: the Buddha-gate, the gate of sentient beings and the mind-gate. The Buddha-gate was considered too difficult, too abstruse, too remote; one had to be a Buddha already to fully comprehend it. The sentient-being gate (the various methods taught and practised by any sort of being) was also too difficult because there are too many different types of sentient beings all with their own types of delusions, so that this gate is a confusing cacophony of disparate methods, some which may not be appropriate for some beings. The easiest and hence preferable gate was the mind-gate. It is no more remote than this very moment of cognition, its diversity can be observed in every thought-instant, and nothing could ever be more appropriately suited for an individual than to observe one's own mind. Tiantai cultivated many types of meditation for that purpose.

THE CHINESE BUDDHIST SCHOOLS: HUAYAN

Drawing on a *panjiao* similar to that of Zhiyi, the Huayan school chose the *Huayan Sutra* (Sanskrit title *AvataCsaka Sutra*, Chinese *Huayan jing*) for its foundational scripture. What immediately differentiates Huayan from typically Indian approaches is that instead of concentrating on a diagnosis of the human problem, and exhorting and prescribing solutions for it, Huayan immediately begins from the point of view of enlightenment. In other words, its discourse represents a nirvanic perspective rather than a samsaric perspective. Instead of detailing the steps that would lead one from ignorance to enlightenment, Huayan immediately endeavours to describe how everything looks through enlightened eyes.

Like Tiantai, Huayan offers a totalistic, encompassing 'round' view. A lived world as constituted through a form of life experience is called a *dharma-dhâtu*. Chengguan, the 'fourth' Huayan patriarch, described four types of *dharma-dhâtus*, each successively encompassing its predecessors. The first is *shi*, which means 'event', 'affair' or 'thing'. This is the realm where things are experienced as discrete individual items. The second is called *li* (principle), which in Chinese usage usually implies the principal metaphysical order that subtends events as well as the rational principles that explicate that order. Often *li* is used by Buddhists as a synonym for emptiness.

The first sustained analysis based on the relation of *li* and *shi* was undertaken by the Korean monk Wônhyo in his commentary on the *Awakening of Faith in Mahâyâna*, which influenced early Huayan thinkers like Fazang. The *li–shi* model went on to become an important analytic tool for all sorts of East Asian philosophers, not just Buddhists. In the realm of *li*, one clearly sees the principles that relate *shi* to each other, but the principles are more important than the individual events. In the third realm, one sees the mutual interpenetration or 'non-obstruction' of *li* and *shi* (*lishi wu'ai*). Rather than seeing events while being oblivious to principle, or concentrating on principle while ignoring events, in this realm events are seen as instantiations of principle, and principle is nothing more than the order by which events relate to each other.

In the fourth and culminating *dharma-dhâtu*, one sees the mutual interpenetration and non-obstruction of all events (*shishi wu'ai*). In this realm, everything is causally related to everything else. Huayan illustrates this with the image of Indra's net, a vast net that encompasses the universe. A special jewel is found at the intersection of every horizontal and vertical weave in the net, special because each jewel reflects every other jewel in the net, so that looking into any one jewel, one sees them all. Every event or thing can disclose the whole universe because all mutually interpenetrate each other without barriers or obstruction.

This form of nondualism is not monistic because *shishi wu'ai* does not obliterate the distinctions between things, but rather insists that everything is connected to everything else *without* losing distinctiveness. Identity and difference, in this view, are merely two sides of the same coin, which, though a single coin, still has two distinct sides that should not be confused for each other. Mutual interpenetration is temporal as well as spatial; past, present and future mutually interpenetrate. Hence according to Huayan, to enter the path towards final enlightenment is, in an important sense, to have already arrived at that destination.

THE CHINESE BUDDHIST SCHOOLS: CHAN

Better known in the West by its Japanese pronunciation, Zen, Chan emerged as a reaction against the increasing scholastic complexities of the Tiantai and Huayan schools and their voluminous, hairsplitting literature, which, some Chan practitioners believed, could be more of an obstacle than an aid to enlightenment. The Pâli term for meditative absorption, *jhâna* (Sanskrit, *dhyâna*), was transliterated into Chinese as *Channa*, and then shortened to *Chan*. Until the early Tang Dynasty, *chanshi* (Chan master) meant a monk adept at meditation, though it did not specify what sorts of meditation he was practising. Some monks were called *dharma* masters (*fashi*), some were called scriptural masters (*zangshi*), some were called disciplinary masters (*lushi*) and some were meditation masters. These titles could be applied to a monk (or nun) of any school, since they denoted one's methodological focus rather than one's ideological leanings.

Chan begins to denote a specific doctrinal and meditative ideology around the time of Huineng (638–713). Although Chan tradition describes a transmission by five patriarchs culminating in Huineng as the sixth patriarch, as noted above, that transmission is more fiction than fact. Huineng's followers established the Southern School of Chan, which unleashed a polemical tirade against the Northern School. Since the Northern School disappeared about a thousand years ago, our only source of information on these schools was the prejudiced accounts of the Southern School, until the discovery at Dunhuang early this century of Northern School documents. We now know that many different versions of lineage histories were circulated, and, more importantly, that the positions attributed to the Northerners by their Southern rivals were grossly inaccurate and unfair. In fact, the Northern School had initially been the more successful of the two, but its success led to its ultimate ruin, since its growing dependence on Imperial patronage made it a vulnerable target during times of Imperial persecution of Buddhism. The Southern School, because it had taken root in remote areas less affected by actions of the Central government, survived the persecutions relatively intact.

Huineng is depicted in the *Platform Sutra* (authored by his leading follower and promoter, Shenhui) as an illiterate seller of firewood who experiences sudden enlightenment while overhearing someone reciting the *Diamond Sutra*. He joins a monastery where, without any official training in scriptures or meditation, he demonstrates that his enlightenment is more profound than all the monks who had been practising for years. Hence sudden enlightenment is one of the main tenets of the *Platform Sutra* (and subsequently for all forms of Chan). Another is 'direct pointing at mind', which, similar to the Tiantai approach, means that what is important is to observe one's own mind, to recognize that the nature of one's mind is Buddha-nature itself.

While some Buddhists had argued that the goal was wisdom, and meditation was merely a means to that goal, Huineng argued for the inseparability of meditation and wisdom. Using an analytic device probably introduced by the so-called neo-Daoist Wang Bi (226–49), the *tiyong* model, Huineng claimed that meditation is the essence (*ti*) of wisdom, and wisdom is the function (*yong*) of meditation. Wisdom does not produce meditation, nor does meditation produce wisdom; nor are meditation and wisdom different from each other. He drew an analogy to a lamp: the lamp is the *ti*, while its light is the *yong*. Wherever there is a (lit) lamp, there is light; wherever there is lamplight, there is a lamp. Lamp and light are different in name but identical in substance (*ti*), hence nondual.

Huineng's style of Chan was still sober, calm, rational, and rooted in commonly accepted Buddhist tenets. New and more radical elements were soon incorporated into Chan, some iconoclastically renouncing meditation and practice as well as scholasticism, and others trying earnestly to work out a rational system by which Chan could be syncretized with the other schools. Zongmi (780–841) considered a patriarch of both the Chan and Huayan schools, attempted just such a synthesis, but his sober approach was soon overshadowed in China by more abrupt, startling forms of Chan.

Of the 'Five Houses of Chan', only the Linji school survives today in China, Taiwan and Korea. Based on the teachings of Linji (d. 867), this school possibly provided Buddhism with its most 'Chinese' voice. Chan literature of the Linji and related schools were among the first texts ever written in vernacular as opposed to classical Chinese. Daoist elements also began to appear prominently. Zhuangzi's 'true man' becomes Linji's 'true man of no rank' who is going in and out of each person's face this very moment, and is always right here before one. The anecdotal humour associated with Zhuangzi's stories and the irreverent exploits of the Bamboo Sages of the Six Dynasties period clearly infused the style of Chan anecdotes. Rather than indulge in elaborate, complicated theoretical abstractions, Chan focused on experience as lived, in terms familiar to anyone immersed in Chinese culture (though often exotic to Western students, which has led to the common misconception that Chan is nonsensical or obscurantist).

Teaching techniques began to overshadow doctrinal content. At the heart of Chan training are the exchanges between teacher and student. Records, called *gongan*, were compiled of classic encounters, and even these eventually became part of the teaching techniques, as they were presented to students as riddles to concentrate on during meditation. To disrupt the sort of idle or pernicious speculation that could prove a hindrance to enlightenment, abrupt and shocking techniques were employed, from radical statements such as, 'If you meet Buddha on the road, kill him!', to exchanges punctuated by blows and shouts (all the more startling in the subdued monastic atmosphere in which they would unexpectedly occur). Linji's methods were designed to make students confront and overcome their mental and emotional habits and crutches, so as to become truly free and independent. Even dependency on Buddhism could be such a crutch. Linji summarized his teaching with the phrase: 'Don't be deceived.'

THE CHINESE BUDDHIST SCHOOLS: PURE LAND

All forms of Chinese Buddhism, including Chan, contain devotional elements and rituals, but for Pure Land Buddhists devotionalism is the essence. The origins of Pure Land Buddhism are somewhat unclear. While undoubtedly devotional practices were imported to China by monks and laity (and these were blended with native Chinese forms of devotionalism), there does not seem to be a distinct school in India devoted to rebirth in Amitâbha's Pure Land. As noted earlier, the traditional lineages are not very helpful for reconstructing the school's history. According to tradition, early contributors to Pure Land thought and practice include Tanluan (476–542), Dao Chuo (562–645) and his student Shandao (613–81). The term 'Pure Land' (*jingtu*) may itself be largely a product of certain license taken by translators. The term *jingtu* appears in Kumârajîva's translation of the *Vimalakîrti Sutra* where the Tibetan version simply has 'Buddha lands' (the Sanskrit version is no longer extant). Apparently, Xuanzang was the first explicitly to associate Sukhâvati (Amitâbha's Paradise) with the term 'pure land'. The main scriptures for Pure Land practice were the Larger and Smaller *Sukhâvati-vyuha Sutras* and the *Guan Wuliangshuofo jing*.

At the beginning of the Tang Dynasty, several forms of Buddhist devotionalism were popular, including cults devoted to Mañjuúrî(Bodhisattva of Wisdom), Guanyin (Bodhisattva of Compassion, at that time particularly popular as a patron saint and protector of travellers), Maitreya (the future Buddha) and Amita (a conflation of Amitâbha and Amitâyus whose names mean 'Infinite Light' and 'Infinite Life' respectively, and are possibly deities of Central Asian origin). Arguably the most popular form of devotionalism was the Maitreya cult. The Empress Wu (r. 683–705), a great patron of Buddhism but generally reviled in Chinese history as an unscrupulous usurper, considered herself an incarnation of Maitreya. Due to her unpopularity once dethroned, people wanted to distance themselves from her and anything associated with her. Unfortunately this effectively extinguished Maitreya worship in China. Worshippers of Amita filled the void.

Pure Land theology maintained that people were living in the age of degenerate *dharma*, when study and personal effort were insufficient for making progress on the path to liberation. Relying on one's own efforts was in fact deemed a form of self-theory, or the selfishness and arrogance that comes from erroneous views of self. Rather than indulge in egoistic fantasies, one ought to rely on the power and grace of Amita. Amita was a *buddha* (whether he was an earlier incarnation of the historical Buddha or another person altogether is answered differently by different Pure Land sources) who, while still a *bodhisattva*, vowed to help sentient beings once he became a *buddha*. He has the power to transfer to anyone he deems worthy sufficient merit to enable them to be born in his Pure Land, the Western Paradise. In the earliest forms of Pure Land devotionalism a variety of practices were cultivated, but these were eventually pared down to chanting the *nianfo*, literally 'remembrance of Buddhas' (in Sanskrit, *buddhânusm[ti*), which in Chinese is 'Na-mu A-mi-to Fo' (Hail Amita Buddha).

SINICIZING BUDDHIST CONCEPTS

Since the time of Mencius, the ultimate ontological issue in China was the question of human nature and mind (which Mencius and most Chinese thinkers treated as synonyms). Pre-Han Chinese philosophers had debated whether human nature was originally good, bad or neutral. The written Chinese character for 'nature', *xing*, consists of two parts: the left side means 'mind' and the right side means 'birth', which led Chinese thinkers to debate whether human nature was determined by what one is born with, namely appetites and desires, or whether it reflects the nature of one's mind, which in Chinese thought invariably carried an onto-ethical rather than strictly cognitive connotation. The word *xin* literally means 'heart', indicating that – unlike Western conceptions that draw a sharp line between the head and the heart – for the Chinese, thinking and feeling originated in the same bodily locus. Feeling empathy or compassion as well as rationally abstracting principles and formulating ethical codes were all activities of *xin*, heart-and-mind.

Indian Buddhism had little to say about human nature, with many forms of Buddhism rejecting the very concept of essential nature. Some of the early polemics against Buddhism in China explicitly attacked it for neglecting to address the question of human nature. The notion of Buddha-nature was developed, in part, to redress that failing. Since Indian Buddhists were deeply interested in the mind in terms of cognitive processes such as perception, thinking, attention and so on, it was a natural step for the Chinese to read these initially in the light of the Chinese discourse on mind, and to further develop interpretations of this material in line with Chinese concerns. Hence passages that in Sanskrit dealt primarily with epistemology or cognitive conditions often became, in their Chinese renderings, psycho-moral descriptions. The Sanskrit term *ekacitta*, a mind with singular focus (but literally meaning 'one mind') becomes the metaphysical one mind of the *Awakening of Faith in Mahâyâna*. Similarly, Indian and Chinese philosophers had developed very different types of causal theories. Indian Buddhists accepted only efficient causes as real, while Chinese Buddhists tended to interpret Buddhist causal theories as examples of formal causes.

SINICIZING BUDDHIST CONCEPTS: EMPTINESS

Before Buddhism entered China Daoists had already embraced a notion of emptiness which it took Buddhists several centuries to realize was significantly different from their own. Laozi had contrasted the empty or open (*xu*) with the solid. What made a wheel functional was its empty hub; what made a vessel or room functional was its open space. Hence emptiness (or openness) is not worthless but rather the key to functionality and usefulness. Later Daoists contrasted existents (*you*) with nonexistence (*wu*), and claimed that all existence emerges from nonexistence and ultimately returns to nonexistence. Some Chinese metaphysicians, such as Wang Bi, wrote about primordial nonexistence (*yuan wu*, *benwu*) as the metaphysical source, destination and substratum for all existent things. Thus form and emptiness were opposed, contrasting poles, and emptiness had primacy.

Some early Chinese Buddhists interpreted Buddhist emptiness in the same fashion, especially in the Prajñâschools. Eventually Buddhists realized, as the *Heart Sutra* says, that form and emptiness are not opposed to each other, but that 'form itself *is* emptiness, emptiness itself *is* form, form is not different from emptiness, emptiness is not different from form.' In other words, Buddhist 'emptiness' did not mean 'open' or 'nonexistence'. Emptiness (*sûnyatâ*) signified the absence of an eternal, independent, self-causing, invariant, essential self-nature (*svabhâva*) or selfhood (*âtman*) in any thing or person. Whatever existed did so by virtue of a perpetually changing web of causes and conditions that themselves were products of other causes and conditions. Stated simplistically, emptiness does not mean that a table is unreal or nonexistent, or that its solid texture or colour are unreal; it does mean that the concept of tableness is unreal, and that the abstractions 'solidity' and 'colour' are unreal apart from the discrete and particular sensations one has at specific moments due to specific causes and conditions. Buddhist emptiness is not a primal void, but the absence of self-essence. To avoid being confused with Daoist concepts of emptiness, the Buddhists eventually chose a new term, *kong*, to render their 'emptiness'.

Emptiness is neither the origin nor terminus for forms; forms themselves at any moment are emptiness. Since everything is causally connected with everything else, and there are no independent identities beyond or behind such causes and conditions, everything, according to Huayan, mutually interpenetrates and conditions everything else. Everything defines and is defined by every other thing.

SINICIZING BUDDHIST CONCEPTS: SUFFERING AND IGNORANCE

For all forms of Indian Buddhism, the fundamental fact with which Buddhism begins, and the problem it attempts to solve, is the problem of suffering (*dukkha*). The first of the Four Noble Truths is: 'All is suffering.' Suffering does not mean simply pain. Buddhism does not deny joy, pleasure, delight and so on; but it claims that all is impermanent, so that whatever the source of a particular pleasure, that pleasure can never be permanent. The more pleasure one feels, the greater becomes one's attachment to the presumed source. The greater the attachment, the greater the pain at the loss of that pleasure. Since everything is impermanent, such loss is inevitable. So, ironically, pleasure itself is 'suffering'. Suffering is the affective reaction to impermanence. According to general Buddhist causal analysis, the causes of suffering are desire and ignorance. We desire permanent pleasures because we are ignorant of the fact that all is impermanent, empty of eternal selfhood. As the Four Noble Truths state, these causes of suffering can be eliminated, and Buddhism is the method or path for eliminating those causes. The purpose of Buddhism, then, is the elimination of suffering.

Chinese Buddhist texts do occasionally mention suffering, but usually in passing. Instead the root problem became ignorance. Discussions of the dialectical conflict between ignorance and enlightenment grew so pervasive that suffering was all but forgotten.

This shift helped reinforce the emphasis on mind and mind-nature. Enlightenment was no longer defined as awakening to the causes of suffering, but instead denoted seeing the nature of the mind itself.

SINICIZING BUDDHIST CONCEPTS: IS BUDDHA-NATURE GOOD OR EVIL?

The pre-Han debate about whether human nature is good, evil or neutral was echoed in debates between Chinese Buddhists about Buddha-nature. Huayan contended that Buddha-nature and *tathâgatagarbha* were pristinely pure and good, filled with infinite good merits and qualities. In the fully realized perfection of Buddha-nature all evil, impurities and delusions have been eradicated.

This position was opposed by Tiantai, which argued that some evil (that is, some ignorance) remains in Buddha-nature. Following the Daoist sense of nonduality, in which good and evil or pure and impure are complimentary opposites as impossible to separate from each other as East from West, Tiantai accused Huayan of dualistic extremism. From the Tiantai perspective, Huayan's 'obsession' with purity and goodness was one-sided and dualistic. Moreover, Tiantai insisted that it is necessary for Buddha-nature to retain some traces of evil and delusion in order to understand and empathize with the plight of ordinary sentient beings. If one becomes too rarefied, too transcendent, one loses touch with the everyday reality in which people wander deludedly, and thus one becomes incapable of effectively saving such people. Buddhahood, for Tiantai, was not simply a matter of correctly seeing or understanding in a 'pure' way, but was at its core salvific; Buddhahood is the active liberation of sentient beings from ignorance.

The debate on Buddha-nature heated up during the Song Dynasty. Heterodox forms of Tiantai tinged with Huayan's 'purity obsession' appeared, and these were challenged sharply by the orthodox Tiantai thinkers from their headquarters on Tiantai mountain (from which the school took its name). The heterodox schools were labeled the Off-Mountain groups, while the orthodoxy styled itself the On-Mountain group. Zhili (959–1028), one of the On-Mountain leaders, had a keen intellect alert to the subtlest hints of Huayan-like thinking lurking in the rhetoric of Off-Mountain thinkers; his writings systematically ferret out and refute those implications with a logical sophistication rarely equalled amongst Chinese Buddhist philosophers.

These debates gain additional importance when viewed in the larger context of Chinese intellectual history. In the pre-Han period, Mencius' contention that human nature is originally good did not prove persuasive. Others argued that human nature was essentially neutral and subject to the influence of external conditions. Another early Confucian, Xunzi, had argued that human nature was basically selfish and greedy, which is why human society needs sages such as Confucius to guide them beyond the baseness of their own nature. Han Confucians sided with Xunzi rather Mencius. The Tiantai position, by insisting that some evil and ignorance exists even in Buddha-nature, was close to some readings of Xunzi's position, while the idealistic optimism of the Huayan view clearly showed parallels with Mencius. Between the Han and Song Dynasties (third through tenth centuries), Confucianism was by and large intellectually stagnant. It found new vitality in the Song in part by reabsorbing back into itself the elements it had 'lent' to the Buddhists (and to some extent Daoists as well). The elements they took back had been modified and expanded by the Buddhists, and given metaphysical foundations that the neo-Confucians retained and continued to rework. Neo-Confucian thinkers, especially after Zhu Xi (1130–1200), rediscovered Mencius and unanimously embraced his view of the original goodness of human nature. Looked at another way, neo-Confucianism adopted Huayan's metaphysics of nature. Zhu Xi's famous dialectic of principle (*li*) and 'material-energy' (*qi*) owed more than a little to Huayan's *li* and *shi* metaphysics.

MODERN CHINESE BUDDHISM

Today the most popular form of Buddhism in both mainland China and Taiwan is a mix of the Pure Land and Chán schools. The central scripture of Pure Land Buddhism, Amitabha Sutra was first brought to China by An Shigao, circa 147, however the school did not become popular until later. Platform Sutra of the Sixth Patriarch is the most important sutra for Chán and this is the only scripture written by ethnic Chinese which is named Sutra. Theravada Buddhism and Vajrayana Buddhism exist mainly among ethnic minorities in the southwest and north, respectively.

Chapter - 4

Buddhism in Japan

To some extent, Japanese Buddhism can be thought of as a series of imports from China. Over the centuries, starting as early as 500 C.E., both lay devotees and monks traveled to the mainland, bringing back with them layer after layer of Buddhist teachings and practices along with other Chinese cultural traditions. At the same time however, as the religion developed in Japan, it often did so along paths not followed on the mainland.

BRIEF HISTORY OF JAPANESE BUDDHISM

The official story of the arrival of Buddhism to Japan states that a political delegation arrived from Korea in 538 C.E.. Among the gifts it brought for the Emperor were a bronze Buddha image, some sutras, a few religious objects and a letter warmly praising the most excellent Dharma. After initial opposition, the gifts were accepted, and a temple was built to house the objects. However, an epidemic which ravaged the land was interpreted as bringing the wrath of the indigenous kami (Japanese Shinto deities) down on the nation. This led to the objects being thrown into a canal and the temple being destroyed.

Nevertheless, during the course of the next half century, Japan witnessed the firm establishment of Buddhism as a religion officially recognized and actively supported by the imperial court, thus overcoming doubts about its efficacy as a means of preventing disease, and also overcoming the fear of the national kami. In these early days, the most important aspect with regard to the flow of Chinese culture into Japan was the introduction of the Chinese script. This provided the means for the Japanese (who did not possess an indigenous writing system of their own) to assimilate the vast tradition of Chinese classics, and the Chinese version of the Buddhist canon. Only very few imported Chinese texts were translated into Japanese; most have continued throughout their history to be used in their original version.

The main three characteristics of the arrival of Buddhism in Japan are as follows:

Firstly, it did not come to Japan on a popular level, but was only accepted by the imperial court and then disseminated in the country from the top. Often, Buddhist faith in Japan is connected with absolute devotion to a leader with emphasis on veneration of the founders of sects, and the majority of sects keep close relations to the central governmental authority of their times.

Secondly, Buddhism was often associated with magic powers, and was used by the court as a means of preventing or curing disease, bringing rain and abundant crops etc.

Thirdly, Buddhism did not replace the indigenous kami, but always recognized their existence and power. This led to numerous varieties of Shinto-Buddhist amalgamation, in which often the kami were considered manifestations of the Buddhas. This is typical of how Buddhism favours harmonious coexistence with indigenous beliefs, and it was to be a similar story when Buddhism subjugated local gods and spirits in Tibet a few centuries later.

During the course of the development of Buddhism in Japan, the prevailing tendency is to search for fulfillment and ultimate truth, not in any transcendental sphere, but within the structure of secular life, neither denying nor repressing man's natural feelings, desires or customs. This perhaps explains why many Japanese arts and skills are pervaded by Buddhist spirituality. Well known examples being the tea ceremony, the arts of gardening, calligraphy and the No play.

The initial period saw the introduction onto Japanese soil of the six great Chinese schools, including the Hua-Yen and Lu, that became respectively the Kegon and Ritsu in Japanese. In terms of geography, the six sects were centered around the capital city of Nara, where great temples such as the Todaiji and Hokkeji were erected. However, the Buddhism of this early period – later known as the Nara period – was not a practical religion, being more the domain of learned preists whose official function was to pray for the peace and prosperity of the state and imperial house. This kind of Buddhism had little to offer the illiterate and uneducated masses, and led to the growth of "people's priests" who were not ordained and had no formal Buddhist training. Their practice was a combination of Buddhist and Taoist elements, and the incorporation of shamanistic features of the indigenous religion. These figures became immensely popular, and were a source of criticism towards the sophisticated academic and bureaucratic Buddhism of the capital.

HEIAN PERIOD (794-1185)

In 794, the imperial palace of Japan moved to Kyoto, and it is from this date that important changes and developments take place which result in the emergence of a more characteristically Japanese form of Buddhism. Two schools – the Tendai and the Shingon – particularly came to the fore, in time supplanting the other established schools, and laying the foundations for future developments.

Two monks, Saicho (767 – 822) and Kukai (774 – 835), effected this change which so decisively affected the future of Japanese Buddhism. By their comprehensive syntheses of the Chinese doctrine, two systems of teaching and practice were created, which effectively furnished all the essentials for the entire further development of Japanese Buddhism .

Saicho, the founding father of the Tendai school, entered the sangha at an early age. After years of study and practice, he became especially partial to the teachings of the Chinese grand master Chih-I and the T'ien-t'ai School, which were based on the Lotus Sutra. In 804, he went to China, and returned with an improved knowledge of various teachings and practices, along with many sutras. He established his base on Mount Hiei, and received permission to ordain two novices every year. Official recognition of his Tendai sect soon followed, and it became one of the two dominating schools of Japanese Buddhism during the Heian period.

The teachings of Chih-I form a far-reaching synthesis of Buddhist tradition inspired by the Lotus Sutra, and Saicho was to add three further elements: the practice of Chinese Ch'an; the commandments of the Mahayana which are based in essentials on the Bonmokyo, and parts of the esoteric teaching of the "True Word", Chen-yen (Shingon in Japanese). All this helped to make a decisive step away from the academic Buddhism of the early period, to a revived active kind of religion based on belief. An essential element in the doctrine of the Tendai was the teaching in the Lotus Sutra that the possibility of salvation is given to all.

Kukai and his secret doctrine, known as the True Word, Shingon, had a mysterious radiance, which encouraged the formation of legends about him. During his early studies in Buddhism, Taoism and Confucianism he came to know one of the principal texts of the esoteric canon, the Mahavairocana Sutra, but did not reach a deeper understanding of it. In 804, he traveled to China where all his doubts and questions with regard to the sutra were resolved; he returned to Japan with many new skills and instructions to impart. He founded his headquarters on Mount Koya on the Kii peninsular. His career was successful to the extent that he was allowed to build a Shingon temple in the emperor's palace, where he performed esoteric rituals and ceremonies. In 835, Kukai sitting in deep meditation fell into complete silence. In the eyes of his devotees he is not dead, but still sits in timeless meditation on Mount Koya.

Esoteric practices were very influential to the point that they dominated the Heian period, and had a decisive influence on the subsequent Kamakura period. Even the more philosophical Tendai school adopted esoteric rituals in order to make it more popular with the general population, whilst figures such as Kukai succeeded by means of esoteric rites in making rain after a time of drought, giving Buddhist esotericism a magical attraction.

Towards the end of the Heian, the dissemination of more popular devotional forms of Buddhism began, which were mainly derived from the Pure Land cult of Amitabha (Amida in Japanese). This was connected with the somewhat pessimistic philosophy of a deteriorating "final period of the dharma", which became widespread during this time. The devotional cults basically propounded the notion that salvation was only possible through the intercession of buddhas and bodhisattvas, for example through the recitation and repetition of simple formula such as the Namu-Amida-butsu (the Nembutsu – "thinking on the Buddha"). There were other faith-based doctrines during this time, the most noteworthy being the belief in the bodhisattva Jizo, who dispenses help to beings on all levels of existence and it is still alive today.

KAMAKURA PERIOD (1185-1333)

From the end of the 11th century, a new military aristocracy in the provinces increasingly evaded the control of the central government, culminating in war between the Taira and Minamoto families. The latter were victorious and thereby acquired absolute power of the country, setting up a military government in Kamakura in the vicinity of present-day Tokyo. Minamoto-no Yoritomo received the title of Shogun with supreme military and police power, thus transferring rule from the court aristocracy to those of the warrior class (samurai). Inevitably, this was to change the whole cultural climate.

This new climate did not favour the study of abstruse philosophy or the performance of elaborate rituals, so more robust and generally accessible teachings became the order of the day. The *Tendai* and *Shingon* schools declined, and more earthy democratic movements such as Zen and the devotional schools advanced.

The first of the three great traditions of Kamakura Buddhism, the doctrine of the Pure Land, continued the development which had begun in the Heian period. There was the founding of an independent Japanese sect of the Pure Land known as *Jodo-shu* by Genku (1133-1212), better known as Honen. He decided that Enlightenment was no longer achievable by the strength man alone, and that the only possible way was to surrender to Buddha Amida and rebirth into the *Western Paradise Pure Land.* New in Honen's philosophy was that, while he recognized the scholastic apparatus of Mahayana philosophy, he concentrated on an intensified religious feeling which found expression in the simple invocation of the name Namu-Amida-Butsu, stamped by unshakeable faith in rebirth into Amida's paradise.

Honen's successor, Shinran-Shonin (1173-1262) founded the *True Sect of the Pure Land, Jodo-shinshu,* which is the largest Buddhist sect in Japan today. In his chief work written in 1224, he explains that the doctrine, practice, belief and realization are all given by Amida Buddha and that nothing depends on man's "own power" (jiriki). Instead, everything depends on the "power of the other" (tariki), namely that of the Buddha Amida. Shinran emphasized that the recitation of the Namu-Amida-butsu was simply the expression of thankfu joy for having received everything from Amida. It is worth noting that Shinran was a monk who decided to take a wife, with which he had five children, and thus he symbolizes a decisive turn in Japan towards lay Buddhism. He stressed that obedience to the Buddhist commandments and the performance of good deeds were not necessary to obtain deliverance; in fact it is precisely the bad man who can be assured of rebirth in Amida's paradise if he wholeheartedly appeals to Amida.

While belief in Amida proceeds from the "strength of the other" (tariki), Zen Buddhism teaches that man can come to deliverance and Enlightenment only from his own strength (jiriki). Zen (Chinese Ch'an, from Pali, jhana and Sanskrit, dhyana) places supreme emphasis on self-power: on the active mobilization of all one's energies towards the realization of the ideal of enlightenment. There had been contacts between Japan and Zen doctrine since the 7th century. However, a lasting tradition that concentrated on Zen practice and led to the formation of a separate sect, was first created by the Tendai monk Eisai (1141-1215). During his studies in China, he had been introduced to the practice and doctrine of a branch of Zen which went back to Lin-chi (called Rinzai in Japanese), and on his return to Japan he started to disseminate the new doctrine.

Eisai established firm relations with the new military government in Kamakura and the military caste that held sway there. They found the simple, hard and manly discipline of Zen more to their taste than the ritual and dogma of the old schools. In contrast to this, Zen Buddhism was greeted with less enthusiasm by the intellectual elite of cities such as Kyoto. There, established practice was represented by Tendai, Shingon and Pure Land with their beautiful rituals. The fierce demands of Zen, with its emphasis on personal effort and the promise of enlightenment rather than heaven, seemed rebarbative and disturbing to the elite. Eisai is also linked to the introduction of tea drinking in Japan, which in time was to lead to the creation of the "tea-way" which, though non-religious, was strongly influenced by the spirit of Zen and the Tea Ceremony.

In general, the monks involved in the transmission of Zen from China to Japan also transmitted Neo-Confucian values and ideas, which were themselves strongly influenced by Ch'an Buddhism and Hua-yen philosophy. The Zen masters added a Confucian moral to Buddhist spirituality, which appealed to the new warrior-class of the Kamakura. For many centuries, the big Rinzai temples in Japan were centres of Chinese learning in general, and Neo-Confucianism in particular. Furthermore, the Rinzai school is closely associated with Japanese arts and the "ways" – the aforementioned "tea way", the "flower way", the "way of archery" and others.

A second Chinese school of Zen, the Ts'ao-tung (Soto in Japanese), introduced to Japan by Dogen (1200-1253). After four years of training in China under Master Ju-ching, Dogen returned to Japan in 1227, and eventually established the Eihei-ji temple in a remote province, which to this day remains one of the two main temples of the Japanese Soto Zen school. The foundation of Dogen's Zen is the constantly emphasized principle that practice does not lead to Enlightenment, but is carried out *in the state of being Enlightened*; otherwise it is not practice. In a logically constructed picture of the world, he equates all being – the believer, his practice and the world – with the present moment, the moment of enlightenment. Striving for enlightenment would therefore be going astray. Dogen's chief work was the Shobogenzo (The Eye and Treasury of the True Dharma).

After Pure Land and Zen, the final great reformer and sect-founder of the Kamakura period was Nichiren (1222-82). After studying in Kamakura and training in Tendai doctrine and practice, he came to the conclusion that the highest, all-embracing truth lay in the Lotus Sutra, known in Japan as the Myoho-renge-kyo, the fundamental canonical text of the Tendai sect. However, Nichiren thought that for the simple ordinary person, Tendai dogma and the reading of the Lotus Sutra were too difficult. He proclaimed that the title, Myoho-renge-kyo, was the essence of the whole sutra, and that it was in fact identical with the state of Enlightenment of Shakyamuni Buddha. It was therefore sufficient to utter the title and find oneself in the state of highest enlightenment. This condition gave rise spontaneously to morally right behaviour, so that it was necessary for the state and society that all should follow the practice of the "invocation of the title."

Two issues isolated Nichiren: the militant style of his presentation, and his insistence that the Lotus Sutra should inform the practice of government. He constantly made his views public, and the hot worded language which he used spared neither secular or Buddhist establishments, and led to his eventual banishment to the island of Izu. He was soon pardoned, but his continued attacks on institutions so provoked government and clergy that he was sentenced to be executed. According to legend, the axe which was raised to behead him was struck by lightning. Off the hook, he again went into exile and further developed his writings. When he finally returned to the mainland, he devoted himself to his missionary activity and to the training of monks on Mount Minobu, until today the main temple of the Nichiren sect. In recent times, certain branches of Nichiren have been connected to nationalistic tendencies within Japan.

LATER PERIODS

The demise of the Kamakura regime inaugurated a new era of internal strife and fighting in Japan, which was to last into the seventeenth century. It also signaled the end of the truly creative phase of Japanese Buddhism. A slide into stagnation occurred, which was to broadly last until the end of the nineteenth century. According to the twentieth century Zen writer D.T. Suzuki, after the Kamakura period "what followed was more or less the filling-in and working out of details."

In the 14th and 15th centuries, the privileged relations of the Rinzai Zen sect with the military government permitted it to gain tremendous wealth. This led to the creation of what is known as the "Culture of the Five Mountains" which constitutes the summit of Japanese Zen culture. It included all the arts, such as architecture, painting, calligraphy and sculpture, as well as printing, gardening and medicine. Ikkyu (1394-1481), a priest of the Rinzai sect, was particularly known for his unconventional character, and he was an accomplished poet, calligrapher and painter.

The Tokugawa Shogunate was to rule Japan from its bastion in Edo (Tokyo) for over two and a half centuries. It was to be the longest period of peace, and for the most part, prosperity in the history of the country. This was basically achieved by closing the country to the outside world, and establishing a regime of inflexible authoritarian control that created stability and order, but stifled all creative change and innovation. The Buddhist clergy was under the strict control of the government, and it was forbidden to found a new sect or build a new temple without special permission.

The Shogunate encouraged the Buddhist clergy of the sects in scholarly pursuits, hoping thereby to divert them from politics. Therefore a huge amount of learned literature was produced, and by the second half of the seventeenth century, editions of the Buddhist canon appeared, the most influential being that by Tetsugen of the new Obaku-shu sect. Obaku-shu had been founded by the Chinese master Yin-yuan Lung-ch'i, a Rinzai Zen priest. It added a new flavour to Japanese Zen, not only by its syncretism (it contained elements of Pure Land Buddhism), but also by the introduction of rituals, customs and a new architectural style imported from Ming China.

From the Zen school during this period, a few influential figures did emerge, the poet Basho and the Rinzai Zen masters Bankei and Hakuin being chief among them. Matsuo Basho (1644-94) was a poet who consciously transformed the practice of poetry into an authentic religious way; many of his finest poems (seventeen syllable *haiku* form) are thought to succinctly catch the elusive, often melancholy magic of the passing moment, and thereby express the true spirit of Zen. Bankei (1622-93) was an iconoclast who challenged orthodox Zen teaching. He spent many years intensively pursuing Enlightenment, and then at last he realized that he had been in possession of what he had been seeking all along, and decided that the term Un-born best described it. He thereafter advocated that people simply awaken to the unborn in the midst of everyday affairs, and he won himself a large audience which did not go down well with the Zen establishment.

Hakuin (1685-1768) is considered to be the restorer of the Rinzai sect in modern times. He revived the use of the koan, statements of Zen masters that are used as problems set to novices in Zen monasteries. They cannot be solved by rational thinking, and are designed to help open the mind to Enlightenment. Hakuin invented many new koans himself, adapted to the need of the times, in that they do not presuppose any scholarly knowledge of the Chinese Zen classics. His most famous koan being, "The sound produced by the clapping of two hands is easy to perceive, but what is the sound produced by one hand only?"

The restoration of the imperial regime in 1868 signaled the end of Japanese isolation. The pressure on Japan to reopen her doors simply becoming too great. There followed a temporary persecution of Buddhism when Shinto was made a state cult, however Buddhism was too firmly established in the affections of the Japanese people for this to last for long, and its religious freedom was effectively soon regained. For the first time in centuries, contact was made with other Buddhist countries, along with Western ones as well, and this served to encourage Buddhist scholarship, and various Buddhist universities were established by the first half of the twentieth century.

During the last 50 years, the evolution of Buddhism has been closely linked to Japan's history. The grip of the government during the Second World War over Buddhist institutions was rigid, and any writings in which Buddhism was placed above the authority of the state or the emperor were suppressed. The only opposition to this came from the Soka-gakkai, founded in 1930 as a non-religious society of teachers, and they were severely persecuted. Since the end of the war, Buddhism in Japan has once again revived, and there has been the foundation of many new sects, along with an ongoing reinvigoration as a result from sustained contacts with other peoples and cultures. Japanese Zen has also been successfully exported to many Western countries, in particular North America.

DEVELOPMENTS OF BUDDHISM IN JAPAN

Buddhism in its spread from India northward and in its triumphant march across China and Korea underwent some radical changes, not only in minor points, but in the very fundamentals of religion. And thus when Buddhism reached Japan in the middle of the sixth century A.D. it was no longer the pure religion of the founder. It was not the Buddhism of the Pali scriptures and the religion which western scholars usually describe when they speak of Buddhism, but it was that expanded and much modified religion which we know as Mahâyâna Buddhism. A part of the original Indian stream and a great many later streams from Hinduism reached Japan through China; so that Japanese Buddhism does go back to India, but the stream had been enlarged by many tributaries from the local cults and religions of other countries, and these were so well mingled with one another that it is impossible to say just what was Buddhist and what was not.

Here we shall trace the flow of this great stream of many waters across Japanese life and we shall see as we go on that in Japan, too, it was fed by other streams — principally by that mighty current of the native Shintô which modified Buddhism so seriously after its union with it in the beginning of the ninth century that the resultant stream was known for many centuries as Ryôbu-Shintô, Two-sided Shintô.

Buddhism reached Korea from China during the last half of the fourth century A.D. and from Korea it crossed the narrow channel which separates the peninsula from the island empire of Japan. Japan and Korea had known each other for many years. The Japanese claim that as early as 32 B.C. the little province of Mimana or Kara sought the protection of Japan against the oppressions of the kingdom of Shiragi, and for several centuries it remained a sort of dependency of the emperor of Japan. Then in the year 202 A.D. the great Japanese heroine, Empress Jingô, made her famous expedition to Korea and apparently reduced the kingdom of Shiragi to a dependency of Japan. Empress Jingô's son and successor, Ôjin Tennô, deified later as the God of War, is supposed to have continued the suzerainty over southern Korea, and during his reign there was probably a real vital connection between the two countries. This is a point on which some of our modern imperialistic Japanese love to dwell, and in connection with the annexation of Korea it was used as an argument by some to justify Japan in taking the step.

Japan's hold on Korea was, however, never very firm, and, as we have said, by the time Buddhism reached Korea in the fourth century the peninsula was occupied by three small independent kingdoms. And this was also the political situation about one hundred and fifty years later, when, in 552 A.D., King Seimei of Kudara sent a gold and copper image of Buddha (probably an image of the Buddha Amitâbha and not of Gautama), Buddhist books, and a letter in which he praised the great merit of Buddhism to the emperor of Japan. As a matter of fact this was but one of many missions sent by this king. It would seem that the three Korean kingdoms were always more or less at war with one another, and it is quite likely that the king of Kudara was moved by political considerations rather than religious when he recommended his religion to the Japanese court. To gain the friendship of this island empire would be a real advantage in his conflicts with his rivals; and all the more did this seem necessary, for the Chinese monarch was showing himself quite unfriendly to Buddhism at this time and in consequence not over-friendly to the Buddhist king of Kudara. Whatever were the motives that lay back of this official Buddhist mission from Kudara, we know that it was sent and that it met with success.

It is an interesting story how these Buddhist beginnings were received. The emperor of Japan was apparently greatly pleased with these gifts, for it must be remembered that images and books were exceedingly rare among the simple Japanese of that early day. He said to the messengers, "I have never heard such sublime teachings, yet I myself dare not decide whether to accept this doctrine or not." The matter was submitted to the counsel of his vassals and one Soga no Iname replied, "Western countries all believe this doctrine and why should not we?" But two other ministers of a more conservative disposition said in substance, "We have our own gods, and if we now change and worship the gods of other nations we are in danger of bringing the wrath of our gods upon our heads." The image was turned over to Soga with the instruction that he was to worship the new god and give the new religion a test; for like the Athenians of old the Japanese did not dare run the risk of leaving any god without an altar even though they already had myriads of their own. Soga accordingly converted his own house into a temple, set up the new image and began the new cult.

But soon after this introduction of the new god a terrible pestilence afflicted the land and the conservative party were not slow in discovering in this the wrath of their native gods. Soga's temple was burned to the ground, and the Buddhist image was thrown into a canal of Naniwa (Osaka). The Buddhist god was, however, to get his innings and show what he could do. A great conflagration suddenly destroyed the great hall of the Imperial residence, and, of course, this could have but one meaning. Furthermore the pestilence seems to have only increased in violence and threatened to extinguish the nation. Some claim that the image was therefore speedily fished up from the sea and reverently placed in a new house of worship. At any rate it seems true that, under the leadership of Soga Mumako, son of Soga no Iname, Buddhism began to take root in Japan.

Thus we see how trifling and chance occurrences may play a great part in momentous issues. Not that these were the only or even the main determining factors, for in the long run the success of Buddhism in Japan was due to its real superiority over the native Shintô faith.

Before we proceed with a narrative of the development of Buddhism in Japan from these small beginnings, it may be well to pause a moment and give very briefly what the native Shintô was and what were the conditions of Japan in general at this time; for the successful entrance of a religion into a country depends more or less upon the religious, social, political and intellectual condition of the people to be won to the new faith.

The population at this time consisted possibly of about two million people — hunters, fishermen and farmers, divided up into many different clans. The center of population was in the Ôsaka-Kyôto region, and the dominant tribe whose head was the Mikado exercised authority over a considerable portion of the main island, though the outlying portions, especially in the north, were still in the hands of the aboriginal Ainus. The people, though very simple in their manner of life, were intellectually well gifted and later proved to be endowed with extraordinary aesthetic ability. Their religion was Shintô — The Way of the Gods. This religion was and is in some of its phases even today an animistic and polytheistic Nature Worship with a strong admixture of Ancestor Worship. The forces of nature are personified and anthropomorphized, while the heroes and ancestors, especially those of the royal family, are deified.

The soul of Shintô is reverence and implicit obedience to the Mikado; and religion and patriotism are made one. Yamato Damashii, The Spirit of Japan, is largely the product of this religion, and it has played a great part in the conquest, unification and civilization of the entire country. Japan is regarded by Shintô as the sacred land of the gods; and every mountain, river, rock, tree and cloud is the abode of some deity. But Shintô was really too childish in many of its conceptions and did not satisfy the deeper needs of the human mind and heart. The rising tide of Japanese civilization, quickened as it was by the introduction of new ideas from the continent, made Shintô more and more inadequate, and Japan was on the whole ready for the new and more elaborate faith of Buddhism.

So much for a summary of conditions which prevailed in Japan when Buddhism was first introduced. It was therefore comparatively easy for the new religion to get a firm hold, especially upon the more progressive element. Its success was, however, not due simply to its superiority as a religion, but even more to the fact that it was the vehicle of a higher civilization, namely, the Chinese civilization from whose fountains Japan has ever drunk deeply even up to almost the present day. We have a modern parallel in what is happening in Korea today. The success of Christianity in that land is due in some measure at least to the fact that it is the vehicle of western civilization and not simply because it is a superior religion.

Soon after the incidents connected with the introduction of Buddhism related above, the ruler of Japan, more anxious for the concrete things of Korean and Chinese civilizations than for the new religion, sent a message to the king of Kudara in which he asked the king to send no more Buddhist priests and images, but to supply him with physicians, apothecaries, soothsayers, almanac makers and artisans of one sort and another. The priests, books and images, however, continued to come together with the things specially asked for. This influx of so many new things had very much the same effect that the influx of western things has had in our own day; it caused a temporary upheaval and led to much internal strife and war. But it was not long till Buddhism had won for itself a place in the heart of members of the ruling family and thus secured protection. Empress Suiko (593-628 A.D.) became an ardent Buddhist, giving over the affairs of state to the Crown Prince Mumayado (better known as Shôtoku Taishi), so that she might have more time for advancing the new faith.

More important than this was the fact that the Crown Prince himself embraced the new religion and administered the affairs of state in such a way that every thing tended towards the spread of Buddhism. In the so-called constitution of Seventeen Articles promulgated by him, he expressly ordered his people to pay all due respect to the new religion. He "bent all his energies to import from Korea, scholars, priests, architects, wood carvers, bronze founders, clay modelers, masons, gilders, tile makers, and weavers; in short, all skilled artisans whose work was involved in creating and installing a great Buddhist temple such as were already known in the peninsula kingdom." In fact, it is held by some scholars that the prince was no mean artist himself and that the famous Hôryûji near Nara erected under his direction has among its art treasures some created by his own hands. It is therefore not at all strange that by the end of Empress Suiko's reign (628 A.D.) there were already 46 temples in existence, and 816 priests and 569 nuns had been consecrated. Not only did Buddhist missionaries pour in from Korea and China, but Japanese were beginning to go in greater and greater numbers to the continent to study at the great centers of religion and culture and then come back with new learning and enthusiasm for the Buddhist faith.

The influence upon Japanese civilization of this close contact with the higher continental civilization can hardly be overstated. In a comparatively short time this simple island people had taken over the fruit of centuries of Chinese culture and made it their own. In fact, the assimilation of western culture in our own day which has astonished the world is no more wonderful than what happened in the history of this people during the seventh century. With the founding of the great monastery of Hôryûji early in the seventh century began that marvelous development of the fine arts which in a few decades issued in the production of world masterpieces, for art critics claim that the famous Shaka trinity with its marvelous lacework screen created at this time has never been surpassed as a work in bronze by any people in any age.

Not only did Japan quickly learn what China and Korea had to teach, but the pupil went beyond his teacher in many respects, so that if one would see the highest development of Asiatic art one has to turn to Japan for specimens. In the political world, too, Japan was quick to learn from the continental neighbors. The great reform, beginning in 645 A.D. and continuing through the rest of the century, known as the Taikwa Reforms, changed the ruler of Japan from what was little better than a tribal chief into a real monarch of an empire. We might say in a word that the impact of Chinese culture fostered largely by Buddhists changed, at least in the upper classes, a simple, unlettered people into a people of culture and refinement.

RISE OF THE NARA SECTS

It is a rather significant fact that Buddhism was firmly rooted in Japan before any sectarian differences were introduced. For a period of about seventy years wise missionaries were content with teaching the general tenets of their faith. Perhaps this was due to the fact that the people of Japan were really not intellectually prepared to appreciate the fine points of the sectarian speculations, and were more interested in the external trappings of religion and the simpler teachings contained in the moral maxims and precepts more or less common to all the sects. Finally, however, the sectarian differences made their appearance early in the seventh century.

Curiously enough the first sect to be introduced was the highly metaphysical Sanron Sect (Mâdhyamika school founded originally by Nâgârjuna). It was brought in from China in the year 625 by Ekwan. Its headquarters was the famous Hôryûji near Nara mentioned above. The Sanron sect belongs to what is called the Provisional Mahâyâna school. Starting with the Hônayûna position of the non-reality of the ego, it carries the principle of negation to the point at which it denies the reality of all phenomenal existence; and the noumenal world, it holds, can only be defined in negative terms.

Synchronous with the establishment of the Sanron was that of the Jôjitsu Sect (Satya-siddhi-sastra Sect). This sect never gained a real independent existence, but was propagated in conjunction with the Sanron. It belongs to the Hînayâna school and represents in its doctrines a rather strong subjective idealism. The third sect to find its way into Japan was the Hossô (Dharma-lakshana Sect, *i.e.*, the Yoga school). It was brought over from China by Dôsho probably about the middle of the seventh century, though some would put it as early as 625. The Hossô, like the Sanron, belongs to the Provisional Mahâyâna school. This is the sect which in the person of Gyôgi Bosatsu, during the eighth century, initiated that syncretistic movement by which the claims of the native Shintô and the new religion were reconciled.

The Kusha Sect (Abhidharma-kosa-sastra Sect) was the fourth to be established in Japan, being introduced in 658 by two Japanese priests who had studied in China, namely, Chitsu and Chitatsu. This sect is usually regarded as the best representative of the Hânayâna school of Buddhism. The center of its teachings is an elaborate psychological analysis through which it seeks to account for the complex of the phenomenal world and yet at the same time denies the reality of the ego.

About three quarters of a century elapsed before the fifth Chinese sect was introduced. This was the Kegon (Avatam-saka-sûtra Sect) brought over in 736. The Kegon was the first sect of the true Mahâyâna school which later was to be the type of Buddhism which really won Japan. Though this sect has now practically disappeared, it has exerted a great influence upon other sects through its chief scripture, the Kegonkyô (Avatamsaka-sûtra), which has ever been popular with Buddhist scholars as one of the chief sources of Mahâyâna philosophy.

Last of these older sects to reach Japan was the Ritsu (Vinaya Sect), introduced in 754, though it would seem that its doctrines, or rather its classifications of the moral laws and precepts contained in the Vinaya scriptures, were among the first teachings to be introduced into Japan. In fact, it was probably these practical moral teachings rather than the philosophical speculations of the other sects which helped win Japan so speedily to the religion of the Buddha. The Ritsu belongs to the Hînayâna school. It, too, like the other Hînayâna sects, has disappeared, but its teachings have been more or less absorbed by the existing Mahâyâna sects, and in that way still exert an influence.

Now these six sects are frequently spoken of as the Six Sects of Nara to distinguish them from the later Kyoto and Kamakura sects. They are called Nara sects because it was in and around Nara and during the Nara Epoch (710- 794) that they attained their highest development. The marvelous progress made by Japan during the seventh century, of which we have spoken above, was continued during the eighth. In fact we may say that the eighth century marks one of the great culminations of Japanese history. Many of the great things of old Japan came into being at this time. Thus, *e.g.* Nara, which was made the capital of the realm in 710, was the first real city Japan had up till that time. And it was no mean city even when compared with the great cities of other lands, its population, it is claimed by some, reaching upward of 500,000. Here, or in the immediate vicinity, were to be found many a noble Buddhist edifice filled with treasures of art, some of which have come down to our own times to be the wonder of connoisseurs.

It was in the Nara epoch, namely in 749, that the enormous Nara Daibutsu, the world's largest bronze statue, was cast. It is 53 feet in height and into its creation entered 500 Japanese pounds (about 666 lb.) of gold, 16,827 pounds of tin, 1,954 pounds of mercury and 986,180 pounds of copper and some lead. The famous Tôdaiji Bell, over 13 feet high and weighing 40 tons, belongs to this century. Early in the Nara Epoch were published Japan's oldest histories, namely, the Kojiki in 712 and the Nihongi in 720. Aston calls this age the "Golden Age of Poetry," for during this period were written the Manyôshû, or "Collection of Myriad Leaves," containing more than 4000 pieces, mostly short poems (Tanka) but also some longer ones (Nagauta).

All this splendor of culture and civilization was largely the work, either directly or indirectly, of Buddhism and shows to what power and influence the new religion had attained by this time. It must not, however, be supposed that the common people of the land had been won over completely to the new faith. This outward splendor and magnificence made, of course, a very strong appeal to the imagination; but, after all, there was deep down in the heart of the average man still a strong loyalty to the old things of the native cults, and he was therefore ever ready to blame the gods of the new religion for the adverse things which befell him or the nation from time to time. It was so even during the Nara Epoch. A great epidemic of smallpox afflicted the realm. Introduced from Korea into the southern island of Kyûshû, it spread northward until in 735 it began to devastate even the aristocratic circles in the capital itself. Offerings were made at the various temples by priests and their royal patrons, but all seemed to be of no avail. It was at this time that the Emperor Shômu contemplated the erection of the great Nara Daibutsu.

However, before he dared to show his confidence in the Buddhas in such an open manner he had to find a way by which to appease the native deities and their devotees. Accordingly, he sent the illustrious Gyôgi Bosatsu, a grandson of a Korean immigrant, to the Ise shrines to inquire of the Sun Goddess what she thought of the emperor's project. Gyôgi remained at the shrine for a week and then he returned to Nara with a favorable answer, viz. that the Sun Goddess had declared herself as identical with the Buddha to whose honor the statue was to be erected. A few nights later the emperor himself is said to have had a dream in which the Sun Goddess said to him, "The Sun is Biroshana." (Biroshana is the Japanese transliteration for Vairochana). This marks the beginning of that syncretistic movement so successfully carried out during the ninth century by Dengyô Daishi and especially by Kôbô Daishi which resulted in reconciling the claims of the two religions in the hearts of the people. It should, however, be added that it also resulted in perverting things, and so in the long run really did more harm than good, as every unprincipled compromise must do.

The influence of Buddhism during the Nara period was great, not only in the spheres mentioned above, but it extended perhaps even more into the field of politics and state affairs. This is only natural, for it must be remembered that Buddhism gained its first and chief hold on the upper and ruling classes rather than upon the common people. Frequently this influence was for the good, as might be expected from the fact that it was the men who had studied in China, or under Chinese priests in Japan, that were best acquainted with politics and matters of government as conducted on the continent. This superior knowledge gave these men a natural place as advisers to the court and other officials. But the temptations which this influence gave to the disciple of Buddha was more than could be endured, and it was not long therefore till the monks and priests became more interested in the "things that are Cæsar's" than in their true mission. In fact things reached such a state that during the reign of Empress Shôtoku (765-770) a Buddhist monk, Dôkyô, had managed to make himself the most powerful subject in the land and was even planning to place himself upon the imperial throne. In this, however, he did not succeed, and while the ambitious clergy continued to meddle in such things, the time was fast approaching when not only the guilty were to suffer for their sins, but the whole Buddhist world which had centered around the old capital of Nara, yea Nara itself, was soon to wane in importance and yield its place to another.

THE KYÔTO SECTS

In the year 782 Emperor Kwammu succeeded to the throne. He must have been a man of daring and originality, for it was he who cut the Gordian knot of the political tangle of his day by simply abandoning Nara to the Buddhists and their schemes and setting up his capital first at Nagaoka and then at a place he significantly called *Heian* (Peace), namely, the present Kyôto. This took place between 784-793, and here at Kyôto the capital of the empire remained for almost 1100 years, namely down to 1868, when the late Emperor Meiji removed his seat of government to Tôkyô. Kyôto soon overshadowed Nara and became indeed one of the world's greatest centers of culture. The decline of Nara had apparently a disastrous effect upon the Buddhist sects entrenched there, for it must be remembered that a Japanese, true to the fundamental principle of his native Shintô, is first a patriot and then a man of religion. When the two conflict, religion is apt to be the loser. To this day this seems to be a characteristic of the average Japanese. Religion is presented by its advocates as something good for the welfare of the state, and by those who oppose it, it is opposed on the grounds that it is injurious to the state. The greatest obstacle which Christianity has met in Japan is the claim on the part of its enemies that it undermines the state. Even a scholar in Japan is very slow to follow where truth would lead him if it should seem to conflict with the sacred traditions of the nation.

Now this running away from the meddling of the Nara sects did not mean that Emperor Kwammu had turned his back on Buddhism as a religion. He simply wanted the monks to keep their proper place and to leave for Caesar the things that are Caesar's. But to make sure that he was getting the right type of religious leaders he sent a promising young man directly to China to bring back a purer religion which would minister in things spiritual and leave the affairs of state in his own hands. This young man was Saichô, better known as Dengyô Daishi, the founder of the powerful Tendai sect in Japan. He was followed a few months later by the equally famous Kukai, known best by his posthumous title Kôbô Daishi, the founder of the other powerful sect of this period, namely, the Shingon Sect. These two, Dengyô Daishi and Kôbô Daishi, are the great names in Japanese Buddhism of the ninth century; and the two sects which they founded have occupied a prominent place in Japanese history down to the present day.

Dengyô Daishi and Tendai

The Tendai sect may be characterized as the harmonizing, comprehensive sect. That is, Tendai tries to hold to all the contradictions of the voluminous Mahôyôna and Hinayana scriptures as being the direct teachings of the founder of Buddhism. It was Chi K'ai, the founder of the Tendai (Chinese, T'ien-t'ai) Sect in China who worked out an elaborate harmonizing scheme by which he tried to show how every Buddhist scripture has its own peculiar place and is the direct or indirect product of S'akyamuni's mind. Humanity has varied needs and these needs must be met in different ways. Thus every scripture has its truth, each giving its own peculiar angle of vision.

This irenic attitude was taken by Chi K'ai in the face of contending sects, each of which seemed to proclaim a different system. There were *e.g.* in China at that time the old Abhidharma sects which tried to define all truth with an Aristotelian precision of detail. On the other hand the Pure Land sects were teaching that all attempts of salvation through knowledge of detailed truth was vain and that there was only one way, namely, the way of Faith in the Grace of Amitabha. And still another group of sects were the contemplative sects which held that neither book learning nor a pious trust in Amitabha saved a man, but that quiet meditation and abstract contemplation was the only true way. Now in the face of these contending schools the comprehensive Tendai Sect arose and it included *all* ways, rejecting none. Thus a Tendai disciple may find salvation through philosophic wisdom, or, rejecting the great mass of doctrines contained in the voluminous scriptures, he may select merely the comfortable doctrine of salvation through faith in Amitabha's great name. Or, again, he may reject all book learning and all simple faith and work out his own salvation through silent meditation and abstract contemplation, as do the contemplative sects.

The broad-minded Tendai philosopher, however, would try to hold to the truth in every way, though as a matter of fact very few ever attained this supposedly lofty ideal. After all, there was developed what we might call an orthodox Tendai system which did reject some things and included others as characteristically Tendai teachings. Thus while theoretically Tendai accepted all scriptures as of equal value, Tendai teachers looked upon the Saddharma-Pun-darîka-sûtra with peculiar reverence. This sûtra together with the Mahâprajna-pâramitâ-sûtra contain, after all, the loftiest teachings of S'akyamuni; and while the teachings of other scriptures are not false they must be regarded as incomplete and only provisional. The Saddharma-Pundarîka breathes a Buddhism quite different from the Buddhism of S'akyamuni. S'akyamuni himself is regarded as but one of the manifestations of the Eternal Buddha, or Buddhas. The identification of the historical manifestation with the Eternal Buddha is the great revelation of this scripture. To know this and to trust in this knowledge far outweighs all merit which man can heap up by practicing the Buddhist virtues and perfections through countless incarnations. Inasmuch, then, as Tendai lays peculiar stress on these scriptures it does have its peculiar doctrines, but it does not thereby exclude absolutely other doctrines even if they should seem to be contradictory.

Now this all-inclusive system was brought to Japan by Dengyô Daishi early in the ninth century. But the Japanese Tendai Sect underwent certain changes and differs considerably from the parent sect in China. This is due to the fact that not only Dengyô Daishi, but also other learned Japanese priests, such as Jikaku Daishi who studied in China, drank not only from the fountains of wisdom which flowed from the sacred mountains of T'ien-t'ai, but also from the deep wells of truth guarded by other Chinese sects. Another factor which was operative was that deep-rooted Japanese characteristic which is quick to adopt anything new but always only after some slight modifications and a mingling with something from other sources. Japanese Tendai claims to be eclectic rather than all-inclusive. That is, it does not simply take everything contained in other schools, but it rather chooses what it regards the best of all schools. But, of course, an eclectic process may be carried so far that it ceases to be eclectic and becomes simply an absorption of things good, bad and indifferent. And that is what seems to have gradually taken place in Japanese Tendai.

It is practically impossible to say for what it really stands. Thus, *e.g.* some Tendai temples you will find littered up with images of Buddhas and Bodhisattvas innumerable. They impress one as religious junk shops. Other temples may have only a trinity of Buddhas, and still others seem to honor but one Buddha. In the temples which sprang from the famous Miidera, Amida (Amitâbha) seems to be the sole object of worship. Thus the Amida teaching was held in Japan long before the real Amida sects came into existence. Again in one and the same temple, one believer may preface his meditations and prayers by the formula, *"Namu Amida Butsu,"* "I adore Thee Thou Buddha of Eternal Life and Light" and another believer may use the equally popular form of, *"Namu-Myôhô Renge-kyô,"* "I worship Thee Thou Scripture of the Wonderful Lotus"; the former being today the special prayer of the Amida sects, and the latter the "vain repetition" of the Nichiren Sect.

Now the Tendai harmonist may believe that he can reconcile the varied beliefs and practices of his own sect by saying that they are but different angles of the same truth; to the Western mind, however, it is difficult to see how such a harmony is anything more than an empty formula. And to the practical Japanese mind it also has appeared so, and that is the chief reason why the Tendai Sect not only split into several sub-sects but also why from it went out many great reformers who could not endure the contradictions. Thus, from the Tendai Sect came forth the founders of the great Amida sects of Japan, the Zen sects and the Nichiren Sect. In these independent sects these conflicting doctrines found their freest development, and these sects in the course of time gradually overshadowed the great Tendai Sect itself.

Kôbô Daishi and Shingon

At the time Dengyô Daishi introduced the Tendai Sect Kôbô Daishi laid the foundations for the beginnings of the Shingon Sect. The latter, like the former, studied at the various centers of learning in China. He remained abroad several years and seems to have come into contact with various influences — Buddhist and others. When he returned to Japan he brought with him many scriptures from the Chinese canon, and these he studied assiduously. He soon began to preach his new teachings, the core of which was that man can even in this present life attain Buddhahood since he is essentially one with the Eternal Buddha. His teaching was naturally challenged by the priests of the older Nara sects, but tradition has it that in his disputations with them he usually gained a miraculous victory on account of which he was held in high esteem by emperor and people.

Especially did he gain the gratitude of Japan when once, after a long drought, the heavens responded to his prayers offered at the request of his Imperial patron. Kôbô was not only a man of prayer but also a man exceptionally gifted in other lines. He is credited by some with the invention of one form of the simple Kana script, and his linguistic ability may be seen in the fact that the Emperor Saga often summoned him to the palace that he might hear his beautiful language. As an educator of the common people he may be said to have been a pioneer, for he it was who founded the Sôgei Shuchiin which was the first institution in which the general public had access to education and which was the forerunner of those temple schools which were often the chief centers of light during the dark ages in Japan. The culture of the silkworm, from which industry Japan to this day draws its greatest revenue, was apparently greatly promoted by him. As a sculpturer he must have been a marvel, for there are many places in central Japan which boast of relics of his work in stone.

But while popular with emperor and people, Kôbô Daishi preferred solitude, and after much searching for a quiet spot he finally found Mt. Kôya, where with the emperor's permission he built a temple. Later when his Imperial admirer gave him the temple Tôji in Kyôto he settled there and made it the center of his sect. But when old age approached and he saw the end coming he fled to his quiet retreat on Mt. Kôya, where he died in 835 in fasting and silent meditation. There he is buried, and the pious followers of this great teacher believe that he is sitting in his tomb wait ing for Maitreya (Miroku), the Buddha of the Future, to come and convert the world. When Maitreya comes Kôbô will come forth from his tomb and join in the glory of victory.

If Dengyô Daishi's teachings may be described as a comprehensive system, Kôbô Daishi's system is characterized by the words Mystery and Magic. In many respects the Shingon Sect is furthest removed from the teachings of S'akyamuni. Strange to say, it, too, holds the Saddharma- Pundaraka in highest regard, and its great Buddha is the Eternal Buddha Vairochana of whom S'akyamuni is but one of many manifestations. Where the Tendai holds to a theory of successive stages in the Buddha's teachings, Shingon divides the doctrines into exoteric and esoteric teachings, and calls its own peculiar doctrines, The Secret Teachings (*Himitsukya*). The great secret is the revealed secret that man can even now attain Buddhahood because he is essentially one with the Eternal Buddha. There are, in general, two ladders by which this pinnacle of all truth may be reached; one is the intellectual ladder and the other the moral ladder, each of which has ten rungs. The intellectual ladder leads upwards, rung after rung, from the lowest being to the highest being, from the finite to the Absolute. The moral ladder is the Buddhist decalogue with its elaborations in the various monk rules which have been handed down from century to century.

In Shingon we have "a world of ideas" (*Kong¯kai,* literally, Diamond World) which is unchangeable and everlasting, having existence only in universal thought. Parallel to this "world of ideas," as a sort of material counterpart, is the world of phenomena. The center of both worlds is the great Buddha Vairochana. In the "world of ideas" the central sun Vairochana (*Dainichi,* literally, Great Sun) tends to draw all bodies to itself, and when one has reached the highest enlightenment one sees that the thought of Vairochana really includes all thoughts, for Vairochana is the All. In the world of the material counterpart, however, the movement is in the opposite direction, *i.e.* the movement is outward and from Vairochana emanate other Buddhas. From these other Buddhas emanate Bodhisattvas; from the Bodhisattvas, in turn, issue other and lesser beings, and so the emanation process goes on till the whole phenomenal world is evolved. The source of all existence, then, is the Eternal Buddha. All other beings have only relative existence. They are not void but neither are they permanent as such. Vairochana as the center of "the world of ideas" is conceived of after the analogy of a planetary system, Vairochana being the sun and Akshobhya, Amitâbha, Ratnasambhava and S'akyamuni being four great planets, each of which has lesser beings as satellites. Vairochana as the center of the world of phenomena is conceived of as the heart of an eight-leaf lotus flower, the eight petals being Amitâbha, Avalokitesvara, Dioyagosha, Maitreya, Ratna Shvaya, Samantabhadra, Muktapushpa and Manjusrî.

Thus as we have said, Vairochana is on the one hand the source of all life and of all beings, and on the other hand he represents the sum total of all truth. Since man is but a fragment of the sum total of all Being his knowledge is fragmentary; but the great and saving revelation of Shingon doctrine is the great secret that man, just because he is an emanation from Vairochana, is really one with him. Man's apparent separateness is not real; deeper than this is the fact of his oneness in essence with the Great All.

This doctrine of the essential oneness of man with the great Eternal Buddha Vairochana differs very little from the pantheistic philosophy underlying the teachings of most Buddhist sects. The difference comes with the method by which this truth is to be reached. We said that Shingon holds that parallel to "the world of ideas" is the world of phenomena, the former being the underlying cause of the latter. From this it follows that ideas are the source of things, and thus if one has the correct ideas one can control things. This is the real meaning of the name Shingon, True Word. The True Word which becomes the Magic Word will become an efficient cause of the desired phenomenon. The one, then, who knows the Magic Word is able to achieve results by simply thinking or speaking the thought expressed by such words. Thus, as we said above, Shingon is characterized by the words Mystery and Magic, and Shingon priests are past masters in all mystery as to magic words and signs made with the fingers and the hands. These occult powers may be used for the benefit of the living or the dead. Especially are the dead to be delivered from the sufferings of hell and lower realms of existence by reciting the correct magical formulæ or making the required signs with the hands and fingers.

Both in its theory of emanations and in its wealth of magic and mystery Shingon seems rather far removed from the teachings of original Buddhism and also from other forms of later Buddhism. Some scholars have sought to find historical connections with other religions and philosophies, and particularly has it been pointed out that there is much affinity with Manichæism. It is doubtful whether it can be shown that Shingon has historical connections with Manichæism, nor does it seem necessary to go very far for the source for these peculiarities of the sect. In the fifth century Asanga had thrown open the flood-gates to all the "magic and mystery" connected with the animism of

India and the lands west and north of India. This stream was increased in volume later on by a powerful current which had passed through Tibet and then joined the Chinese Buddhist stream again. But whatever was its source, it is clear that this prominent aspect of the Shingon Sect is in flat contradiction to the teachings of S'akyamuni, who branded such things as superstition and folly and the real enemy of the ethics of the Middle Path.

We said that Kôbô Daishi was a great benefactor of Japan, and his piety and good works must have done much to recommend his religion to his people. The thing, however, which had more to do with making his religion acceptable to the people of Japan than anything else he did was his clever compromise with the native Shintô. We have already stated above how during the preceding century Gyôgi Bosatsu had begun the movement of religious syn-cretism by the clever answer he brought back from these shrines, viz., that the Sun Goddesshad declared herself to be identical with the Buddha Roshana or Birochana (Vairo-chana) to whose honor Emperor Shômu erected the great Nara Daibutsu. How far Gyôgi carried his scheme is hard to say, but as he was one of the greatest artists of his day it is quite likely that with his marvelous creations in bronze and wood he made the union of Shintô and Buddhist deities very real to the people of his day. But, after all, it was Kôbô Daishi who must be given the honor of being the one who really succeeded through his Ryôbu Shintô in making the two religions but two sides of the same thing.

The Sun Goddess, Amaterasu, was made identical with Vairochana, the great Buddha of Shingon (Vairochana is usually called Dainichi, Great Sun), and the lesser Buddhist deities were identified with the lesser Shintô gods, or the latter were declared to be just so many manifestations of the Eternal Buddha. The Shingon theory of emanations lent itself unusually well to this syncretistic movement, for it was easy thus to account for the essential oneness of the Buddhist and Shintô pantheons. One and all of the many gods of both religions were but emanations or radiations of the Central Sun which Buddhists knew as Vairochana and Shintôists as Amaterasu. Since the Central Sun is one and the same in both systems the emanations must be essentially alike, no matter what different names they might have.

This movement, of course, resulted in bringing into Japanese Buddhism many elements which were quite foreign to original Buddhism, and carried still further the tendencies which manifested themselves as early as the third century B.C., namely, the tendency to overcome alien beliefs by compromise and absorption. From the deification of its founder, Buddhism went on step by step to the admission of gods upon gods, the greatest of whom being the Buddhas Amitâbha and Vairochana, both of whom were symbolized by the sun. And when these had been declared to be identical with the Sun Goddess, Amaterasu, the next steps in this religious syncretism were comparatively easy to take. Even the Shintô War God, Hachiman, was not refused entrance into this new religion which in the mind of its founder was to have been above all else a religion of peace and one which subdues the passions which lead to strife and war. It is not strange, then, that Japanese Buddhism has always been and is to this day — at least as far as the uneducated masses are concerned — a polytheistic and idolatrous religion. And Kôbô Daishi, the saint par excellence of early Japanese Buddhism, who succeeded in making his religion popular with the people, may be regarded in a true sense as a perverter of Buddhism.

This clever compromise made not only Kôbô's sect popular but also the Tendai Sect, for Dengyô Daishi, too, had worked out a scheme by which he harmonized the claims of Shintô and Buddhism. All over the land temples were built in which both the old Shintô deities and Buddhist saints and Bodhisattvas were worshipped. The two new sects grew with leaps and bounds, so that they soon overshadowed the old Nara sects. Mt. Hiei was gradually being covered with monastery after monastery, and soon branch temples of the famous Enryakuji were being built in other parts of the land. The same was true of Mt. Kôya and the Shingon sect.

Just as in the Nara period so in the Heian period Buddhism was closely identified with the ruling classes. Kyôto became the capital of magnificence and splendor that it was largely because the Buddhist monks who went back and forth between China and Japan kept the latter country in close contact with the superior civilization of the former. The light of culture and refinement which radiated from Japan's new capital in ever widening circles till it reached even the more remote places of the empire was strongly tinged with Buddhist colors. What Chamberlain says so well of Japanese Buddhism as a whole is especially true of the Heian epoch when he writes: "All education was for centuries in Buddhist hands, as was the care of the poor and sick; Buddhism introduced art, introduced medicine, molded the folk-lore of the country, created its dramatic poetry, deeply influenced politics and every sphere of social and intellectual activity. In a word, Buddhism was the teacher under whose instruction the Japanese nation grew up."

A few instances from the time of Emperor Shirakawa (1072- 1086) may indicate how extensive must have been its influence by that time. It is said that *e.g.* the Buddhist injunction against taking life was so strictly enforced that "eight thousand fishing nets were seized and burned; no gifts of fish were to be offered to the court; hunting and hawking were rigidly prescribed, and the hawks set at liberty." This same emperor spent immense sums of money upon Buddhist temples and equipments. "Besides 5470 scrolls or hanging pictures painted and presented to various fanes, Shirakawa was responsible for the erection of one huge idol 32 feet in height, 127 half that size, of 3150 life-size, and of 2930 three-feet images. Then of seven-storied pagodas the tale was twenty-one, and of miniature pagodas as many as 44,630." And what he did so lavishly others imitated to a considerable extent; so that all central Japan was literally studded with Buddhist structures of one sort or another.

From this the reader should not infer that all was well with the Buddhism of the Heian period. Though it did much to advance civilization in Japan in many ways, it must be admitted that there was not a corresponding advance in the moral and spiritual life of the people. In fact, towards the end of the tenth century the great centers of religion themselves began to be hotbeds of vice and intrigue rather than seats of learning and virtue. The age itself, of course, was partially responsible for this, for it was beginning to be an age of political disturbances and military conquest as a result of a complex of causes for which no one in particular was responsible. But, after all, the Buddhist leaders must be blamed for not doing their duty as spiritual guides. In truth, they sank to the level of their surroundings and in many cases became the blind leaders of the blind. "By the end of the eleventh century," writes Murdoch, "any one of these great fanes (*i.e.* Enryakuji, Miidera and Kôfukuji) could readily place several thousand men in the field at very short notice.

Each of them had become a huge Cave of Adullam, — a refuge for every sturdy knave with a soul above earning a livelihood by the commonplace drudgery of honest work. Each of them had in truth assumed the aspect of a great fortress garrisoned by a turbulent rabble of armed ruffians. And each of them had degenerated into a hotbed of vice, where the most important precepts of the moral code were openly and wantonly flouted. . . . And yet in spite of the foulness of their lives, the prestige of the priests had never stood higher, while the resources of the monasteries had never been greater; and year by year they were adding to their wealth." The ex-Emperor Shirakawa well expressed the situation in a witticism when he remarked that although he was the ruler of Japan there were three things in the Empire beyond his control, — "the freaks of the river Kamo (which often inundated and devastated the capital), the fall of the dice, and the turbulence of the priests."

Thus we see the irony of history; the very Buddhism which Emperor Kwammu had fostered in his new capital of Peace to counteract the influence of the old Nara sects, in the end turned out to be a greater nuisance and meddler in the affairs of state than the older rival ever dared to be. Not infrequently did these occupants of Hieizan set at defiance both the entreaties and threats of the imperial court itself. Truly Buddhism had wandered far from the path of quiet meditation and peace in which its founder had sought to lead his followers.

THE SECTS OF THE GREAT AWAKENING

But as out of decadent Catholicism sprang the great Protestant Reformation, so out of this prosperous and degenerate Heian Buddhism came the great religious awakening in Japan during the twelfth and thirteenth centuries.

What might be regarded as a voice in the wilderness was that of a half-witted wandering priest called Kûya who according to some was really an Imperial prince, a son of Emperor Daigo. He went dancing from place to place, repeating incessantly the

Nembutsu (the prayer, Namu Amida Butsu) by which he hoped to direct the attention of the people to the spiritual side of life which had been so utterly buried in the confusion and tumult of the age. He did not, however, confine his activity to preaching and praying, but gave expression to his faith in a real concrete way; for he built bridges, improved roads, repaired temples, dug wells in barren lands, tunneled mountains and labored with his hands unceasingly — all with the purpose of turning men's minds to the better and higher things of life. It is difficult to say whether Kûya's preachings did more than arouse a passing curiosity.

A man who indirectly exercised a great influence on the generation of religious reformers which was to appear later was Genshin. While still a youth of tender years he dreamed that a priest gave him a small mirror and asked him to polish it. He did not understand the significance of the dream until later when he entered, at the age of thirteen, a Tendai monstery on Mt. Hiei, where under the great priest and scholar Jie he was led into the deep truths of Tendai doctrines. At the early age of fifteen he began his lectures on the sacred scriptures and was greatly admired by the emperor who gave him many beautiful garments as a token of his esteem.

Young Genshin was much elated over this recognition and sent these gifts to his mother. But his mother was not so pleased as he expected her to be and sent him the following reprimand: "The idea of your leaving home was that you might enter the path of true enlightenment and not to gain any profit or make a name for yourself. Do not be led astray by these things. I thought you would be a bridge to connect this world with the next, but I am sad to find that you are only a monk of this world." These words were sufficient, and the young Genshin turned his back on worldly ambitions and gave himself to a diligent search for the truth. He wrote to his mother in reply to her rebuke, "I regarded books as bridges that lead across this life (*i.e.* learning as a way of success in life), but now happily I have entered the Way of Truth through them." It is said that when his mother was on her deathbed Genshin spent the last hours at her side leading her into the joy of the faith and trust which he had found, namely, the faith in the name of the great Buddha Amida.

The books which Genshin wrote attracted attention not only in Japan but even learned priests in China were deeply impressed by his learning and marveled that Japan should have men of such profound insight and piety. And the Chinese emperor, when he learned of Genshin's death, built a special pagoda in which he had an image of Genshin placed. Genshin was not the founder of a new sect nor did he inaugurate any great reform in the decadent Buddhism of his own day. He remained a priest of the Tendai Sect though he is regarded as one of the great church fathers of the Amida sects which arose soon after his day. This is due to the fact that by his writings he helped lay the foundation for the reforms and new sects of the Kamakura period. His three small volumes on Paradise, the Intermediate States and Hell have exerted a great influence and should be of special interest to Western readers, especially to students of Dante. His description of the eight Buddhist hells, each with its sixteen compartments, affords particular interest to one familiar with Dante's Inferno. Genshin probably received most of his ideas on this subject from Indian sources, and one cannot help but wonder whether Dante may not have drawn from the same. Genshin, of course, wrote several centuries before Dante's day.

Ryônin and the First Amida Sect

Genshin was followed by Ryônin (1072-1132) who, too, was a student at the Tendai monasteries. Ryônin also studied the doctrines of the Shingon sect, but he felt that in all his studies he was not really entering the way of true enlightenment. Not only did he himself fail in his search but he saw that this was the experience of other monks. All of them were so busy with their much learning that they did not really take time to find the heart of truth. He therefore retired to a quiet spot and spent his time in reading and repeating the prayer "Namu Amida Butsu," "I adore Thee Thou Buddha of Eternal Life and Light." It is said that he repeated this prayer sometimes as often as 60,000 times in one day, thus concentrating his mind and heart on Amida. One day when he was thus absorbed in prayer and deep meditation Amida appeared to him in a vision and said: "Great is the merit of Nembutsu (*i.e.* repeating the prayer, Namu Amida Butsu). If by your own prayers you teach others to pray the Nembutsu, their prayers will become your merit and in this way there will be mutual benefit. This is entering Paradise through the power of another." This thought impressed Ryônin very much and so he formed the Yûdzû Nembutsu Sect (Society of Mutual Benefit through Nembutsu). He went to Kyôto with a roll-book and enrolled the Emperor Toba and many courtiers and officials. Afterwards he wandered from province to province enlisting people in his new sect.

The Yûdzû Nembutsu Sect is the oldest of the four Amida sects in Japan and the first outward expression of that great religious development which took place during the twelfth and thirteenth centuries. It is the first distinctively Japanese sect; the Six Nara sects and the Tendai and Shingon sects having been introduced from China. But while it is the oldest of the Amida sects and as a sect the first Japanese product, it must not be regarded as the beginning of the Amida teaching in Japan nor as even a fair representative of this great division of Japanese Buddhism. The truer representatives of this type of Buddhism are the Jôdo Sect introduced from China but greatly modified in Japan, and its main offshoot, namely, the great Shin Sect of which we shall speak presently. But before we come to these we wish to make a few remarks about the beginnings of the Amida doctrines in Japan.

The idea that one can be born into Amida's Western Paradise by praying sincerely the prayer "Namu Amida Butsu" is a very ancient one in Japan. To begin with, it would seem that the image sent by the king of Kudara to the emperor of Japan in the year 552, when Buddhism was officially introduced, was an image of the Buddha Amida, and so the Amida faith may be said to date from the very beginning of Japanese Buddhism. This may be stretching a point and so we lay no stress upon it. It does seem true, however, that Shôtoku Taishi, the first great royal patron of Japanese Buddhism, expressed longings for the Western Paradise, and during the reigns of Kôgyoku and Kôtoku (642-654),

Enon is said to have lectured on the Paradise scriptures in the palace. Gyôgi Bosatsu, the Father of religious syncretism in Japan, preached salvation through the name of Amida; and Chikô of the old Sanron Sect drew pictures of the Western Paradise and wrote an essay on Paradise.

Coming down to the end of the Nara period, *i.e.* at the end of the eighth century, we find pictures of Amida and his Western Paradise in most of the head temples of every province. Besides this it seems to have been the custom at this time to copy on the forty-ninth day after a death occurred the Shosan Jôdokyô (a hymn on birth into Paradise), and on the first anniversary it was the custom to erect an image of Amida six feet in height. All of this goes to show that the Amida doctrines were more or less known at this time. After this Dengyô Daishi, the founder of the Tendai Sect in Japan, gave Amidaism a prominent place in his comprehensive system, and another great Tendai priest, Jikaku Daishi, carrying out Dengyô's wish, built a special hall in which he placed an image of Amida. We have already stated above that the Tendai temples which were connected with the famous Miidera give Amida the highest place of honor. The half-witted priest Kûya, as we have said, went everywhere repeating the Nembutsu, and the learned Genshin laid a more lasting foundation for this doctrine in his writings. But Amidaism as a separate sect did not come into existence in Japan until Ryônin founded his society of Mutual Benefit through Nembutsu, *i.e.* the Yûdzû Nembutsu Sect.

Hônen and the Jôdo Sect

Ryônin's conception of Amida's way of salvation was, however, a very inadequate one. He laid too much stress on the idea of merit of the believer, *i.e.* the merit of repeating the Nembutsu. This was really too much of "a vain repetition of the heathen" to satisfy thoroughly the deeper religious sense of the people of Japan. The great teacher of Amida Buddhism was yet to come. This was Genku, better known as Hônen Shônin. When Ryônin died in 1132 Hônen was a baby boy of two. It was an age of civil wars, wars in which not only the Samurai took part, but also the monks of Hieizan, Miidera, Kôfukuji and the other great monastic centers of the time. One day the father of Seishimaru (Genku's name as a boy) was mortally wounded in the conflict, and the little lad, reared in the atmosphere of war, attempted to kill his father's enemy. The father praised his son for his loyalty and courage, but in his dying words he said: "I now die through this misfortune, but you must not take vengeance on my enemy. My death is only the reward of my former life. If you avenge my death you will in turn be subject to the vengeance of your enemy's descendants. All living beings fear death. As I suffer from my wounds, other men suffer; and as I cling to life, shall not others cling to life equally? Henceforth pray only for salvation for yourself and your fellowmen. Cast away all vengeance and malice and seek to attain enlightenment."

These words made a profound impression on the boy, and soon after this incident he entered a monastery of the Tendai Sect on Hieizan. He was a diligent student and penetrated far into the various doctrines of not only the Tendai Sect but of all the sects.

But in all his seekings he found no peace for his soul. Like Luther more than three centuries later, Genku longed for a deeper assurance of salvation and a more vital religious life than was offered at the centers of learning on the slopes of Hieizan. One day, as if by chance, he hit upon Genshin's "*Ôjôyôshô*" (Collected Essays on Entering Paradise). A little later he became acquainted with the writings of Zendô Daishi, from which he drank deeply; for here he learned that man's salvation does not depend upon his own strength so much as upon the grace of Amida.

Even the lowest sinner may find a way of escape from this life of misery and suffering into a life of happiness and peace if only he has learned to pray in faith to the great Buddha Amida who has prepared for those who believe in him his Western Paradise. When Genku read these great words of hope, he flung away then and there the ordinary way of salvation which Japanese Buddhism had usually been proclaiming, namely, the way of salvation through one's own wisdom and virtue; and he became the prophet of the new way, the way of faith in the mercy of Amida. He became the founder in Japan of the great Jôdo, Pure Land or Paradise Sect (1175) which has as its chief tenets a semi-theistic conception of God, a doctrine of a personal future life and salvation for all men who believe in the grace of Amida. This way of salvation, it holds, was worked out for man by the vicarious sufferings of the (divine) man Hôzô Bosatsu.

With the founding of Hônen's sect, Amida Buddhism may be said to have been thoroughly established in Japan. The influence of Hônen's teachings soon became far-reaching. People from all classes of society — from the nobility and the royal family down to the lowest peasants — entered the new sect. Priests of other sects, one after another, began to give their allegiance to this new school and helped spread the way of salvation through faith in Amida. Among Hônen's followers were a great many men of real ability and this naturally gave prestige to the Jôdo Sect. But strong men are often "strong-minded" men and that frequently becomes a seed of discord. It was not long therefore before the new sect began to divide into several branches or factions, all of which seem to have had a remarkable vitality and so hastened to spread the influence of the sect. The differences were usually very minor and not sufficient to make any serious break.

Shinran and the Shin Sect

There was, however, one disciple, Hônen's greatest disciple, namely, Shinran Shônin, who thought that his master had not gone far enough in his exposition of the Amida doctrine, and so felt compelled finally in 1224 to establish an independent sect. This sect is the powerful Jôdo Shinshô, The True Pure Land Sect, usually spoken of by the shorter term, Shin Sect.

When Hônen founded the Jôdo Sect in 1175, Shinran was two years old. He was of noble birth; being a descendant on his father's side of the great Fujiwara family, and on his mother's side, of the illustrious Minamoto family. As a lad of four he lost his father, and in his eighth year his mother also died. Acquainted early with the vicissitudes of life, neither his social standing nor the luxury of his condition could at all satisfy his heart. His mind became more and more set upon deeper things and at the age of nine he became a pupil of Jichin, the abbot of Shôrenin monastery on Hieizan. He is said to have composed the following beautiful line when he took this step: "The heart that thinks there is a tomorrow is as transient as the cherry blossom, for is there not the midnight wind?" He spent a good many years on Hieizan studying the deep things of Tendai philosophy. He also visited Nara and there learned what he could from the scholars of the older sects, among whom there were a great many men of real ability at this time. So profound was his learning that he was popularly known as "The Genius of Hieizan" and "The Famous Priest of the Future." He was made abbot of one of the monasteries on the mountain and was in a fair way of becoming a high priest of the Tendai Sect and of being placed at the head of the Sansenbo, the 3000 monastic buildings which studded Hieizan, thus over-shadowing with his dignity the whole mountain and the neighboring capital of Kyôto. But like the founder of Buddhism, Shinran, having given up all worldly ambition when he first entered the way of enlightenment, was not to yield to the temptation of occupying a conspicuous place as a high priest. He rather gave himself the more diligently to the search after truth and to prayer.

One day Shinran happened to hear Hônen preach on the way of salvation through faith in Amida's great name. After the sermon he called on Hônen in his study and after an earnest inquiry as to the fuller meaning of this teaching he then and there gave up the old way of salvation through the Law (Shôdomon) and accepted the doctrine of salvation through faith in Amida (Jôdomon). This was at the age of twenty-nine. Two years later, influenced by a vision of the Goddess of Mercy (Kwannon) and urged on by his master Hônen, he married Princess Tamahi, the daughter of Prince Fujiwara Kanezane, thus setting an example to the Buddhist world of a new type of priesthood. By this step he broke down the barrier between priest and layman, seeking to demonstrate to the people of Japan that religion should not make a man live an abnormal life and break up the most sacred institution of humanity, namely, the family. Shinran also ate meat and other food forbidden to the priesthood, and in his dress he conformed to the style of ordinary citizens of the land. In short, he lived as a man among men, for he felt that religion has to do with the ordinary things of life and should enable the ordinary man to live this life in the best way possible.

It is not strange that he was attacked fiercely by the priests of the other sects, for his innovations were every whit as extraordinary as any thing Luther ever thought of. He was accordingly banished in 1219 to the province of Hitachi, but he looked upon this exile as an opportunity rather than a hardship. "If I do not go to my place of banishment," said he, "how can I convert the people of those remote parts? This, too, is a blessing flowing from the master's teachings." After six years the ban was removed, but he was in no hurry to get back to Kyôto and civilization. He took a roundabout way through the outlying provinces, preaching the new way and building temples as he went. After an absence of twenty-eight years he finally reached Kyôto, rich in his experience and confident in his gospel of salvation through Amida's Name. The remaining years of his life he spent in writing and preaching. People came even from the distant places to sit at his feet and learn from this great teacher how to walk in the way of Amida's grace. He died at the ripe age of eighty-nine, true to the end to his determination not to know anything but Amida and salvation in his Western Paradise. "Vain thoughts flee at the prayer Namu Amida Butsu. Both the mouth which utters these words and the heart which believes them are in Paradise." "When you see the change which befalls all men, arouse your heart to rely upon Amida." (Shinran.)

At no point in the history of Buddhism would a comparison with the founder of Buddhism and his teachings be so interesting and instructive as just at this point. It is impossible to give here in detail the doctrines of the Shin Sect and the reader is referred to the author's translation of *"A Catechism of the Shin Sect,"* but we must give at least an outline of the main tenets of this remarkable form of Buddhism.

As we stated above, Shinran taught salvation through faith in the Name of the Buddha Amida and rejected the old way of salvation through one's own wisdom and virtue. Just what does this mean? Briefly stated it means the following:

There may have been a time back in the "golden age" of the human race, said Shinran, when it was possible for man to save himself through his own strength, but in "these latter days" this is quite out of the question; for man is entirely too corrupt and lost in ignorance and sin for this task. There is for him now only one way of salvation, namely, the way of simple faith and trust in the great mercy of Amida. But who or what is Amida? Not trying to give the history of the Amida faith we shall give simply what is believed about this Buddha Amida. Amida Butsu (Buddha Amitâbha), before he became a Buddha and while he was still the Bosatsu Hôzô (Bodhisattva Dharmakara) many æons ago, made a great vow in which he vowed that he would not enter the full bliss of Buddhahood until he had worked out a way of salvation for all men, including even the lowest sinners. He remained true to his vow and after many incarnations of self-sacrificing lives he finally succeeded in heaping up so much merit that he became the great Amida Butsu, the Buddha of Eternal Life and Light who offers every man entrance, or rather birth, into his Pure Land of Bliss.

There is but one thing which man must do in order to win this birth into Paradise, and that is to accept the gift that is offered in a spirit of simple faith and trust. The believer is told to call upon the name of Amida in the prayer Namu Amida Butsu which probably means, "I adore Thee," or "Have mercy upon me, Thou Buddha of Eternal Life and Light." He who does this shall be saved. Some go even so far as to say that the faith itself which enables the believer to utter this prayer effectively is also a gift of Amida. The works of the Law, i.e. the good works of a man's daily life, which most Buddhists regard as a heaping up of merit or good Karma, are of no avail, according to the followers of Shinran. Faith in Amida's great Name and that alone can save. Good works are not excluded, but they are regarded as only expressions of the believer's gratitude to Amida for his gift of salvation. That is, good works are not the cause of a man's salvation, but they are the effect of his having been saved through faith.The teachings of the Shin Sect in regard to the way of salvation do not only differ widely from the teachings of the founder of Buddhism and those of the older Japanese sects but also somewhat from the teachings of other Amida sects. The Yûdzû Nembutsu Sect, of which we spoke above, also preached salvation through Amida's name; but, after all, salvation had to be earned by a faithful repetition of the Nembutsu. That is, the believer made merit, or heaped up a good Karma, by repeating his simple prayer over and over again. Then the great Jôdo Sect, of which the Shin sect is really an offshoot, also continued to lay a good deal of stress on making merit.

While Amida's grace was held to be sufficient to say, still the believer was warned to be strict in his observance of certain rules of conduct and was made to feel that, after all, good works had a great deal to do with one's salvation. The follower of Shinran, on the other hand, is taught to rest in perfect peace of heart and to trust solely in Amida. He should not even worry about his moral condition or have any anxiety as to his growth in character. "Whether we are saved because our sins have been blotted out or not we do not know; it is as Amida has ordained. We have nothing to do with it; we have but to believe." And Rennyô, one of the great lights in the Shin Sect, says, "The important thing according to the founder's (*i.e.* Shinran's) teachings is nothing else than this heart of faith. He who does not know this is to be regarded as an outsider; he who knows what faith is has the true marks of a follower of Shinran."

Now this way of salvation proclaimed by Shinran, and to a certain extent also by other Amidaists, obviously signifies a rather radical departure from the fundamentals of S'akyamuni's religion. In the first place it would seem that Amidaism, at least in the minds of some of its adherents, not only makes room for a real God-idea, but this idea seems to come very near a theistic conception. It is significant that the Buddha S'akyamuni almost disappears in the Shin Sect and is regarded simply as the teacher of the gospel of Amida. He is revered as a great man and the founder of Buddhism, but he is not usually held up as an object of worship. If he is worshipped at all it is only because he is regarded as an incarnation or partial manifestation of Amida; never as the highest Buddha as such. As we have just said, we shall treat of this subject more fully later and show that Amida Buddhism is not a real monotheism, but for the present we may treat it as pointing in the direction of a truer conception of the divine than is found in the other schools of Buddhism.

Another fact about these Amida sects and the Shin Sect in particular is that salvation means the salvation of the individual into a future life where there seems to be a real continuity and identity of the individual and not a mere Karma continuity and identity. The Shin Sect teaches that at death the believer really enters Amida's Western Paradise, and to many this hope of a future life of happiness seems to have been a real source of joy and peace. There are even cases on record where men have committed suicide in order to hasten their departure from this world and enter Amida's Paradise. Others have lived in such a joyful anticipation of this that this world was turned into a Paradise for them; in fact, Shinran rather emphasized the thought that salvation begins in this life.

A third point of difference is in the conception of sin which one finds in the teachings of the Shin Sect. Man is regarded as totally depraved and beyond the possibility of saving himself. Sin is not regarded as mere outward evil or misfortune, as it is so often in Buddhist thought, but rather as a condition of the heart which may cause outward evil and misfortune. The one thing necessary, then, is to have a change of heart, and this change of heart comes through faith and not through an effort on the part of man to cleanse his heart through his own wisdom or strength. When Amida is received through faith he controls the heart and so uproots all sin. "When we firmly believe in this vow (*i.e.* Amida's vow to save all living beings) and do not doubt it for a moment, Amida graciously governs our heart. Our evil heart at once becomes united with the good heart of the Nyôrai (*i.e.* Amida)." (Shinran.)

Thus in some of the great fundamentals of religion, namely, the God-idea, the doctrine of the future life, the conception of sin, and especially in the conception of the way of salvation, Amida Buddhism in Japan seems to differ rather widely from the rest of Buddhism and the teachings of the founder S'akyamuni; particularly is this true of the great Shin Sect founded by Shinran Shônin.

A further difference, which though it may not be a fundamental of religion is nevertheless of great importance, is the attitude towards the duties of men as citizens of this world. Where other sects divide the teachings of Buddhism into esoteric and exoteric, or into higher and lower truths, the Shin Sect divides its teachings into doctrines which relate to salvation into a future life and doctrines which relate to a man's duties as a citizen of this world. Buddhism has always been exceedingly other-worldly, and from the very beginning it has held up the life of retirement from the world, the ascetic life of the monk or nun lived in some secluded spot, as the highest type. All through the long centuries the chief function of the average Buddhist priest seems to have been to officiate at funerals and to take charge in one way and another of those who have passed into the great beyond. The Shin Sect, too, is other-worldly; in fact, it has the clearest doctrine of a future life, but it also has a good deal to say about a man's duty as a citizen of this world. We saw above that Shinran himself married and lived the normal life of an ordinary citizen of Japan. This was not a mere accident, but it grew out of a profound conviction that a man of religion should be a model citizen. Household rather than temple or monastery religion was the thing the world needed.

This emphasis on the everyday duties of life really grew out of two things. One was the conviction that salvation has its beginning in this world, *i.e.* the believer is even now united with Amida and so can live in the world without being in bondage to the sins of the world. "How happy the thought," says Hônen, "that though we are still here in the flesh we are numbered among the holy ones of Paradise." The other reason is the fact that in Japanese Buddhism in general and in the Shin Sect in particular there is much less emphasis put upon the evils of our present existence than in Indian Buddhism. This world, S'akyamuni had said, is a world of suffering and sorrow and therefore its hold on us should rigorously be reduced to the lowest terms possible. The Japanese mind has never accepted this doctrine fully, and the Shin Sect, which is the purest Japanese product of all Japanese sects, has been least influenced by it.

It is more natural for the Japanese mind to look upon life and the things of life as good, for Japan is above all else "the land of the gods," and Japanese are the offspring of "the sons of heaven." Thus the religious life cannot be so very distinct from the normal life of a man as a citizen of Japan, and any teacher who can show how religious faith and practical conduct may be harmonized is bound to have a great following. Shinran did have a great following and his sect is today the strongest of all sects of Japanese Buddhism. In fact, it has a vitality which is rather unique among the old religions of the orient. Unhampered by any elaborate metaphysical system, it seems to be able to adjust itself to the great changes — political, economic and social — which have come over modern Japan, and to continue its hold upon the people of this generation while most of the other sects seem to be on the decline. If Buddhism has any future in Japan it will be the Buddhism of the Amida sects in general and the Shin Sect in particular.

With these few remarks we must leave for the present this most interesting of all Japanese Buddhist sects and pass on to an account of the other great sects.

Introduction of the Zen Sect

Between the founding of the Jôdo and the Shin sects there was introduced from south China one of the main branches of the Dhyâna school, namely, the Rinzai branch of the Zen Sect. The Dhyâna school of Buddhism reached China from India in the year 520 A.D. when Bodhidharma came to China as a missionary. Bodhidharma (Japanese, Daruma) is regarded as the twenty-eighth patriarch, being in direct "apostolic succession" from S'akyamuni. With his removal to China the center of the school passed from India, and so he is also looked upon as the first Chinese patriarch. At this time China was being flooded with Indian books and the bewildered Buddhist did not know to what book or books he was to turn for the correct teaching. Bodhidharma came with the message that the true teaching of the master was not contained in any one book nor even in all the books put together, for truth is too great and deep to be expressed in any written or spoken word.

Truth is in the heart itself and it must be transmitted from heart to heart by a sort of spiritual telegraphy; or even better, the heart must teach itself through silent meditation. The chief characteristic, therefore, of the Zen Sect is silent meditation and abstract contemplation. The true follower seeks thus to penetrate into the inner recesses of reality, into what might be called "the white silence of Truth." It is said of Bodhidharma that he sat seven years staring at a blank wall and that when he was asked questions as to religion and himself he kept silent. And of another Zen philosopher it is said that when he fell into the hands of bandits and they tried to intimidate him by thrusting a sword at his face he did not so much as bat an eye but sat unmoved. No wonder that the ruffians were themselves terrorized and fled leaving this holy man in peace.

Now this method of approach to the truth and salvation as a resultant of the knowledge thus gained was known in Japan from the early days of Buddhism on, being introduced by the high priest Dôsho who established the old Hossô Sect in this land. After him Dôsen, Dengyô, Jikaku and other prominent leaders in religion practiced and preached the Zen way of salvation. By the twelfth century there were a great many, especially men of deep natures, who were acquainted with this quiet way of approach to the truth, but still the followers of Zen had never organized themselves into a separate sect but continued to remain in the existing sects, especially in the all-inclusive Tendai Sect. Finally, however, late in the twelfth century appeared Eisai. Like other great leaders of his day he, too, studied Buddhism at the famous monasteries on Hieizan belonging to the Tendai Sect. He also became a student of the "Secret doctrines" of the Shingon Sect, but finding no satisfaction in this he returned to Hieizan and for eight years studied profoundly the voluminous canon of Mahâyâna Buddhism.

An opportunity presenting itself he carried out a long cherished wish and sailed for China where he studied for a while at the headquarters of the Tendai Sect. Here he secured thirty volumes of rare books and with these he returned to Japan, hoping thus to find the object of his earnest quest. A few years later, however, he felt again constrained to go to China and there at the Tendai center he was initiated into the true teachings of the Zen Sect. When he started for home his teacher bestowed upon him, as a special mark of his achievements, the Great Mantle, the symbol of his having mastered the truth as known by the Zen school. The Zen Sect dates its origin in Japan from about the time of Eisai's second return from China, i.e. about 1191. In 1201 the reigning shôgun invited him to establish himself at the Kenninji in Kyôto, and later at the Kenkôji in Kamakura, which city became the center for the sect. And having its center in this military capital of Japan is one reason why the Zen Sect has always had and why it has to this day a great many military men among its adherents.

Not many years after the founding of the Rinzai branch of the Zen Sect a sister branch of this contemplative school, namely, the Sôtô branch, was established by Dôgen, or Shôyô Daishi, with headquarters in the province of Echizen. The chief difference between the Sôtô and the Rinzai branches of the Zen Sect is that the former puts more weight upon book learning as a subsidiary aid to silent meditation on the truth.

It is the claim of the Zen Sect that it represents most truly the spirit and teaching of the founder of Buddhism. This claim seems substantiated by the facts in the case. Not only does the historic connection with early Indian Buddhism seem more direct than in the case of other sects, but its emphasis on meditation and self-discipline seems nearer to the practice and teachings of S'akyamuni. To be sure, Zen philosophy does not give the

Four Great Truths and the Noble Eightfold Path the same importance as S'akyamuni probably did, but still it insists, as he had done, on the doctrine that man must save himself through his own strength and must not depend for help upon God, or the gods. In fact the Zen Sect makes little or no room for the God-idea, or for the idea of the real permanency of the individual in a future life. It has nothing to say about an Eternal Buddha, though it does recognize an ultimate reality transcending the power of the human mind to grasp, which reality S'akyamuni himself, as we saw, did not deny. While S'akyamuni laid his chief emphasis upon the idea of "escaping from the evils of this life," the Zen teachings of Japan lay the emphasis on the escape from the limitations of the present and empirical self into the glorious liberty of the union with the Greater Self; without stating, however, what that Greater Self is or what the nature of such a salvation might mean.

The practice of Zen, or Zazen, is a kind of mystical self-intoxication by which the believer seeks to rise above the world of sense with all its limitations and differences into the freedom and harmony of the Reality which lies beyond and in which there are no differences and jarring contrasts. Naturally not all who practice Zazen pass exactly through the same experience. With some it is entering into a feeling of oneness of all reality, so that the consciousness of the self and all individual existence fades into nothingness and only a "holy vacancy" remains. With others it may go no further than a heightened sense of the oneness of all reality, so that no matter what loss may come to the individual, there can be no permanent loss since the self is regarded as being really one with the Greater Self, or the Universal Self. But in any case, the believer who has entered this ecstatic state feels himself no longer bound by the ordinary laws of our every-day experience. "He has ceased to think of good or evil, released himself from a relative idea of wise and common beings, given up any discussion or consideration of ignorance and intelligence, and delivered his mind from an idea of the boundary between Buddhas and sentient beings. He gives up doing all works and abandons perceiving all objects, does nothing at all, and abstains his six organs of sense from performing their respective functions."

All our ordinary knowledge, *i.e.* the knowledge of the sense-world in which we make differences between things, is regarded as illusion. Even our moral distinctions have no value and must be treated as the product of the unenlightened mind. "The ancients say: 'When illusion vanishes, quietude will appear; when quietude appears, knowledge will arise; when knowledge arises, truth will make its appearance.' If you want to put an end to such illusive thoughts, you should abstain from thinking of good or evil, and without perceiving objects or performing works, you should not think with the mind and do anything with the body. This is the first precaution to be taken. When illusive objects vanish, the illusive mind will consequently vanish. If the illusive mind vanishes, the entity that never changes will appear. It always knows things distinctly. It is not an object of quietude, nor an object of activity."

In order to attain this state of mind which is void of all sense objects and in which Reality Itself will appear, the student of Zazen is given minute directions as to how and where he is to sit in his silent meditations. We can do no better than quote rather at length from a translation of the works of the founder of Sôjiji, one of the two headmonasteries of the Sôtô Sect, from which the above excerpts are also taken.

"As for the place of meditation, a quiet place is good; the cushion you use must be thick; you should prevent wind and smoke from coming in, and rain and dew from moistening you; you should take good care of the place where you sit, and always keep it clean. . . . The place of sitting should not be too bright in the daytime, nor too dark at night, it should be warm in winter and cool in summer. . . .

"While you sit, you should abandon the ideas of heat, will and consciousness, put an end to the thoughts of recollection, perception and contemplation; you should not intend to become a Buddha and care for right or wrong; and valuing time highly, you should be so urgent in the practice of Dhyâna as though you were trying to rescue your head from fire. . . . Shih-hsiang taught his disciples to become like dead trees, and Ju-ching of Tai-pai used to warn his disciples against dozing. For the Dhyâna man there is no need of burning incense, worshipping, invocating the Buddha-name, making confession, reciting Sûtras, or performing daily services; he has only to sit on in meditation and thereby he will attain enlightenment.

". . . There are two ways of sitting: full cross-legged sitting, and half cross-legged sitting. According to the former way, you must put the right foot on the left thigh, and the left foot on the right thigh. Your clothes must be loosely tied and well arranged. Put the right hand with the palm upturned on the left foot and the left hand on the right palm. The thumbs of both hands stand supporting each the point of the other, kept closely to the body. The points of the thumb must be kept just in front of the navel. Keeping the body upright and sitting erectly, you should not incline or bend the body to right or to left, nor should you lean your body forwards or backwards. Your ears and shoulders, nose and navel should be kept respectively in perpendicular lines. Your tongue must be stuck to the upper gum. Breathing must be made through the nostrils. Lips and teeth must be stuck to each other. The eyes must be opened moderately, neither too widely nor too narrowly.

Thus making proper arrangements of the body, you should inhale and exhale a few times through the opened mouth. Next, settling your body, you should move your body from side to side, each time decreasing the degree of the motion, and finally coming to a firm upright sitting, when you should consider unconsiderableness. How could unconsiderableness be considered? It is considerationless, which is an important means of Dhyâna sitting, by means of which you must forthwith destroy evil passions and obtain full enlightenment. "When you want to rise from sitting, first of all you must put both the upturned hands on the knees and move the body from side to side seven or eight times, each time increasing the degree of the motion and breathing out of the opened mouth. Putting your extended arms on the ground, stand up easily and walk slowly along the left side of the room, ever turning to the right."

As one reads these detailed instructions given to those who would practice Zazen, one cannot but be struck with the contradiction involved in the means of achieving this goal of abstract contemplation and the goal itself. The one is the most careful — almost puerile — regard for the details of the sense world, while the goal is a state of mind in which the sense world has no existence. The follower of Zazen may say that this regard for the detailed arrangement of the body is only provisional and these things vanish with the illusive mind when once the believer has entered the state of perfect quietude and truth. Quite so; only then it should not be necessary for one who has reached such a state to return again to an ordinary state of consciousness in which the details and differences of the sense world seem so very real. That is, the student of Zazen should not be given any rules as to how to arise from his posture of sitting in meditation; for why should he wish to arise and return to the sense world if he has really entered a state in which Truth has appeared and in which he knows that the objects of our every-day consciousness are illusive?

Obviously the world of sense is too real to be disposed of in this way for any length of time, and the problems of truth and reality must be approached in another way than by a mystical self-intoxication lasting under favorable conditions for only a few hours at best. That the "quiet mind" is the most favorable condition in which Reality may be apprehended, no one would question; but it cannot be apprehended simply by a process of elimination and evacuation of the content of our ordinary conscious states. This can only end in an abstraction and vacuity which may be a pleasant feeling to those who would escape for a little while from the "evil of existence" in this "incurably evil world," but it can hardly satisfy permanently the hearts of those who would overcome the evils of Life and enter a life of a Positive Good.

It seems a curious phenomenon that a sect which lays such an emphasis on the contemplative life and which holds out the "white silence of truth" as the highest goal should have always had among its followers a great many men of the military class. Even in modern industrial and bustling Japan it is the fashion of military men to practice "Zazen." Besides the reason already given above, namely, the fact that the Zen Sect made the military capital of Japan its center of activity, there are two other reasons. One is that the Zen Sect has always shown itself very friendly to Confucian ethics and made it a part of its practical teachings. From the earliest times Confucianism has been a sort of religious philosophy for the military classes and never has it been regarded in Japan as antagonistic to Buddhism. The vagueness of the God-idea in Confucianism is exceedingly congenial to the Zen mind, and the definiteness of the Confucian ethics, especially the ethical teachings which deal with the relationship of lord and vassal, formed a good substitute for the ethics of the Noble Eightfold Path.

At any rate, the former were not regarded as contrary to the latter. The other great reason for the popularity of Zen thought with military men is the fact that it lays a strong emphasis upon self-discipline and self-control, the primary qualification of any true soldier.

Even the physical discipline of a true student of Zen is Spartan, and the mental discipline is often such that men become indifferent to all dangers and face death without a tremor. The capture of Port Arthur in the Russo-Japanese war was in part at least the fruit of Zen discipline.

NICHIREN AND THE NICHIREN SECT

There is one more great sect which arose during this remarkable period of Japan's religious history, namely, the Nichiren Sect founded by Nichiren Shônin in 1253. Of all the founders of sects in Japan or leaders in things religious, Nichiren is the most picturesque and in many respects the most powerful personality. He was born in 1222 in an unknown village of Awa Province. As a lad he became somewhat acquainted with the teachings of the Shingon Sect, but later he went to Mt. Hiei and studied under the great priests of the Tendai Sect. For about ten years he gave himself to these studies and then returned to his native province ready for his great campaign. Like all great reformers, Nichiren did not start out to found a new sect. He began by denouncing what he regarded as a real perversion of the master's teachings.

Such perversions he found especially in the teachings of the sects which were just then coming into great popularity, namely, the Jôdo, the Shin and the Zen sects. In his *Rissho Ankoku Ron,* Nichiren's chief writing, he makes a vehement attack on Hônen, the founder of the Jôdo Sect, and upon all the followers of the Amida doctrine. He laments that the teachings of Dengyô Daishi and the older type of Buddhism were being neglected and that the people had ears only for the writings of Zendô and the Amida scriptures. This bears testimony to the wonderful success the Amida sects had soon after their coming into existence. The Zen sects, too, he could not endure and opposed them as the invention of the devil. Even his first love, the Shingon Sect, he denounced as "a traitor to the country."

The reason Nichiren so bitterly opposed these other sects was because he felt that they were dividing Buddhism, and especially that the Amida sects were taking away the glory of S'akyamuni and giving it to another, namely, Amida. And on the other hand, with a divided religion Japan would be a divided nation, and so both religion and state would be destroyed. That is why he cries in one of his impassionate utterances, "Awake, men, awake! awake, and look around you. No man is born with two fathers or two mothers. Look at the heavens above you: there are no two suns in the sky. Look at the earth at your feet: no two kings can rule a country." But this, he felt, was exactly what was happening in Japan. Politically the country was divided into factions, some giving their allegiance to the emperor, at Kyôto, others to the shôgun or regent at Kamakura. Spiritually some were true to what he thought was the real teaching of the founder and others were followers of Amida, Dainichi or some other Buddha. And as the former was the real outgrowth of the latter division, there was but one thing to do, namely, to uproot the sects which had proved themselves disloyal to the pure teachings of the founder.

Not only was the political and religious world divided and disintegrating, but because of this the nation was being destroyed, he felt. Evidence of this seemed abundant on every hand. In 1257, *e.g.*, a terrible earthquake shook things from their very foundations. This was followed the next year by an equally terrible hurricane; and as a result of these two calamities, famine and pestilence completed the work of destruction. And still further, there were signs that what was left by these natural calamities would fall a prey to a foreign invader, the Mongols who in 1264 had established themselves in Peking under Kublai Khan and were threatening to subdue the whole of eastern Asia, including the islands of the Sunrise Kingdom. To avoid this impending peril Japan must be a united nation both politically and spiritually.

That Nichiren was not a mere alarmist is shown by the events which followed in the political world. The predicted invasion of the Mongols actually materialized, and apparently the only reason it did not succeed beyond the occupation of a few minor islands and a narrow strip of coast line in Kyûshû was the timely appearance of a severe typhoon which caused the Mongol ships to share the fate of the great Spanish Armada. The proud Japanese, however, prefers to lay greater stress on the valor of his illustrious forefathers, who, he claims, were the only people of that age able to check the advancing hordes of the Mongols which at one time or another overran great portions of the two continents of Asia and Europe.

Nichiren was equally right in his estimate of the religious situation. The new sects, especially the Amida sects, were doing much to dethrone the founder of Buddhism from his place of honor; for it is a fact that most Amidaists regard Gautama as simply the great teacher and not the Buddha to be worshiped. If he is worshiped at all it is only because he might be regarded as one of the historic manifestations of Amida. The Shingon was equally a departure though in quite a different way, as we have already shown above. Whether his attacks on the Zen Sect were justified on the same grounds is a question; for, as we have said above, the Zen is nearer the teachings of the founder in many ways than, perhaps, any other Japanese sect. But on the whole Nichiren was correct in raising an alarm and trying to bring his people back to the historical Buddha S'akyamuni if Japanese Buddhism was to follow the teaching of him whom they professed to follow.

But while Nichiren was zealous to restore Buddhism to its pristine purity it does not at all follow that he even knew what the pristine purity of Buddhism might mean. Both the spirit of his religion and the content of his doctrines prove that he knew really very little on this subject. As a student of the Tendai he became acquainted among other books with the Saddharma-Pundara-sûtra (Japanese, Hokkekyô) which he made the main foundation of his teachings. As we have already pointed out, this is a comparatively late writing and breathes a Buddhism quite different from the Buddhism of S'akyamuni. The great Buddha of that scripture is the Eternal Buddha of Original Enlightenment with whom S'akyamuni is identical, or of whom he is one of many manifestations. But the historical Buddha S'akyamuni had nothing to say of such a Buddha, and he certainly never claimed to be identical with or the manifestation of such a Buddha. Then further, Nichiren and his followers lay great emphasis on faith, faith in this sacred scripture which is regarded with a superstitious reverence. The prayer which is so constantly upon the lips of Nichiren's disciples, "Namu Myôhô Renge Kyô" (Hail, Thou Scripture of the Lotus of the True Law), seems of all "vain repetitions of the heathen" the most vain; especially is this true when judged from the standpoint of what S'akyamuni regarded as the kernel of his teachings.

Then Nichiren's bitter attack on other sects was also a great departure from the spirit of older Buddhism, which was nothing if not tolerant of views that differed. This tolerant attitude was especially characteristic of the Tendai Sect, from which Nichiren learned practically all that he knew about Buddhism. This characteristic of Nichiren was not altogether a bad one, for if there is anything that Buddhism needed it was a firmness which would enable it to hold to some definite things and reject others that were incompatible. But we simply wish to point out that Nichiren, in trying to give Buddhism some backbone, was infusing into it his own vigorous personality to whom distinctions were real and vital, and he was not restoring a characteristic of the older Buddhism. In his *Rissho Ankoku Ron* this comes clearly to light, for in this dialogue between the master of a house and a guest the latter frequently makes the point that the spirit of Buddhism is one which tolerates all views and persecutes none, and the master has great difficulty in proving from the sacred scriptures that heretics should be opposed.

The truth of the matter is that Nichiren was anything but a reformer of Buddhism. He thought he was one, but in reality he was a man who gave Japanese Buddhism a new turn. This new turn was not in the doctrines he taught, for there is nothing new in the teachings of the Nichiren Sect, but in the spirit which he infused into the new sect which he founded. The very fact that it is the only Japanese sect which calls itself by the name of its founder shows that it was founded on Nichiren's spirit and personality rather than upon any new doctrine or upon any old Buddhist teaching restored to life. Nichiren has transmitted his positive spirit to his followers, though it must be admitted that the positiveness which made him a towering figure in Japanese life, in most of his followers assumes a fanatic character which is the enemy of all true progress and has made the sect, as one has put it, "the Ishmael of Buddhism."

Nichiren's bitter attacks upon the political and religious leaders of his day naturally led to counter attacks from his many enemies. By the priests of other sects he was accused of promulgating heresy, and his political enemies accused him of inciting rebellion. In 1261, he was arrested and brought before the regent's court at Kamakura. It is not strange that he was found guilty and that he was banished to the peninsula of Idzu. Three years later, however, he appeared again in the streets of Kamakura, more outspoken than ever. For a while he was safe, for the people believed that it was in response to his prayers that the heavens sent rain after a long drought. Like Elijah of old, he mocked the "false prophets" and came off victorious. But even so, it was impossible for a man of his temper to keep out of trouble, and we soon find him again before the regent's court. This time the charges were so serious that the court felt constrained to condemn him to death.

He was led to the sands on the Kamakura beach and the executioner's sword was about to strike the fatal blow when, as if by miracle, a messenger from the regent appeared upon the scene and saved his life. Nichiren was instead banished to distant Sado, where he remained till 1272, when he returned once more to resume his preachings and warnings. By this time, he had won so many followers that he was quite safe. The remaining ten years of his life he spent at Minobu and Ikegami, which two places are regarded to this day as the chief seats of the sect. At Ikegami Nichiren entered into rest from his strenuous life, and there is his tomb, which is still a sacred shrine to thousands. Every autumn his numerous followers gather there from all quarters to do him honor. But the thoughtful student, when he listens to the deafening noise of those drunken worshipers — drunken not with Nichiren's enthusiasm and inspiring message but with cheap *saké* — mourns the thought that one so earnest and on the whole so sane should have such unworthy followers. For it is true that while there are some educated people in the Nichiren Sect the rank and file come from the most ignorant and lowest classes; and the religion which they profess, instead of lifting them to a higher and purer life, seems only to rivet upon them more tightly the superstitions and follies of a darker age.

The Ji Sect

Another sect which came into existence about this time and which we mention just in passing is the last of the four Amida sects, the Ji Sect founded by Ippen Shônin. Some hold that it was first founded by Kûya and that Ippen is the second founder, but if it was founded as early as Kûya's day it made no place for itself before Ippen's day. It is of little consequence now as it has only about 500 temples in all Japan, but in its early history it promised to be of great influence and at one time had even an imperial prince for its head. Ippen Shônin was remarkable for his zeal in trying to spread his message, going from one end of the land to the other to teach men the Easy Way, the Way of Faith in the Mercy of Amida. He seems to have transmitted this characteristic to his followers, for the sect has apparently always laid great stress upon itinerant preaching. One naturally wonders why such efforts have produced no greater results, unless it be that they are reaped by the more powerful Amida sects from which the Ji Sect really does not differ enough to warrant a separate existence.

All four of these great sects, the Jôdo, Zen, Shin and Nichiren came into existence within a period of about three quarters of a century, namely, between 1175-1253, and their beginnings undoubtedly represent the greatest outburst of religious life to be found in Japan's long history. The student who reads with an unbiased mind this movement and the lives of the great men who led the way, cannot fail to be impressed with the positive contribution made by Japan to at least one of the world's great religions. To know this period of Japanese history will cure any man of the superficial thought so often expressed by Westerners that the Japanese have borrowed everything they possess and that they are only imitators. The religion of these four great sects is as truly a real development of Indian and Chinese Buddhism as is the Protestantism of Germany, England and America a development of medieval and early Christianity; the only difference is that it took place some three centuries earlier.

The old Nara sects and the two Kyôto sects of the ninth century had their influence on Japan because they represented a higher civilization than that of Japan, but these four great sects of the Kamakura period gained their hold because they were the first real expression of Buddhism in terms of things Japanese, i.e. with them Buddhism may be said to have been thoroughly planted in Japanese life. It was planted not only in the life of the upper classes, as was largely the case with the older sects, but in the life of the people at large. It is only natural that these sects should become very popular, and while the old Tendai and Shingon sects continued to exercise a great influence they were relegated to a secondary place, especially in the new Kwantô region, the center of the military rulers of Japan. Out of a total of 72,000 temples in existence today over 53,000 belong to the above-mentioned four great sects, and they represent the dominant forces of Japanese Buddhism today.

Unfortunately this reformation of Japanese Buddhism in the twelfth and thirteenth centuries had in it also some of the evils of the Protestant Reformation. It had in it from the beginning the seeds of schism and divisions. We saw above that Nichiren was alarmed at the influence the new sects were having and that he sought to rally Buddhists around the one standard of loyalty to S'akyamuni and one earthly ruler; but as a matter of fact his efforts resulted in making further divisions and in bringing in a period of strife and hatred among the various sects. Not that Nichiren was responsible for all these fights and divisions but that he marks in himself the tendency of the age. Any account of these divisions, or even the barest outline of them, would try the patience of even an interested student. It is enough to say that the process went on and on, old schisms dying out and new ones taking their place, until to-day, Japan has over fifty Buddhist sects recognized by the government.

Of these there are thirty-six divisions and subdivisions within the four sects of the Kamakura period. The differences between the main divisions of Japanese Buddhism, of which it is customary to make twelve, are often much greater than the differences between the great divisions of Christianity. On the other hand the differences between the subdivisions of a sect are often very minor. Thus, *e.g.*, the ten subdivisions of the Shin Sect are due not to any doctrinal differences but sometimes simply to the fact that some temple, harboring perhaps a royal or other important personage, became thereby too prominent to be regarded as a branch-temple and so was made independent and the center of a new subdivision.

In other cases sub-divisions were caused by the rise of some great priest who by his own personality impressed himself so powerfully upon his followers that they banded themselves together into a brotherhood without thereby intentionally cutting themselves loose from the parent body but which nevertheless in the course of time became independent. In still other cases, the divisions were due merely to geographical conditions, for in a mountainous country like Japan, before the advent of the railroad, travel and intercourse were exceedingly difficult. This fact had made the political divisions very real for centuries before the advent of Buddhism, and these political divisions in turn made the religious differences very natural and easy.

Thus Japanese Buddhism is quite accustomed to the idea of schisms and divisions, as indeed Buddhism in India and China was from the early days; but it must be added that the average Buddhist, especially the average Buddhist philosopher, sees in this nothing to be regretted, but only a sign of life. Even a Christian must admit that schisms are often a sign of life, though frequently a misdirected life. The Buddhist philosopher on the other hand would hold that because Truth is many sided and men's minds are so finite, it is the glory of a religion to have many divisions each of which brings out its own peculiar angle of the whole truth. So far do some philosophers carry this half truth that they do not hesitate to regard the most glaring contradictions as but the opposite sides of the same truth. But of this characteristic of Buddhism, when we take up the Buddhist theory of knowledge, and so we leave it to pass on with the historical narrative.

POLITICAL STRIFE AND RELIGIOUS DECLINE

The wonderful religious outburst of the twelfth and thirteenth centuries was followed by a sad decline. For about one hundred years after the founding of the Kamakura shôgunate Japan enjoyed peace and a measure of prosperity. The Hôjô regents who supplanted the descendants of the great Yoritomo were on the whole strong and capable rulers, and under their administration the country was able to recover somewhat from the devastating wars which had preceded this period. But in the beginning of the fourteenth century things began to change for the worse again. In 1333 the Hôjô regents were overthrown, and upon this followed the long Wars of Succession when Japan had two rival lines of emperors, and for more than fifty years civil war and private wars were the order of the day. Finally in 1392 the Ashikagas succeeded in bringing the land once more under one central authority, but this did not mean much gain to the average citizen.

As a matter of fact the peace under the Ashikaga shôguns was often less endurable than war, for the tax-gatherer was more to be dreaded than the soldier or the plague and famine which in those days usually followed in the wae of war. It is claimed that in one form or another the poor peasants had to pay about 70 per cent of the produce of their fields as taxes. The money thus extorted from the people was not used to repair the ravages of preceding wars but was squandered in extravagant and luxuriant living by the shôguns and their hangers-on. The third Ashikaga shôgun, Yoshimitsu, *e.g.*, spent enormous sums on magnificent palaces and private residences. One writer states that his "Flower Palace" cost about five million dollars; a single door costing as much as $150,000.

In this mad craze he was followed by the upper classes who could — and more often could not — afford it; so that the city of Kyôto had at this time between six and seven thousand such extravagant residences. Even when the land was stricken with a severe plague and famine, as it was, *e.g.*, in the time of the eighth Ashikaga shôgun, Yoshimasa, when in two months about 80,000 people perished, this extravagant style of living was kept up.

It is therefore not strange that in such days the heart for quiet and industrial living was taken out of the common people and that industry and the constructive forces of life lagged. Nor is it strange that finally Japan was so impoverished that when, *e.g.*, in 1500 the Emperor Tsuchimikado II. died it was forty-four days before enough money could be gotten together to defray the funeral expenses, while his successor, Nara II., had to wait twenty-one years before he had sufficient means to celebrate his coronation appropriately.

That this should be a period of religious decline goes without saying. Of course, in one way religion seemed to gain a firmer hold on the people just because of the adverse circumstances under which they lived. Especially those sects which held out to the common man the hope of a speedy entrance into paradise from this "vale of tears" found a rather congenial atmosphere in which to propagate their doctrines. In fact the pessimistic spirit of Buddhism as a whole, which was one born in a world-weary civilization and which regards life as incurably evil and everything as evanescent, fitted in remarkably well with the temper of the age. The very woes of the people became a source of prosperity to the unscrupulous priests, who were usually quite ready to exchange their "spiritual treasures" for deeds to broad acres and stately manors. The pleasure-loving Yoshimitsu and his successors were indeed ever ready to spend goodly sums upon temples and temple decorations. Yoshimitsu was specially generous towards the Zen Sect and gave liberal gifts to the five great fanes of Kamakura (Go-zan) and the five great fanes in Kyôto and its vicinity.

He went so far as to direct that each province should have its own great Zen monastery. The land owned by all the temples and monasteries was exempted from taxation, and many monasteries received funds from the special tax known as Dansen. And still further, certain ones received directly the custom duties and transit duties collected at the various barriers which were now being erected all over the land. Thus, *e.g.*, the great Kôfukuji of Nara received the customs of the port of Hyôgo.

With such favors extended to the Buddhist monks and priests it is only natural that outwardly at least religion was flourishing in this age of bloodshed and misery. But a religion which lives on the fears and tears of its adherents is not a healthy product; and as a matter of fact this period of the great Succession Wars and Ashikaga shôguns was not great in spiritual realities. Very few indeed were walking in the Noble Eightfold Path of the founder. Not only had the Buddhist layman wandered far from this path but the priests and monks seem to have gone even farther astray. Even the new sects which had been founded as a protest against the corruption of the old Kyôto sects had gone the way of all the rest. The great monasteries were great only as formidable camps of fighting monks, for the military monk was the order of the day. Some authorities claim that in the early part of the sixteenth century the Buddhist priests were on the whole the strongest political force in Japan.

This is probably not an exaggeration, for it must be remembered that by this time all semblance of a central authority had vanished. The emperors were figure-heads and even the shôguns were mere puppets, and the various feudal chiefs were each a law unto himself. And often greater than the authority of these feudal chiefs was that of the rich monasteries with their extensive lands and their mountain fortresses. But, of course, the priests did not wield this authority as a unit nor in the interest of what might work for the good of the land. When they were not taking part in the general civil wars of the age on one side or the other, the various monasteries fought among themselves. Hieizan, Miidera and Kôfukuji had been in the habit of doing this for centuries, but now they were imitated by the new "centers of light." Particularly fierce was the feud between Jôdo and Nichiren sects. Even the followers of the great Shinran apparently believed in the power of the mailed fist as much as the rest, for we read that towards the close of this age a great monastery of this sect was able to resist successfully Nobunaga's besieging army of sixty thousand.

But it was not only that the religious leaders of this day had exchanged their spiritual weapons for steel swords and spears and that the foes they were fighting were their own brethren and not the hosts of sin and darkness, that marks the spiritual decline of the times. These "centers of light" were guilty of far more infamous deeds of darkness. We read, *e.g.*, of the abbots of monasteries, after taking the customary vows of poverty and celibacy, spending their days in riotous living with lewd women. And the worst of it was that apparently nobody regarded this wrong or inconsistent. In the middle of the fifteenth century, when famine and plague stalked through the land and daily between seven and eight hundred peasants fell by the wayside, it was quite common to dispose of the daughters of poor families by selling them to brothels, while the boys were frequently sold to the priests, "who shaved their eyebrows, powdered their faces, dressed them in female garb and put them to the vilest of uses, for since the days of Yoshimitsu, who had set an evil example in this as in so many other matters, the practice of pederasty had become very common, especially in the monasteries, although it was by no means confined to them."

It would, however, not be correct to infer from what we have just said that Buddhism did not exert any influence for good during this period of bloodshed and misery. In fact there are many cases in which Buddhist priests intervened with the mercy of Buddha to stay the wrath of men. Buddhist monasteries were often like the cities of refuge in ancient Israel, and political criminals frequently were allowed to choose between the tonsure and the sword. It is true that the guilty occasionally escaped thus from well-deserved punishment, but more often the law from which they escaped was not the law of right but only that of might. Then here and there were individual priests of real power who exercised a great influence for good over the rulers of the day and so helped guide them through these periods of storm to days of peace.

Perhaps the most conspicuous case of such an influence was that of the relation between Ashikaga Takauji and the famous Zen priest Soseki. Not only did such men give spiritual consolation to these leaders in their trying times but perhaps more often gave them real solid advice as to the affairs of state. Soseki especially seems to have tried to apply the truths of religion to the practical problems of life. He sought to show Takauji that mercy, patience and serving others were not only the expression of the Buddha heart but also the quickest and surest road to a reign of peace. "If one rises above the clouds, the moon can be seen without an obstruction," he once wrote to the founder of the Ashikaga shôgunate. Little did he realize how few would be able to do this during the two centuries which followed.

Then again, should it be said to the credit of Buddhism, that this period marks a wonderful development in pictorial art, viz., the rise of the great Zen school of painters which has dominated the ideals of artists in one way or another down to almost the present day. Of course, such an influence may not have been very far reaching in that age, but the fact that this development of at least one of the fine arts was possible at all goes to show that, after all, there were individuals here and there who had time and taste for the higher aspects of life.

But after this has been said it must be confessed that the period of the Ashikaga shôguns was in general one of religious decay. Buddhism though outwardly strong was really bankrupt morally and spiritually. Here and there a man, *e.g.*, like Rennyô (1415-1499) of the Shin Sect appeared and tried to make Buddhism a real spiritual force in society, but the darkness of the age was against them. Rennyô, *e.g.*, was compelled to write out the doctrines of his sect in the simple Hiragana script, as not only the lower classes but also the middle and some of the upper classes were unable to read or understand anything written in Chinese characters in which all the Buddhist scriptures were published. It is true, some light continued to stream into Japan from China during these dark days, but it was rather faint, for the Neo-Confucianism which was to exert such a great influence during the Tokugawa shôgunate had not yet taken a firm hold, though a number of Zen scholars had been more or less under its influence from the end of the thirteenth century onward.

RELIGION IN THE TOKUGAWA PERIOD

Reconstruction Days and the Catholic Mission

The long period of strife and bloodshed of which we have just spoken was followed finally by the great peace of the Tokugawa shôgunate. By the middle of the sixteenth century the movement had begun which was gradually to bring about a unification of the empire and restore peace and prosperity to a much afflicted people. There are three great names around which the history of Japan centers during these reconstruction days, viz., Nobunaga, Hideyoshi and Tokugawa Ieyasu. Of course, there were other great men who helped in the unification of the empire, but these three stand out like great peaks. We shall not stop to give even an outline of their lives, though it would not be out of place in even such a hurried review of the development of Buddhism, for while they were not men of religion they had a great deal to do with determining the religious development of the empire for several centuries.

All three were men who rose from an obscure environment, and Hideyoshi, the greatest of the trio, was the son of a simple peasant. A Japanese wit has well expressed their respective characteristics as follows: "If you do not sing," said Nobunaga to a nightingale, "I will wring your neck." "If you do not sing," said Hideyoshi, "I will make you." "If you do not sing," said the more diplomatic Ieyasu, "I will wait until you do." The nightingale finally did sing the song of peace and unity for Ieyasu, but each of the three had a big part in making it sing. Their work resulted in the great Tokugawa shôgunate, which ruled the land with such skill and firmness for about two centuries and a half that there was hardly so much as a dogfight on this blood-drenched soil.

It was just at the beginning of this reconstruction period that the Catholic mission under Xavier came to Japan in the year 1549. The mission landed from a Portuguese ship in the southern island of Kyûshû. The missionaries were well received, for in their train came the merchants and traders with guns and other implements of war so much appreciated by a warlike age. We are told that even the Buddhist priests received these Christian missionaries in a friendly spirit, for they regarded their religion as simply one more form of the comprehensive Mahâyâna teaching. And besides, they were not half so much concerned with rivals in things spiritual as in worldly power and prestige. It goes without saying that the Catholics were not willing to compromise with the Buddhists, though they did not take an openly hostile attitude until they had first ingratiated themselves with certain political factions to whom they looked for patronage and protection.

We find thus the missionary Froez, in the year 1568, seeking an interview with the great Nobunaga. At this conference, apparently, an understanding was reached by which the Catholics were to be utilized for fighting and crushing the Buddhist monasteries, which had incurred Nobunaga's enmity. We do not know the details of the arrangement, but it is a fact that Christianity in Japan at that time advanced with leaps and bounds and that Nobunaga in 1571 exterminated the three thousand monasteries which studded Mt. Hiei. This wholesale destruction of the historic center and home of Buddhism was but the beginning of similar operations against the other monastery centers in the land. By the zealous Catholics Nobunaga was regarded as the "true scourge of God." Nobunaga, however, was not a Christian himself; he simply used the Jesuits to serve his purpose. His religion was his own ambition, for he built a great temple and placed in it a stone image of himself which he expected the people to worship. But as in the case of vain

Herod of old, his self-exaltation was speedily followed by his downfall. The hand of the assassin, inspired by his trusted general Akechi Mitsuhide, brought his career to a sudden end.

Nobunaga was succeeded by his friend and lieutenant Toyotomi Hideyoshi. Hideyoshi was quick to conserve what Nobunaga had begun. He "made the nightingale sing," not so much by threatening "to wring its neck" as by less drastic measures, though he, too, resorted a good deal to the sword to carry out his program of harmonizing the nation. Hideyoshi, too, was not a friend of the Buddhists and continued the work of Nobunaga in reducing their military strength, though he showed some consideration for certain monasteries which he could use to an advantage. He had begun to suspect the Jesuits of political intrigues and in 1597, he suddenly dropped his mask of friendship and had twenty-six of them crucified on Martyr's Peak near Nagasaki. This did not mean that all Christians were put under the ban, for later on he entrusted the Christian general Konishi with a regiment of Christians to carry out a military expedition against Korea, though he took the precaution to send also some Buddhist troops with them, the idea being that the two groups would spy on each other and so neutralize their influence. Hideyoshi like Nobunaga made his own ambition his religion as may be seen from the fact that he erected a magnificent temple to the New War God which was to be none other than himself.

Hideyoshi was succeeded by Ieyasu, the last of the great triad. Nobunaga and Hideyoshi had done preparatory work for the unification of the empire, Ieyasu consummated and consolidated it. He had but one great battle to fight, namely, the famous battle of Sekigahara, and then he could wait till the "nightingale sang" its song of peace. And sing it did, for Ieyasu became the founder of the illustrious Tokugawa shôgunate which gave peace and order to Japan for more than 250 years. The emperor at Kyôto was allowed the nominal rule of the empire but it is an open secret that the shôgun's word at Yedo (Tôkyô) was supreme, and when Commodore Perry opened the closed doors of Japan in 1853 it was with the shôgun that he dealt as the real ruler of the land. The relative power of emperor and shôgun may be best appreciated when it is remembered that the annual appropriation for the royal family and its dependents was only 150,000 koku of rice and this was not taken directly from the national revenue but was given by the shôgun out of his own fat income of 4,000,000 per year.

Ieyasu's attitude toward religion differed from that of his two predecessors in that he was himself a professing Buddhist and took a more or less active interest in religious reform. Whether he was really a religious man is another question. The truth of the matter seems to be that he was very liberal in his views and looked upon organized religion as a force that might help him in the affairs of state, for Ieyasu was above all else a shrewd statesman. That is why he was so intimate with the priest Tenkai who became his right hand man to control not only the Christians but also the Buddhists themselves. And that is also why he encouraged the revival of Confucianism in Japan, for he saw in the Confucian philosophy of state and its emphasis on the spirit of loyalty a desirable force to help him in his great work of national unification.

The Closing of the Doors and the Suppression of Christianity

It may seem strange at first sight that a man so liberal minded should be the one who closed the doors of Japan to the outside world. The truth of the matter is that this policy which seems so narrow to us moderns was really in the interest of peace and order. The only mistake was that the doors were kept closed so long after the danger which Ieyasu sought to avoid had passed. It is safe to say that if his successors had been as open minded as he was they would have changed the policy long before they actually did. Ieyasu's reason for cutting Japan off from the outside world was simply to enable him to consolidate his work of unification. He did not wish any disturbing element to come in from the outside and upset the peace that had been bought at such great cost. Too long had Japan bled from the wounds of discord.

Now Christianity was undoubtedly a foreign element and in the form in which it had been propagated in Japan from the beginning it meddled entirely too much with the things that belong to Caesar to be allowed with impunity. The Buddhists, of course, meddled even more than did the Christians but Buddhism had been the religion of the people for centuries and could not be opposed too much. It was enough to regulate it through the priests themselves. But Christianity was a new outside element and if it was not willing to be merged in the national religion of the land there was but one thing left, namely to exterminate it. An additional reason for this attitude towards Christianity was the fact that the Jesuits were the real agents of the pope at Rome and that all true disciples were called upon to regard the pope as not only the spiritual head but as also superior to earthly rulers in temporal matters. It is only natural that Ieyasu should see in the rising Catholic church in Japan the seed of future political troubles.

We find accordingly that step by step the regulations against Christianity became more and more severe until it was positively forbidden by law after 1611. Whereas under Nobunaga's régime the Catholics were used as an instrument to fight Buddhist monasteries, Ieyasu turned the tables and used the Buddhist monks to suppress Christianity. In every city and village of the land certain officials were set over well-defined districts, their sole duty being to spy out those suspected of being Christians. (It is an interesting fact that the second man to become a bishop in the Japan Methodist Church, Bishop Hiraiwa, is the son of such an official, the office having been hereditary in the family for several generations.)

The story of the suppression of Christianity in Japan has been told by others and we need not repeat it here. We simply state that after the first severe persecutions the majority of the thousands and tens of thousands of the nominal Christians who became such in the period of governmental patronage recanted and entered the Buddhist ranks. One of the requirements of the day was the registration of every Japanese citizen as an adherent of one of the Buddhist sects. This, we might remark in passing, accounts for the fact that to this day the great majority of the people regard themselves as Buddhists, though as individuals they may not care a fig for the religion or know the barest outline of Buddhist teachings. But not all these Catholic Christians recanted. Many of them died the martyr's death, and in spite of the closest watch on the part of the government for 250 years Christianity kept cropping up again and again. There are many people still living who saw the edict boards against Christianity along the highways of the empire; and the brass crosses worn smooth by the feet of those who thus proved that they were not Christians, may be seen in the museums of the nation. But when the edicts were finally taken down there were several thousand Christians in and around Nagasaki who had kept the faith. And in other parts of the land there are Christians in whose families precious Christian relics have been handed down in secret from generation to generation.

Partial Revival of Buddhism

The Buddhists were used as an instrument of the government to suppress Christianity. This does not mean, however, that Buddhism under the Tokugawa shôguns ever got back its former vitality or even its outward prestige. The truth of the matter is that the blow which Nobunaga dealt to the famous Tendai monastery on Mt. Hiei proved almost fatal. And as Mt. Hiei was really the mother of all the great leaders who founded the leading sects this blow proved serious to Japanese Buddhism as a whole. All the more serious was it for the religion of Buddha when it is remembered that other great centers of the faith were equally disturbed during the stormy times that preceded the great calm.

After peace was restored and prosperity and culture began to return, Buddhism, too, recovered somewhat from the shock. In almost every one of the leading sects appeared men of real ability and character. It is therefore customary among Buddhist writers to speak of the "Middle Reformers," *i.e.* the men who after the devastating wars of the Ashikaga period brought new prosperity to the various sects. Thus, *e.g.* the Tendai Sect, while crushed in and around Kyôto, began to show new activity in the Kwantô with Nikkô and Yedo as centers. In the Shingon Sect we see the New School party growing in power and influence. The Rinzai and Sôtô branches of the Zen Sect had suffered most severely from the wars, for as we have said, these sects had a great many military men as adherents, and the old law that he that takes the sword shall perish by the sword held good in Japan as truly as elsewhere. But when peace was restored these sects became quite flourishing, especially in outward things, for it was the fashion of the day among the various feudal lords who were usually military men to bestow much property upon Zen temples and monasteries.

The Jôdo Sect seemed specially favored from time to time by the Tokugawa shôguns and it recovered much of its former glory, having among its strong temples such places as the famous Chionin of Kyôto and the Zôjôji of Tôkyô, and counting among its priests many men of real ability. And what is true of the Jôdo is equally true of the Shin Sect. Its great temples built in the modern period and some during the past few decades are numerous. The headquarters of the two Hongwanji branches in Kyôto are especially a credit as magnificent specimens of temple architecture. The Nichiren Sect, too, had its reformers and shared with others a certain degree of prosperity during the peaceful days of the Tokugawa period.

This day of renewals saw even the introduction of a new sect from China, namely, the Ôbaku branch of the Zen Sect founded in 1659 by a Chinese priest named Ingen and by Chinese refugees who came to Japan after the fall of the Ming dynasty. This sect has never attracted many adherents but it has exerted a great influence and counts among its few followers a number of the strongest men of Japan. The distinguishing feature of the sect is its use of modern Chinese for its scriptures whereas other sects still use the ancient Chinese, though in very recent years they have begun to use Japanese translations for the general public. But after all this has been said about the renewal of Buddhism during the Tokugawa period it cannot be held that the religion of Buddha ever reached again the heights it had attained during the great period of religious awakening in the twelfth and thirteenth centuries. In spite of this outward prosperity and activity which led in some cases to the formation of new subdivisions, the period as a whole cannot be regarded as a great period for Buddhism as far as real spiritual influence and strength is concerned. The truth of the matter is that the springs of the spiritual life for this age were really outside of Buddhism, namely, in Confucianism.

Neo-Confucianism

Confucian thought had influenced Japan from the earliest days — even before Buddhism was introduced during the sixth century. But while this is true it cannot be said that Confucianism before the Tokugawa age was ever the dominant life-current in this land. It was rather like a number of minor tributaries which fed the main stream; particularly was its influence felt in the realm of practical ethics. In fact, as we have said before, much of the ethical teachings of Japanese Buddhism is really only a restatement of Confucian ethics. That is, the strongest influence which Confucianism exerted on Japan before the Tokugawa age was exerted through Buddhism.

Now it is a peculiar coincident that at the very time when Buddhism in Japan burst forth into the four great sects of the Kamakura period, namely, the rise of the Jôdo, Zen, Shin and Nichiren sects, Confucianism in China was being reshaped in the Neo-Confucian schools of Shushi (Chinese, Chu Hi 1130-1200) and Ôyômei (Chinese, Wang-Yang- Ming 1472-1528). The foundations for the Ôyômei school were really laid by Riku-Shôsan (1042-1094), and so while Ôyômei, who gave the school its permanent influence, belongs to a little later period we may say that these Neo-Confucian schools arose about the time of the great Buddhist awakening in Japan. It was this type of Confucianism which was to overshadow Buddhism during the Tokugawa period. Particularly was the Shushi school to become the dominant force in the official world of Japan, for it was made the authorized system of education by Ieyasu and became so firmly entrenched that any one opposing its teachings was regarded as a traitor to the state.

This reshaping of Confucianism in China into the Shushi and Ôyômei schools was really more than a restatement of an old system; it was in fact a syncretism of Confucianism and Buddhism. Even as early as the days of Mencius and a little later Confucianism was being strongly influenced by Taoism. That is, Confucian scholars, while clinging to the practical ethics of the Five Relations, began to seek for a metaphysical and religious basis for their ethics. Then with the coming of the Zen philosophy in the sixth century A.D. and the general development of Mahâyâna Buddhism in China, the movement in Confucianism from the external and formal to the internal and spiritual continued.

This was the period when Chinese Buddhism took up into itself much of the practical teachings of Confucianism which have ever since constituted the practical ethics found in Chinese and Japanese Buddhism. But not until the days of Riku- Shôsan, Shushi and Ôyômei did Confucianism develop a real metaphysical and religious basis for its teachings. These philosophers and their followers were always talking about the "Ri" and the "Ki" and the relation between the two. That is, where the older Confucianism was always talking about the human relations these Neo-Confucianists were more concerned with the problem of the relation of the human to the divine, of the finite to the infinite, of the phenomenal world to the noumenal world. The "Ri" becomes in Confucianism what the "Tao," or Way, was in Taoism, and what the Eternal and Monistic Substance or the Rational Principle was in Mahâyâna Buddhism. And the "Ki" in Confucianism takes very much the same place which the transitory and phenomenal world occupies in Buddhism.

The chief difference is that the "Ri" in Confucianism is usually more than a mere Rational Principle but frequently has a moral quality. That is, it is the personification of Moral Wisdom rather than the personification of mere Reason. In some writers the conception of this Moral Wisdom approaches very near the conception of a personal God, though in others it remains rather pantheistic. And as the Absolute is thought of in terms of Moral Wisdom rather than mere Reason, the relation of man to the Absolute is also thought of more as a moral relation, i.e. man's chief duty is expressed in terms of righteous conduct rather than in terms of right knowledge, as is usually the case in Buddhism.

While these two Neo-Confucian schools are alike in that both are the expression of a union of Confucian and Buddhist thought, they differ somewhat from each other in other respects. The Shushi school regards itself as a true transmitter of orthodox Confucianism and consequently lays a great deal of stress upon a knowledge of the classics and erudition in general. The Ôyômei school, on the other hand, while claiming to be a follower of Confucius in spirit, is more free in what it regards as orthodox. It lays not so much stress upon erudition as upon intuitive knowledge. Very much like the Zen Sect in Buddhism, which holds that the true teaching of the master is transmitted from heart to heart and not through books, so the Ôyômei school holds that books are only guideposts to the truth and that the heart must find the truth in itself. Or as Kumazawa Banzan, one of the chief representatives of the Ôyômei school in Japan, has so well put it when he compared books and the teachings of wise men of the past to the foot prints of a rabbit which one wishes to catch. Obviously the foot prints are a help in catching the rabbit, but they are not the rabbit itself. But if one has once caught the rabbit the foot prints are no longer necessary. Where Shushi said, know before you act (and by knowing he meant a knowledge of what wise men of the past have said), Ôyômei said that one can know fully only as one acts. Both schools lay emphasis on practical moral wisdom, but the one looks upon transmitted knowledge as a guide to conduct and the other rather emphasizes the mutual influence of knowledge and action which alone gives true wisdom.

It is not our purpose to give here a detailed account of the introduction of this Neo-Confucianism, nor of its real place in the life of Japan. As already stated before, it was brought in gradually by priests of the Zen Sect who have always been among its chief exponents. The first representatives seem to have been two Chinese Buddhist scholars, Sôgen and Ichizan, the former coming to Japan in the latter part of the thirteenth century. These were followed by other Chinese teachers and by Japanese scholars who studied in China, but the political strife and bloodshed which caused Buddhism to degenerate in Japan also kept Confucianism from gaining much of a hold. It was not therefore until the famous trio, Nobunaga, Hideyoshi and Ieyasu, had restored peace that Neo-Confucianism became fully established in the person of the scholarly Fujiwara Seigwa (1561-1610) who is usually regarded as the first real exponent of the Shushi school in Japan.

He was followed by Hayashi Razan (1583-1672), also a descendant of the great Fujiwara family. Both these illustrious scholars had been Buddhist scholars and the latter became a Buddhist priest after retiring from his position in the Tokugawa government. His opposition to Christianity was pronounced and the account of his interview with one of the Jesuit missionaries is of special interest to the student of Christianity in Japan. Other great lights regarded as disciples of the Shushi school in Japan are such men as the scholarly Muro Kyuso, the famous educator Kaibara Ekiken, Yamazaki Anzai and a whole host of strong and earnest men.

Just as the Shushi school had been recognized in China as the orthodox school by the government during the Ming era (1402-1644), so it was made, as we have said above, the authorized system of education by the Tokugawa shôguns. Ieyasu and his successors encouraged this teaching because of its great emphasis on loyalty and obedience which a subject owed to the ruling powers. So general became this teaching and so deeply was it planted into the Japanese mind that we see its effect to this day in the intense loyalty and patriotism so characteristic of the people of Japan. In fact, it was the spirit of this teaching so zealously fostered by the Tokugawa shôguns which finally, in the teachings of the Mito branch of the Shushi school, resulted in the overthrow of the shôguns and the restoration of the emperor as the real ruler of Japan.

But while the Shushi school was recognized and encouraged as the official teaching and while opponents to this system were often suppressed, there were in Japan, as there had been in China before, men whose thought-life could not be confined to a fixed rut by government edicts or persecutions. These became the followers of Ôyômei and constituted the Ôyômei school. The first and in many respects the greatest of these was Nakae Tôjiu, the Sage of Ômi. In his philosophy of life Japanese thought reaches in many respects its loftiest form, and it is not strange that he is still regarded with great reverence. Some say he was really the only true sage Japan has produced. His conception of the nature of the "Ri" and man's relation to it and to his fellow man was indeed a close approach to the best Christian thought, and should be a real schoolmaster to bring men to Christ. Another man of this school was Nakae's greatest disciple, Kumazawa Banzan, who was perhaps the most independent thinker of all these Neo-Confucianists and whose views on Buddhism and Christianity are of special interest. The Ôyômei school, like the Shushi school, counted among its exponents many of the leading men of the Tokugawa era. In fact the stream of Confucianism in this school kept purer and fresher than in the official Shushi school, for the latter was too closely hemmed in by official regulations to allow the freedom so essential for the spiritual life. The official school became really corrupt and helped rivet upon Japan that formalism and dead uniformity so characteristic of much of the life during the Tokugawa period.

In addition to these two Neo-Confucian schools, found both in China and Japan, there developed in Japan, during the latter part of the seventeenth century, a third school of Confucianism known as the Classical school. The founders of this school were Yamaga Soko and Itô Jinsai, of whom the latter is of greatest importance, though the former is of peculiar interest in that he is regarded as the father of Bushidô *"The Way of the True Knight."* This school may be said to be a protest against the emphasis which both the Shushi and Ôyômei schools were placing upon the thought-life as over against the life of action and emotion. That is, Confucianism was becoming much like Buddhism, which conceives of life too much in terms of the intellect and not enough in terms of the feelings and the will.

The school has a right to be called the Classical school in that it made a conscious effort to get back to Confucius and even back to the life-ideal of the wise rulers before him and of which he was only a transmitter; but, after all, the philosophy of life held by the chief exponents of this school is a great advance over the older Confucianism. Particularly is this true of the philosophy of Ogiu Sôrai. Though he claims to go back to the teachings of the sages that preceded Confucius, it is clear that his lofty conception of the divine and man's relation to it and to his fellow-man is more than the exposition of these ancient texts, but rather shows that, keen scholar that he was, he was a true heir of all the ages. Ogiu Sôrai and Nakae Tôjiu represent the best blending of what is loftiest in the teachings of the old philosophies and religions of Japan. Other great names in this Classical school are Itô Togai and Dazai Shundai, the latter being of special importance as a vigorous opponent of Buddhism.

Of less importance in the life of Japan during the Tokugawa period than the above three schools of Confucianism is a fourth one, known as the Eclectic school. The tendency towards eclecticism is always strong when too many schools of philosophy and religion occupy the field, and there were a number of such movements in Japan at this time. But this Eclectic school of Confucianism must be distinguished from the others in that it professed to draw its material only from the existing Confucian schools. When it is remembered, however, that the schools of Neo-Confucianism are themselves a syncretism of Confucianism, Taoism and Buddhism, this so-called Eclectic Confucian school is really a wider eclecticism.

Now from this brief summary of Confucianism in Japan during the Tokugawa age it is clear that Buddhism had indeed a strong rival, for while, as we have said, this Confucian thought was first introduced by Buddhist priests as a part of Buddhist teachings, the movement gradually became independent of its foster mother and in some cases even opposed. In fact, some of the most bitter enemies which Japanese Buddhism ever had were among these great Confucian scholars who came to Confucianism through Buddhism. Gradually the intellectual leadership and the guidance in matters of moral education passed from the hands of the Buddhists into the hands of men who drew their inspiration from Confucian thought. The function of the Buddhist priests was more and more limited to matters pertaining to the future world and to taking care of men's dead bodies rather than directing their daily lives. The official world in Japan and the military classes and men of affairs had indeed little to do with Buddhism and so it became more and more the religion of the ignorant masses, who knew nothing of its better teachings or of its past glory. Even the better minds in Buddhism could not cope with the new situation. When challenged by the progressive Confucianists to state their religious views in terms applicable to Japanese life they could not do it acceptably. The simple truth of the matter is that the Buddhist philosophy of life, being itself the expression of a world-weary civilization, cannot be made a constructive force in an age of reconstructions.

Neo-Shintô Opposition to Buddhism

But Neo-Confucianism was not the only force with which Buddhism had to divide the field after the rise of the Tokugawa shôgunate. There developed also what might be called a Neo-Shintô. We saw how at the beginning of the ninth century Shintô and Buddhism were merged into one system known as Ryôbu Shintô. What this really meant was that Shintô was virtually swallowed up by Buddhism. Not that Shintô disappeared entirely, for the religion of the masses in Buddhism was often more like the old Shintô than Buddhism, but that it was Buddhist thought which dominated the minds of the thinking sections of society. But when, through the civil wars that preceded the Tokugawa age, Buddhism had been weakened, the spirit of the native Shintô came to life again.

It is rather difficult to account for this, but one factor in the matter seems to have been a growing national consciousness caused, on the one hand, by the influx of the Neo-Confucianism, and on the other hand, by the enforced unification of the empire under Ieyasu. That is, the growing knowledge of things Chinese naturally led men to think of things Japanese by way of comparison. We know, *e.g.*, that Hayashi Razan and other Confucian scholars went so far as to work out a theory of a relation between Japan's first emperor, Jimmu Tennô, and the Chinese Emperor Taikaku of the Shu era, and that these views led Tokugawa Mitsukuni (1628-1700) to gather together many great scholars into an institution called the "Shôkô Kwan" for the purpose of investigating Japanese history. It was these scholars of the Mito branch of the Shushi school who wrote the Dai Nihon Shi, *"Great Japanese History,"* which was to play such a big part in the Restoration of 1868. But this movement in the Mito school was only a part of a wider movement, namely, a movement to know and restore things Japanese.

A better knowledge of things Japanese showed men that Buddhism, which had dominated Japan so long, was really a foreign importation and that it could be justly blamed for having played a big part in the civil wars which had for centuries devastated these beautiful islands. In fact, it could be shown with a degree of fairness that Buddhism had broken the spirit of the native Shintô, the heart of which was loyalty to the ruler and a deep patriotism. Of course, Confucianism was also a foreign element and for that reason there was some opposition to it on the part of certain Shintôists, but still Confucianism, with its emphasis on filial piety and loyalty, was much nearer to Shintô in spirit than was Buddhism, whose highest ideal was the celibate monk, and which treated human life and the world as evil. As time went on, therefore, this Neo-Shintô gained momentum until finally in the persons of Motoöri Norinaga and Hirata Atsutane it became a fierce opponent of Buddhism and all for which Buddhism stood. "Back to the pure Shintô of the early days!" was the cry of these men. "Back to the religion which is the only real basis for the teaching that the Imperial household descended from the Sun Goddess Amaterasu." Buddhism had made of emperors mere puppets to plotting priests and so destroyed the very foundations of the Japanese state.

Even among Buddhists themselves there was a searching into the facts of the past which helped weaken its hold on Japan and shook men's faith in its authority. Attacked from all sides and on historic grounds, some of the more earnest priests took a more critical attitude towards their own religion, and we have what we might call the birth of higher criticism in Japanese Buddhism. Two learned men, Tominaga Nakamoto and Hattori Tenyû, were elected to make a special study of the Buddhist canon; and particularly the work of the former, though attracting little attention at the time, laid the foundations for future criticisms. We wish to state here simply that he came to the general conclusion that Mahâyâna Buddhism was not the pure Buddhism of the founder. It is only natural that such views should have a rather serious effect on the minds of those who placed all the emphasis on external authority.

Now this religio-patriotic movement led by the Shintôists and the Confucian scholars of the Mito school not only undermined the authority of Buddhism, branding it as a foreign and undesirable importation, but it also reacted on the Tokugawa shôgunate itself, which had been instrumental in establishing the Shushi school. If Buddhism was a usurper in the spiritual world, then surely was the shôgunate itself a worse criminal, for had it not robbed the emperors at Kyôto of all real authority? Little did Tokugawa Mitsukuni dream that when he founded the "Shôkô Kwan" at Mito and encouraged the scholars to study Japanese history he was helping in the overthrow of his successors. We would not say that this was the only factor in the situation, for the Tokugawa shôgunate, long before it was viewed as a usurper, had degenerated and lost its control over the powerful clans in the south, but still the leaders from these southern clans, which took the lead in the movement that ended in the Restoration of 1868, drew much of their inspiration from the Mito scholars. The Restoration was, of course, hastened by the appearance of Commodore Perry's ships in 1853, but it was not really caused by this as some Westerners fondly imagine. It was really a very minor factor in a very complex movement the core of which was in the religious and philosophic life of the nation during the two centuries preceding.

BUDDHISM IN THE MEIJI ERA

With the passing away of the Tokugawa shôgunate and the restoration of the emperor as the real ruler of the empire Buddhism passed into a new world. However much opposition there had been to it during the Tokugawa period and however much it had lost its intellectual and moral leadership to men reared in a Confucian atmosphere, it still occupied a place as a state religion. Even the fierce advocates of the native Shintô could not succeed in dislodging Buddhism from its nominal position as the religion of the land or in breaking the union of Shintô and Buddhism. But a few years after the Restoration, namely, in the year 1870, Buddhism was finally disestablished as the state religion and separated from Shintô. An attempt was even made to make the divorced Shintô the state religion, but this was pressing matters too far and did not succeed.

Instead Shintô was separated into two parts, namely, Shintô as a religion and Shintô as a system of rites and ceremonies to be used on state occasions as the official form for such things. This second division (Shinshoku) takes charge of all national shrines and tombs of great statesmen and patriots which are not officially regarded as having any religious significance. Shintô as a religion (Shintô shûkyô), on the other hand, with the granting of the Constitution in 1889, was placed on the same footing with Buddhism as one of the religions of Japan, In fact, the Constitution of Japan recognizes the principle of religious liberty, and so puts all religions on the same footing before the law. The fact, however, that the government takes its ceremonies for state occasions from Shintô and has Shintô priests officiate at such times, and the fact that the great Shintô shrines are made national shrines gives the impression to the people that the government regards Shintô as the state religion. The distinction in Shintô referred to above has no meaning to the average Japanese and all the explanations of government officials as to what they mean by it has not changed matters much. The simple fact is that the people at large regard the great Shintô shrines as having religious significance and as more than simply nurseries for patriotism.

As a result of this disestablishment of Buddhism as a state religion it has found it rather difficult to readjust itself. All through its history in Japan it had depended a good deal upon government patronage, and frequently its interests had been identical with those of the rulers of the nation. Thus to be cast off and thrown upon its own resources naturally led to a good many hardships. A good many temples have found it impossible to continue and have been abandoned, and still more are in a dilapidated condition. What impresses one who visits the numerous beauty spots in Japan so frequently occupied by Buddhist temples is that their glory belongs to a past age rather than to the present.

The pilgrims who visit these sequestered spots are not so much the pious believers with their rosaries and much repeated prayers but troops of Middle school students out on an Autumn or Spring excursion with little knowledge or interest in the things for which these decaying temples stood in the past. Of course, there are certain parts of the country where these temples still stand for the authority of the past; especially is this true in some of the non-progressive sections on the west coast of the main island, but no serious student of Buddhist history would hold that Buddhism plays anything like the rôle in Japanese life which it played up to or even through the Tokugawa period.

In certain quarters, however, attempts have been made to reform Buddhism and restore it to its erstwhile place in Japanese life. Two or three of the leading sects seem to have found themselves again and are succeeding fairly well in meeting the stress of economic readjustment that has come over Japan in our day. Some of the more progressive leaders say that the disestablishment of Buddhism as the state religion is really a good thing and will enable it to fulfill its mission as a spiritual force in society. These sects are even trying to extend the field of their activity by carrying on mission work in the newer portions of the empire and by trying to rejuvenate the decadent Buddhism of Korea and China.

New methods of propaganda are being adopted, taken over bodily from Christianity. Thus on all sides we see springing up Young Men's Buddhist Associations, Buddhist Sunday Schools, Women's Societies, Orphanages, Homes for Ex-convicts, etc. Even street preaching and special "evangelistic campaigns" are getting quite common, and the content of some of the sermons and hymns is sometimes taken bodily from Christianity, only that the name Buddha takes the place of Christ. It must be added, however, that the recent scandals connected with the headquarters of almost every one of the leading sects go a long way to counteract this forward movement and many earnest Buddhists are wondering what will be the fate of their religion in Japan.

THE PLACE OF BUDDHISM IN JAPANESE LIFE

THE INFLUENCE IN THE PAST

An interesting but exceedingly difficult problem is the one as to what place Buddhism has had in the life of the Japanese people. The answer to this question is peculiarly difficult because Buddhism is not and has not been the sole religion of Japan, but during the greater part of its long history in this land it has been closely bound up with Shintô and Confucianism; so that even today, though it is officially separated from Shintô, a great many Japanese are Shintôists, Confucianists and Buddhists at one and the same time. Some writers speak of Shintô as the root, Confucianism as the branches and leaves, and Buddhism as the flowers and fruit of the tree of Japanese civilization.

This conception is not altogether wrong, for it is true that historically Shintô comes first, and that in organizing legal and educational institutions Confucianism has played a prominent part, and that finally the chief contribution of Buddhism lies in the realm of art, philosophy and religion. But since art, philosophy and religion are not only the flower and fruit of a civilization but also in turn become the root and branches of the succeeding stages, Buddhism from the ninth century on has been a real part of the roots, branches, leaves, flowers and fruit of the Japanese tree of life. That is, its influence has been so profound that there is no aspect of Japanese life which has not been greatly modified by it. This influence cannot be measured by enumerating simply the major points, though this is all that we can do here, but so far reaching has it been that one can see it also in countless minor ways which apparently have little to do with religion as such.

Among the major contributions which Buddhism made to Japanese life we must place first and foremost the fact that it has been a vehicle of the higher civilization of the continent. This was true not only during its beginnings in this land when it so obviously was the means of bringing in the wealth of Korean and Chinese culture, but down to the Tokugawa period the Buddhist monks and priests continued to be the chief means by which Japan kept in touch with the rest of the world. The point cannot be overstated, for just as truly as Christian missionaries from Europe and America have been the apostles of a superior civilization to the backward nations of the world, so have the Buddhists often been to Japan the messengers of progress and light. In a real sense has Buddhism been the "Light of Asia," and perhaps no part of Asia has received as much through it as has Japan. In saying this we do not wish to imply that Japan would have remained in darkness if it had not been for the religion of the Buddha. It is naturally impossible to say just what would have taken its place. Perhaps Shintô, though a very primitive religion, would have developed into a higher, and on the whole, a more satisfactory religion. Nor do we wish to imply that Buddhism is not today an actual hindrance to the coming of the "Greater Light," the "Light of the World." But the history of Japan having been what it was, it is correct to say that Buddhism has been a determining factor, and that the sources of Japanese culture have been either directly or indirectly mainly Buddhist.

As Buddhism was both a vehicle of a higher civilization and itself the expression of such a civilization naturally its influence on the intellectual life of the nation was incalculable. Shintô was the religion of an immature people, Buddhism a philosophy of life as worked out by a profoundly meditative and speculative India. Thus the first really deep-going influence which Buddhism exerted upon Japan was that it led the people to think more profoundly upon the problems of human life. This intellectual stimulus extended in all directions. First of all it affected the native religion, and Shintô was raised from a jumble of contradictory legends and myths into what was at least the semblance of a reasoned philosophy of life. The various legends were systematized and built up into a more or less connected whole.

The Japanese began to work out a connected account of the past and wrote the first history of their race. It is true that the Kojiki and Nihongi are not real histories, but they are attempts to weld together in some way the traditions of the past into a historic narrative. Then further, this intellectual stimulus soon showed itself in its effect upon the language. With the coming of Buddhism the Japanese language was raised into a real medium of education and culture. A very large per cent of the present vocabulary came either directly from Buddhism or was added from the Chinese to give an adequate expression of the new ideas which came in the train of the new religion. The spread of the art of reading and writing, and thus education in general, was largely due to the influence of the Buddhists.

Buddhism taught Japan the elements of logic, psychology, natural sciences as then known in India and China and the subtleties of philosophy and metaphysical speculations. The first sects introduced laid special stress on dialectics and psychological analysis, and this certainly had a great deal to do with sharpening the intellectual powers of the people. And what was true in the early days remained true for centuries; namely, that whatever the Japanese knew of philosophy and science they owed largely to Buddhism. This intellectual development accounts for the fact that when Western culture came to Japan in the modern period the Japanese were able to assimilate it in such a surprisingly short time, and that today there are Japanese scholars in every field of learning who can hold their own with the scholars of any nation. In short, Japan has been a cultured nation for centuries and she owes to Buddhism a great debt for the major part of this culture.

Now this spread of general culture and this development of the intellectual powers of the people naturally had a profound effect on every phase of life. Thus *e.g.*, in the political world it helped create a new Japan. When Buddhism reached these shores, Japan was not yet a real nation. It was rather a land inhabited by various tribes with the tribe in the Kyôtô-Osaka region gradually gaining the ascendancy. Buddhism enlarged the horizon of the people with its constant emphasis on universals, so that the tribe-idea naturally had to give way to the national ideal. It is true, as we said above, that the organization of the political institutions came from Confucianism, but it came largely through the Buddhist missionaries and educators. And again it is true that Shintô has been the political weapon through which patriotism was cultivated and the various tribes subdued and unified, but, after all, it was a Shintô profoundly modified by Buddhism, and it was the Buddhist philosopher who laid the real foundations of the Japanese state by inspiring the early historians to build up the myths and legends of prehistoric times into a more or less concatenated whole.

Even to this day the Japanese state has for one of its main pillars the legendary history of the Kojiki and Nihongi which, in an indirect way at least, owe their very existence to the impact of Buddhist culture upon early Japan. Then further, the part which Buddhist monks and priests played in the actual political development of the nation through the centuries is beyond measure. It is true that this was far from being a noble part in all cases. In fact there were times when the rulers of the nation were little more than mere puppets of ambitious priests who shielded themselves behind the sacred mantle or the hallowed walls of a powerful monastery. What we wish to point out, however, is that whether for good or evil the part which Buddhism has played in the political life of Japan has been not only an indirect influence but often a very direct and decisive one.

But not to claim for Buddhism too much either of good or evil in a field usually claimed for Shintô and Confucianism, let us come to the sphere in which the influence of this religion is self-evident, we mean the field of art, philosophy and religion.

In the field of art it is more correct to say that Buddhism created certain branches of Japanese art than simply that it influenced them. Thus Japanese architecture, sculpture and painting are what they are because Buddhism has made them so. Music and poetry have also been influenced, though perhaps to a lesser degree.

If in the field of architecture we were to remove from these pine-clad hills and valleys the Buddhist temples, monasteries and flights of stone steps leading up to them, very little of grandeur or beauty would remain. The average Japanese house seems to be a development of the primeval hut and as a work of architecture it cannot claim a very high place. What makes it attractive is not any architectural feature but rather the cleanliness, neatness and simplicity of the interior; or it may be its picturesque environment. The Shintô shrine, too, cannot be said to rank very high, though the shrine entrance, the Torii, may be regarded as a real work of art. But it is really only when we come to Buddhist buildings that Japanese architecture can make any claims. We are not saying that these measure up to the architectural monuments of the West, but only that whatever there is in Japan that merits any attention along this line belongs to Buddhism.

In the field of sculpture Japan is relatively much richer, and this is almost purely the product of Buddhism. What existed of this art before the introduction of Buddhism may be classed with the crude clay figures produced by most primitive peoples. It is surprising in what a short time really world masterpieces in bronze, clay and wood were produced. Within a hundred years after Buddhism had reached these shores, the Buddhist sculptors were doing wonders. The world's largest bronze statue belongs to Japanese Buddhism of the eighth century.

It is true that this does not rank so very high as a work of art, but there are many smaller relics of that period which do rank high. And not only during that first period did the Buddhist sculptor carve his ideals in wood and bronze, but all down through the centuries he dominated this art. The thousands and tens of thousands of images and statues which are to be found in temples, temple grounds, along the highways and byways, in cities, towns and villages, in valleys, on hills, mountain sides and mountain peaks, — all these are the handiwork of the Buddhist artists. And not only is the Buddhist pilgrim surrounded on his journey through life by the symbols of the things invisible, but when he is dead and buried Buddhist art in stone and bronze marks his resting place and "implores the passing tribute of a sigh."

And if Buddhist ideals have guided the chisel and the knife, they have also inspired the pencil and the brush. Here the influence, though perhaps less evident to the casual student, is equally striking. In a land of such natural beauty as Japan one would naturally expect the painter to be inspired largely by his wonderful environment, but instead of that, practically all the older schools of painters were inspired by Indian and Chinese masterpieces introduced by Buddhism. Thus one student of the subject says that "it may safely be asserted that not one in twenty of the productions of these painters, who to the present day are considered to represent the true genius of Japanese art, was inspired by the works of nature as seen in their own beautiful country." In fact the very neglect of perspective in landscape paintings and the "impossible mountains" in these are well-known characteristics. It may be that the very exquisiteness of the scenery in Japan has made the artist despair of ever producing it on canvas, and so instead he seeks only to suggest it, leaving everything but a few bold strokes marking the outline to be supplied by the imagination.

The oldest Japanese painting, dating as it is believed from the seventh century, is a mural decoration in Hôryûji, a Buddhist temple near Nara. Practically all the leading schools down to the present day had their birth in a Buddhist atmosphere. Thus the great painters, Chô Densu and Jôsetsu, the most famous names in the most glorious period of Japanese painting, were Buddhist priests. The great men who succeeded them and founded independent schools, all kept true to the old traditions and preferred the models introduced from China by the Buddhist monks from century to century to the infinitely more perfect models which nature itself supplies to every artist in Japan. Thus while Buddhism has created and nurtured the art of painting in Japan, it may also be said to have hindered the highest development in that it has imposed a slavish adherence to classic Buddhist models, and only occasionally have artists been able to break away from this tyranny, and paint as they really saw with their own eyes.

The influence of Buddhism on music, the most subtle of the arts, it would be difficult for any one not a real student of oriental music to estimate. And for a Westerner the subject is practically impossible, for there is nothing among things oriental which seems more weird. It takes years for one whose ears are attuned to the harmonies of our Western masters to be willing to admit that Japan has anything worthy of the name. It often seems more like the twang of loosely strung chords terribly out of tune. One of the best authorities on the subject of the scale in Japanese music says that it consists "of five notes of the harmonic minor scale, the fourth and the seventh being omitted, because, as there are five recognized colors, five planets, five elements, five viscera and so on, there must also be five notes in music." Being written in the minor key its dominant note is that of melancholy and despair, and not that of joy and victory. Because of this, Japanese music, whether influenced by Buddhism or not, is after all a real expression of that pessimistic philosophy of life of which Buddhism is the best formulation.

As one's understanding of this philosophy of life grows, one's ears also become more sympathetic with the music of it, and especially do one's ears respond to the one distinctively Buddhist instrument of Japan, namely, to the rich, mellow tones of the temple bell. In the words of Captain Brinkley, "The suspended bell of Japan gives forth a voice of the most exquisite sweetness and harmony — a voice that enhances the lovely landscapes and seascapes, across which the sweet solemn notes come floating on Autumn evenings, and in the stillness of Summer's noonday hazes. The song of the bell can never be forgotten by those that have once heard it. Their notes seem to have been born amid the eternal restfulness of the Buddhist paradise, and to have gathered, on their way to human ears, echoes of the sadness that prepares the soul for Nirvâna,"

Japanese poetry, to continue the Hegelian order of the arts, also shows the influence of Buddhism. It may be difficult to prove that the form of poetry has been much influenced but its contents reflects every aspect of Buddhist thoughts and ideals. This is peculiarly true of the short stanzas called Tanka, consisting of not more than five lines and thirty-one syllables, and still more of the Hokku, consisting of only seventeen syllables. These short poems are really more like epigrams and so are apt vehicles of sentiments too deep for thought, or ideals too lofty for many words. The favorite subject matter of these short poems are "the flowers, the birds, the snow, the moon, the falling leaves in autumn the mist on the mountains . . . and the shortness of human life," but the point of view from which these are treated is usually the Buddhist. Thus the favorite cherry blossom is the symbol of the brave knight who does not cleave selfishly to this life; the moon is the symbol of the change to which all things are subject, the falling leaves in Autumn point the way of all life, and the shortness of human life is, of course, an ever-recurrent note in Buddhism; and the short stanza is especially well suited to give expression to a sigh over life's fleetingness. Even the subject of love is dealt with in Japanese poetry from the standpoint of the Buddhist doctrine of Karma. Thus lovers imagine themselves to be destined for each other because in their Karma preëxistence they had loved; and the conjoint suicides so popular in this land are often inspired by the thought that the law of Karma will bring the lovers together in a future existence under more favorable conditions than the present.

Then a form of poetry which is distinctively Buddhist is the Wasan or Buddhist hymn. Though the Wasan is not ordinarily ranked very high as literature, occasionally these hymns rise to high levels and compare not unfavorably with our Christian hymns and songs.

But if the influence of Buddhism on Japanese life has been strong in the field of art, it has been perhaps even greater in the realm of philosophy and religion. It is true, of course, that it had to divide the field with Shintô and Confucianism, but largely on terms laid down by itself. In fact, it is very doubtful whether Shintô would have survived at all if it had been opposed by Buddhism, and not incorporated into it; for Shintô was entirely too primitive to have satisfied much longer the growing intelligence of the Japanese. Buddhism's victory might have been delayed but it would have been inevitable. And Confucianism, too, gained its hold in Japan largely because Buddhists propagated it. It was fostered by them because it supplemented the Buddhist teachings, especially in the field of practical ethics. Thus, as we have said, both Shintô and Confucianism had their place in Japanese life largely on terms laid down by Buddhism. This, of course, in turn affected Buddhism and made it quite different in Japan from what it was in other lands. But still the genius of the religion of the Japanese people, especially in its higher intellectual and philosophical aspects, has been for centuries and still is today, more Buddhist than anything else.

What, then, are the chiet contributions to the distinctively religious life of Japan which Buddhism has made?

First of all, Buddhism elevated and enlarged the conception of the Divine. Shintô was a rather puerile animism and crude polytheism, and the Japanese had not yet advanced to the idea of the universal or the monistic whole. The elements of monism or monotheism found in present- day Shintô were not there when Buddhism first reached these shores; for, as we have said above, not until Buddhism had made itself felt was there even an attempt made to build up the various legends and myths of the native religion into a connected and reasoned whole. But it is the very breath of the philosophy of Mahâyâna Buddhism to reduce the plurality of being to an all-embracing Divine Whole, and to regard the myriads of gods and individual beings as in some way the expression of the All-One. It is true, of course, that in popular Buddhism the gods of polytheistic Shintô and other cults have always played a prominent part; and, on the other hand, it is true that the conception of the Divine All in philosophic Buddhism frequently faded away into thin mist or the "Unknowable" of agnosticism; but even so, it must be admitted that Buddhism did give the Japanese a loftier conception of the ultimate source of all reality than Shintô had. In fact, as we have seen, Amida Buddhism in particular entertained a conception of the Divine which did not differ very far from the Christian conception of God.

Secondly, Buddhism greatly enlarged the conception of man's destiny. The early Shintô ideal went very little beyond the conception of man as a creature of sense-experience. The gods were implored or propitiated in order that they might bestow upon the suppliant what he wanted for a prosperous and happy existence. And the happiness of existence lay not so much in the realm of an enriched personality, as in the realm of those things which satisfy the desires of the senses. What lay beyond the realm of sense or the point in time when the sense organs are dissolved in death, did not concern the early Shintôist so much. Buddhism, however, taught Japan that man's present life is but a moment of his existence and that the real life is more than the life of the body. In spite of the doctrine of the non- reality of the self, Buddhism has impressed, through its doctrine of Karma, the thought of the far-reaching effects of the psychic forces in human life.

It taught the Japanese to think of all things *sub specie œternitatis* and to regard especially the individual human life in its relationship to the past and the future. Thus it both minimized and magnified the place of man in the universe. It minimized man in that it exhibited him as but a fragment of the Whole. But it also magnified human life in that it showed that however small this fragment might be its destiny is wrapped up with the destiny of the Great All. To be sure, Buddhism did not always have a very clear idea as to what this destiny might be, and often it seemed to be the destiny of Vacuity, but occasionally at least it held out to man a hope of a future life which was truly inspiring. And even in quarters where the hope of a larger future was not emphasized, or where it was left among the great uncertainties, the emphasis which such Buddhist thinkers placed on self-culture carried with it by way of implication the thought of a higher destiny; for what would self-culture mean if at the end of the road lay no real positive goal? That is, the schools in Japanese Buddhism which apparently denied the future life, after all, held out some sort of desired future to the individual and so ennobled the conception of man's destiny.

A third great contribution which Buddhism made to the religious life of Japan is the conception, or conceptions, regarding the way by which man can reach his higher destiny. Whatever have been the perversions of these conceptions — and they have been gross and many in popular Buddhism — the higher Buddhism has always insisted that it must be by way of obedience to the truth. Man must know the truth, and the truth shall set him free from the bondages of his little self into the liberty of the greater Something. The doctrine of Karma, which runs all through Buddhist thought, on its better side means that this universe is under law. To know this law is to know the truth, and to obey the truth is to become superior to the law, or rather to direct the operations of the inexorable law in such a way as to bring man into a better and fuller life.

Even the schools which teach the doctrine of salvation through faith in Amida do not deny the necessity of obedience to the law of Karma, only they hold that the obedience was rendered once and for all by Amida. Thus as we have said, whatever perversions there have been in popular Buddhism, and whatever superstitious practices of magic the ignorant masses may indulge in, the higher side of Buddhism has always stood for the conception of a universe of rational laws which man must obey if he would advance into a larger and nobler life.

This thought of obedience to the truth naturally leads us to the moral and ethical side of the religious life. There may be nothing distinctive in these ethical teachings when compared with the ethics of other advanced religions. But when seen in the light of Shintô ethics — if it is possible to speak of such a thing — it will be realized what a great contribution Buddhism has made. And when it is further remembered that Buddhist priests were largely the medium through which Confucian ethics were made known in this land, we will have to say that practically all the moral training which the people of Japan have had up to the modern period they owe either directly or indirectly to Buddhism.

Not only did Buddhism influence the thought side of religion and the practical working out of this in ethical conduct, but also in the less important side of the outer trappings of religion did it exert a great influence. One reason why Buddhism appealed to the ancient Japanese was the fact that it had much more elaborate and impressive outward settings than their native religion had. It brought with it images, statues, pictures, bells, incense and all that goes to make an impressive ritual; and, in the course of time, it developed in Japan a complex ecclesiastical machinery. So rich in these outward things is Buddhism that even a Roman Catholic might feel perfectly at home in these surroundings. A few years ago a writer in one of the leading Christian papers made a comparison between Buddhism and Catholicism, and he showed over thirty points in which the two were in agreement in these externals of religion. It is not strange that when Xavier and his fellow workers came to Japan they were regarded at first by the Buddhist priests as but one more sect of their own religion.

Such, then, are some of the main influences which Buddhism has exerted upon the life of the people of Japan. In some fields these have been so determining that of the major Asiatic states Japan is most Buddhist, and certainly in no other land has Buddhism so much to its credit. It has been the dominant religion in this land for about a thousand years, and during that time Buddhism has developed aspects which make it more nearly an adequate religion for an advanced people than the forms it has taken in other Asiatic countries. That is to say, Buddhism has not only exerted a great influence on Japan, but the Japanese genius has also in turn impressed itself upon Buddhism.

But after we have said this much about the influence which the religion of Buddha has exerted upon Japanese life in the past, we must now come to the question as to what place it has in present-day Japan, and then the still more difficult question as to what its place will probably be in the future, for no one is more ready to admit than educated Buddhists themselves that a new day has arisen for the old religions of this people, and that, though the past may have belonged to Buddhism, the present and especially the future are problematic.

Chapter - 5

Buddhism in Korea

In order to understand Korean Buddhism, we must first take a look at its history. Although there is evidence of earlier contact with Buddhism, the usually accepted date for the introduction of Buddhism to the peninsula from China is 372 CE (Common Era). Today Buddhism is woven into every aspect of Korean culture from customs to artifacts.

SHAMANISM

When Buddhism was first brought from China to the Korean Peninsula in 372 CE, Shamanism was the indigenous religion. Shamanism is the ancient religion of animism and nature-spirit worship and its origins in Korea are lost in antiquity. It is based on the belief that human beings as well as natural forces and inanimate objects all possess spirits or that they are gods. Since Buddhism was not seen to be in conflict with the rites of nature worship, it was able to naturally blend in with Shamanism. And so many of the special mountains believed to be the residences of gods in pre-Buddhist times, soon became the sites of Buddhist temples.

Korean Shamanism regarded three gods with special reverence and importance: the Mountain God, Sanshin (who is usually depicted as an old man with a tiger at his feet), the Toksong, or recluse, and Ch'ilsong (the god of the seven stars, the Big Dipper). Buddhism accepted and absorbed these three gods and, even today, special shrines are set aside for them in most temples. The Mountain God, in particular, receives due veneration following the ceremonies honoring the Buddha in the Main Hall. And thus Chinese Buddhism blended with Korean Shamanism to produce a unique form: Korean Buddhism. As in other Buddhist countries, the fundamental teachings of the Buddha remained the same, even though the form, influenced by indigenous culture and customs, was uniquely Korean.

KOGURYO

In 372 CE, a monk was invited from China to the northern Kingdom of Koguryo. He brought Chinese texts and statues with him. Buddhism was quickly accepted by the

Koguryo royalty and their subjects. This original Buddhism was elementary in form. The people believed in the law of cause and effect — "as you sow, so shall you reap" — and the search after happiness. This simple philosophy had much in common with the indigenous Shaman beliefs and may have been a reason for the quick assimilation of Buddhism by the people of Koguryo.

PAEKJE

Buddhism was carried from Koguryo to the southwestern kingdom of Paekje in 384 CE and there, too, the royal family received it first. The teaching seems to have been similar to that in Koguryo. King Asin (r. 392-405), for example, proclaimed that his "people should believe in Buddhism and seek happiness." In the reign of King Song (r. 523-554), there is a record of a monk, Kyomik, returning from India with new texts and especially the Vinaya (monks' rules and the stories leading to their formulation). He is considered the founder of one of the main schools of Buddhism of that period.

From 530 on, monks traveled to Japan and there taught the people Buddhism. Architects, painters, potters and other craftsman and artists often accompanied the monks and it was these people who constructed the great temples of Japan.

KARAK

For a short time, a small, separate federation known as the Karak Kingdom (1st to 6th century CE) existed. It was a small kingdom in the Kimhae area situated on the southern coast between mighty Paekje and fast-growing Shilla. Kaya could not repel an invasion in the mid-sixth century and so was annexed to Shilla before reaching full maturity.

The Samguk-yusa says that there was a stone pagoda in Hogye-sa in Kimhae. This pagoda had four sides and five storeys, and the carvings on the sides were famous for their magnificence. It is known that this pagoda was brought by sea to Korea by an Indian princess from Ayudhya a kingdom of southern India. She came to marry King Suro (r. 42-199) the first king of Karak and she was later known as Queen Hohwang-ok. As far as the records show, until the arrival of the Indian princess, there were no temples and no Buddha statues and the people knew nothing about Buddhism. Because of this, there was no place to keep the pagoda. It was only later, in 452, in the 2nd year of the 8th Karak king, Chilji (r. 451-492), that Wanghu-sa was built.

Information about the Karak Kingdom is of particular interest because the princess came from a Buddhist stronghold in India and most probably brought statues and texts with her. However, according to the above record, Buddhism was not popular in Karak before the building of the temple. This is not surprising considering that this would mean that Buddhism was accepted in Karak before Shilla and even before Koguryo. Unfortunately, we know very little about Karak but there are a few legends concerning Buddhism told about the kingdom.

One is about the story of King Suro's decision on where to place the capital of Karak. Another is about Mano-sa (the temple of 10,000 fish). There are also two stories one about the temple Changyu-sa and another about the hermitage Ch'ilbul-am. But these stories do not necessarily contain any historical truth and so cannot be considered too seriously. Till we have certain new historical evidence, we must think of the above legends as indications of Karak Buddhism only.

SHILLA

In Shilla, it was the common people who were first attracted to Buddhism. Among some of the aristocrats, there was considerable resistance to the new culture. It was only after the martyrdom of Ich'adon, in the reign of King Pophung (r. 514-540) in 527 CE, that Buddhism gradually became the national religion of Shilla.

STORIES ABOUT THE ARRIVAL OF BUDDHISM IN SHILLA

Firstly, "the Koguryo monk, Ado, came to Shilla in the 2nd year (263) of the reign of the 13th King Mich'u (r. 262-284)." This information comes from a record quoted in Samguk-yusa. Master Ado's father was an envoy to Koguryo and his mother, a Koguryo woman, was called Kodonyong. Ado went to Wei to meet his father at the age of 16 and then he studied under Master Hsuan-chang. He returned to Koguryo when he was 19 and went to Shilla to teach Buddhism, following his mother's advice. This was in 263, the 2nd year of King Mich'u. Before journeying to Shilla, Master Ado heard from his mother that there were seven temple sites in Shilla where the past seven Buddhas had been. But when he tried to teach Buddhism to the Shilla people, they tried to kill him. Ado hid himself at the house of Morye at Ilsson and stayed there until he cured a daughter of King Mich'u of a terrible sickness. Only then, was he able to build a temple in Ch'on-gyong forest and teach Buddhism. As soon as King Mich'u died, the people tried once more to harm him. And so he returned to Morye's house and lived there till he died.

Secondly, we have another record concerning a different monk. "Master Mukhoja stayed at the house of Morye at Ilsson in the reign of the 19th King Nulji (r. 417-458)." This is quoted in the Samguk-yusa. Mukhoja secretly lived in the cellar inside Morye's house and then left. Before he left, he taught the people about the use of incense, and he cured another princess.

Thirdly, we have another reference to Master Ado. "Master Ado came to Morye's house with three attendants and stayed there, in the reign of King Pich'o (r. 479-500)." There we read that Master Ado stayed at Morye's house for a number of years with his three attendants and then he returned healthy to Koguryo. He left his three attendants in Shilla to teach sutras and the Vinaya and they made many followers. This record adds that Ado looked like Master Mukhoja.

Fourthly, Master Ado came to Morye's house on the 11th of the 3rd month, 527, the 14th year of King Pophung. Morye, on seeing Ado, was surprised and frightened. He hid Master Ado in a secret place inside his house, explaining that two Koguryo monks, Chongbang and Myolguch'e who had come before him had been killed. And so Morye cared for and served Master Ado. Just at that time, Ado found out that a foreign envoy had brought incense to King Pophung. And so Master Ado went to the palace. The foreign envoy showed Master Ado respect and "this showed the king, for the first time, that Buddhist monks should be respected. The king then allowed Buddhism to be accepted."

This record is of particular value as it introduces a new aspect of the beginning of Buddhism in the Shilla Kingdom. At first the two monks were martyred. Then the king accepted Buddhism after seeing the foreign envoy show respect to Master Ado. Here the martyrdom of Ich'adon is not mentioned, unlike other records.

According to the four above records, there are three different Master Ados who introduced Buddhism to Shilla. Though the contents are very similar, the chronology of events is unreliable. We must therefore conclude that we can neither know who introduced Buddhism to Shilla nor when it was introduced precisely. The above records are all legends which were handed down among the people and it seems that the transmission was not achieved on the level of a national exchange but rather as a continuous series of missions of monks. Legends tell us that a few Koguryo monks secretly introduced Buddhism again and again, and that the area they worked in was around Ilsson and especially Morye's house. The missionary monks were not just one or two, they were many. Also they had to work secretly without revealing their proper names or identity.

In addition, the names, Mukhoja and Ado (or Adu), might not be the specific names of individual monks, but words used to indicate monks in general. For we are told that "... when the name of a monk is not known, he was called `Adu-samma.'" This is the long form of "Adu" or "Ado," a common name for a monk.

Since Buddhism was introduced to Shilla in that way, we can guess that the next king, Chinhung (r. 540-576), wanted to make Buddhism official as soon as he acceded to the throne. However, this was not to be. Stubborn, conservative ministers and officials of the court objected to Buddhism. King Chinhung, who was deeply convinced that Buddhism would bring good fortune to the people and help his kingdom, was greatly troubled by the resistance of his ministers. It was under these circumstances that a young minister, Ich'adon, knowing the king's problems, died a martyr for the kingdom, the king, and Buddhism.

THE STORY OF ICH'ADON

In the Samguk-sagi and the Samguk-yusa, Ich'adon is said to have been a nephew of King Pophung. The Samguk-yusa adds that Ich'adon's grandfather, Ajinjong, was a son of Suppogalmun. According to the Samguk-sagi, Suppogalmun was the father of the 22nd king, Chijung (r. 500-514) whose son was King Pophung. Therefore King Pophung was Ich'adon's uncle. According to the story, Ich'adon decided to help the king and so he and the king developed a plan which would finally convince the ministers.

At that time, anyone who claimed they were a Buddhist was beheaded. And so, according to the plan, one day Ich'adon proclaimed his belief and the king ordered him to be beheaded. Ich'adon announced, "If Buddhism is good then, when my his head is cut, the blood that flows will be white." True to his belief, as soon as his head was severed from his body, white blood poured out. Seeing the greatness of Ich'adon's sacrifice, the ministers no longer objected to Buddhism and it was accepted from then on.

One year later, in 528, King Pophung ordered that the people cease from killing any living things. In 535, King Pophung started to build Hungnyun-sa in Ch'on-gyong forest which was east of Kumkyo, the bridge over the river So-ch'on in Kyongju. When some parts of the temple had been completed, the king went to live in the temple and ordained as a monk; he took the Buddhist name of Popkong, meaning "Dharma Emptiness." The queen followed her husband's example and, when Yonghung-sa had been built, she was ordained and took the Buddhist name of Myobop, meaning "Marvelous Dharma."

Thus Buddhism was established in Shilla during the reign of King Pophung. Apart from the few legends mentioned, we know nothing of the policy and achievements of Buddhism in the reign of King Pophung.

THE PATRONAGE OF BUDDHISM BY KING CHINHUNG

Shilla Buddhism did not take on its own specific character until the reign of King Chinhung (r. 540-576), the 24th king of the Shilla Kingdom. He, through his policies, was responsible for the unique nature of Shilla Buddhism and the immense impact which it had on the culture of Korea. In 540, King Chinhung ascended the throne when he was still young and so his mother ruled Shilla as regent. King Chinhung was a devoted Buddhist throughout his life and his achievements as a Buddhist have been carefully recorded, here are some:

- In 544, Hungnyun-sa was completed and in the 3rd month of that year many men and women were ordained as bhikkus and bhikkunis.
- In spring 549, an envoy from Liang brought the Shilla monk, Master Kaktok, who had been studying in Liang, back with a Buddha relic. At that time the king told all his ministers to go and bow out of respect in front of the temple.
- In 550, the king appointed Master Anjang to an important government post.
- In 551, the king nominated Master Hyeryang from Koguryo to be the leader of the monks and entrusted him with all sorts of plans to make Buddhism grow and prosper. Hyeryang held large Buddhist assemblies for the first time.
- In 565, an envoy, Liu-ssu from Ch'en, and Master Ming-kuan brought about 1,700 volumes of sutras and sastras to Shilla.
- In 566, the temples Hwangnyong-sa, (which had been commenced 13 years earlier), Kiwon-sa, and Shilje-sa were completed.

- On the 20th day of the 10th month, 572, a huge ceremony was held for the war dead at Oe-sa for seven days.
- In 574, the king made three Buddha statues at Hwangnyong-sa.
- In 576, Master Anhong came back from China and he offered the Lankavatara-sutra, the Srimala-sutra, and Buddha relics to the king.

All of these records show that King Chinhung promoted Buddhism very enthusiastically. Not only did he believe in Buddhism fervently, building temples, ordaining bhikkus and bhikkunis, and doing other Buddhist work, but he also applied Buddhist principles to his way of governing the people. He was always delighted to receive sutras and the relics of the Buddha from any monk returning from China. Due to his enthusiasm, Buddhism was firmly established as a national religion. Towards the end of his life, King Chinhung became a monk. named Popun, "Dharma Cloud" in his old age and his wife became a nun at Yonghung-sa. (Several Shilla kings were ordained and their queens and families often followed the example and entered monasteries.)

THE ARTS

The arts flourished during the Shilla Period. A huge temple, Hwangnyong-sa, was built and it became the center of Buddhism for Shilla.There is a record which clearly demonstrates the position and excellency achieved by such a great king as Chinhung. It is the story of the three Buddha statues of Hwangnyong-sa: The three statues were made in the 35th year of the reign of King Chinhung. They were cast from of 34,200 kilos of iron ore and gold which had been sent in a big vessel by the Indian King Asoka (r. 270-235 BCE) who, during his reign, unified most of India for the first time. There is a story about him which concerns the origin of the gold and iron.

One day, lamenting that he could not be born at the time of the Buddha, he tried to make a Buddha statue triad out of gold and iron. Three times he tried and each time he failed. So, thinking that the failure must be due to his bad karma, he decided to put all the gold and iron in a vessel with a letter, saying, "We hope that this metal can be used to make a triad in a country which has good karma." He sent the vessel carrying the gold, the iron, and the letter away. It went from country to country but the triad could not be made until the ship arrived in Shilla. This story shows the strong connection between Shilla and Buddhism. It also suggests that King Chinhung was very powerful as he was able to make the triad that Asoka could not make.

POLITICAL ORGANIZATION

At the time of King Chinhung, Shilla was a politically and geophysically weak kingdom surrounded by the stronger kingdoms of Paekje and Koguryo.

During the years of King Chinhung's reign, Shilla gained in territory and made political and religious reforms. Therefore, King Chinhung is considered to have been one of the greatest kings in Korean history.

We are also told that King Chinhung established the P'ungwoltto which was an organization for training young men. It was founded on Buddhist ideas and contributed to the settling of national thought. According to a stone monument, which is still standing today, the king was always accompanied by monks. Also the names of monks were written before the names of all government officials.

i) P'ungwoltto, Youth Organization

The P'ungwoltto was a system or organization established on a national level by King Chinhung. It provided much of the moral and military leadership necessary for Shilla in her drive to unify the peninsula. We find the story of the creation of this organization in the Samguk-sagi and Samguk-yusa.

ii) Wonhwa

King Chinhung chose beautiful girls and made the "Wonhwa," a record states. This was an organization to educate young girls in order to develop their talents; it was very important to the administration of the affairs of state. The king began with two girls, Nammo and Kyojong (or Chunjong) and soon each one had 300 followers. But Kycjong was jealous of Nammo and killed her. And when this murder was discovered, Nammo was put to death and the institution of "Wonhwa" was abolished.

iii) Hwarang

"A few years after this event, King Chinhung again thought about the education of the young. This gave rise to the formation of the 'P'ungwoltto' for the prosperity of the nation. He ordered virtuous, superior and refined boys from good, aristocratic families to be chosen, and he made them 'hwarang,' or 'Flower Boys,' a name probably derived from the fact that the boys were beautifully decorated. Among these young men, Solwon was chosen to be the head of the group, or kuksson. This was the beginning of the hwarang, the members of the organization, and creation of the kuksson, the leader." This P'ungwoltto has been wrongly called "hwarangdo" by many scholars who very carelessly misunderstood hwarang to be the center of the organization. However, the so-called hwarangdo did not have any authority: It is clearly recorded that this organization of young men formed by King Chinhung was called P'ung-woltto in the history books. Furthermore, some scholars have long considered the organization as consisting of warriors or soldiers. This, too, is wrong. It was an organization formed to train the youth purely in self-improvement and so that the nation might prosper. The organization consisted of a head, the kuksson, hwarang, and his followers, the nangdo, consisting of monks and laymen. The young men were usually from about 14-15 to 17-18 years of age. There were also monks who were much older than the boys called nangdo monks. The kuksson was chosen from among the hwarang and he held a position of national authority, being the head of the organization, and was even respected by the king. He was considered as a symbol of Maitreya Buddha, the Future Buddha, and was treated as the little Buddha of the nation.

It is recorded that the boys were beautifully decorated with flowers and other ornaments. We can imagine that the reason for this came from the relationship between the hwarang and Maitreya who is always depicted wearing rich clothes and jewels. The monks, the nangdo, in the organization were under the kuksson and their prime function was to give guidance. The hwarang lived according to Buddhist principles but, as they were warriors, they had slightly different precepts. (The adjustment of the precepts is very indicative of the effort Buddhism has always made to adapt to circumstances.)

1. Serve the king with loyalty.
2. Serve and tend parents with filial devotion.
3. Treat friends with sincerity.
4. Do not retreat from battle fields.
5. Be discriminating about the taking of life.

There were two main influences on P'ungwoltto. One was the idea of the Chakravatin, the universal monarch and the other was the belief in Maitreya, the Future Buddha. These beliefs were very important to King Chinhung and so he named his two sons, Tongnyun, or "bronze wheel," and Kumnyun, or "gold wheel," proof of the influence of the concept of Chakravatin on the king. The hwarang were also known as the yonghwa-hyangdo, "Incense Group of the Dragon Flower," the followers of Maitreya. The Maitreya-sutra and the sutras mentioning the Chakravatin show that the Maitreya Buddha and the idea of Chakravatin were intimately interconnected. It is interesting to note that incense was introduced from China during this period. The people, not knowing its use, thought it magical and so employed it for curing disease!

BUDDHIST CULTURE OF THE THREE KINGDOMS

The transmission of Buddhism to the Three Kingdoms brought significant development in many aspects of national culture. Before the advent of Buddhism, there was hardly any culture established on a national level. After the arrival of Buddhism, the arts flourished with the making of bells (the huge cast iron ones beautifully decorated with relief work to be seen at temples in Korea), pagodas, statues, carving, architecture, painting and industrial arts. Buddhism contributed to the development of the spiritual civilization greatly. But today, because of many invasions and the lack of careful preservation, only a few records exist. These consist of archaeological sites, historical remains and books.

TEMPLES

The first Korean temples to be built, according to records, were Songmun-sa (or Ch'o-mun-sa) and Ibulran-sa. They were built in 375 by Koguryo King Sosurim. Koguryo King Kwang-gaet'o built nine temples in P'yongyang in 392. And other Koguryo temples like Kumgang-sa, Panyong-sa, Yongt'ap-sa, were also built very early on according to the records. Sadly, we know nothing about the form or style of these temples.

However, an ancient temple site, believed to be that of Kumgang-sa, was excavated at Ch'ong-am-ni, near P'yongyang and the Taedong-gang River in 1938. The arrangement of the temple compound seems to have been centered on an octagonal building. Traces of two other buildings are found to the east and west of the octagonal building. To the north, there are traces of a big building, and to the south a trace of a gate. Further north, there are traces of four more buildings, one quite separate from the rest.

A temple was built on Han-san as soon as Buddhism was brought to Paekje. Later on, during the reign of kings Pop and Mu, Wanghung-sa and Miruk-sa were built respectively. In the record, some names of other temples such as Yoak-sa, Oham-sa, Ch'onwang-sa, Toyang-sa and Paeksok-sa were also mentioned. Some of these temples have been excavated but some remain to be dug. Wanghung-sa was a very magnificent temple in Puyo, the capital of Paekje at that time. The site of Miruk-sa is the largest of the sites of Korean temples and it shows a unique arrangement of the three buildings. Hungnyun-sa, which was finished in 545, the 5th year of the reign of King Chinhung, was probably the first and the largest Shilla temple. Yonghung-sa and Hwangnyong-sa were built at the same time as were Chiwon-sa and Shilje-sa. All of these temples were large and magnificent; many more were to be built as the years went by.

Such great temples influenced the architectural style and the building techniques used at that time enormously. In this way extraordinary developments occurred. Special roofs to cover the huge halls had to be created and the arrangement of beams to support the roofs required great engineering ability.

PAGODAS

Today, most famous Korean pagodas are made of stone. But originally, pagodas were made of wood, earth, bricks, or other materials.

As far as the records show, the first pagoda to have been constructed was Yukwang-t'ap in Lia Tung in Koguryo. According to the Samguk-yusa the precise date of the construction of this pagoda is unknown. It was made of earth, and consisted of three parts, the top resembled a Korean traditional kettle turned upside down. A king (one record says it was a sage king, but it is not certain who the king was), after finding the earthen pagoda, built a seven-storey wooden pagoda out of devotion.

Another record tells of a stone pagoda at Yongt'ap-sa. A legend says that Master Podok found the pagoda under the ground following the instructions of a supernatural being. It had eight sides and seven stories.

Besides these few records, not much else is known about Koguryo pagodas. We do not know how many there were nor do we know their style.

According to Chinese records, Paekje had many temple pagodas. However, specific records of these pagodas are very rare. Among the existing stone pagodas, the oldest in Korea and largest in the east is on the site of Miruk-sa, together with the stupa of

Chongnim-sa site, they show us the excellent technique and style of Paekje pagodas. In the making of pagodas in particular, Paekje had many great artists and so they were sent to Shilla.

One particular example is the Paekje artist Abiji who was sent to Shilla to help build the nine-storey, wooden pagoda at Hwangnyong-sa, the oldest, recorded, Shilla pagoda which was finished in 645. It stood 68 m. high and was outstandingly magnificent. The story of the building of this pagoda is recorded in Samguk-yusa. The Diamond Altar (actually made of stone) of T'ongdo-sa, where Master Chajang enshrined the Buddha's relics which he had received from Manjusri, and a pagoda of Taehwa-sa were built at the same time.

Master Cha-jang recommended the building of that first pagoda for the security of the nation. It was thought that such religious actions as the building of a pagoda would protect the nation against disasters and the nine neighboring, hostile countries including Japan and China. Pagodas were held to be lucky and also they were considered as able to "balance" or "mend" "wounds" in the earth. These are unlucky spots recognized by geomancers.

The present pagoda at Punhwang-sa is the oldest brick- shaped, stone pagoda among all those which were built before the unification of the peninsula in 668.

STATUES

Most of the gold-plated, bronze Buddha statues which existed up to this time were from Koguryo and Paekje; the technique and beauty of these statues is wonderful. Paekje King Song, in 545 made a huge Buddha statue, wishing that all living beings in the world attain enlightenment. He also sent a Buddha statue to Japan when he introduced Buddhism there, following it later on with more, including Maitreyas. Even today, great Paekje Buddha statues such as Ma-aebul are occasionally discovered in the ground.

We have already seen that King Chinhung, in 574, made a Buddha triad for Hwangnyong-sa. This triad, together with the nine-storey pagoda and a jade belt received by King Chinp'yong from heaven are three national jewels of the Shilla period.

Master Yangji, during the reign of Queen Sondok, made: a Buddha triad; the four temple guardian statues for Yongjo-sa; the arahant statues on eight sides under the pagoda of Ch'onwang-sa; and a Buddha triad and temple guardians for Popnim-sa. He also made roof tiles for the pagoda building of Yongjo-sa, as well as writing the Chinese characters on the boards of Yongjo-sa and Popnim-sa. He built a brick pagoda and kept 3,000 Buddha statues at Sokjjang-sa where he lived. In this way Master Yangji did a lot for Buddhism as he was a master of making statues and pagodas, carving and painting. Legend says that he had supernatural powers.

Japan was helped by this flourishing culture of the Three Kingdoms Period. Paekje, in particular, sent many Buddha statues, including a stone Maitreya Buddha statue, and other Buddhist instruments. Moreover, all kinds of technicians and artists talented in such fields as the making Buddha statues, building temples, Buddhist paintings, and making roof tiles were sent to Japan. There they trained apprentices in their special talents so that the techniques could be handed down. Apart from Paekje, Koguryo also sent many artists to Japan. In particular, Master Tamjing excelled in painting so he taught the Japanese how to paint for the first time. And he also imparted techniques in making colors, paper and inkstones.

In the Three Kingdoms Period, there are many legends about pagodas and Buddha statues. Some tell that they were not made by human hands but that they appeared out of the earth or beneath some body of water, or that they came down from heaven. Some of the more famous legends include: a Koguryo pagoda at Yongt'ap-sa; a stone Maitreya Buddha statue at Saeng-ui-sa which was discovered in Samhwaryong pass by Master Saeng-ui in the reign of Queen Sondok; Sabul-san, a big stone, of Taesung-sa which was "dropped" from heaven in 597 and had Tathagathas on four sides of it; and three Maitreya Buddha statues which rose up from a big spring on Yonghwa-san in the reign of King Mu.

Not only did the arts flourish, but there were many famous monks living at this time. One of the most celebrated in the entire history of Korea was Master Wonhyo. Here is one of the most celebrated stories about him. It is important because it led to his main, original contribution to Korean Buddhist philosophy and this development is still central to Korean Buddhism today.

MASTERS WONHYO AND UISANG

Master Wonhyo (617-686), one of Korea's greatest scholars, was born in a simple family. After living as a monk for many years, he renounced religious life in order to better serve the people. Married for a short time to a princess, he had one son. As a scholar he wrote many important treatises in which he explained his philosophy of oneness, Ekayana, the interrelatedness of everything in the universe. The development of this view is due to an event in his life.

At the time that Master Wonhyo lived, many monks went to China to study and look for teachers. Wonhyo and his close friend, Uisang, also set out for China together; both of them wanted to study Buddhism there. One night on the way, Wonhyo awoke thirsty and, searching round, he found a container with delicious cool water in it. He drank the water and, his thirst quenched, he went back to sleep.

In the morning, he found that the vessel from which he had drunk was a skull. Suddenly he saw that everything depends on the mind — thirsty, he had found the water so refreshing and the vessel so welcoming but on awakening, in the light of day, he was disgusted to find a dirty skull — and he attained enlightenment. Realizing that it was no longer necessary for him to go to China in search of a teacher, he returned home. Master Uisang continued the journey. After ten years studying in China under a great master, Uisang offered a special gift to his teacher: a poem in the shape of seal which, when written down, geometrically represents infinity. This poem contained the essence of the Avatamsaka-sutra (an extremely long text explaining the universe); it is one of the greatest offerings of the Korean people to the world.

BUDDHISM FROM UNIFICATION UNTIL TODAY

UNITED SHILLA PERIOD (668-935)

In 668 CE, Shilla conquered the other kingdoms and Buddhism became the central cultural force uniting the peninsula. This period came to be known as the United Shilla Period. Various rituals were developed and performed as spiritual requests for protection from foreign invasion which was seen to be a constant problem to the little peninsula standing between the two vastly larger civilizations of Japan and China. National sentiment was strong and the people worked hard for unity and understanding, with everything tending towards the realization of their patriotic aspirations. From the very start, the Buddhism studied used a unified approach, the "One Mind," the universal interrelatedness of everything, as taught by Wonhyo. Throughout the United Shilla Period, Buddhism continued to prosper and grow, both academically and culturally. This was the time of the creation of some of the finest Korean art; the main temples of Korea were built; pagodas were erected; beautiful statues fashioned — all of this was of profound significance to the country's Buddhist heritage. The famous rock statue of the Buddha in Sokkuram cave, in Kyongju, was carved in 732: today it still evokes a sense of wonder and is one of the items on the UNESCO World Heritage List.

The Avatamsaka-sutra and the Lotus Sutra were the main focus of study. Much of the chanting concentrated on Amitabha, the Buddha of Universal Light, and Avalokitesvara, the Bodhisattva of Compassion.

Towards the end of the United Shilla Period, the Chan School (Son in Korean, Zen in Japanese) was introduced from China and this added a new dimension to Korean Buddhism. Meditation and direct experience were emphasized over concentration on studying the texts. Nine different schools emerged and they were known as the Nine Mountains of Son.

KORYO (935-1392)

After the glory of Shilla faded, the Koryo Dynasty assumed power in the 10th century. Buddhism continued to be the national religion, with the kings establishing shrines and temples throughout the country. However, excessive focus was placed on rituals and this created an unfavorable atmosphere for spiritual development.

In an attempt to purify and renew the spiritual aspect of Buddhism, several monks struggled against the ritualistic trend. One of these monks was Master Uich'on (1055-1101), son of King Munjong (1046-1083), who collected about 4,000 volumes of Buddhist texts while studying in China; from these the Tripitaka Koreana, the complete collection of Buddhist texts carved on wood blocks, was produced. This eminent Koryo monk emphasized the importance of bringing the contemplative, Zen, and Textual, Avatamsa, traditions together under a new school: he called it Ch'ont'ae. It was this development which brought new life to Koryo Buddhism.

Buddhism remained the dominant intellectual influence during the later years of Koryo, as Confucianism, introduced to the peninsula at the same time as Buddhism, had not yet gained much popularity.

Master Chinul (1158-1210), usually known as Pojo- kuksa, became the leading monk of Korea. He founded Songgwang-sa Temple on Mt. Chogye, and this large temple remained the headquarters of the Son sect for over 300 years. The Nine Schools of Son (Zen) were unified by Master T'aego (1301-82) under the name Chogye which has remained the main sect to this day.

CHOSON/YI (1392-1910)

With the downfall of the Koryo Dynasty in 1392, Buddhism slowly declined as the new rulers of the Choson Dynasty adopted Neo-Confucianism. Prior to this, many Buddhist monks had become overly involved in politics, resulting in royal strife. The new interest in Confucianism led to the oppression and restriction of Buddhism by some Choson kings. Temples could not be built near towns and had to be constructed in the mountains; many temples were pulled down; monks were looked down on and, for many years, not permitted to enter the capital city. While some kings persecuted Buddhism, the common people continued to go to the temples. Scholars, too, frequented the temples.

At the beginning of the Choson Dynasty, geomancers were consulted in order to find the ideal site for a new capital. They chose an ancient place called "Hanyang" which was then renamed "Seoul" and which has been the center of culture and learning for the peninsula since that time. The name means "capital" in Korean and was probably derived from the ancient Indian place most dear to the Buddha: Sravasti. In Chinese, "Sravasti" became "Sarobol" and finally "Seoul" in Korean.

In the late 16th century, during the Japanese invasion by the armies of Hideyoshi, Buddhism came to the country's rescue. At the age of 72, Master Sosan (1520-1604) and his disciple Samyong (1544-1610), trained and led a band of 5,000 Buddhist monks against the Japanese troops who had invaded the peninsula and won. For a short time, the persecution of Buddhism was reduced because the government was grateful to the monks who had saved the country. Following the defeat of the Hideyoshi Invasion, Master Samyong, was sent as chief delegate to Japan and in 1604 he completed a peace treaty.

MODERN TIMES: RENEWAL

In 1910, the Choson Dynasty came to an end with the annexation of the country to Japan. During the Colonial Period, Buddhism was greatly favored and supported by

Japanese policies. However, the celibate sects were discouraged and monks were encouraged to take wives, following Japanese custom. Also, contrary to tradition, the heads of temples were appointed by the Japanese occupation authorities.

Unfortunately, during this period, many Buddhist art treasures were taken to Japan. Today the Buddhists, in co-operation with the Korean government, are negotiating with Japan in order to have these stolen treasures returned.

After Liberation in 1945, the celibate ordained members of the main sect of Korean Buddhism, Chogye, superseded the married monks who had taken over the principle temples during the Japanese Occupation. Large numbers of men and women were ordained and there was a great revival of Korean Buddhism.

Recently, many new temples and centers have opened in the towns. Programs for people of all ages include: learning to chant, studying of texts, all night meditation classes, social gatherings.

About half the population of Korea is Buddhist as many people still see it as old fashioned to call themselves Buddhists and do not own up to the fact. In addition, most Koreans, even though they may not call themselves Buddhists, maintain a Buddhist view of life and the afterworld. Those who follow other religions keep many customs which are Buddhist in origin and everyone knows that Korean culture is primarily rooted in Buddhism.

THE HISTORY FROM ANOTHER PERSPECTIVE

Originally, Buddhism was introduced to Korea as a foreign thought system. Growing up in India and coming to Korea through Central Asia and China, the initial phase of introduction and the subsequent integration was difficult and only slowly did Korean Buddhism emerge and a new development take place. This then became the ideological foundation and cultural backdrop of the Korean people, influencing every stage of history and every aspect of culture. The process of the creation of Korean Buddhism was, like the development of Buddhist culture in other countries, the welding together of the teachings of the Buddha with the indigenous culture. Thus Koreans added their own characteristics to the basic Buddhism which they received, creating a totally new form of Buddhism which differs from that of India and that of China.

The individuality and unique characteristics of Korean Buddhism are seen through the whole of Korean culture. In particular they are vividly confirmed in the tracing of the development of Korean Buddhist thought.

This overview of the Buddhist philosophical trends will help the reader to understand the overall process and the main characteristics which have persisted throughout the evolution of the development of Korean Buddhism: The Process of Philosophical Development. Ever since its introduction to the peninsula, Korean Buddhist thought has undergone various stages in its evolution. These are summarized as follows:

a) Period of Introduction: the initial contact and subsequent adjustment;
b) Period of Settlement: the beginning of Hinayana and Mahayana studies in the Three Kingdoms Period;
c) Period of Expansion: enlargement and development of various fields of Mahayana studies in the middle Shilla Period;
d) Period of Spreading: introduction of Zen in the late Shilla Period and encouragement of Buddhist studies in the early Koryo Period;
e) Period of Transfiguration: development of community movements and acceptance of Linchi (Kor. Imje; Jap. Rinzai) Zen in the late Koryo Period;
f) Period of Stagnation: oppression of Buddhism in the early Choson Period;
g) Period of Taking a New Direction: union of Zen and Academic study and three approaches of practice after the middle Choson Period.

The above divisions are purely arbitrary and defined for convenience's sake. However, they do trace the process of development through the different periods of history and so delimit the advancement of Korean Buddhist thought. Let us now briefly examine the content of Buddhist thought in conformity with each period.

THE PERIOD OF INTRODUCTION

After its initial introduction in 372 CE, Buddhism was faced with the problem of settling into a new environment. The socio-philosophical milieu of the time was centered on Shamanism. Accordingly, the main task of Buddhism, as is the case with any new religion, was to try to educate the people by inspiration and sometimes the use of miracles. The main principles of Buddhist teaching were then offered to the people. These consisted mainly of the teachings of karma and cause and effect. So that Buddhism developed its philosophy in Korea centering around the theory of karma, which is a basic doctrine of Buddhism, and this tenet alone reformed the primary Shamanistic culture. The existing gods were naturally assimilated into Buddhism and the foundation was set. Buddhism was welcomed and supported by the kings and royal families of the Three Kingdoms because it could offer a more useful governing ideology for social development, compared to the original system of thinking and culture. It was seen as a much needed element around which the confrontation of the Three Kingdoms could take place. For they were all eager to be the focal point of unification and centralization. Accordingly, Buddhism was accepted by royal families and aristocrats and then it gradually developed into a national system.

THE PERIOD OF SETTLEMENT

As a result of the usefulness with which Buddhism was perceived, it was able to settle into Korea not long after its introduction. It is hard to pinpoint the exact time of this settlement, but it can be considered to be one or two centuries after the initial contact. With establishment came the impetus for a high level of Buddhist research and development, from about the early 6th century. The research carried out at this time was into purely doctrinal questions which were not related to the national trend in Buddhist thought and it was this development which is seen as proof of the final amalgamation of Korean Buddhism into Korean culture. Existing Korean records of the research carried out at this time are very few but the trends and outlines can be considered from Chinese records dating from that period.

According to these records, the research of scholar-monks of the Koguryo Kingdom — which accepted Buddhism initially — was most active. Koguryo Master Sungnang systematically researched and developed the study of the Three Treatises, that is, Chung-non (Mulamadhyamika-karika-sastra, Treatise on the Middle), Shibimun-non (Dvadasanikaya-sastra, Treatise on the Twelve Gates), and Paeng-non (Cathusataka, Treatise in One Hundred Verses), which are fundamental texts of Indian Buddhism, especially Mahayana Madhyamika philosophy. Hence he directly influenced the establishment of the Chinese School of the Three Treatises. Besides him, many Koguryo masters were active either in China or in Koguryo. Master Chihwang studied the philosophy of Sarvastivada, a major branch of Hinayana Buddhism, Master Podok is known to have been a great scholar of Yolban-kyong (Nirvana-sutra), and Master P'ayak studied Ch'ont'ae. In Paekje there was also a lot of research carried out. After Master Kyomik returned from a pilgrimage to India in 526, research and writing on Vinaya philosophy was especially popular, and belief in the Lotus Sutra and Maitreya, the Future Buddha, increased dramatically. The doctrinal study of Paekje, which introduced Buddhism to Japan, became the foundation of Japanese Buddhism.

Shilla recognized Buddhism officially later than Koguryo and Paekje. Belief in the Pure Land of Maitreya was eagerly accepted as a kind of governing Buddhist ideology from the beginning. Later, from the early 7th century, studies on various Mahayana texts such as sutras and Mahayana vinayas became popular.

The Buddhist thought of the Three Kingdoms does not seem to have gone much beyond research into the texts of Hinayana and Mahayana. But Koguryo Master Sungnang's study of the Three Treatises is considered the origin of Korean Buddhist philosophy. Because of this, only some of the studies of this period are selectively seen to be important.

THE PERIOD OF EXPANSION

After the middle 7th century, Korean Buddhist thought developed greatly but this growth was very different from the early days. For about 130 years from the time King Munmu (r. 661-681) who unified the Three Kingdoms in 668 and King Hyegong (r. 765-780), research into the Mahayana was very active and many books were written. The research of this period was varied enough to cover most fields of Buddhist studies such as Vinaya, Three Treatises, Vijnanamatravada (Kor. Yushik), Avatamsa (Kor. Hwaom), Esoteric, Maitreya and the Pure Land. But especially Avatamsa philosophy developed by masters Uisang and Wonhyo formed the main focus of study. In addition, the Vijnanamatravada study of Master Wonch'uk and succeeding Shilla masters occupied an important place in Buddhist research of the time.

Master Uisang continued in the line of orthodox Chinese Avatamsa study, and after his return from China, he devoted himself to advocating Avatamsa doctrines and establishing the tradition of Shilla Avatamsa. Master Wonhyo made a comprehensive study of Hinayana and Mahayana, and developed very creative, innovative theories on the philosophy of the Awakening of Faith centered around the idea of the tathagatagarbha (Tathagata's womb) and the theory that everything arises from the mind. Such philosophy as that of the Awakening of Faith shares a mutual understanding with Avatamsa philosophy, hence Master Wonhyo is also considered to be an established Avatamsa philosopher. The Avatamsa philosophy advocated by these masters corresponded well to the socio-political integration which was required for Shilla to head for unification.

However, Shilla Vijnanamatravada philosophy which, along with the Three Treatises philosophy, is one of the representative trends of Mahayana study, originated from Master Wonch'uk who studied in T'ang. Master Wonch'uk greatly contributed to the new Vijnanamatravada study which was introduced to China from India by Chinese Master Hsuan-tsang. Master Wonch'uk's Vijnanamatravada philosophy is well known in the context of its confrontation with that of Master K'uei-chi who was also a disciple of Master Hsuan-tsang. Master Wonch'uk's philosophy was inherited by Shilla masters and it was the point of departure for more active research. Apart from all the other fields of Mahayana studies such as Pure Land, Esoteric Buddhism, research into the Lotus Sutra, and belief in Avalokitesvara, this new direction developed enough to attract close attention in the middle Shilla Period.

THE PERIOD OF SPREADING OUT

But the above research met limits of development in the late Shilla Period. Exegetic studies replaced the earlier research which gave rise to new philosophy and theory, and exceptional writing, as was previously common, was hardly ever produced. Shilla Buddhism needed fresh stimulation and a new impetus to get it going again. This new dimension, one which differed radically from existing trends, was introduced by Shilla masters who had studied in China. It was Son. In particular, it came in the form of the Hung-chou School of Master Ma-tsu Tao-i (709-788), which can be traced to the Sixth Chinese Zen patriarch, Hui-neng (638-713), which denied all ideological studies, such as Avatamsa, and emphasized on sitting meditation. This dealt a powerful blow to the formal, scholastic schools of Buddhism which had fallen into the habit of dry academic pursuits.

During the Koryo Dynasty (918-1392), Zen philosophy was fully accepted and developed greatly. The founder of the Koryo Dynasty, King T'aejo, eagerly supported the movement and summoned many Zen masters who could be useful to the management of his new kingdom. Accordingly, after the foundation of Koryo, various philosophies overwhelmed current Buddhist studies, even though Koryo Buddhism intended to follow the tradition of Shilla Buddhism in principle. Therefore, the Shilla Buddhist studies carried out after the middle period were continued into Koryo and formed the basis of the new direction taken. Thus there was diversity in the studies. These included: Avatamsa philosophy and Yogacara and Vijnanamatravada philosophy were newly develop along with the sudden rise of Zen; Vinaya, Esoteric Buddhism and Shinin or thought of the Divine Seal evolved; and Ch'ont'ae (Ch. T'ien-t'ai) study suddenly became important.

Avatamsa was still the most representative study of the Koryo Period. Master Kyunyo (923-973) inherited the Avatamsa philosophy of Shilla Master Uisang and developed his own Avatamsa theory of "reconciliation of nature and characteristics." Master Kyunyo's Avatamsa philosophy was criticized by Master Uich'on (1055-1101) being biased in its view on doctrines. Master Uich'on adopted a new tendency of Chinese Avatamsa, and proclaimed the theory of dual practice of study and meditation, that is, that doctrinal studies and actual practice should be carried out together. Master Uich'on, on the other hand, went one step further and established the Koryo Ch'ont'ae School from the standpoint of dual practice of study and meditation.

It was at this time that the Ch'ont'ae doctrine and meditation, which had been studied from the early Koryo Period, became the main stream of the new philosophy. Besides Avatamsa and Ch'ont'ae, Yuga and Vijnanamatravada also became prominent from the reign of King Hyonjong (r. 1009-1031). But Master Sohyon (1038-1096), during the reign of King Munjong, did not continue in the tradition of Shilla Vijnanamatravada which had originated from Master Wonch'uk, but he turned towards the Vijnanamatravada philosophy of Chinese Master K'uei-chi, which claimed to be orthodox Chinese Vijnanamatravada.

THE PERIOD OF TRANSFIGURATION

The rapid development of Ch'ont'ae philosophy influenced the whole of Buddhist studies in the early Koryo Period. Especially the Zen School was deeply affected. The result was that many Zen masters moved to the new Ch'ont'ae School. This shows that the Ch'ont'ae philosophy of Master Uich'on who claimed that the dual practice of study and meditation was necessary, had absorbed Zen philosophy. The result was that the hitherto active Zen made poor progress once the Ch'ont'ae School was founded.

It was Master Chinul (1158-1210) of the middle Koryo Period who overcame the hardships of Zen and created a fresh direction in the Zen tradition. He fiercely criticized the existing Buddhist communities like the Avatamsa School which revealed excessive political interests and conspiracy with aristocrats on the one hand, and developed community movements centered around Zen in local places far from the capital, Kaegyong, aimed at renovating Buddhism on the other hand. His Meditation and Wisdom Community emphasized the equal, balanced practice of meditation and wisdom in order to keep the religious purity of Buddhism from the pollution of political power. At the same time, it was aimed at the study of all aspects of Zen.

Master Chinul's intentions are well seen through his creative Zen philosophy of the three approaches: the approach of "equal maintenance of alertness and calmness," the approach of "complete and sudden faith and understanding," and the "shortcut" approach. His creative Zen attitude forms a good contrast to that of Uich'on who intended to include Zen in the Academic School by founding the Koryo Ch'ont'ae School.

When the Koryo Zen tradition was again roused from stagnation and stimulated by Master Chinul's community movement, the Ch'ont'ae School founded a similar community. Called the White Lotus Community, it was created by Master Yose (1163-1245) and based in a local temple. Master Yose developed three approaches to repentance as taught in the Lotus Sutra as well as emphasizing the wish to be reborn in the Pure Land and the Ch'ont'ae practice of Concentration and Insight. In that way he advocated popular Buddhism which made this movement different from Master Uch'on's Ch'ont'ae philosophy. The White Lotus Community together with Master Chinul's community affirm the philosophical change of Buddhism in the middle Koryo Period.

Then a new tradition of Zen was introduced from Yuan in the late Koryo Period. It was at the time when military rule, which had been encouraged in order to fight against the Mongols, was over and imperial rule was restored. Hence from the 13th century, Koryo's internal affairs were intervened upon by Yuan, and Koryo Buddhism found itself in a new situation: the new Chaun School and the Ch'ont'ae School coming from another lineage became active. However this was merely a social influence and not one that affected the philosophical movement at all. In fact it was the direct result of aristocratic Buddhism which had taken up a position closer to politics.

At that time, Ch'ont'ae Master Unmuk of the White Lotus Community persisted in his wish for the purification of folk Buddhism, and so he advocated having deep belief in Amitabha. Also Avatamsa Master Ch'ewon inspired belief in Kwanum (Avalokitesvara) based on the Flower Garland Sutra. In addition, one Master Wonch'an, of unknown origin, formed a peculiar esoteric group which practiced the pure conduct of reciting mantras and prognosticating rebirth in the Pure Land. What was common to the above tendencies was that they all relied on other power, that is the help of the Bodhisattvas or Buddhas, a very different trend from that of Zen.

It was in the middle of the 14th century, that Zen was introduced from Yuan by masters Po-u, Hyegun, and Kyonghan. The Zen School was one of five Chinese Zen families of the seven Chinese Zen schools. This family tradition was more active than any other. Zen prospered greatly in Koryo and an effort was made at reviving and renovating Zen Buddhist thought through this new direction. From the time of the development of the community movement by masters Chinul and Yose until the flourishing of Zen was a period of transfiguration for Korean Buddhist thought.

THE PERIOD OF STAGNATION

From the late 14th century on, the Choson Dynasty (1392-1910) which was founded on the political ideology of Neo-Confucianism, oppressed Buddhism and caused it to fall into stagnation. The second Choson king, T'aejong (r. 1400-1418), started implementing a strong policy of suppression and control so that Buddhism economically and culturally began to be destroyed. This harsh policy was enforced with political or socio-economic reasons in mind rather than any philosophical reasons. Therefore in spite of the general trend of persecution, some kings and members of the royal household personally followed Buddhism and had relationships with monks. Thus oppression and encouragement of Buddhism were both practiced during the Choson Dynasty.

THE PERIOD OF TAKING A NEW DIRECTION

The variation of the oppression and encouragement policy towards Buddhism ended after the middle of the Choson Period. In the earlier part of the dynasty, Buddhist thought and belief had some influence on the general trend of events. But Neo-Confucian scholars led the Korean academic community and they became more and more powerful from the middle period on. Accordingly, Buddhism which had to survive in the mountains from the time of King Chungjong (r. 1506-1544) had a more urgent task in merely existing than it did in developing any new thought. Therefore Buddhism tried hard to find a way to harmonize Confucianism and Buddhism.

In an effort to reconcile the differences and put an end to the conflict, various books were written. Master Kihwa clearly states this intention in his Hyonjong-non (Clarification of the Right) written in the early period. The book was aimed at putting an end to Confucian scholars' misunderstanding of Buddhism and informing them of the true meaning. It was a kind of philosophical confrontation of the Confucian theory of the reasons for the rejection of Buddhism, but the conclusion was about the harmonization of Confucianism and Buddhism. Another book by an anonymous writer, Yusok-chirui-ron, was written with the same purpose in view and therefore contains the same material. Master Po-u's theory of "one right" was developed for the same purpose and it concerned the "one" as a universal principle and the "right" as an ethical principle.

Through these means different master worked to harmonize Confucianism and Buddhism. Efforts at reconciliation continued. Master Sosan Hyujong who led the Buddhist community of the middle Choson Period, tried hard to bring about peace. In his Son-ga-kui-gam (Paragon of Zen Family), he advocated the reconciliation of the three teachings, Confucianism, Buddhism, and Taoism. The task of Buddhism, which had been the union of Meditation and Study up to the middle of the Koryo Period, became the harmonization of Confucianism and Buddhism in Choson Dynasty.

In spite of all these negative influences, the Buddhist philosophical tendency of the early Choson Period moved forward. Though eight Meditation Schools and various Study

Schools were amalgamated into two, Meditation and Study, by force, Zen and Ch'ont'ae communities were still active, and Zen philosophy was constantly trying to embrace Study. Besides, the project of writing Korean Buddhist texts, translation from Chinese into Korean was continued by kings Sejong and Sejo who actively encouraged Buddhism. The project was magnificent in scale, and it had an important philosophical meaning as well. The main Mahayana texts involved were: Surangama-sutra, Lotus Sutra, Diamond Sutra, and Heart Sutra. In addition, esoteric Buddhist texts, and various Zen texts were also published in hangul, the new Korean script which King Sejong had invented. The extensive publication of these traditional Study texts is proof that, even though Choson Buddhism was mainly concerned with Meditation, Study also played an important role.

The project was of further importance because of the use of hangul which was only employed by the masses and innovative Buddhist monks and supporters. This was of special interest as it attests to the popularization of Buddhism. In spite of these events, Buddhism was mainly oppressed and suffered greatly under the persecution of the government. The policy continued without change after the middle period. However then there was also a new trend in Buddhist thinking. Now, the main task of the Choson Buddhist community became the transmission of Dharma lineages. That is, whereas the interpretation of Study from the standpoint of Meditation was prominent in the early period, the so-called theory of "throwing up Study and entering Meditation" became pervasive in the late period, hence the system of Dharma transmission appeared. But this does not indicate the absolute disappearance of the Study approach. Traditional Study systems like Avatamsa, Lotus Flower, Pure Land, and Esoteric Buddhism still continued. Besides these, Zen accepted Avatamsa especially the Madhyamika School and Pure Land chanting, even though Zen finally intended to resolve the other thoughts into itself. As a result, the unique phenomenon of the simultaneous practice of the three approaches, that is, Zen meditation, studying texts, and esoteric chanting was followed in the late Choson Period.

The above phenomena of Dharma transmission and the practicing of the three approaches was the Buddhist way of existence under the attack of the government. All official religious activities of Buddhism were blocked and so in order for anything to take place, it had to be done in the seclusion of the mountains. It was inevitable that the Buddhist community could only be sustained by way of the Zen transmission of Dharma lineages. Also it was only natural for a community which had already lost its own particular characteristics to practice various doctrinal teachings such as Avatamsa, Pure Land, esoteric and belief in Avalokitesvara simultaneously.

But the above attitude, besides being a method of handling historical hardship, can be understood as the establishment of a new philosophical direction which was holistic. In fact, it is not excessive to say that Korean Buddhist thought has pursued a holistic approach ever since the time of its introduction right up to the present moment. Though Buddhist thought from the middle to late Choson periods was formed under the stress of oppression, it, too, was holistic. This is the reason that the middle and the late Choson periods are here described as the time during which a new direction in the sense of further development was created.

This, then, is most of the important information on the history of Korean Buddhism. Now we will pass on to a brief consideration of some of the features which make Korean Buddhism unique.

THE CHARACTERISTICS OF KOREAN BUDDHIST THOUGHT

Throughout its long history, certain attributes are almost always evident in Korean Buddhism. These are interesting to identify because they offer a whole picture. For, whatever the period or stage of development, there have always been certain prominent factors which affected the general Buddhist climate and so the culture and the people of the country.

INDIVIDUALITY

Korean Buddhist thought is basically closely related to the philosophical thinking of Chinese Buddhism. Therefore the initial Buddhism to be introduced was directly or indirectly Chinese and it was the new research done by Korean masters which created what came to be called Korean Buddhism. This was a form of Buddhism which was different from Chinese Buddhism, even though some of the basic ideas were Chinese in origin.

In Koguryo, Master Sungnang's research on the Three Treatises become the foundation of the Chinese Three Treatises School. Another example of individual development is to be seen in Shilla Vijnanamatravada which also developed apart from the teachings in China. Thus Vijnanamatravada followed the teachings of Shilla Master Wonch'uk who advocated a different view from his comrade, Chinese Master K'uei-chi. In the case of Paekje Vinaya thought, Paekje Master Kyomik had already introduced the original Indian vinayas in five parts one century earlier than the foundation of Chinese Vinaya School during the T'ang Dynasty. The Vinaya texts were translated in Paekje and published in 72 volumes, so that an individual Vinaya thought, one suited to the Paekje social system, was established. Master Uisang's Avatamsa thought is also very different from his Chinese Dharma friend Master Fa-tsang. Whereas Master Fa-tsang attached weight to the philosophical understanding of Avatamsa doctrine, Master Uisang emphasized the practical part of Avatamsa centered around the idea of Ocean-seal Samadhi. Master Wonhyo also developed Avatamsa thought with his unique theory on the Awakening of Faith, without any Chinese influence.

Such original thinking and development of Korean Buddhism is again revealed in the introduction of Zen and its establishment in the late Shilla Dynasty. Shilla masters introduced Zen Dharma from various Chinese Zen schools, but they never proclaimed to belong to those schools. Instead, they either founded their own or joined the already existing Korean Nine Mountains of Zen and so held on to the Korean Zen tradition. This tendency is also seen in the Zen thought of Master Chinul in the middle Koryo Period. To devise a method of harmonization of Meditation and Study, he formed his own very individual Zen thought. To this end he accepted orthodox Chinese Zen thought on the one hand and quoted other studies like the Avatamsa theory of Li T'ung-hsuan — which is considered a non-orthodox Chinese Avatamsa School — on the other hand.

The holistic Buddhist practice of three approaches, meditation, studying sutras, and chanting in the period of forming a new direction can be seen as one example of the individuality of Korean Buddhism. This is due to the fact that, though it was a phenomenon which appeared in the process of overcoming problems, it certainly was a conclusion derived from Korean Buddhist thought which differed from its Chinese counterpart. In this way we can conclude that Korean Buddhist thought, in close connection with Chinese Buddhist thought, has firmly established its own individual identity.

MENTAL FOUNDATION AND IDEOLOGY

Korean Buddhism offered a mental framework and ideology which corresponded to each phase of social development in the historical process. The important task of Buddhism in the initial period of introduction was the problem of establishment. Buddhism embraced the primitive thinking of Shamanism and so developed traditional thinking. Concepts such as the theory of karma replaced Shamanistic belief, hence it brought about social development and functioned as a prop and strengthener of the sovereign power. All the Three Kingdoms made Buddhist thought their central ideology. Especially Shilla before unification of the peninsula, made the best use of Buddhism, letting it influence every aspect of life so that the culture developed greatly. The ideology which was particularly popular was the Pure Land of Maitreya. Examples are the Shilla thought of Sankha, the universal monarch (Chakravatin) and the system of P'ungwoltto, the organization for training young men called hwarang.

The Shilla kingdom went one step further. There Buddhist thought was used as a pivot point for the accomplishment of the unification of the Three Kingdoms and then it was taken as the foundation ideology of the new unified state. Buddhism, especially Avatamsa philosophy, then became very influential as a socio-political ideology for the reconciliation and the integration which were needed by Unified Shilla. The foundation ideology of Koryo was also based on Buddhist philosophy. The theory of reconciliation of Confucianism and Buddhism in the Choson Period, was an active effort made to overcome the ideological gap of the time.

PHILOSOPHICAL REFORMATION MOVEMENT

Korean Buddhist thought devoted itself to philosophical reformation and the overcoming of fixed concepts from the beginning. Just after becoming thoroughly established, Korean Buddhism entered a phase of philosophical settlement already at the time of the Three Kingdoms and immediately began to make full use of the research being carried out. This openness and willingness to receive new thinking shows the reformation oriented character; this trend continued throughout the history, long after the period of establishment.

After unification, Buddhist philosophy was on a different level and Mahayana philosophy became fully developed. For it was not possible for the philosophy to stagnate at the level where it satisfied social ethics and sovereign ideology. And then once again, when Mahayana Buddhist philosophy met the limit of its conceptual development, Zen, which denies conceptual Buddhist thought, was introduced. It was a philosophical reformation movement. Encouragement of Buddhist studies in the early Koryo Period was done with the same view in mind. Thus Koryo masters did not merely continue the traditional thought system of Shilla Buddhism. They imported and integrated new thinking from Chinese studies. The community movements after the middle Koryo Period and the introduction of Zen in the later Koryo Period show stronger characteristics of philosophical reformation.

PURSUIT OF HARMONIZATION AND UNIFICATION

The pursuit of harmony and unification were constant focal points of Korean Buddhism. This is most remarkable in the history of Korean Buddhist thought, and it originated from Shilla Master Wonhyo's Buddhist thought. His whole thinking is centered on the idea of reconciliation. Through his creative theory, he harmonized the two different Buddhist values of categories of reality and ordinary categories which had been considered a problem. Also, he brought together the concept of the "void" (of Madhyamika philosophy) and that of "existence" (of Vijnanamatravada philosophy) — a subject of argument in Indian and Chinese studies — in the structure of his concept of the "One Mind."

This characteristic of harmonization and unification is also seen in the Vijnanamatravada thought of Master Wonch'u k and the Avatamsa thought of Master Uisang. Even more so, we find this dimension in the writings of Master Uich'on whose theory of dual practice of study and meditation aimed at the harmonization of doctrinal theories and actual practice, and so the unification of Meditation and Study which were in great conflict at that time. Master Chinul's Zen thought is the same. He boldly accepted Study, especially Avatamsa, which had been denied by the Meditation Schools and by that act he brought Meditation and Study together. Once again in the Zen thought of Master Sosan, during the Choson Dynasty when Buddhism was being persecuted, Confucianism, Taoism and Buddhism were brought together.

These trends of individuality, ideological foundation, reformation, and harmonization continue today. With 16 centuries of history behind it, Korean Buddhism now has a big responsibility to continue in the same vein. Korean Buddhist thought and culture are the ideological foundation of the Korean people and the driving force behind the development of the country. Today as much as ever, Korean Buddhism is Korean history.

Therefore Buddhism is now being strongly urged to once again bring a fresh philosophical ideology and way of practice applicable to modern society.

THE ORDERS

The Main Order: Chogye

The name of Korea's main sect, Chogye, comes from the mountain in China on which the Sixth Patriarch, Hui-neng (638-713), lived. The name "Chogye" was probably brought back from China by Master Toui in about 820 CE. It is an order which stresses meditation, originating from the Chan teachings of China. Slowly, many different Zen sects formed in Korea. Master T'aego (1301-82), a great monk, returned from China in 1346. After that he united all the Zen sects and called the resultant order "Chogye."

During the Choson Dynasty, when Buddhism was not favored, the Chogye Order continued to exist but with less force than before. After the Japanese colonization of Korea in 1910, the Chogye Order received yet another blow: married monks were introduced and Korean monks were encouraged to take wives.

It was only after liberation in 1945, in an age often referred to as the era of purification, that Korean Buddhism once again began to flourish. Public support grew and most of the large temples were once again run by the celibate monks of the Chogye Order.

The Chogye Order emphasizes meditation which is considered by most Buddhists to be the best way to attain enlightenment. The most venerated texts are: the Heart Sutra, the Diamond Sutra, the Platform Sutra of the Sixth Patriarch, the Avatamsaka Sutra, and the stories of ancient Zen Masters.

There are 1,632 (1997) temples belonging to the Chogye Order; this does not include numerous little hermitages dotted about the mountainous areas. These temples are organized into twenty-five geographical regions; each region has a main temple. Of the twenty-five main temples, there are four major temples: T'ongdo-sa Temple, Haein-sa Temple, Songgwang-sa Temple, and Sudok-sa Temple. These four temples have a meditation hall and a major monks' training center within the same compound.

The scale of operation of the Chogye Order has been renewed and enlarged since 1986. The Buddhist newspaper published by the Chogye Order has an increased circulation. Monks are assigned to the military to serve soldiers, and teachers have been sent to Korean Buddhist centers established in countries such as United States, Japan, Hong Kong, Australia, and Europe. Now there is a radio station and TV network which function in collaboration with the Chogye Order.

The Order consists of about 12,000 ordained members. There are 8.1 million active registered lay members and many, many more who are not registered (1997).

Other Orders

There are many other Buddhist sects in Korea. Although they share identical philosophy, the teachings of the Buddha, they differ in the area on which they lay stress and in the choice of principle text. All are Mahayana sects and some incorporate tantric influences into their teaching. The second largest sect, T'aego, has mostly married monks. The Hwaom, Chonghwa and Wonhyo sects all stress the Flower Garland Sutra, Avatamsaka. The Pophwa, Purip and Ilsung, among others, concentrate on the Lotus Sutra. The Pure Land sect venerates the Lotus Sutra and the Pomun is the only all women Buddhist sect in the world.

Most of the Korean Buddhists sects were founded after the liberation from the Japanese in 1945. Since then Korean Buddhism has been changing rapidly: programs have been more diversified and education has been emphasized. Country and mountain temples have been attracting more and more people. Increasingly there are also more Buddhist places to go to in the cities. (In the past, during the persecution of Buddhism in the Choson Dynasty, temples were not allowed to be built in the cities.) Another activity is the translation of Buddhist texts from Chinese into Korean so that people can read them more easily and the recording of the texts. At present the entire collection of wood-blocks at Haein-sa Temple is being put onto CDs and there is a plan for translation into English in the future.

In the area of education, many temples now have kindergartens or other schools attached to them. This is interesting because traditionally, in most Buddhist countries, young children learned to read and write from monks. One Buddhist University, Dongguk, has campuses in Seoul and Kyongju and there is a special university for monks and nuns called Sangha University.

Youth movements are greatly increasing. There are youth groups in schools and universities engaged in many special activities such as studying texts, traveling to different temples, reviving traditional folk dancing, and doing social work.

MONASTIC LIFE

GOING FORTH

After the Buddha Sakyamuni attained enlightenment in northern India, at first men and later women, attracted by his teaching, decided to follow him. They left their homes and joined the order that thus grew up around the Buddha. This was called "the going forth" from home to homelessness; it is still considered the first ordination ceremony in all Buddhist countries. The men and women who chose this way of life accepted to try to live according to ten training precepts as they continue to do today:

1) not to kill anything;
2) not to take anything that is not given;
3) to be celibate;
4) not to lie;

5) not to take intoxicants;
6) not to eat outside of mealtimes;
7) not to use adornments;
8) not to delight in singing, dancing or shows;
9) not to seek comfort;
10) not to amass wealth.

Soon another, more formal ordination ceremony was instigated; now, this is considered as the second ordination ceremony in all Buddhist countries. This ceremony consists of the acceptance of trying to live according to more training rules. These rules — recorded in the first part of the Buddhist texts, the Vinaya — initially came into being as solutions to problems which arose as the community lived together and grew at the time of the Buddha. Little by little rules were created according to circumstances. The men and women who received this second ordination became known as "bhikkus" and "bhikkunis" respectively.

In order to support themselves, the bhikkus and bhikkunis went on a daily alms round, gratefully receiving whatever they were given to help them on their spiritual quest. "Bhikku" means "a person who receives a share," they received a portion of the common wealth. After the Buddha's death, the bhikkus and bhikkunis traveled and as they did, Buddhism spread. People were attracted to the Buddhist teachings of peace and tolerance and temples were built all over India, Sri Lanka, China and, eventually, most of Asia. A monk brought Buddhism to Korea and started an unbroken tradition of ordained men and women which continues up to the present day. Let us now consider the life of bhikkus and bhikkunis in Korea. (Throughout this description, "monk" and "he" refers to men and women: their respective life-styles in Korea are identical.)

RENUNCIATION AND STUDY

Anyone in Korea who wishes to be ordained in the main Buddhist monastic order, Chogye, should have completed high school and be normally healthy in order to endure the rigors of the training. Usually a man or a woman wishes to ordain in order to attain enlightenment and to help living beings. The method used to accomplish this work is careful training and ardent practice for as long as possible — even the whole life. Communal living, meditation, religious practice, the study of texts and listening to the words of great monks and nuns all form part of this way of life.

At first, the candidate becomes an aspirant. On entering the monastery, he cuts off relations with the outside world for a time, symbolized by shaving hair and beard and wearing gray or brown clothes. (Women do not shave their heads at first: this being a trial period, they would have difficulty returning home, if they so chose.) Traditionally, shaving the hair is a renunciation of rank, as well as a way to reduce vanity and to be more hygienic. During this period, the aspirant learns chanting, does chores about the monastery and cares for the senior monks. In addition, and probably most importantly, he must learn what the Buddha taught and the spiritual path ahead. For this he relies on the ancient texts as well as the commentaries written by practitioners through the ages.

Books have always been of central importance to Buddhism. Intrinsic to Buddhist philosophy is the fact that each person must study and test the teaching for himself. In all Buddhist countries, people have always been literate and the books as freely available as possible. In fact, books started with Buddhism

Books, Binding & Printing

Most of us buy paper back books these days. Piled at airports and in book shops, they look just exactly what they are: mass produced. Obviously they pop out of a machine ready-made and that is exactly how we treat them: with no respect. We carry them around in a pocket or a bag and the covers get bent and messy but we don't really care because that is what they are meant for. No-one seems to care, even the editing is lousy!

It wasn't always like that. We used to carefully bind books, covering them in leather, embossing them with gold and silver and there were even covers made of ivory and beautiful wood. In the west, the library of a great house was very important and a special place for delving into life's secrets. The books were treasures and even today, to be left a library in someone's will is a wonderful thing.

Books started with Buddhism. One of the most important practices in Buddhism since ancient times is studying the texts and therefore they had to be available to everyone. In Sri Lanka, the texts were written down on palm leaves (specially dried, the letters were scratched into the leaf with a needle and powdered ink rubbed into the marks) in about 80 BCE.

The leaves were strung together and the resulting book was preserved between two slabs of beautifully decorated, often bejewelled, wood. The result could be carried around easily and, as it was often in the local script, everyone could read it. In China, the texts were carved on strips of bamboo, silk, stone and on wood but there seems to have been a tendency of preserving the texts in one place rather than spreading them around. It was in Korea that printing really developed. The first example of a printed "book" in the world is a Buddhist text consisting of 12 separate sheets from separate wood-blocks, stuck together to form a scroll dating from between 706 and 751.

Today, now a World Heritage treasure, the over 80,000 wood-blocks completed in 1251 of the entire collection of Buddhist texts can be seen at Haein-sa Temple, near Taegu. These blocks are truly marvelous because of the evenness of the carving and the fact that there is not a single mistake in the whole collection — unlike the paper backs of today!

In order to make copies of wood-blocks, ink is spread on the surface so that it soaks in for a few hours and then a new layer of ink is applied, a piece of mulberry paper is smoothed on top, the surface is carefully brushed with a ball of human hair (to remove any wrinkles and see that the letters are well formed on the paper) and then it is carefully peeled off and set to dry.

Due to the need to study so emphasized in Buddhism, books were in heavy demand. The labor intensive method of printing from the wood blocks was time consuming and costly. So a more available method had to be sought out: someone had to invent moveable type. And this is what happened. The characters were cast in the same way as coins and then lined up to print texts. The first book to be printed was The Selected Teachings of Buddhist Sages and Son Masters in 1377 — long before Gutenberg in the middle of the fifteenth century!

From single sheets, to many stuck together in a scroll or in a screen, to printed sheets, the evolution of the book has played a central role in the development of culture. Once moveable type was invented, then the printed sheets had to be fixed together and protected. This is where the creation of book covers came into being and more efficient binding techniques were used.

Books were always prized and loved. In order to express and underline this feeling, beautiful covers were created. In Korea, embossed mulberry paper was usually used. The embossing formed a back-drop pattern and the covers were often dyed and sometimes oiled. The designs used were mostly traditional ones like water chestnuts, one of the most popular because, as the plant grows near the edge of ponds, people regarded it as a good luck charm for preventing the burning down of their homes — and of the books. Also popular was the swastika, a symbol of peace and good luck in Asia. Lotuses, thunder clouds, tortoise shell and bats — the Korean name is similar to the word for good luck — were common motifs.

Binding was traditionally done with cord. The whole book was put together with a strand running length-wise on the back and on the front and then four horizontal strands held the pages together. Of course the technique was specialized and required dexterity and experience to execute well. Alas, all of this is long past and only available at great expense today. So, as paper backs are the current book form, maybe we have to learn to love them and treat them more decently!?

After about one year, it is then decided whether or not the candidate is suitable for monastic life and, if so, he chooses a teacher — or they choose each other. The aspirant is given ordination and takes the first set of basic training rules: the ten precepts which constitute the going forth" The teacher takes care of the disciple, now called a sami, (samini for women), materially and spiritually. The disciple, in turn, serves his teacher.

Next the young monk is sent to one of the Monks' Colleges. These are special institutions where the sami (or samini, separately) study the texts more deeply, learn

Chinese characters, chanting and all the other talents required for a fully ordained member of the Buddhist community. In addition, these days there is a large number of more modern subjects available. Examples include English, psychology, techniques for teaching the young and the old are included in the curriculum. The most important lessons are in the art of communal living. As all the members of one year will stay together in one large room for the four years, they must learn to live harmoniously.

FULL ORDINATION

After five years, if the teacher sees fit, the novice is sent for the second ordination and becomes a bhikkhu (bhikkhuni for women) or a full member of the monastic community or Sangha. This ceremony is preceded by five days of extra training and lectures.

BHIKKUNIS

Since the introduction of Buddhism to Korea, many Korean women have become bhikkunis. Examples include records of queens and women members of the court being ordained in the sixth century. From that time until the present day, Korea is the only country to have a clear, unbroken tradition of women receiving both ordinations. Since 1981, the traditional Chinese system of ordination, known as the Double Platform, requiring ten bhikkus and ten bhikkunis, all of ten years ordination, has been reinstated as well.

Taiwanese bhikkunis also receive the second ordination, which was brought from China at the time of the Cultural Revolution. In other countries, invasions and famines resulted in there being insufficient long-term ordained women members to officiate. Therefore, women could only have the lower ordination in Sri Lanka, Burma, and Thailand until recently. In December 1996, the first group of Sri Lankan women received higher ordination and, although it is seen as highly controversial, the movement is gaining popularity and more and more Theravada women are becoming bhikkunis.

As so little is known and there is much interest in bhikkunis, here is a more in-depth look at the history, life and customs of ordained women in Korea.

THE HISTORY OF KOREAN BHIKKUNIS

Introduction

It is a difficult task. The low position of women in society and the 500 years of the persecution of Buddhism are probably responsible for the obliteration of most of the information that was recorded. Therefore, with the little that remains, an attempt at interpretation, often a little far-fetched, has been made. The resulting picture is, at best, vague but we can obtain some kind of an idea of the lives, status and activities of bhikkunis as well as some sense of the evolution of the Korean Bhikkuni Sangha throughout the long Buddhist history of Korea, from 372 CE to the present day.

The Buddha and the Bhikkuni Sangha

The Buddha, twelve years after his Great Renunciation and six years after his Great Enlightenment, visited his hometown, Kapilavastu. At that time, Queen Mahapajapati, the Buddha's aunt and step-mother, asked him to ordain her as a bhikkuni. Though the Buddha did not accept her request at first, his disciple Ananda Thera managed to convince the Buddha that women, being spiritually equal to men, were entitled to a life of homelessness. The Buddha agreed and then ordained Mahapajapati as the first bhikkuni. Leaving the household life, Mahapajapati was thus the founder of the Bhikkuni Sangha.

After Mahapajapati, many women left their homes, were ordained and practiced sincerely. Women from aristocratic families and ordinary families alike, sought a life of homelessness. Queens and laborers left their parents or husbands and followed the Buddha; many bhikkunis attained enlightenment and became Arahants, fully enlightened ones. The stories of some of these women are recorded. The trend continued as Buddhism spread and records show that when Buddhism was introduced to China, many great women became bhikkunis there, too.

The Bhikkuni Sangha of the Three Kingdoms

Unfortunately extremely little information is available for Paekje and Koguryo, so it is necessary to concentrate on Shilla. In spite of this we are able to make various serious speculations and even come to some conclusions.

Koguryo

There are no existing records of Koguryo bhikkunis. So we can only guess at their way of life and type of activities through the records of the Bhikku Sangha. Considering the development of Buddhism in Koguryo and the active achievement of Koguryo bhikkus, there must have been many bhikkunis in Koguryo and the Bhikkuni Sangha must have flourished, too. According to a Japanese record, in 587, Koguryo Master Hyep'yon ordained three Japanese bhikkunis for the first time in Japan before they traveled to Paekje in order to study. So there definitely was an ordination ceremony for bhikkunis in Koguryo. Bhikkuni Popmyong became the teacher of the three Japanese bhikkunis in 587 and this shows that the Koguryo Bhikkuni Sangha had formed its own system to practice and educate the people with bhikkunis who were sufficiently experienced to become teachers.

Through Japanese records it is seen that Koguryo bhikkunis came to Japan and educated people. But it is not possible to know about the background, activities and the status of the Bhikkuni Sangha. Although most probably differing in many characteristics, we can assume that the Koguryo Bhikkuni Sangha was quite similar to that of Paekje. It is most probable that the toyunarang system existed.

During the reign of the 27th Koguryo King Yongyu (r. 618-642), Taoism was introduced to Koguryo and gained a lot of power. Due to this many monks left Koguryo.

During the reign of King Pojang (r. 642-668), Buddhism declined to such an extent that Master Podok was refused by the king when he applied to revive Buddhism. So he left for the south and went to live there on Kodal-san mountain at Wansan-ju. The Bhikkuni Sangha must have also been greatly affected by these political changes.

Koguryo, the first of the Three Kingdoms to accept Buddhism, had a Sangha which was well supported by the kings. The Bhikkuni Sangha produced bhikkunis like Popmyong who educated the Japanese which shows that they must have been well enough organized to train bhikkunis from abroad.

Paekje

The 27th king, Widok (r. 554-593), in the 24th year (577) of his reign, sent sutras, abhidharmas the Vinaya, a meditation monk, a magician, technicians for building temples, and bhikkunis to Japan, 194 years after the introduction of Buddhism to Paekje. What is interesting in this record is the official despatch of bhikkunis. It is not known whether bhikkunis were sent abroad before King Widok or not, and if so, whether, as one would suppose, the reason was because the Paekje Bhikkuni Sangha was so well established that it could send representatives abroad.

The bhikkunis must have been well educated and had much experience in the practice of Buddhism, at least sufficiently to be sent abroad in order to represent the Paekje Bhikkuni Sangha. It also suggests that there were large numbers of bhikkunis and it is even reasonable to suppose that most bhikkunis were from aristocratic families, as in Shilla, for Buddhism in Paekje, too, was supported by the royal family.

Then in the 35th year of the reign of King Widok, in 587, a Buddha relic, bhikkus, technicians for building temples, roof tilers, and painters were sent to Japan. A record states that the Japanese minister, Soga-no-umako, asked for a monk from Paekje to learn about the ordination ceremony. Two or three nuns – depending on the interpretation – including one named Zenshin, traveled to Paekje in order to study there. The three then ordained twelve more for the first time, on their return to Japan and thirty-five years after the three bhikkunis returned, there were 569 Japanese bhikkunis.

Before traveling to Paekje, the three bhikkunis received precepts (probably samini precepts) from Koguryo Master Hyep'yon and then studied under Koguryo bhikkuni, Popmyong. The bhikkunis, not satisfied with learning Buddhism in Japan, came to Paekje to learn about the ordination ceremony properly.

There are many reasons that the Japanese bhikkunis chose Paekje. Among the Three Kingdoms, Paekje was the most involved in the exchange of culture with Japan, in particular Buddhism. Paekje directly brought the Vinaya from India, and was therefore considered the most developed in the precepts. Also the social activities and development of the Paekje Bhikkuni Sangha may have been more vigorous than that of Shilla or Koguryo.

Unfortunately most extant records about bhikkunis are from Shilla. Though the records of Paekje and Koguryo are rare, considering the achievements of the successive generations of Paekje kings who were all deeply involved in Buddhism, the Paekje Bhikkuni Sangha was most probably as developed as Shilla. There is a Chinese record of a traveler to Paekje giving his impressions of the kingdoms. He said, "There are so many pagodas of bhikkuni temples in Paekje."

The more precise records of the Paekje Bhikkuni Sangha come from Japan. According to one record, there were separate bhikkuni temples in Paekje, and the bhikkunis received precepts according to the original procedure written down in the Vinaya. When a Paekje envoy to Japan was questioned about the program of the ordination ceremony by a Japanese, he answered, "At first, ten bhikkunis are invited to a bhikkuni temple and they, as teachers, give precepts. And then, at another temple, ten bhikkus are invited and so, together with the former ten bhikkunis, there is a total of twenty teachers. Together they give precepts."

The speaker, not being ordained, could not give more precise details of the procedure. However, the sequence of the ordination is the same as the text: first precepts are given by ten bhikkunis and then again together with ten bhikkus.

When we consider that even a layman knew something about the ordination procedure, we realize that everyone was well informed about Buddhism. Also, it indicates that trouble was taken in the keeping of the regulations of the Bhikkuni Sangha during the reign of King Widok and the discipline was carefully developed. There is also an indication of the stability and authority of the Bhikkuni Sangha of that time.

In 655, during the 15th year of the reign of King Uija (r. 641-660), Bhikkuni Popmyong went to Japan and cured a sick person by chanting the Vimalakirtinirdesa-sutra. The fact that this case is recorded in a history book tells that the bhikkuni was considered to be great. It is also good evidence of the traffic between the peninsula and Japan from the time of the 27th King Widok until the last (31st) King Uija, a period of about 130 years.

The mission of Paekje bhikkunis in Japan speaks of the high learning and great virtue of the bhikkunis, and the existence and activities of the Bhikkuni Sangha as a whole. From the above cases, the scale and activities as well as the social status of Paekje bhikkunis can be sufficiently understood.

Shilla

It is not very clear when Shilla women started to accept Buddhism. It is simply guessed that it must have been some time after the official recognition of Buddhism in Shilla in 527. There were many women supporters of the temples as well as many bhikkunis. Some women became temple servants, others devoted themselves as patrons. With the great devotion and variety of activities which women gave themselves to in the temples, their contribution was considerable.

The First Bhikkuni of Shilla

The first recorded bhikkuni was Sa-ssi, the sister of Morye who was a Shilla lay Buddhist. It appears that she was ordained before the official acceptance of Buddhism in Shilla žwhich makes the record all the more interesting. (From Samguk-yusa, Legends of the Three Kingdoms, 3rd volume.) The record says:

"Morye's sister, Sa-ssi, was ordained by Master Ado who was being hidden in her house because he wished to spread Buddhism. She lived in a temple which she had built called Yonghung-sa at Samch'ong-gi. Later, when King Mich'u passed away (284), people tried to kill Ado and so he returned to Morye's house and, eventually, died there. Buddhism could not be taught in Shilla any more."

Apart from this record, it is not known whether or not Master Ado ordained any other women. The record refers to the period before the official introduction of Buddhism to Shilla, after Master Ado's death, there were no other recorded ordinations until Buddhism had been formally introduced.

THE FIRST BHIKKUNI SANGHA OF SHILLA

Bhikkuni Myobop, King Pophung's Queen

The 23rd Shilla King Pophung (r. 514-546) protected and encouraged Buddhism. He built Hungryun-sa and became a monk, being given the dharma name of Pop-un (Dharma Cloud) and also the name of Popkong (Empty Dharma) (Samguk-yusa, the 3rd volume). King Pophung's queen also had a deep yearning to become a bhikkuni and so she followed in the footsteps of the first bhikkuni, Sa-ssi, who had built Yonghung-sa. The queen was also ordained and she went to live in Yonghung-sa. Her dharma name was Myobop (Marvelous Dharma).

If we accept the foundation of Yonghung-sa by Sa-ssi, the first bhikkuni, then it seems that the later Yonghung-sa founded by the queen was established in memory of the former and is unlikely to have been the same temple. One thing is clear: from the beginning of Buddhism in Shilla, women participated actively. The fact, that the queen became a bhikkuni and followed Sa-ssi about 252 years later tells us that Sa-ssi must have made a great impression – maybe through her character and practice – causing the legend to be passed down so that the queen, on hearing it, followed the example.

The queen could not have been ordained alone and have lived by herself in the temple, Yonghung-sa. There must have been other women from aristocratic families and even other members of the royal family who followed Myobop. All of them would have lived together in the temple and spent time chanting for the welfare of the country and the people. As there is no mention of ordinary women being ordained, maybe it was not permitted and only queens and aristocratic women could become bhikkunis. Possibly, the queen's servants could have been ordained or maybe they just lived in the temple to serve the queen.

Thus the Bhikkuni Sangha was established. Later, during the reign of King Chinhung (r. 540-576), special positions were made within the sangha.

Bhikkuni Popun, King Chinhung's Queen

The queen of King Chinhung, Pak-ssi was a daughter of Minister Youngshil. After the king had taken ordination and become a monk, the queen became a bhikkuni and lived in Yonghung-sa temple. Some records say that her Buddhist name was Popun, but as this is the same name as that of her husband, King Chinhung, it is not sure whether the record is correct. A further record tells that in 614, a statue at Yongch'on-sa fell down by itself and was smashed to pieces. Soon after that, the bhikkuni passed away. (Often when a great person dies, a symbolic event which foretells the death of that person, occurs. The falling of the statue was a preliminary announcement of the death of the bhikkuni who was, after all, the most important member of the Bhikkuni Sangha and so a major influence on the women of that time.)

The Social Status of the Bhikkuni Sangha

Enthusiastic devotion to Buddhism was thus started by the queens of kings Pophung and Chinhung, and it influenced many aristocratic women of Shilla. As Buddhism gradually filtered down through the society, it reached ordinary women, and many of them must have been ordained. Some probably became bhikkunis when they were young and unmarried, and some, like Chiso, the wife of General Kim Yu-shin, became bhikkunis after losing their husbands. Due to the many aristocratic women involved, the Bhikkuni Sangha must have held quite a high position in the society of the day.

There were some objections to kings and queens being ordained due to the social system of the time. The highest members of society belonged to the group known as the bone-rank and the people found it hard to accept that its leaders left to live in temples. But with the strong will and dedication such as the Buddha and his step-mother had shown, these social restrictions were overcome and it was possible for the kings and queens who wanted to be ordained, to leave and live in temples. The socio-political status of the queens must have been reflected in their position in the Sangha so that the relationship between the queens and the other bhikkunis, who were often the queen's maids, couldn't have been equal.

These bhikkunis seem to have lived more freely than the original Indian ordained women. One of the reasons was due to the evolution of Buddhism itself constituted by the influence of different cultures as Buddhism moved from India through China. In addition, the social status of the women involved must have affected the way they lived. The evidence for this supposition is well found in the system of ordained officials.

Toyunarang, Head of the Bhikkuni Sangha

During the reign of King Chinhung, the Sangha developed enormously, particularly the Bhikkuni Sangha.

King Chinhung was a grand nephew of King Pophung. He became king when he was only seven, and it was the queen of King Pophung, a devoted Buddhist, who ruled as regent. King Chinhung performed many great services for the development of Korean Buddhism due to the powerful influence of the Queen Regent. For example, he officially permitted anyone, men or women, to be ordained in the 5th year of his reign. This was the year of the completion of Hungnyun-sa, a great temple. After giving permission for ordination, the king established a rank system of monks and nuns to promote the well-being of and to organize the Sangha. He became a monk later on in life and chose Sammaekchong (which means sami, sramanera) as his posthumous designation. From the 11th year of his reign, King Chinhung appointed monks to various important positions. The job of these officials was to superintend the other monks and nuns. The mere fact that special people were elected to oversee the Sangha suggests that there were quite a large number of ordained people, possibly, also, the monks and nuns may have been too powerful for the king and so had to be controlled by special officials from their own group.

Toyunarang was the title given to the head of the Bhikkuni Sangha and the very existence of this post suggests that the number of bhikkunis must have been considerable and that their role in society could not be overlooked. Unfortunately, there is no record of the precise duties and activities of this position existing today.

There are, however, two different views about the role of the toyunarang. One comes from a Japanese scholar who says, "the toyunarang could have been a woman who was a kind of priest." But the Korean scholar Lee Ki-baik, in his article entitled The Transmission of Buddhism to the Three Kingdoms and its Social Characteristics, states that toyunarang was a bhikkuni. He points to the social status of women in Buddhist society during the early Shilla Period, and adds that toyunarang was one of the official positions which was the same as that from the Chinese Northern and Southern Dynasties; it was originally introduced from China to Koguryo.

The Word "Ani"

In the Three Kingdoms, the word "Ani" is often found in the names of king's mothers, queens, or king's sisters. Originally "Ani" is related to women, either as a proper noun indicating a particular woman, or it can also have been used in reference to bhikkunis.

In the Japanese history book, Ilbonso-gi, it is written that the first Japanese bhikkuni, Sonshin, went to Paekje to learn the discipline, the Vinaya, and she is recorded as having been called "Sonshin-ani." Then in the Korean book Kyerim-yusa, it is recorded that bhikkunis during the Koryo Dynasty were called "Ani," showing that this was a usual way of calling bhikkunis.

"Ani" was a term used in the names of high ranking women in the Shilla Dynasty. Some records show that some of these women were appointed to the position of supervisor of national ceremonies or as managers of ancestral temples of the royal family. All these records support the present writer's opinion about the word "Ani" — it was originally the title or name given to aristocratic women, and when Buddhism was introduced, the title was used for bhikkunis whose status prior to ordination was that of a queen or an aristocratic woman. (It is interesting to note that Ani is the title used to address women ordained in Tibetan Buddhism today.)

The Social Background

The Buddha, when he permitted women to be ordained, gave eight extra rules especially for women in addition to the already established rules. These rules were concerned with the social behavior and the safety of the ordained women. It is highly debated why the Buddha did this but one reason was probably to establish a social form for the Sangha to operate under. Many see this as a reason for considering bhikkunis to have been lower in the social order than bhikkus.

However, in the Shilla Period, men and women were equal and the same was true of the members of the Sangha. Queen Sondok belonged to the hallowed-bone group, the highest rank in the society. Even though a man from true-bone rank, who was actually lower in the social system could be chosen to be king, Queen Sondok was anointed. Therefore at that time, women had the right of succession in the family lineage and they probably had the same rights in the inheritance of property also. The fact that Queen Sondok became a bhikkuni raised the status of ordained women and, therefore they were probably considered to be on the same level as men.

During the late Shilla Period, the 50th king, Chonggang (r. 886-887) abdicated the throne in favor of his sister, Queen Chinsong (r. 887-897), saying, "My sister is bright and her body is like that of a man. You, the people, should follow the example of queens Sondok and Chindok."

The Social Activities of the Bhikkunis

There is no record concerning the role of bhikkunis in society and their practices. But there is a record about a bhikkuni called Chihye who lived during the reign of King Chinp'yong who is reported to have held a special ceremony every spring and every fall, 10 days each for laymen and laywomen. She lived in Anhung-sa.

There is a special story recorded about her. Once, when she was preparing to repair one of the main halls, she had a dream in which it was revealed to her that there were over 5 kilos of gold under the statue ready to be used as payment for the repairing of the hall.

As in the case of Bhikkuni Chihye, other bhikkunis in the Shilla Kingdom had to be vigorous in helping Buddhism to become well settled and familiar to all classes of people.

The Bhikkuni Sangha of Unified Shilla

Considering the changes in the lifestyle of the people of the Unified Shilla Period, the consolidation and general spread of Buddhism to all parts of society, the Bhikkuni Sangha of Koguryo and Paekje seems to have been absorbed into the Shilla Bhikkuni Sangha without much conflict. This probably happened with unification. As the Bhikku Sangha developed rapidly, the Bhikkuni Sangha must have done likewise. Thus the simple chanting and praying of the early days could not have sufficed the new extended demands. Five doctrinal schools emerged and these developed separately, therefore it seems logical to suppose that the bhikkunis probably belonged to different schools and pursued different courses of study.

Still, aristocratic women formed the majority of bhikkunis, as far as we know. The royal family even donated relatives to the temples to be servants.

>From the fact that most bhikkunis were from aristocratic families, we can guess at the high status and authority which the Bhikkuni Sangha probably held in Shilla society. When the Meditation Schools started to flourish, there must have been a bhikkuni sect which was mainly concerned with practicing meditation.

Koryo Period to the Modern Era

During the Koryo and Choson periods, more and more ordinary women were ordained, some for secular reasons and others for philosophical reasons. Some were ordained simply to spend their lives praying for their dead fathers; some were forced to be ordained by the fathers, for they had no money for their daughters to get married; wives and daughters of rebels were also ordained or became lifelong servants.

During the late Koryo period, as temples accumulated wealth with the help of kings, the Sangha became corrupted. The Bhikkuni Sangha was also spoilt and the temples concentrated on producing various goods such as hemp cloth and so became rich and lacking in concentrated practice as they spent more and more time on providing goods.

The Choson Period was the worst time for women. During that period, a woman was more concerned with preserving her chastity than with saving her life. When a woman remarried, her children badly treated and could not rise in the world. At times, women as well as men were prohibited from ordaining by government order and many young bhikkunis were forced to disrobe. As a result, only ordinary women who had run upon hard times seem to have been able to become bhikkunis. The consequence of this movement was that the status of bhikkunis in society became lower and lower. Besides, the severe social rules that were kept at that time prohibited them from doing anything to improve their lot.

When Korea was colonized by Japan in 1910, the Choson law which had prohibited bhikkus and bhikkunis from entering the capital for most of 500 years, was revoked and so the Sangha was able to regain some of its freedom of movement and outlook. Buddhism was used by the Japanese in their aggression and thus became heavily influenced by the Japanese style. In this way the Sangha which had been centered around celibate ordained members, was forced to change into one of married monks; because of this the bhikkunis lost their independence. They could only continue to exist by staying near bhikkus, who, having been driven out of their temples in towns and cities, were forced to live in the high mountains, far from civilization. In the early part of the twentieth century, the western movement of emancipating women influenced Korean society enormously. In addition, women also joined the movement for Korean Independence on an equal footing with men. After independence, as democracy became more imminent, women acquired a better status than that of the Choson Period. These social changes were reflected in the Bhikkuni Sangha. Educated women again started to be ordained and the bhikkunis joined the bhikkus in the Sangha purification movement. At that time, the celibate Sangha fought against the married monks and the bhikkus and bhikkunis were comrades in a common struggle. Now, the number of women being ordained is far greater and their level of education far higher than earlier on in the century. The increase in women seeking ordination was possibly initially due to the mass of female orphans from the Korean War in 1950 and the baby boom after the war.

Whatever the reason, the trend continues and today as many women seek ordination as men, sometimes more. The increase in more educated women coming to the temples may be due to the fact that bhikkunis are very well supported and now run beautiful temples, whereas before they had to spend time repairing old temples to make a place to live. Also, today, the value of education has been accepted. With the general improvement in educational level, women have come more into contact with Buddhism due to the presence of temples and centers in the cities, on university campuses and in society as a whole.

These days much time and effort is spent in order to carefully train women who wish to become bhikkunis. They are sent to university and many even go abroad to study. Now there are even bhikkuni professors and teachers.

Conclusion

Unfortunately, the records about bhikkunis which still exist almost exclusively only mention the personal background of the aristocratic women or queens who were ordained during the Shilla Period. There are almost no records of the activities, achievements, or way of life of bhikkunis in general.

The reason for this lack of records is: firstly, perhaps the bhikkunis did not often get involved in vigorous enough activities or achieve great enough fame for records to be made. Secondly, though there were great bhikkunis, the position of women in the society was such that records were not kept. Thirdly, women of the time in general were not active enough or educated enough to keep records about themselves.

All of these reasons point to the fact that the bhikkunis probably lived quite a passive life due to the lack of education. Women were not educated and, therefore, unable to become bhikkunis who were able to keep records and to be active enough in the society for there to be something to record.

In spite of this lack of information there are strong indications that the Bhikkuni Sangha flourished from the time of the introduction of Buddhism and that it almost always led a life that was independent and equal to the Bhikku Sangha. In addition, as far as we can tell, the Sangha never died out and there has been a continual succession of bhikkunis in Korea. Today, the bhikkunis are strong, independent and extremely active. They run temples which vary from 275 members to tiny hermitages for private practice. They are active as professors and teach at all levels. It is hard to imagine that they are not the continuation of a long and strong heritage which has been passed down through the ages.?

LIFESTYLE OF BHIKKUNIS TODAY

"Anyone who sees me here, probably feels sorry for me. But I couldn't be happier." This was the conclusion of a young Samini (a woman who has completed at least a year in the temple and taken the first ordination) in a traditional Zen temple near Taegu in southeastern Korea. It is a temple belonging to the traditional Chogye-jong, the main Buddhist Order of Korea. (The following account pertains only to the Chogye Order.) Representing the principle line of traditional Korean Buddhism, at present (1997) the Chogye Order has about 1800 temples, 800 of which are run by ordained women. There are about 3,500 ordained men and 2,900 ordained women — those who have received the two ordinations. In addition, there are about 2,700 men and 2,900 women who have received the first ordination. Registered lay members of the order number about 8.1 million. Buddhism was introduced to Korea in 372 CE from China. As far as we know, the ordination of women started from about the same time.

"What on earth do you mean by that?" I asked.

"Well, I prepare food and cook and clean from 5 a.m. to 6 p.m. every day. In addition, I do my bowing, learn my chanting and take care of my teacher. At night I am so tired. Doesn't sound very exciting, does it? But I am really and truly happy! Eventually I will go to the meditation hall but first I must prepare myself."

I thought over this conversation and realized that most people would think her life dull. There is a Japanese proverb that those who live in the temple see outsiders as a little strange. And once you leave the temple, you see the people living in the temple as a little strange. From a worldly point of view, she looked "strange." And I began to wonder. Why would anyone chose to spend years on end working without monetary gain or any other the tangible benefits which are valued by most people.

"I thought about life," she answered when I asked her. "Is money important? No, I decided. Is fame important? Absolutely not. Then what is important? To understand life and death. The Buddha taught us a way to find an answer to this. We go to live in a community, practice hard and constantly in order to understand things properly. Our ancient teachers said that this is the best way. So I decided to leave my family and go to the temple. I knew that I was free to leave the temple life at any time and I was free to stay as long as I wished."

"Wasn't your family terribly upset?"

"Yes, at first. Now they have become used to it and are happy for me."

These days most of the women who walk up the long road to the temple gates and ask to be accepted are well over 20 years old, they are often college graduates and mostly motivated by a love for temple life and the Buddha's teaching. Many see the futility of life — sleep, get tired, eat, eliminate, grow old, die and take nothing with you, the hollowness of money and fame — and aspire for true understanding of the meaning of life. A very few just want to escape from society, marriage and responsibility. In order to be accepted, they must have completed High School, be healthy and normal (because of the rigors of the way of life, it is no place for anyone who is handicapped), if possible they should have obtained permission from the family and must be single. Their introduction has usually come from a school or college Buddhist group or their family has a close relationship with a temple. The families do not usually want their children going off to the temples, for obvious reasons as well as the fact that Korea still has strong Confucian influences. Temples never encourage anyone, it is strictly a personal choice.

Having informed the family of their intention, the aspirant leaves for a temple which is usually quite far from home so that they won't be disturbed by well-meaning relatives. Often, in order to train hard, she does not see her family for a while. This, too, is a strictly personal choice. The aspirant starts life with working, bowing, learning chanting and trying to adjust. For many it is the first time away from the home, the first experience of vegetarian food and everything is strange. She cuts her hair very short (not shaving it in case she wants to leave) and wears brown clothes.

After a year, she chooses a teacher and the teacher chooses her — it is a mutual agreement. The teacher is a woman, usually over 40 years of age. She can accept as many disciples as she wishes, depending on how many ask. To the best of her ability, she provides them with necessities like clothes, teaches them the philosophy and how to live in the temple. The main job of the teacher, however, is to encourage her disciples to practice hard. "We are all just trying hard and practicing together," Sunim — the title used for any ordained member of the Korean Buddhist community — explained when I asked her whether her teacher was enlightened. "We are all here to help, encourage and inspire each other. That's all!"

The group of disciples form a family and they identify themselves according to the number of generations they are in their lineage. Then the aspirant has her head shaved and takes her first set of precepts, 10 training rules. These days there is a formal ceremony preceded by three weeks of intensive training. The aspirant is now a samini and wears gray clothes. At the ordination ceremony, she also receives her ceremonial robes: a long gray robe with flowing sleeves and a patch-work brown one which is fastened at the left shoulder.

After the ceremony, she returns to her temple. The young samini all live in a big room, where they sleep, study and eat. "What kind of work did you do when you returned to the temple?" I asked. "I did almost everything" said Sunim. "I helped prepare the vegetables and rice, worked in the fields, looked after the older members, rang the huge bell and so on. Unfortunately I was much younger than others and so I never did the gentler work like cleaning the Main Hall. Temple life is very regulated, but there's an air of freedom as well. Every three months we changed our job. It was interesting and challenging." Korea has four distinct seasons and temple life adjusts to the changes. Older — not necessarily in physical years but in the number of years lived in the temple — bhikkunis go to the meditation halls in the summer and winter, called the "meditation seasons" and visit teachers during the spring and autumn, the "free seasons." The younger members change jobs. To mark the change there is a huge clean out, the temple is dusted and washed from top to bottom.

"How do you keep the community functioning together? What is a typical day like?" I asked. "Well, there are various means. First of all there is the big bell which is sounded every morning at 3 a.m. to wake everyone up and again in the evening before chanting. Some temples also sound it at lunchtime. Then there are the periods of activity. The mokt'ak (a hollowed wooden "bell" used for chanting, also) is sounded before activity periods and meals. Those who are studying assemble in the big room, get out their little desks (they sit on the floor) and wait for the teacher. Those who have other duties go to perform them. The first period is from about 4 to 6 a.m. Then everyone has breakfast together. The next period is from about 7 to 10 a.m. After that there is chanting and lunch. The next period is from 1 p.m. until about 4 p.m. Then there is dinner and chanting. Afterwards there is another period from about 7 to about 10 p.m. The times change with the seasons and vary from temple to temple. Every two weeks there is a special day when we all take an extended bath, wash and mend our clothes and relax. The next day there is a lecture, often given by a visiting teacher. It is strange that within such uniformity, an air of individualism pervades. This is probably due to the fact that each person looks after herself and by doing so frees the others from worrying about her, allowing them to get on with their own lives."

After two more years, the Samini go to the special training temples where they spend four years learning texts, Chinese characters, chanting, and living together. As they advance they are given more and more responsibilities. The training is very strict.

"If we were so much as a second late for any of the chanting ceremonies, classes or meals we had to pay. Also, an absolute taboo was leaving even a single sock on the laundry lines after the start of the evening chanting." I was quite surprised. I wondered how adults who had chosen freely to live in the temple could possibly "pay." "Oh, that's simple," replied Sunim. "We had to do extra vegetable peeling or rice cleaning duty." (I thought of the soldiers peeling potatoes and realized that it was truly international!!!) "The worst was cleaning the toilet..."

The fourth year they are seniors and so have to help the teachers and take charge of the younger students. This is the year that they receive final ordination, 348 training rules or precepts, and become a bhikkuni, a full member of the ordained community. ("bhikkuni" is the Korean pronunciation of the Sanskrit bhiksuni. Originally it meant "a person who receives a share." Traditionally all ordained members of a Buddhist community went on alms round every day and received their share of the community food. In return they taught the people philosophy and helped them with their problems and also instructed the children.) These training rules make up the total description of the way the bhikkuni is to live for the rest of her life.

The bhikkuni ordination ceremony is very elaborate. The precepts are received from ten senior ordained bhikkus and ten senior bhikkunis who preside over the ancient and formal ceremony preceded by five days of intensive training and lectures. Each Samini is given a copy of the 348 precepts and a beautiful certificate.

Afterwards, many bhikkunis return to their temples to do kido — the Korean word for religious practice which usually consists of bowing, chanting or a mixture of the two for a definite period of time like one week, 100 days or three years. "Why do you do such a strenuous activity as going up and down as many as 3,000, even 10,000 times a day when you do the bowing?" I inquired. "First of all it is important to understand that we are not bowing to the statue or the picture. We could bow anywhere but we find the statue inspiring. We bow to everything, we bow to teach ourselves humility, we bow because we hope that once we begin to practice meditation there will be no disturbances to our practice. We just hope." Another friend told me, "I wanted to prove my determination to myself. It is symbolic of my determination to attain enlightenment. I wanted to show myself that I could complete something so difficult as bowing 3,000 time a day for 100 days. Then I would know that I had the ability to study to the end."

A note about the word "study." In Korean Chogye Buddhism, the traditional Zen way of koan practice is observed. Called "hwadu" in Korea, this cryptic, non-logical question is usually received from a meditation master. It is supposed to occupy the mind 24 hours-a-day until a "solution" is achieved. When sitting in the meditation halls, this question is "studied" in the hope of obtaining the answer which can only come from a total change of consciousness allowing the person to see and understand things as they truly are, free from conditioning, prejudice and preconception. The questions are now famous, for example, "Who am I?" or "What is the sound of one hand?"

Then the bhikkunis set out for the meditation hall. This is a great step for them for it is the culmination of years of training. Life in the meditation hall is hard. All live together, practicing as much as they are able to do. The smaller halls have place for about 10 people, the bigger ones up to 50, whatever the number, they stay in the hall for three months and sometimes three years. They sit 8, 10, 14 or 20 hours a day depending on the period of the meditation season. About 25% of the entire, fully-ordained community are in the meditation halls in any particular season. They are cared for by the community. A few will wander from hall to hall throughout their lives, the rest will return to the temples to help in the organization or go to university.

"What will you do when you are old?" I asked as I gazed at her fresh, bright face. (Traditionally, the temple was a total community. Anyone in trouble, orphans, the old would all take refuge in the temple. Even nowadays there are still many orphans accepted and many old people chose to end their days in a temple. The orphans go to school and the old people help out, living the end of their lives useful and loved.) Sunim thought for a moment and then answered, "I'll probably return to my temple and live with the others. As much as possible, I want to continue life in the meditation hall. By that time," she smiled, "I'll probably have my own disciples and maybe I can teach them a thing or two. But that is a long way away..."?

Morning

The day begins at 3 a.m. One monk rises a little earlier, washes, and puts on his ceremonial robes. Slowly, he walks to each part of the monastery beating a mokt'ak (a hollowed, wooden, bell-shaped percussion instrument) and chanting as he goes. The clear sound of the mokt'ak breaks the stillness of the pre-dawn hours...

"Pray that the whole universe will hear this sound and may all painful places be brightened. May the hells, ghosts and animals be relieved of suffering, and may all problems disappear so that all living beings may properly awake."

This wake-up ceremony is carried out every day of every year regardless of the weather. On hearing the mokt'ak, the monks get up, fold and put away their bedding, and wash (they sleep in their clothes). In the countryside, traditionally, they often wash in a stream or from a large stone bowl where water collects. After a short time, the large bell, followed by the drum, gong and wooden fish, are sounded and all monks go to the Main Hall for chanting. The large bell, drum, gong and wooden fish each represent a section of the world of living beings. The large bell calls those who have become decadent. The drum, made of an animal skin, calls the animals; and the cloud-shaped gong calls the beings of the air. The log carved into the shape of a fish calls all that live in water. Every living thing is called to listen to the chanting of the words of liberation taught by the Buddha and to follow that wisdom, if they so wish.

After communal chanting, each monk returns to his place. The students go to the study hall; the meditating monks go to the meditation hall (in the meditation seasons they merely bow in the meditation hall and sit); and the working monks go to their place of duty. At about 6 a.m., breakfast takes place.

Breakfast traditionally consists of rice porridge and pickles which the community eats together in silence in a formal style from a set of four individual bowls. A spoon is used along with chopsticks, a custom which is unique to Korea.

Spoons & Chopsticks: History, Culture and Etiquette

Koreans are the only far easterners to use spoons to eat both rice and soup regularly. The Chinese have those chinaware spoons for soup but eat the rest with chopsticks only.

Koreans use spoons all the time; two theories prevail about this practice. Eighty percent of Korean food consists of soups, often served in a communal pot in which everyone dips. Also Koreans love to put rice into the soup and eat the two together: impossible to eat with chopsticks. Another plausible reason lies in the habit of mixing rice with other grains making the whole rather non-sticky and therefore difficult to carry to the mouth with chopsticks because the mass lacks in adhesiveness. This is particularly true in the case of adding barley and millet which were and are wide spread customs. In fact in hard times, rice became a luxury to Koreans and they subsisted mostly on barley — no stick there!

Whatever the reason, bronze spoons and chopsticks have been unearthed from the royal tomb of King Munyong of Paekje (r. 501-523), among other places, which are very similar to those found in China making it highly likely that either Koreans copied Chinese spoons or they used imported ones. But the Chinese stopped using spoons on a regular basis and Koreans continued... Other spoons, dating from the Unified Shilla Period (668 - 932) were excavated. These show straighter handles and are not found in China. Those dating after the eighth century were absolutely unlike any Chinese ones. As a similar style is found in Japan, it is surmised that Korea exported them to that country. Members of the royal court had to use silver chopsticks and spoon because poison discolors silver, warning the user. Women of the court had a silver spoon which accompanied their personal dagger which they always carried so that it was ever available. The dagger was small with a very sharp blade just long enough to reach the heart, ready for suicide in order to avoid being raped in times of invasion.

Ancient spoons and chopsticks were made of copper, brass or silver. From the Koryo Period (932-1392), the spoons had curved handles which looked like a swallow's tail. Sometimes the handle ended in a knot. The spoon was also quite long and not very wide. It was not until the early Choson Period (1392-1910) that the spoons became flatter and wider and shaped like a lotus petal. After the middle of the Choson Period, the handles became longer and thicker and straighter and the round part became very round. As far as chopsticks are concerned, it is claimed that Korean chopsticks are the easiest and most convenient to use. Japanese chopsticks are too thin and Chinese chopsticks are hardly shaped at all. Many a foreign visitor would dispute this claim when faced with the highly slippery prospect of eating with the common metal Korean chopstick!

Even though history is not of the greatest interest, it is extraordinary to think that such mundane things as eating implements carry history, geography, art and technology all wrapped up in them. In addition, there is a tremendous amount of culture and etiquette contained in the lowly spoon. Customs concerning spoons are very strict. When setting the table each place is set with rice, soup, spoon and chopsticks. Rice comes first, then the soup followed by the spoon and then the chopsticks. (Is this in order of importance? In which case is the spoon more important than the chopsticks?) As far as table etiquette is concerned, Koreans never put the spoon down on the table until they have finished eating. When laying it to rest during the meal, the spoon is placed on the side of the rice bowl or in the soup bowl. The chopsticks can be placed on the table when the eater is occupied with other aspects of the meal but never the spoon. Also a spoon held too high up the handle foretells a marriage far from home. And anyone holding the spoon too far down the handle is simply uncouth — and might have to suffer dirty fingers.

If you really want to change your fortune, here's how. You go to a fortune teller who decides on a more lucky or more auspicious name and has it engraved on your spoon. You then proceed to only use that spoon for a long time (one year?) and the new, luckier name changes everything for you. At least that is what a friend of mine did. I'm sorry to report that, as I lost sight of the person, I don't know the outcome so let's just believe the fortune teller and expect the best of all possibilities Traditionally newly weds prepare the spoons and chopsticks (and other things) which they will use until their death. The sumptuous 100 day celebration of a baby (feted because it has lived through the many perils of early infancy) is when the child receives his first set of spoon and chopsticks.?

After breakfast is the most important part of the day because the air and minds of the monks are clear. Activities continue with the studying monks often receiving their main instruction at this time.

Midday

Chanting and offering rice, thus remembering the Buddha's custom of eating once a day, take place at 10:30 a.m. After the ceremony, the monks have lunch. They chant before and during the meal and remind themselves to take food to sustain the body, not from greed or from a desire to beautify themselves.

"Let us reflect upon the human efforts that have made this meal possible, and ask ourselves whether we deserve this offering. Let us rid ourselves of greed and regard this meal as medicine to help us to see the truth and to reach the great wisdom beyond."

Lunch is the main meal of the day for the Buddha did not eat in the evening. In China, due to climatic changes — being often much colder than India — this was changed. However, if the monks do eat, the food is taken in the spirit of medicine. (Traditionally, in Korea, as monks did not eat in the evening, they merely rubbed their grumbling bellies with a stone. Thus evening food is referred to as "medicine rock," in Korean.)

Afternoon and Evening

After lunch and a short free period, all return to their respective activities until suppertime at about 5 p.m. (depending on the season—it is earlier in the winter than in the summer). An hour or so later, the sound of the big temple bell announces chanting: "May all living things who hear this bell be relieved from suffering, develop wisdom and attain enlightenment. May we all live in peace..."

Quiet study or meditation follows. Then at about 10 p.m. the beds are rolled out and the lights switched off.

Meditation Life

Meditation is very much stressed in Korean Buddhism and many monks and nuns spend their whole life in meditation. In all Buddhist schools in all countries, meditation is considered the main means for attaining enlightenment. The year is divided into meditation seasons, winter and summer, and free seasons, spring and autumn. The winter retreat begins on the 15th of the 10th lunar month and continues until the 15th of the 1st lunar month (roughly November to February). The summer season starts on the 15th of the 4th lunar month and ends on the 15th of the 7th lunar month (roughly May to August).

About two weeks before the season begins, monks and nuns start to look for a meditation hall where they can spend the season. Once the season starts, they are not permitted to leave the monastery until it is over. To eliminate distractions, there is neither chanting, nor reading and even talking about the Buddha is discouraged. All potential obstructions to concentration are eliminated to permit the meditator to make the breakthrough to enlightenment. Many monks observe silence and others may give up reclining for a certain period. There are four meditation sessions a day: pre-dawn, morning, afternoon and evening. Silent meals are taken with the rest of the residential community.

Before a session starts, a hollowed-out bamboo rod ("chuk-bi" in Korean) is struck three times. Fifty minutes later, the chuk-bi is sounded once only before the ten minute walking meditation period. Then all sit down again to continue the sitting meditation. At the end of the session, the chuk-bi is again struck three times.

Once a year, in many temples—twice in the bigger ones—there is an intensive, one-week period. At that time, the meditators practice up to twenty hours a day and do not recline. After this, many continue the exercise and occasionally even extend it to years!

Traditionally, meditating monks have few possessions and what they have can be packed into a backpack together with their bowls for eating and robes for chanting. In the search for enlightenment, meditating monks are unattached as clouds in the sky, or as flowing mountain streams. Some remain in the same temple for three or five years, others move about. Some only meditate for a short while, others for the whole life. Once enlightenment is attained, the monk has a duty to teach others.

The Year

Each year is naturally divided into four seasons. Temple life, ever as close to nature as possible, follows the seasons and Korea's climate has a sharp distinction between the very cold, dry winter, the balmy spring and autumn and the humid, sweltering summer. Thus the summer and winter are reserved for meditation and retreat, and the spring and autumn for wandering, seeking instruction and doing service.

The ordained members of the Sangha have their own distinctive robes. Based on traditional Korean clothes, the season are well accommodated.

Clothes to Suit the Climate

Some say that each color has a meaning, at least that is what I've been told. This results in certain customs. In India the young bride-to-be is dressed in red and in Korea the young bride on her traditional honeymoon wears a crimson coat. Red is considered the color of passion. In the western world, the bride-to-be wears white, the color of purity. Buddhist monks in Sri Lanka wear saffron (yellow) because it is the color of intelligence. Originally the wandering philosophers (sadhus) of ancient India wore gherva, a reddish color derived from rubbing bricks on white cloth. This signified the five elements — earth, water, fire, air and ether — and the fact that the person had passed out of society, passed out of the established norms and duties of human life in an effort to gain wisdom and understanding.

When Buddhism passed to China in about 1st century CE, the Chinese changed the yellow, of which they are not so fond, to grey and so in Korea, ordained Buddhists (and lay people doing special practice) wear grey. The color of ashes — recalling Buddhists' customary future cremation — and all colors mixed, grey comes in many shades from light to almost black. The cloth used for the robes is in varying thicknesses and textures of fabric in order to be suitable for the rigorous extremes of the Korean climate. Traditionally the clothes were made of the cheapest and most readily available cloth. Special kinds of hand woven cotton (which were not so special way back when) suitable for the very distinct seasons of spring, autumn and winter were used and ramie or linen were considered best for the summer. As the clothes were large, many layers could be heaped on below the outer grey wear. Therefore, even though the fabrics used were of varying thicknesses, compensation for the basic lack of warmth of cotton could be acquired by heaping up layers below.

Basic monks' clothes consist of an array of garments. Based on the traditional Korean hanbok, monks' clothes are made one "ch'i" larger everywhere (a ch'i is a traditional measurement which equals the width of the base of the first finger.) The clothes consist of very baggy pants, bhaji; a short working jacket, choksam; a longer formal jacket with a flowing tie in front, dongbanga; and an overcoat, drumagi. In addition, there is the ceremonial dress. The main robe is called a changsam and as it is made of 10 meters of cloth, it is very large and flowing, reaching down to the ankles and has pleats in the skirt part. Over this is worn the Buddhist robe, a garment made of patches of brown cloth and secured to the left with a Turk's Head knot, leaving the right shoulder uncovered — a sign of respect in ancient India.

It is made of patches because it therefore has no commercial value and some say that it is an image of the paddy fields through which the Buddha spent many years wandering... Let us take a look at the clothes in more detail. There are the pants, bhaji in Korean, which are very baggy and comfortable. The fabric is gathered at the waist with a belt which is tied at the side. At the ankle, the bagginess is gathered and folded using another piece of cloth to tie it, traditionally, or elastic, these days. Then there is the working jacket, choksam. It is short, with short sleeves, large pockets in the front and it is done up with buttons or press fasteners. If you are going out of the temple, you put a coat, drumagi, on top of this. The coat is long and flowing and it is secured with a tie on the inner left and a long flowing tie on the outer right. The sleeves are long and it usually has no pockets, just two holes through which you can put your hands to adjust the inner garments! If you are receiving guests in the temple, you wear a dongbanga. This is a short jacket — longer than the working one — which has a tie in the front like the coat and deep pockets inside.

Probably the most interesting types of monks' clothes are the summer, heavily starched ramie and linen, and the wonderful padded winter fare. Korean summers are hot (35 degrees Centigrade) and humid (85%-95%). Ramie and linen are not only porous allowing the skin to breathe but when starched, the clothes stand out from the body. Everyone always wants to touch the cloth because it looks so rough and coarse, but I can assure you, there is nothing so comfortable for the climate! Unfortunately, these clothes used to be cheap but are now terribly expensive... Korean winters are cold, the temperature often going down to -10 or -20 degrees Centigrade. Although layers can and are worn under the loose clothes, this is not enough. You need a barrier against the wind and the dry cold. Originally introduced from China, cotton-wool padded clothes, nubi in Korean, are worn.

To make nubi clothes requires an enormous amount of time. However, once made, if they are well cared for, they last a long time. (While writing this, I am wearing a nubi joki, vest or waistcoat, which is at least 15 years old!) First of all the clothes are cut out and then, traditionally, straight parallel lines are ironed on with an indo, a small cast-iron, iron which is thrust into hot oak embers, wiped off on a piece of cloth and used to make the lines to be stitched through the layers to keep the cotton wool in place. This piece of cloth is placed on top of a layer of cotton wool which has been placed on top of another layer of cloth. The lines are stitched in perfectly even stitches using waxed thread. (Some people hold a candle below to catch the needle when it is pulled through so that it doesn't go into the fingers.) Before this kind of nubi, Koreans used to stitch around the edge only. Then, when the garment was dirty, it was unstitched, the cloth washed, boiled and starched and then it was all sewed up again! Needless to say, these days, not many people have time to unsew and sew up clothes all the time. Therefore nubi clothes are popular. Although the ordained Sangha's robes are rather interesting to the visitor, they are very practical and comfortable to wear. The bagginess means that they last a long time and life on the floor (continual getting up and down, sitting cross-legged) is easy. Don't ever try these clothes yourself because you may find them so convenient that you never want to take them off!?

At different times during the year, there are changes in schedule. When more manpower is required for agricultural activities, all join in. In the early spring there is a special week for lay people. During that week, the monks look after the lay people, who are doing special religious practices, and do some extra practice themselves. Bowing, reading texts, reciting sacred words and so on are all part of the way people practice Buddhism and try to improve themselves.

Later Life

Once training is completed, monks chose from different ways of life. Some monks go to university; some are called upon (especially as they get older) to do administrative jobs. Sometimes a group will decide to do a three-year long meditation retreat; sometimes monks will go abroad to teach. Often, they will change, too. A teaching monk, for example, may return to meditation for a time.

Many monks and nuns specialize in a particular activity. There are famous artists, there are professors, doctors, a dentist and so on. One of the most popular "professions" to chose is calligraphy. Because of the heavy reliance on Chinese characters and the traditional respect given to the learned and artistic, a calligrapher is a special person in Korean society. Below we have used the Confucian gentleman as our subject. Today, although there are a lot of monks who do calligraphy, there are still many laypeople as well. (In fact, if you should visit a class, you'd be surprised at the number of people who plan their life around calligraphy!) Let us take a look at:

The Four Friends: Brushes and Loyalty

What is a friend? Someone you can rely on, someone you can turn to, someone who is constant, unchanging in loyalty, whose company you enjoy. Well, every self-respecting Korean (Confucian) gentleman had four friends: his brush, his ink stick, his ink stone, and his paper: constant, loyal and a source of joy. These four things were always available in the gentleman's room and whenever he was bored, it was to their friendship that he turned. We tried to find a finer analogy between the Four Friends and the life values that they might represent which could have been handed down through the long generations of the rich cultural heritage of Korean humor, but failed. So it seems to be up to us to invent something! The brush you can imagine easily. It represents steadfastness, companionship. It accompanied that self-respecting gentleman everywhere because in those days there were no places to rush to and everyone wasn't "busy." In fact non-busyness was the order of the day. In spite of this hard adherence to doing nothing, boredom hit every now again and so, according to the National Treasure of brushes, Mr. Kwong Jin-tae, the gentleman would take up his trusty brush and paint a picture — to relieve the boredom. In order to create the art work, he needed an ink stick and an ink stone which represent constancy, loyalty, and paper, the fourth of the Four Friends, which represents enjoyment because it comes in many different forms.

It seemed a good idea to begin with the brush because it was the most constant friend. In order to learn about brushes, we turned to the maestro, Mr. Kwong Jin-tae, who is the National Living Treasure of Brushes. It was a joy to meet him. The story of his life consists of brushes and almost nothing else. He started making them when he was

14 years-old; of course I asked why. "Well," He replied, "a man visited our house and, because we were so poor and I had no other idea, I thcught it was a good choice." He learnt with his teacher for ten years and then set out on his own.

His big break came after the Korean war, when everything was destroyed: the first thing that everyone wanted and needed was a brush. "There were only 28 brush makers in Korea at the time, so we all did a roaring business!" He continued, " You have to remember that in those days the brush was everything. Starting from the carpenter who marked the place where he was going to cut the wood, brushes were central to every aspect of life. After all there were no pens and no pencils then. In the past, men didn't rush around attending power luncheons or doing international deals. They carried their brush in the sleeve of their coat (rolled up in a little rice stalk mat to keep it straight) and went around to contests, or joined friends to write poetry."

"Can you do calligraphy?" I asked Mr. Kwong. "Oh no," he replied, " I only know how to make brushes. In fact for most of my life I get up in the morning, eat something and then just make brushes until midnight." "Yes" said his wife, "We've been married for 43 years and all we've done is make brushes." Sounded like a complaint so I checked "Are you bored?" "Oh no! There's no time to be bored, we just make brushes." Her husband quickly explained, "In those days there was no TV, no radio and we didn't know what was going on in the world at all, we just made brushes."

Brushes in Korea have a sketchily known history, like many things Korean, either there were no records kept or they were destroyed. Apart from a brush found in a tomb dating back 2,000 years, little is known about brushes beyond about 500 years back. There were 200 kinds of brushes when Mr Kwong started. Brushes were not only used for marking something (carpenters) and writing, but they played an important role in cloth making and designing, and many household jobs. Nowadays, Mr. Kwong only makes calligraphy brushes.

By this time I was really curious, I hadn't expected brushes to be so interesting. "So what are brushes made of?" I finally asked. "The best brushes are made of the hair of a big male goat. The hair should be smooth, strong and straight and so the best hair is cut after snow falls of January and February. The absolute best is the hair of the white goats from Northern Cholla Province by the sea and the hair from under the legs is really fine because it has been protected. Live goats are not shorn, the hair is removed from dead animals." In addition to goat's hair, a baby's first hair makes an excellent brush — Mr. Kwong's personal favorite. Feathers can be used and sometimes small brushes can be made from squirrel tail hair. Unusual brushes are made of bamboo finely shredded with a needle (must take forever) and tightly bound pine needles.

Once you have the goat hair, it has to be treated in order to remove the natural oil in it — otherwise it won't hold the ink. The hair is laid down with layers of ash and a heavy, flat weight is placed on top in order to squeeze out the oil. This is the traditional method, nowadays they use an electrically heated iron block which squeezes the oil — with the ash — in just five minutes. Then the bristles are put together and tied with string. For the king or famous scholars, gold and silver thread was used. The end which is to be fitted into the handle is burned to make the base more solid. Mr. Kwong showed us that the properly made base cannot be squeezed. After that, the bound bristles are fitted into the handle.

Brush handles are made of almost anything: china, silver, iron, brass, horn, and bamboo. Mr. Kwong prefers bamboo but his son complains that in the shop sometimes the bamboo warps and no-one wants to buy the brush. There are no rules as to the length of the handle, it should just look and feel nice. When not in use, brushes are stored hanging on special stands made of wood. In this way they dry and don't rot.

Finally, I asked Mr. Kwong about how to judge a good brush. "It should be very soft, should look nice, be even pretty. And when you squeeze the bristles together, the tip makes a very slight curve, it isn't straight." I looked around the apartment as we were leaving. "So, how many apprentices do you have to carry on?" He bowed his head, "No-one is interested these days. They all want to go and learn driving. Brush-making is difficult, it's a craft, you can't be greedy, you can't be interested in money if you really want to do it." "And your son?" I asked brightly. "Oh, he learnt in the womb, of course," Mr. Kwong's wife said, "he knows how to make brushes." "But he never does..." Mr Kwong interjected.

Ink, Ink-stones and Constancy

Every self-respecting Confucian gentlemen had Four Friends, four constant companions to his life. These things, brush, ink stick, ink stone and paper, provided him with enjoyment as well as the constancy and loyalty you would expect of a friend. Let us now take a look at the ink and the stones that it was ground on.

Traditionally ink came in sticks, very small ones long ago. Pine wood was burnt and the soot collected. This was then mixed with pine resin, formed into rectangular sticks and dried. As it was a precious substance, it was decorated with special, auspicious Chinese characters which were engraved on the stick. Sometimes the characters were painted another color, or gold and silver was applied. Nowadays, when everything has to be in such huge quantities due to the enormous population of the world, carbon is used and it is mixed with different substances to produce rather larger sticks which are decorated in the same fashion and even, sometimes, perfumed.

Now the aforementioned gentleman had a problem if he was in a hurry to relieve his boredom. In order to have the ink to paint the picture, he had to spend a number of hours rubbing the ink stick on the fine surface of the ink stone with a little water to create the right consistency of ink for his amusement. It is just possible that his ink stone was of superior quality and had a tightly fitting cover. If so, then the ink of the last time had not dried up but if not, he had to make new ink. He had to rub the ink stick in rhythmic, circle motions on his fine ink stone, adding a drop of water every now and again until he had the ink he needed. (Machines are used today, of course.)

Usually ink stones are made of a black stone which is relatively soft to carve. Elaborately decorated on the top, they vary enormously from the smallest which can be about the size of a finger, to the biggest, about the size of a roof tile. The usual design is one in which there is an elevated area and a slope with a smaller area in which the ink can collect as you grind away. The edges are raised and the grain of the stone is very fine. Additional, non-essential tools accompanied the gentleman. A water dropper, a ceramic or porcelain closed jug which had a small hole so that the quantity of water can be regulated. (These water droppers are now collectors' items because they come in many different sizes and shapes and are often made of fine ceramic, beautifully gazed and decorated.) A useful tool is a very interesting holder made of bamboo with small, two-ended, bamboo buttons to lock the ink stick into place. The hands remain clean and even a very used, thus short, ink stick can be ground to the end. There is one more "appliance" in the ensemble: an ink pot. This is a lovely round or oval ceramic object, often exquisitely painted, with a top and bottom of the same size. Ink can be kept from drying out in it. Back to the ink stones...

Ink stones are made in various shapes and with various designs. Usually rectangular, some stones are round, oval, square, hexagonal or octagonal and occasionally they come in no particular shape or in the form of the design which has been carved on the back. The expensive variety are actually carved, the cheaper ones are made from the powder of the stone, reconstituted with a binding substance and pressed into a mold. The carvings on the lid of the ink stone are, of course, highly symbolic. Most popular are the classic ten symbols of longevity; one or more are combined to form the decoration. These are: the sun, clouds, water, rocks, tortoises, cranes, deer, pines, bamboo and pullch'o, the fungus of immortality. Other favorites come from the group known as the "four gentlemen" (noble symbols): bamboo, pine, chrysanthemums and orchids. Sometimes there is a dragon, a crane, a turtle, a phoenix, grapes, plum blossom, an elixir bottle, a persimmon, a fish, or Chinese characters. As far as the shops seen these days, tortoises seem to be the front runners in popularity for decorating an inkstone.

And so the Confucian gentleman passed his days grinding his ink stick on his ink stone, smoothing out the paper to cover with lovely strokes from his brush – and he didn't die of stress-related diseases.

Chamber Pots, Hats and Vases

You may wonder what on earth chamber pots, hats and vases could possibly have in common. In most places, nothing, it is true. But in Korea, they are (let's make it were) all made of paper, yes paper. In Korea, paper was not only essential, it was involved in every aspect of life... and still is. Traditionally in summer, the elegant Confucian gentleman sat in his wooden floored room with the windows/doors hitched up so that the air could circulate freely and create a lovely soft, cool breeze. Dressed in white, flowing, finest ramie clothes, his hair carefully knotted under his horse-hair hat, he would sit on an intricately woven mat or cushion and, drawing his lovely little wooden desk to him, he set to occupying his time with his Four Friends: his brush, ink stick, ink stone and paper. After grinding the ink stick with occasional drops of water on the ink stone, he would smooth out a piece of fine, fresh paper on his desk, carefully placing special long weights at the top and the bottom. Then, dipping his brush into the ink, he would write a few lines of poetry in energetic, emotional strokes. The Four Friends had once more proved loyal, constant and a source of enjoyment.

The paper will have been chosen from among thousands of different kinds. Korean paper is made of mulberry pulp mixed with what is called "pulp" — which is recycled paper. There is no right/best/good paper for any given thing, everything depends on your personal taste. "Some prefer smoother paper, some prefer more absorbent paper, some prefer more pliable paper; it all depends on the individual taste. Generally though, good calligraphers like very absorbent paper," said my interviewee, Chi-kwang Sunim. An ordained Buddhist in Korea for nearly 20 years, one of her constant interests has been paper. "You can't imagine the variety! When we were making paper during a special workshop recently, we chopped up grass, pine needles, flowers, almost anything to create a different texture, a different smell, a different color of paper. (Actually, I had never really thought much about paper, just used it. As the world of variety and possible uses opened up before my eyes, I became quite engrossed! I imagined rose paper, lily paper, lilac paper and so on...) Then we used only natural materials so the paper would be stronger, last longer and stay the same color, not fading or discoloring with age."

Chi-kwang went on to explain that natural bleaches really make a difference. I knew normal bleach, chlorine water, but didn't know anything about natural bleaches, and so I asked. "Oh, the stalks of different plants like rice or better still buckwheat are burnt and the pulp is boiled with the ash. This produces a really marvelous paper."

I began to wonder just how far paper could go. And then I was told. "There are paper umbrellas, raincoats, vases, boxes, floor panels, chamber pots and even shoes." (Shoes of cardboard, yes. But paper shoes?) The soles, I was soon told, are made of layers of paper stuck together with glue and the rest of the shoe is made of woven paper, the basis of many traditional household articles — all carefully varnished, or more traditionally oiled — stitched together with paper string.

Paper is cut into long strips and then rolled into long worm-like pieces. It is these that are woven. Rather naively I began to wonder about the practicality of walking in the rain in a paper raincoat with my paper umbrella in my paper shoes! "All are woven from these worm-like pieces of paper string and treated. The umbrella and shoes are varnished with lacquer and the raincoat is treated with wild sesame oil. They're very strong, you know," Chi-kwang assured me.

Cushion covers, table and floor mats, book covers, and vases are all made of woven paper. Vases are carefully lacquered on the inside to make them able to hold water. And then there is the traditional Korean floor covering — before linoleum.

Korean floors in the rooms traditionally inhabited during winter, when the temperature hovers between 0 and -20 degrees Centigrade, were heated under the floor. The floors were made of huge stones and earth under which flues conducted hot air from a fire made in the adjoining kitchen to the external chimney. The floor was covered with paper.

Large sheets of pulp-rich paper were stuck together in layers and then dipped in vats of soya bean oil. The result was a very strong, thick paper which was laid down on the floor in squares with the edges overlapping, stuck down with glue. (Of course things have changed and now fish oil is usually used.) The paper was then lacquered a number of times. These floors start life a bright yellow which mellows to a rich chestnut as time goes by. In fact, if the floor is sand-papered and lacquered again every year, the paper lasts for ever.

Long ago, clothes were made of paper and this is a new trend on the catwalk. Wedding dresses, scarves, hats and suits are all being made of paper. The best is 100% mulberry paper. The sheets are crumpled up over and over again to make the paper strong and give it a lacy look. Then the clothes are stitched and worn and even washed — though carefully.?

Whatever the activity, each member of the temple continues throughout his life to do his best to attain enlightenment. Living a simple life, being vegetarian, abstaining from cigarettes and alcohol, being celibate, and dedicating his actions to the welfare of all beings are ways in which Buddhist monks try to improve the world.

Buddhist Ceremonies

Apart from the three daily chanting periods, there are special ceremonies for other occasions. Memorial services are quite frequent. Offerings of food are placed on an altar and monks chant, accompanied by the periodic ringing of small hand bells and the rhythmic beating of the mokt'ak. Every two weeks, on the day the monks shave their heads, and wash and mend clothes; there is a ceremony and teaching delivered by a senior monk; the ceremony is open to the public. This is the time for large meetings to take place in order to discuss temple problems or changes — Buddhist temples are very democratic.

The five main Buddhist holidays are richly celebrated each year, according to the lunar calendar: the Buddha's Leaving Home (2nd month, 8th day), the Buddha's Death (2nd month, 15th day), the Buddha's Birthday, the main event of the year, (4th month, 8th day), "All Spirits' Day" (7th month, 15th day), and Enlightenment Day (12th month,

8th day). For the Buddha's Birthday, in particular, Koreans resort to a purely Korean phenomenon: the lotus lantern.

Unique to Korea: Lotus Lanterns

It's really hard to pinpoint what it is that makes a lantern so special. Faces glow in the light and there seems to be some hidden delight and gentleness in carrying a lantern. I know that this is true for Seoul, Korea, because every year there are many small local parades of lanterns to celebrate the Buddha's Birthday in May and people come in droves to see the lanterns and many more than you would expect come to carry a lantern around the neighborhood. It seems such a simple activity and yet people of all ages love it.

In Korea, lanterns are a major focus of one of the most important yearly events called Buddha's Birthday. Celebrated on the 8th day of the 4th lunar month every year, Koreans believe that that is the day the Buddha Sakyamuni was born in northeastern India. (The Buddhist year is calculated from the Buddha's death which was 2500 years ago in 1956.) The Buddha was a man who spent his life teaching anyone who was interested in trying to understand reality. He taught people how to develop from a state of ignorance into true wisdom, symbolized by lotus lanterns.

Unique to Korea, lotus lanterns consist of the symbols of the lotus flower and a candle. The lotus, a common symbol in Buddhism, represents the process of shedding ignorance (darkness, growing towards the light from the mud) to attain wisdom (light, the opening of the flower in the sunlight).

Making lanterns in the shape of lotuses renacts the aspiration of everyone for wisdom. The candle inside symbolizes the attainment of wisdom. The occurrence of these lanterns is first recorded in 551 in the Shilla Kingdom and their popularity reached a climax in the Koryo Dynasty when there were parades of up to 10,000 lanterns. King T'aejo (r. 918-943) mentions in his Ten Injunctions — a summing up of the founder of the Koryo Dynasty's political philosophy and religious belief — that "the hanging and parading of lotus lanterns is serving the Buddha." (Injunction No. 6 adapted.) As at Hallowe'en in the USA or Guy Fawkes in the UK, children used to carry the materials for the lantern-to-be from house to house collecting money, candies or food.

Lotus lanterns have to be seen to be believed. The beauty of them hanging and casting a mystic light filtered through pink, vermillion, yellow or cyclamen into the dark night is breath-taking. Maybe it is the beauty, maybe it is the spellbinding atmosphere that causes people to be unable to imagine how these lanterns are made. Lotus Lantern International Buddhist Center made the biggest lotus lantern in the world which went into the 1989 Guinness Book of World Records, and therefore they consider themselves expert in the art. Here is the process.

Traditionally, the frames were made of bamboo. The strips of bamboo were molded into hexagonal shapes and the joints secured. A long thin piece of bamboo made the handle. Nowadays, wire is used and the frames come ready made. For the petals, lightweight paper was dyed, cut into the desired size of rectangles and piled in stacks of 20 or 30 pieces. Then each stack was dampened and strapped tightly to a bottle. The string securing it to the bottle was wound round and round with a little space between each turn. A piece of wooden board with a hole the size of the circumference of the bottle (looking a little like a toilet seat) was placed over the neck of the bottle and then pressed down with enormous power forcing the string and paper to the bottom of the bottle and creating the pleats of the petals. After a couple of minutes, the string is carefully unwound and the paper cautiously removed and set aside for drying on the warm, heated floor — Korean houses and apartments have heated floors, a traditional luxury. These days the petals come ready made, too!

Once each stack of pleated, curved paper is dry, it is ready for separating and making into petals. Each piece of paper is gently held and the tip is twisted with a little paste to form a point. Now, back to the frame. Over the frame, white paper is pasted. When the frame and the petals are dry, then the lantern is ready to be assembled. Paste is applied to about two or three centimeters of the base (away from the point) of the petal and then it is stuck at the upper end of the lantern with the point just going over the edge of the frame. After that the petals are stuck all the way around in layers until the bottom of the lantern. There one to three layers of green petals are stuck, sometimes with the petals pointing downwards. Next the lantern is placed upside down to dry. When the time comes to use the lantern, a candle is placed inside and lit — this is the magic.

If you happen to visit a temple on or around Buddha's Birthday, you will be surprised to see the lanterns hanging with pieces of paper with writing on them dangling from the bottom. These pieces of paper have the names of people on them. Anyone who wants to can "buy" a lantern and write anything he or she likes on it. A donation is given to the temple. Buddhists believe that the more we give, the more generous we are, the happier we are. The money given helps the temple for its expenses as well as helping for any of the numerous welfare projects that most temples have.

There are also ceremonies for marriages, births and special birthdays.

Childless couples may have a ceremony in the hope of bearing a child;

nervous students may chant for good exam results.

Lay Life

If anyone wishes to become a Buddhist, he often decides his own course of spiritual training, taking advice from the monk or nun he chooses as his teacher. Usually he receives the five training precepts: not to kill, not to steal, not to indulge in sexual misconduct, not to lie, and not to take intoxicants. These are not vows, but conscious decisions to train in certain areas. Failure is met with sorrow and a greater determination to try harder.

Then, in order to confirm his desire to help living beings, he may later take the 48

Bodhisattva precepts. The gist of these rules is repeated at the end of every ceremony:

"May all beings be saved.

May all sufferings be ended.

May we learn all Dharma teachings.

And may we attain enlightenment.

I vow to save all beings.

I vow to end all sufferings.

I vow to learn all Dharma teachings.

I vow to attain enlightenment."

Each temple has its own program. Lay people choose any temple they like and go there as often as they like. Usually they choose a temple for its beautiful position, or because some member of the family used to go there or because they like the monks. Then they chose the program they wish to follow. There are chanting classes, text study classes, lectures, ceremonies and religious practice, bowing and reciting. There are youth groups, older people's groups, chorale groups, study groups, social work groups and groups that go on temple tours. In addition, there are possibilities for individuals to stay in a temple and do a retreat or special religious practice. The variety of activities is infinite and can be adjusted according to the wishes of the individual involved.

VISITING TEMPLES

INTRODUCTION

Everyone is welcome to freely visit a Korean Buddhist temple at almost any time. In order to make a more pleasant visit, we have put together this information for you. When you tour a temple, please enjoy the beauty of these treasuries of culture, the homes of people seeking spiritual understanding, and places where Buddhism is taught and practiced. As temples vary enormously we decided to put the information about temples into sections rather than to write a guided tour. We have used a variety of sources and tried our best to make the data accurate. Sources include the information boards in front of temples, Korean Buddhism, a compendium printed for the 1988 Olympics, and an article by Greta Diemente Sibley, Who's Who in Korean Iconography.

There is a way to make your visit more enjoyable. Although Buddhists suffer from the normal human failings, they do try to live up to the ideals of the Buddha who taught a way of life, philosophy or religion — depending on the way you look at it — based on taking total responsibility for oneself and behaving with total tolerance towards others. Thus the monks and nuns who live in the temples try to be tolerant and open-minded, living to the best of their ability. In order for harmony to prevail, there are a few restrictions.

Making a Pleasant Visit

Firstly, when you come to any shrine, please either take a quick look in from the door-way and move on or take your shoes off and go into the shrine. Don't linger in the doorway as it is considered rude. If you enter, sit down for a few moments and feel the atmosphere. If there are people inside, they will be chanting, or reciting a special word or phrase with a long string of beads, or meditating. They are there because this is their main practice place and they can come at any time they wish.

Secondly, although the temple is magnificent, it is the home of the monks or nuns who live there. Although there are no restrictions to taking pictures of the exteriors of buildings, pagodas, stone lanterns etc., sometimes there are objections to taking photos inside. Ask someone with a gesture and respect their reply. Consider how you would feel being photographed in similar circumstances... Put yourself in their shoes: would you like to be photographed at breakfast (even if you eat it in such a novel way)? So, if someone makes a gesture of "NO" (don't take that picture/go in that area), please respect it.

Thirdly, if a monk, nun or layperson should stop and put his/her hands together and bow, they are greeting you. Please return the greeting by stopping and bowing, or by making the same gesture.

THE TEMPLE COMPOUND

A Buddhist temple compound is far more than just a collection of buildings—it is a microcosm: a home to the ordained members of the Buddhist community, a shelter for people in trouble, a place for orphans and the old, as well as somewhere for students who want to do intensive studies. Built at different times under different circumstances, temples vary enormously, each one having its own special features. They do, however, follow a basic pattern.

First of all, the land is chosen according to the ancient science of geomancy which considers the shape of the mountains, position of water and the cardinal directions. Next the Main Hall is built, accompanied by special ceremonies. The other religious buildings (like shrines) follow, set out so that the visitor is carried from the mundane world of human beings, through three progressive gates, to the spiritual world of the Buddhas and Bodhisattvas. The whole arrangement, if seen from the air, forms a mandala, a cosmic pattern. Last of all the buildings necessary for the ordained members who live there are built. These include kitchens, eating areas, living places, bathing facilities and so on.

Outside the Compound

At the entrance to most temples, there is an information board which is in English at all the larger temples. It recounts the history of the temple and also alerts the visitor to associated hermitages that are beyond the main temple and, sometimes, hiking trails around that particular mountain area. It also points out special temple treasures: statues, monuments, halls. Apart from the information board, usually there are a number of free-standing, stone objects on the way to the first gate. These are monuments, including stele, pudo and pagodas.

Monuments

Monuments of various kinds are plentiful and their meaning can be guessed by their location and amount of inscription. Many lines of three Chinese characters is a listing of names of people who donated funds for building or restoration. Many characters on a stele with a turtle base will recount the history of the temple. If it is done by a famous person, there may be a separate information sign nearby, such as the one at Chikji-sa near Kimch'on by the famous philosopher-statesman, Yi Yulgok. If a stele and turtle base is near a pudo, it is a dedication to the monk whose ashes are enshrined in the pudo.

Pudo

Pudo, stone monuments to famous monks, sometimes have the sari ("jewels" or small stone-like calcified relics left after cremation — much venerated and respected by Buddhists everywhere) of the monk buried beneath them. Bulbous in shape, older or simpler ones often have small or large caps on top of them.

Pudo can be found in front, behind, or to the side of a temple complex. In Pomo-sa, in Pusan, they can easily be missed because they are so far to the side of the temple compound. In Kumsan-sa, near Kimje, they are several hundred meters beyond the compound walls. Sometimes, they are found standing alone and, it seems, forgotten in a remote area where other traces of the temple have disappeared.

The Three Gates

After passing the above mentioned objects the real tour begins. You walk along a gently winding path which leads up to the first gate which is called "One Pillar" Gate. Then you pass through the second, "Four Guardians" Gate—a two-door building. Here the four awesome protectors of the temple greet you.

Nearby is the third gate called, the "Gate of Non-duality." This gate represents the fact that, though the visitor is passing from the secular world into the spiritual world of the temple, these two worlds are not different from one another, they are not-two, non-dual. Somewhere before reaching the main entrance to the temple, the path crosses a bridge over a stream. This crossing is a symbolic purification.

Inside the Compound

Within the confines of the temple compound there are many different places to see. The buildings are varied and, like the kitchens, rather evident. However there are various other objects which will be totally new to the unaccustomed visitor. These include pagodas, stone lanterns, and often objects special to that temple.

Pagodas

These are usually monuments to great personalities and enshrine their ashes or calcified remains. Pagodas are said to have evolved from the dome-shaped stupas of India and now resemble multi-storied buildings with "roofs" on each level and often pilasters on the corners and sides. They always have an uneven number of storeys and also once had an ornate metal finial, a decoration on the top. Sadly, the iron bars on which they were secured have deteriorated and most of the pieces have been lost. (These days, there is a fashion to replace the finial with a modern replica.).

Originally pagodas were built of wood. This can easily be seen in the older ones because the brick and later the stone subsequently used was fashioned in the same manner — as if it was wood. As time went by, brick-like stone became the common building material. A fine example of this is the pagoda at the site of Punhwang-sa, in Kyongju. The oldest and largest is the partially destroyed pagoda at the Miruk-sa site on Iksan which was built in seventh century Paekje. Although most of the extant pagodas are from the Koryo Period (916-1392), there are still many dating from the Shilla period. These pagodas stand out because of the loveliness of their proportions and the lightness, almost elegance of the design. At Sonam-sa in Songju, standing by the path to the temple together with other pudo and monuments, is a most unusual sari container. On the base sit four animals holding up a little three-storey pagoda.

Stone Lanterns

These are usually found in the main courtyard (and at royal tombs). Usually stone lanterns are made of granite, beautifully decorated with different motifs. Near the top there is a square or octagonal shaped section where the oil lamp or candle was burned; the light is diffused through four openings, one in each direction. These lanterns are often lit so that the monks and nuns can see their way to the Main Hall for the 3 a.m. chanting ceremony.

Buildings

Buildings include the Bell Pavilion; the Main Hall; one building for the Disciples; one building for the Judges; a museum; a building for the portraits of great monks; and a building for the pictures of the Buddha's life. Often there are many smaller buildings which include shrines to different Buddhas and Bodhisattvas as well as local folk gods. Then there are the monks' buildings which vary in number and size depending on the number of inhabitants and needs of the temple; occasionally there is one building unique to that temple.

Just before entering the main compound, sometimes just over the main entrance, there is a pavilion-gate. The pavilion portion above may be open or may have walls, it may be neglected or used for meetings and study or as a Bell Pavilion. The lower section is open and makes a thorough-fare to the courtyard.

BUILDINGS

The Bell Pavilion

On the way to the Main Hall, you may pass an open, two-storey structure, within which were the four instruments that call all living things to hear the words of the Buddha and which regulate the timetable of temple life.

The Main Hall

There is usually little doubt about which building is the Main Hall. Location, contents and the attention it receives separate it from the other buildings. The number of statues therein depends on the wishes and wealth of the temple, so they can range from one to at least eleven as in the Taejok-kwang-jon at Kumsan-sa in Kimje. There is generally a certain system followed in the number, disposition and personalities chosen.

The Main Hall is usually called Teung-jon or Taeungbo-jon (Great Hero Hall) and so the central figure is usually Sakyamuni, the Historical Buddha (Sokamoni-bul in Korean). However, if the Main Hall carries the name of Kuknak-jon, then the image within is always Amitabha, Buddha of the Western Paradise, (Amit'a-bul in Korean). These two Buddhas are the most popular. However, as in Haein-sa, near Taegu, the main statue is Vairo-cana (Pirojana-bul in Korean), the Cosmic Buddha.

The Disciples' Hall

The Disciples' Hall is called the Nahan—jon. There statues representing specific enlightened disciples of the Buddha are to be found. The statues are usually made of wood and number between sixteen and 500 serious-looking men, often brightly dressed, seated cross-legged or on stools with hands on legs, or holding books, or gesturing, and one is always holding a resigned tiger by the hind legs with his head and fore paws dangling. Each statue represents a disciple of the Buddha who attained enlightenment and each one has an individual story. If you look carefully, you can enjoy the humor inherent in temple life!

The Judgment Hall

At the larger temples without exception you will always find the Myongbu-jon (Judgment Hall) which contains Ksitigarbha, the Bodhisattva of the Suffering (Chijang Posal in Korean) his two attendants, Modukkuiwang, a wise man and cousin of the Buddha, and Tomyong-jonja, a disciple, as well as the Ten Judges who determine one's fate after death according to the deeds performed during life. The Ten Judges may be statues, rarely portraits only, but often there is a combination with pictures depicting the punishments of wrong-doers. Around the judges are errand boys to carry writing brushes and paper; near the door are messengers; and just inside the doorway, two ferocious, ready-to-strike guards. One attendant holds a box which contains the keys to paradise. Usually, too, there will be a mirror somewhere. This is actually the instrument of Yama, the God of Death who shows us a reflection of ourselves so that we may judge ourselves, for we know what we have done.

The Museum

Most of the large temples have a museum. There, ancient and valuable objects are stored and made available to visitors at special times.

Smaller Buildings

Another building often seen is the Yong-san-jon, named for a sacred mountain in India where the Buddha delivered the Lotus Sutra. Within is found Sakyamuni Buddha with numerous nahan (Arahants: enlightened disciples of the Buddha). The total number ranges from sixteen to 500.

Portraits of special monks are in the Pyochung-won in larger temples and in the Main Hall in smaller temples.

Halls for the secondary Buddhas and Bodhisattvas are often named according to the statue that they house. Piro-jon is the small shrine housing the Vairocana Buddha, the Cosmic Buddha. The Yaksa-jon is for the Universal Healer, Yaksayorae. Miruk-jon is for the Future Buddha, Maitreya (Miruk-bul in Korean). The Kwannum-jon is important as it houses Avalokitesvara, the Bodhisattva of Compassion (Kwan-seum Posal in Korean) a source of succor for all who suffer.

The Palang-jon, another building at larger temples, honors the eight important events in the life of the Buddha with large murals. These are often very magnificent and sometimes old and celebrated, as in Haein-sa.

The Monks' Buildings [ssh]

The living quarters, guest rooms, kitchens and eating hall are usually a little off to one side of the compound. In larger temples, there is also a study hall where monks live while learning the basic texts and chants. And there is almost always a meditation hall, at least in larger temples, carefully built in the quietest corner of the temple compound. These days, because there are so many visitors, there may a cafeteria-type eating place where anyone is welcome to come and eat at the meal times.

ICONOGRAPHY

Here are some basic indications of the different characters figuring in Korean Buddhist Iconography.

Guardians

Whether they be mighty wooden statues or paintings housed in gates, or simply two figures painted on doors, the first personalities to be encountered at a Korean temple are generally the Four Guardians.

If the temple one is visiting is not particularly grandiose, it is usually the two gate gods one must pass in order to enter the temple grounds. These deities prevent evil spirits from entering the temple precincts. In China they are called Heng and Ha. They boast the power to send forth deadly Buddhas & Bodhisattvas rays of light, one from his nostrils giving forth the sound "heng," the other from his mouth with the sound "ha." The mouth is the door of the face, and, symbolically, Ha's open mouth indicates that the temple is protected whether the doors are opened or closed. The two gods protect on another level as well, that of wisdom over ignorance.

In the larger Korean temples, one is likely to find, in addition to the two gate gods painted on the doors, the Four Guardians housed in their own gate structure. In statue or painted form, these figures are imposing, often as much as five meters tall.

These protectors are of Hindu origin, and are said to have helped Siddhartha Gautama, the Indian prince who became the Buddha, to leave his father's house on the night of his renunciation by each taking hold of one hoof of Siddhartha's horse and lifting him over the palace walls. In another legend, Siddhartha (now the Buddha Sakyamuni, the Silent One of the Sakya Clan) was setting out on his alms round. The guardians all rushed to present him with bowls made of precious stones. The Buddha refused them. The guardians then offered him bowls of ordinary stone. Accepting them as more suitable to his position, Sakyamuni piled the four one atop another, and miraculously, they became one vessel. The guardians served Siddhartha throughout his earthly life.

The Four Guardians all bear a fierce countenance and trample the opponents of Buddhism under their feet. Each of them represents one of the cardinal directions.

The guardian of the North, Tamun Chonwang, holds a pagoda, or tower. The tower represents a reliquary stupa, symbolizing death. The stupa consists of three basic parts: the base, which represents the earth, the dome, which represents heaven, and a connecting piece, or cosmic axis.

Chonjang Chonwang is the guardian of the southern quarter. One may identify him by the sword he bears, usually poised for action. He is reputed to have the power to multiply his sword so that he can always outnumber his opponents.

Chigook Chonwang guards the East. He is easily spotted by the lute he holds, the strings of which control wind, thunder, hail and other weather phenomena.

The guardian of the West, Kwangmok Chon-wang, holds a dragon in one hand and a jewel in the other. The original meaning of these symbols seems to be lost in time.

The Four Guardians should be looked for in the corners of temple murals where variations may be observed between Koryo and Choson style painting, for even within the history of Korean Buddhism the objects which the guardians hold have changed.

(Which guardian governs which quarter of the world is often disputed.)

Regardless of iconographic variations, one may identify the guardians by their ever-present battle dress and imposing facial expressions. Their variety in appearance only serves to provoke thought and make us more aware of their function. They forever remain routers of evil demons and protectors of Buddhism and the Buddha's teachings.

Buddhas & Bodhisattvas

Most of the other statues which one sees in the temples are either Buddhas, enlightened beings, or Bodhisattvas who are beings who have given themselves to helping others. Most of the Bodhisattvas represent one particular aspect of either wisdom or compassion while the Buddhas are the embodiment of perfect wisdom and perfect compassion.

BUDDHAS

Sakyamuni (Sokamoni-bul, in Korean)

The Buddha Sakyamuni is the main statue in most temples. He is the historical Buddha, the Sambhogakaya. He was born as a prince called Siddhartha Gautama in northeastern India in the fifth century BCE.Frequently, pictures of various episodes from his life will be found on the exterior of the Main Hall. Sometimes these pictures are housed separately, sometimes they are found in the back of the Main Hall (Haeinsa). One may follow Siddhartha through the process which brought him to enlightenment. Often pictured are: his mother, Queen Maya, having the auspicious dream of a white elephant; his birth in the Lumbini Garden; his childhood bath in the fire of nine dragons; his meditation in the Himalayas; his struggle with desires; his enlightenment under the Bodhi Tree; scenes of him teaching, and his death.

The mudra, hand position, of "calling the earth to witness" which is most often associated with the Buddha Sakyamuni, recalls a story about the Buddha (it is found in the Sokkuram statue in Kyongju). Just after his enlightenment, he was challenged as to his right to sit on the small piece of ground that he was occupying. He called the earth to witness his many good deeds of past lives and so justified his seat in that place. The figure is of a seated Buddha, the right hand hanging over the knee, palm inward, sometimes pointing with one finger, usually with the whole hand, towards the earth.

Vairocana Buddha (Pirojana-bul, in Korean)

Vairocana is the Cosmic Buddha who spreads the light of Buddhist Truth in every direction, the Buddha who embodies the Wisdom of Universal Law. He is the center, Buddha Incarnate, the Original Teacher, the Dharmakaya. Vairocana is the embodiment of Truth and Knowledge. As is the case with all Buddhas and Bodhisattvas, Vairocana is not exclusive of other Buddhas but represents a particular aspect of Buddhahood: in this case, the aspect of Cosmic Energy.

Vairocana is usually depicted with his hands in one of several positions. A common example is the mudra of the "knowledge fist." This mudra is made up of the right hand "diamond fist" and the left hand "diamond finger." The "diamond fist" is formed by making a tight fist with the thumb at the center. The "diamond finger" is the left index which is inserted into the right fist. The mudra of the "knowledge fist" dispels darkness. One of Vairocana's names is Diamond Buddha. The diamond represents the supreme strength and durability of Buddhist knowledge. The left index finger represents the world of sentient beings, the surrounding right hand, the protection of the world of Buddhas. Generally the left hand refers to the passive pole and the right hand to the active pole. The left represents the physical plane and the right the metaphysical. This mudra is a divine representation of the passions, and a comment on the intensity with which one aspiring to wisdom pursues the goal. The mudra represents the union of the sexes with Vairocana as the procreator.

Other mudras of Vairocana are variations on the joining of the hands, palm to palm, fingers crossed over one another and thumbs erect, or the right hand encompassing the left hand which has been closed in on itself. These mudra also represent the universal knowledge of the Buddha.

Vairocana is sometimes enshrined in his own building called the Great Light Hall. He is usually unattended when in his own shrine. In other halls, he is the central figure of a trinity. He is often attended by Manjusri and Samantabhadra.

Amitabha Buddha (Amit'a-bul in Korean)

Amitabha Buddha emanates from the meditation of the primordial Buddha; he is the Nirmanakaya. He is the Buddha of Infinite Light and governs the Pure land, the Western Paradise. In India, where Buddhism began, people felt relief from the extreme heat of the day when the sun reached the western sky. Thus, Amitabha's paradise came to be associated with the west.

Appropriately, he sometimes wears the color red.

Amitabha has vowed to save all beings who call on him. He assists them by admitting them to his Pure Land where they will know no hindrances to achieving enlightenment. The Pure Land is no different from the Pure Mind, the state in which one is free from illusion.

Sometimes it is almost impossible to know if one is looking at a figure of Amitabha or Sakyamuni because their faces are so similar and their symbolic hand gestures are often the same. Each is generally depicted as the central figure of a triad. When trying to discriminate between the two, it is helpful to identify the images which flank the central figure. For example, if the side figures are Avalokitesvara and Mahastamprapta (Taesaeji Posal, in Korean) the Bodhisattva of Power, the central Buddha is Amitabha. If there is a separate building for this triad, then it is called the Temple of Supreme

Bliss. Amitabha often holds his left hand in the "fulfilling the vow" pose, the palm turned outward in a gesture of offering. This pose is found most commonly in standing figures. When he is seated, the left palm is often simply held face upward in the lap. The right hand is raised, a gesture of fearlessness. Three forms of this right hand gesture are: the thumb touching the index, middle, or ring finger.

The thumb and index finger form a circle which represents the perfection of wisdom.

Bhaisagya Buddha (Yaksayorae-bul, in Korean)

Bhaisagya Buddha is the Universal Healer or Medicine Buddha. He provides relief not only from disease and misfortune, but also from ignorance, which is the greatest ill to Buddhists.

Usually Bodhisattvas, not Buddhas, hold attribute objects. The alms bowl and the medicine bowl (which evolved as a symbol from the alms bowl) are the only exceptions. Sakyamuni and Amitabha hold the alms bowl, or sometimes hold their hands in a mudra suggestive of holding the vessel, and Bhaisagya Buddha holds the medicine bowl.

The alms bowl is one of the very few personal possessions of Buddhist monks. It represents the sincere offerings of believers and the humility of monks.

Images of Bhaisagya Buddha closely resemble those of Amitabha except that the latter is usually golden, while the former is almost always white. Though Bhaisagya Buddha usually holds the medicine bowl in both hands, he sometimes holds it in only one hand, the left. In this case, the right hand assumes the pose of the "absence of fear" which, although certainly appropriate to his role as a healer, is usually associated with Amitabha.

Maitreya Buddha is the Future Buddha. He lives in the Tusita Heaven where he waits until his time to be born on this earth arrives. He is the embodiment of love and compassion.

Paintings of Maitreya are virtually nonexistent, but statues of him are still extant. They were particularly popular during the days of the Three Kingdoms (before 668 CE) and devotees carried miniatures of this Buddha in their pockets.

The Korean form of Maitreya is very special and unusual. Most people know the jolly, fat, laughing Buddha of Chinese iconography. He is the Chinese Maitreya, promising plenty in the future. The Korean counterpart is thin and easily identified when in the "posture of reflection." He sits with his right elbow resting on his right knee. His right foot or ankle is on his left knee. The left hand rests on the right ankle or foot. His head is slightly inclined, suggesting contemplation. The index and middle fingers of his right hand are slightly inflected and just touch the face. (The statue in the National Museum is hauntingly beautiful and well worth a visit.)

Many large statues in Korea are called Miruk-bul, Maitreya Buddha, but there is speculation about their true identity.

BODHISATTVAS

Avalokitesvara (Kwanseum Posal, in Korean)

Avalokitesvara is the Bodhisattva of Compassion. Although in India, Avalokitesvara is clearly male, she is most often depicted as neither male nor female or female by today's artists. A bit of mustache is visible in some contemporary paintings, but these works are generally of an old style. In her Buddhist context, Avalokitesvara's sex is irrelevant, the idea is an artistic impression of the idea of perfect compassion.

Born from a ray of light emanating from Amitabha's right eye, Avalokitesvara is thus closely related to Amitabha and so assists those who request access to the Pure Land. The name means "Hearer of Cries," and she is often pictured with her head slightly inclined as if listening to the pleas of the suffering. She is frequently pictured with a vase and willow spray. The vase contains amrita, the nectar of her compassion, or the waters of life. The willow branch represents her ability and willingness to liberally sprinkle "sweet dew" on the afflicted. The willow, which has long been considered to have medicinal value, also symbolizes her role as a healer. She is often shown near water, suggesting her paradise, Potala. In paintings she wears white clothing and, like other Bodhisattvas, is sometimes adorned with jewelry, including a crown.

Avalokitesvara also assumes a thousand-eyed/ thousand-armed form. Each hand bears an eye so that the Bodhisattva can see how to help those in distress.

Her eleven-headed and nine-headed forms (the most famous one is behind the Sokkuram statue in Kyongju) often accompany her multi-limbed depictions and remind us of her all-accepting and all-inclusive nature. In her eleven-headed form the left three heads bear an angry countenance; the right three, a serene smile; the three at the back, an expression of compassion; the front and largest face exudes serene equilibrium; and the eleventh face, at the very back, is laughing: a testimony to her wisdom.

Situated at the apex of a multi-headed Avalokitesvara, is a head or miniature Buddha representing the Bodhisattva as an emanation of the wisdom of Amitabha.

Ksitigarbha (Chijang Posal, in Korean)

Almost without exception, Korean temple compounds include a special shrine to Ksitigarbha. An interesting and colorful building containing pictures of the Buddhist hells and heavens, it is also the place where photos or memorial tablets of recently deceased persons are installed and where services for the benefit of the dead are conducted.

The central figure is Ksitigarbha, the Bodhisattva who helps the suffering of the nether world. This Bodhisattva is greatly loved by Mahayanists for his commitment to remain until no more people suffer in hell. Ksitigarbha is usually bald, or has closely-cropped hair (the surest clue to his identity when he is present in a painting of many figures) and holds in one hand a staff or a sistrum, and in the other, a jewel. This is the "wish-fulfilling gem," a magical jewel which grants all selfless requests. Ksitigarbha is usually flanked by one of two sets of figures: two guardians of the Underworld, Dokmyang Jonja and Mudok Kweiwang, or Yama and Ksitigarbha's mother from his former earthly existence — he offered to take her to the lowest hell.

On each side of Ksitigarbha stand five imposing figures. These are the Ten Judges. The judges are usually in statue form, either standing or seated. Some more elaborate halls contain, interspersed among and in addition to the Ten Judges, many smaller statues of celestial deities and servants to the judges.

The judge who receives the most attention is Yama (Yama Daewang, in Korean). He is considered to be the most powerful of the ten and sometimes he occupies a prestigious position beside Ksitigarbha. Yama, a deity borrowed from Hinduism, is the Lord of Death. Various Hindu texts describe him as splendid, others as ugly and deformed. Always depicted with a mirror ready to show us our own reflection when the time comes, the feeling evoked by Yama is one of dread.

Behind each of the judges is a painting of the territory each governs. The ten territories (six belonging to common people and four to Bodhisattvas) are not only to be thought of as places the deceased must traverse, but should be considered allegorically, as either levels of existence or stages in an individual's immediate life — for we all create our own hells.

TRIADS

Buddhist triads are composed as follows: three Buddhas, three Bodhisattvas, one Buddha and two Bodhisattvas, one Buddha and two historical personages (usually enlightened ones), or one Bodhisattva and two historical or mythical personages. In addition to specific attributes, emblems, and mudra, there are some simple ways of discriminating generally between Buddhas and Bodhisattvas.

Bodhisattvas are sometimes adorned with jewelry and crowns while Buddhas generally are not. Though there are certain celestial trinities of three Buddhas,(often the Past, Present and Future Buddhas) one can often identify Bodhisattvas by their secondary position in a trinity, relative to the main image.

Buddhas bear the "thirty-two marks," some of which are easily spotted, for example: the tightly knotted black hair; the protuberance on the head; the white, curled hair at the center of the forehead; the long earlobes (without earrings); and three rings, or creases, around the neck. Certain basic configurations are apparent in the composition of triads of images. One combination is Amitabha attended by Avalokitesvara and Mahastamprapta, the Bodhisattva of Power. The two Bodhisattvas are emanations of Amitabha.

Sakyamuni is usually flanked by his two favorite disciples, the young Ananda (representing the intellect) and the aged Kasyapa (representing experience and wisdom) or by Samantabhadra and Manjusri. When alone, Samantabhadra is seen seated on an elephant, Manjusri on a lion. Manjusri is the Bodhisattva of Wisdom (knowledge of the true, non-dualistic identity of the world). Samantabhadra is the Bodhisattva of Power and Compassion. Wisdom is identified with the intellect and with unification or non-duality, while compassion is emotion and multiplicity. Manjusri often holds a sword with which he severs earthly attachments, revealing wisdom. Holding a trident, he spreads Buddha's teaching through thought, speech, and action.

Manjusri and Samantabhadra are frequent attendants of Vairocana Buddha as well. In this case, the three make up a metaphysical triad as opposed to the historical triad of Sakyamuni, Ananda and Kasyapa.

Vairocana is sometimes depicted with Sakyamuni and Bhaisagya Buddha, composing the Trinity of the Preciousness of the Teachings.

Guardian Painting (Shinjung Taengwha, in Korean)

The Shinjung Taengwha, a painting featuring Tongjin Posal, is commonly found in Korean temples. Its frequent presence, however, in no way seems to make its meaning well-known. The only point on which most people agree, Buddhists included, is that they don't know much about the Shinjung Taengwha.

There are twelve to twenty figures depicted in the Shinjung Taengwha. The central image is of Tongjin Posal, who is easily identified by his elaborate headdress which resembles a fan of feathers. One of a number of beings who guard the doctrine, Tongjin Posal is the Bodhisattva who protects the Saddharma pundarika, the Lotus Sutra of the True Law, one of the most revered Mahayana texts which explains that the truth is conveyed by silence and gestures as well as words.

There are different interpretations of the Shinjung Taengwha. One is that the figures surrounding Tongjin represent beings who are well-acquainted with the Three Refuges: the Buddha, his teaching (Dharma), and the Buddhist community (Sangha). Another is that the figures are historical personages such as Confucius, or lesser deities like the Kitchen God. The four, or sometimes five, figures at the base of the painting or to the sides of Tongjin Posal, are clearly guardians. One guardian often carries a rolled-up scroll, representing the doctrine which he protects.

Depending on the size of the temple, and consequently on the number of halls or shrines therein, the Shinjung Taengwha is found in any one of many buildings, but most often on the right wall of the Main Hall.

It is interesting to note that, as the gods are beings in the realm of pleasure, they cannot attain enlightenment. Therefore the monks and nuns turn to the Taenghwa when they chant the Heart Sutra in order to help the gods attain a human birth in their next life and so reach enlightenment. In addition, as humans need help from the gods, often people will bow towards the Taenghwa as a gesture of respect and humility in the understanding of the fact that it is difficult to reach attainment alone.

The Mountain God (Sanshin, in Korean)

Every Korean temple has a place for Sanshin, the Mountain God, whether it be a painting and small altar set up in one of the larger halls, or, as is most often the case, a small separate building off in one corner of the compound. Sanshin is not depicted in statue form, but instead is always painted.

As belief in mountain spirits preceded Buddhism's entry into Korea, Sanshin is not of Buddhist origin but was absorbed into Buddhism. Little by little it came to be suggested that Sanshin had been a Bodhisattva all along. Sanshin is particularly popular among women hoping for sons. However, visitors to most temples pay their respects to Sanshin.

The paintings of the Mountain God all follow the same basic pattern. Pictured is an old man seated with, or sometimes on, a tiger. Because tigers were a constant threat in mountainous areas, their ferocity came to be associated with powerful spirits. The Mountain God is not exclusively the old man or the tiger, rather he is both. Perhaps the tiger's presence also suggests the close relationship in geomancy between mountains and tigers. Commonly the old man and tiger are pictured in a deep valley with a stone cliff on the right.

The Recluse (Toksong-in, in Korean)

Toksong-in is commonly known as the Recluse. Toksong-in is not an historical personage or a paradigm of isolation. He represents in the Mahayana tradition of Buddhism what the arhant represents in the Theravada. The arhant is a holy person, perfect being, a disciple of the Buddha Sakyamuni. Toksong-in is a timeless being, a reminder that one should not seek enlightenment outside of oneself, for, "alone and holy," he is enlightened within.

Mahayanists are wary of the illusion of the ego appropriating external self-definitions. Toksong-in urges us to seek the Buddha within, to realize that everything is inside of us and not external to us. Demonstrating Chinese iconographic and cultural influence, a young manservant is sometimes present holding tea, a platter of fruit, or a fan.

The Big Dipper (Chilsong, in Korean)

Chilsong, the Big Dipper, has roots in Taoism and Shamanism. The Great Bear Constellation, which is Chilsong, is visible year round, partly accounting for the great reverence with which he is regarded. Chilsong is thought to control both good and bad fortune. He is particularly popular among women hoping for children.

On the left hand side of the Main Hall or the Judgement Hall, a large painting of Chilsong is sometimes hung. The painting is colorful and impressive. It contains many figures and festive scenes. Presumably, when Buddhism came to Korea, people assumed that they were a manifestation of the compassionate Buddha. Seven Buddhas, one for each star, run in a row along the top of the painting. The seven stars pictured as Buddhas demonstrate the incorporation of originally Shaman concepts into Korean Buddhism.

Some large Korean temples have an entire shrine dedicated to Chilsong. In this case Chilsong is depicted economically in one statue. Like Bhaisagya Buddha, he holds a medicine cup in his left palm which rests on his left knee. In his other hand he sometimes holds a lotus flower. In addition to the statue, he is further depicted in seven paintings, one of each star deity, which are found on the walls of the shrine. In keeping with Chilsong's celestial nature, to the left and right, respectively, of the central Chilsong, are figures of Ilgwang and Wolgwang. Ilgwang's crown has at its center a red sun, Wolgwang's, a white moon. Both hold lotuses.

The Oxherding Pictures

On the outer walls of the Main Hall, along with the paintings depicting the life of the Buddha Sakyamuni and other pictures, there are often the ten Oxherding Pictures (called Shim-oo-do in Korean). Coming from the Sung Dynasty (1126-1279) in China, they were conceived by Buddhist masters as a teaching device. The pictures represent the training of the mind by the metaphor of tethering an ox; the herder is you, the ox is your mind.

The progressive whitening of the ox indicates the gradual awakening of the oxherd to his true nature; it is a process of purification. The original series ended with an empty circle, for it was inherently understood that the ox herder carried on with life as usual, now an enlightened life. In an effort to dispel the frequent misunderstanding of Buddhism's "enlightenment" as mere emptiness, the series was expanded to include the oxherd's return to the world.

i) Searching for the Ox illustrates the separation of the herder and the ox, and the former's seeming violation of his true nature. The oxherd is dissatisfied with his environment, he is subject to passions, and desire for possessing a satisfactory self-definition and fear of losing that identity have him in a vulnerable position and a painful predicament.

ii) Seeing the Footprints illustrates the awareness gained by the oxherd that there is the possibility of transcending his pain. He has a preliminary understanding of the origin of his pain. Though he is unable to see the ox, the ox's presence is known.

iii) Perceiving the Ox illustrates the oxherd's realization that nothing exists outside of himself, and, therefore, that "himself" as an individual entity is non-existent. He is comforted by the loss of objective perception. The herder is free from the need to defend his objective self-definition.

iv) Catching the Ox illustrates the struggle which is the result of incompletely transcending aggression. The oxherd has laid hands on the ox, but has not developed the energy to keep it under his control. He knows his ego to be untrue, but the ego (attempting objectification of the self) struggles to control the herder.

v) Taming the Ox illustrates the oxherd's determined and concentrated efforts to attain wisdom despite his still prevalent vulnerability to confusion, for the ox and herder are not yet one. The herder must keep his whip ready to prevent the ox from wandering, just as the student of Zen must discipline himself to prevent his mind from wandering.

vi) The properly tended ox is pacified. When the fuel of the passions is burned up, the fire is forgotten. The oxherd is pictured Riding the Ox Home. The oxherd's concentration is not subject to the calls of the world. His mind may no longer be deceived, but instead has begun to engage in truly creative activity. He may not be led astray. With a joyful heart, he meanders home.

vii) The Ox Transcended/The Oxherd Alone illustrates that the ox was never real. Not only has the ego no chance of gaining control, but there is no longer even a notion of an individual mind to be deluded by the ego. The light of wisdom shines. The oxherd is no longer born, and no longer dies, the phenomena that previously caused so much pain. He is unborn.

viii) The Ox and Herder Transcended, illustrated by the empty circle, shows only the slightest remaining distance, which is yet an infinite separation, between mind and self. With the non-existence of dualism, Buddhism cannot be exclusive or inclusive. At this point, it is not a path to be followed, but a truth to be lived. The oxherd no longer follows, but knows the immediacy of wisdom.

ix) Reaching the Origin, one is not enriched by anything external. It is apparent that one was never in fact enriched, but was eternally pure and compassionate. There is only a "source" or "origin" in the sense of eternally present, inexhaustible, serenity.

x) In the World, the awakened, enlightened being follows no example. He is what he knows to be true and projects his Buddha-nature to those who need his care.

Eight Scenes of the Life of the Buddha

Paintings of the eight scenes of the life of Buddha can be found in the Palsongjon, the Eight Pictures Hall, or on the outside walls of the Main Hall of Buddhist Temples. When inside, they are skillfully artistic and colorful as well as quite complex. In addition to the specific episodes, associated ones are shown and the background of the scene is elaborated. When on the outside walls, they are of simple design in a more naive style.

In either case, there are eight clues by which each can be identified: (1) elephant; (2) baby; (3) sick or dead man; (4) white horse over a wall; (5) starved figure; (6) tempters; (7) halo; (8) bier.

i) ***(Elephant)—Announcement of the imminent birth***

A white elephant is a sacred, auspicious symbol in India, where the Buddha was born, and is depicted as the vehicle that brought to earth the Buddha-to-be. Between the right ribs he entered Maya's womb.

In more detailed indoor paintings, the background is of the palace in which he was born with many people in the rooms and gardens. A whole host of heavenly beings surround the elephant and the Buddha-to-be in a cloud that trails to earth above Maya's head.

ii) (Baby)—The birth

The well-developed babe emerged from the right side of a fully clothed mother and began walking immediately after birth. He was born into a royal family and bore the title of Prince. He was named Siddhartha; Gautama was his family name. Seven days after his birth his mother died. At sixteen he married and had a son. His life in the palace was one of comfort and luxury.

In compound pictures there are nine dragons washing the baby with many earthly attendants.

iii) (Sick/dead man)—The world outside the palace

Eventually Siddhartha began to see, outside the sanctuary of the palace, sickness, old age and death. Then he saw a recluse and realized that the only way to overcome sickness, old age and death was to leave home and attain enlightenment. Siddhartha decided to leave his family and home for solitude and meditation.

In the simple pictures one emaciated body tells the story. In the complex ones, life goes on as usual in the palace, but outside the walls in the lower right can be seen illness and in the lower left, death.

iv) **(White horse over wall)—Renunciation**

His father, learning of Siddhartha's intentions to leave the palace, placed extra guards by the gates and others to watch over his son at all times.

But Siddhartha, with the aid of the four guardians and other spirits, was able to escape over the wall on his favorite white horse.

A white horse taking to the air, with his master astride it and the groom hanging on to the tail, represents renunciation.

v) (Starved figure)—Asceticism

For six years he studied and meditated. As was the custom in those days, he punished and disciplined the body until he was nearly dead. Finally realizing that this was not the right way, he began to live moderately and to maintain a healthy body in order to practice in his quest for understanding and enlightenment.

vi) (Tempters)—Temptations

The demon Mara sought to break the spirit of the meditating man and sent various lures away from the path Siddhartha had chosen. First he sent worldly pleasures. When these failed, he sent his army-cum-monsters but the power of the nearly enlightened Buddha was able to stop them and turn their weapons into lotus blossoms. Evil, in the guise of Mara and his tricks, was defeated and righteousness prevailed.

The three voluptuous women trying to seduce him leave no doubt that this is the temptation scene!

*vii) **(Halo)—Enlightenment***

After overcoming temptation, enlightenment is complete. Siddhartha had become the historical Buddha, Sakyamuni. For forty-five years, he wandered and taught anyone who was interested in his understanding of reality.

In addition to the halo there are disciples at his feet, but in the complex pictures this scene is subordinated by a confusing array of celestial and worldly beings and structures.

*viii) **(Bier)—Death***

At the age of eighty the Buddha died. His disciples and many animals gathered around the bier to mourn his passing.

In elaborate paintings, there is a colorful shower of relics from the burning casket. Around the body are crowds of both heavenly and earthly mourners.

CONCLUSION

Please don't fall into the trap of thinking that all temples are the same; they are not. Each one has distinctive characteristics and a different story. Having visited a few and worked out the basic structure, you can start to concentrate on the individuality and appreciate the finer points of each setting, each building, and each painting or statue. But don't be in a hurry, there are over 2,000 temples in Korea, not to mention innumerable hermitages!

THE MAIN TEMPLES OF THE KOREAN BUDDHIST CHOGYE ORDER

Korea has many large temples. Here is some basic information about the main ones. First we will consider three special temples which represent the Three Jewels of Buddhism. These are: T'ongdo-sa Temple, representing the Buddha; Haein-sa Temple, representing the teaching; and Songgwang-sa Temple representing the Buddhist community. Then we will cover other major temples of interest and finish up with a few temples in Seoul which, though often not as grand as those in the mountains are, nonetheless, well worth visiting.

THE TEMPLE WITHOUT A BUDDHA STATUE: T'ONGDO-SA

THE THREE JEWELS TEMPLES

The Temple Without a Buddha Statue: T'ongdo-sa [sh]

T'ongdo-sa, "Pass into Enlightenment," Temple is the first of the "Three Jewels" temples of Korea representing the Buddha. It is traditionally a Zen Temple and as far as the number of buildings is concerned, 65, it is the largest temple in Korea.

T'ongdo-sa Temple, once a center of Korean Buddhism, was built in 646, in the reign of Queen Sondok by Master Chajang on his return from China. One of Korea's greatest monks, Master Chajang, brought relics of the Buddha with him and these he enshrined at T'ongdo-sa Temple.

Master Chajang, coming from a royal family, could have advanced well in the court; instead he chose to be a monk. The king, appreciating his abilities, continued to request him to accept a court position which he refused. In exasperation, the king threatened the monk with the death penalty if he refused again. Master Chajang calmly replied, "I would rather die keeping the laws of the Buddha for one day than live for one hundred years breaking them." Seeing the wisdom of this reply, the king permitted Master Chajang to continue his monk's life.

Master Chajang went to China with ten other monks in 636. There he received relics of the Buddha from Manjusri Bodhisattva and then returned to Shilla with different sets of texts. He built a small hermitage on Yongjuk-san Mountain and from there oversaw the building of T'ongdo-sa.

Before entering the temple compound, the visitor has to pass over the "windless" bridge which leads into a forest of "windless" pines. Most temples have a bridge — often over a wonderful rushing torrent — before the gates to the compound. This is a symbolic purification of the individual as he or she passes from the secular world into the spiritual world.

The Main Hall at T'ongdo-sa Temple, (National Treasure No. 144), was reconstructed in 1601 in the reign of King Sonjo; the previous one had been destroyed in the Hideyoshi Invasion. It is one of the only ancient buildings (with the Great Hall of Light) in the temple compound. The Main Hall is unique in that it has no statue, only a window looking out to a stupa. The ceiling of the hall is especially marvelous as it is covered with a beautifully executed pattern of chrysanthemums.

Behind the Main Hall are the Diamond Stairs which lead up to a platform. On the platform is a bell-shaped stupa or pagoda, surrounded by a stone barrier. The gate to enter into this little enclosure is very finely decorated with dragons, clouds and two protector guardians which have been hewn out of the granite doors. At the four corners of the platform there are protective deities. This bell-shaped stupa is perfectly proportioned. The base and upper part are decorated with lotus patterns, lotus blossoms, lotus petals, the Four Virtues and gods; it is believed to enshrine the relics of the Buddha which Master Chajang brought from China and is therefore the focal point of the temple. As the stupa contains relics of the Buddha, it represents the Buddha and so there is no need for a statue in the Main Hall as well.

Pagodas developed from stupas, the symbol used to represent the presence of the Buddha after his death because they enshrined his remains. After the Buddha was cremated, his remains were divided up between the eight different clans who had been his followers during his lifetime and each clan built a stupa. These cupola-shaped structures, being symbols of the Buddha, then continued to be constructed in the grounds of every new temple which came into being and their shape evolved as Buddhism was accepted in other cultures. As time went by, they were used to enshrine the remains of great monks as well. In China, the stupa evolved into a pagoda which also took on different forms. Today you can see pudo, bell-shaped pagodas, many-storied pagodas and simple, few storied pagodas all varying in shape, design and decoration depending on the period in which they were made, the amount of money offered by the donor and the skill of the craftsman.

There are many buildings at T'ongdo-sa. Of special interest are: the museum which contains many precious ancient objects; the memorial shrine to Chajang built in 1727 containing a portrait of the master; and the Great Hall of Light. This last is a hall dedicated to Vairocana Buddha and was constructed 600 years ago; it is reputed to be the oldest in Korea. The statue and decorations are magnificent.

Of note is the lovely Nine Dragons Pond. Originally it was very large and nine dragons lived in it. However, after some time it was reduced in size and now the monks who live in the temple believe there is only one dragon (referred to as a snake) which never comes out...

There are many small hermitages in the valleys behind the temple.

THE TEMPLE OF THE TEACHING: HAEIN-SA

Haein-sa Temple is the second of the Three Jewels Temples, representing the Teaching. "Haein" means "reflection on a smooth sea." It is the description of a state of meditation (samadhi) taken from the Avatamsaka Sutra. In this sutra, Haein Samadhi is a stage in which an enlightened person sees everything as it is: a world in which all dualities cease. Such a world has a surface like that of a calm sea. This total tranquility, unperturbed by the vicissitudes of life, is the stage of the Buddhas and it is also our True Nature.

At first a hermitage, the temple was built by Master Sunung and Master Ichong on their return from studying in China in 802 under directions from a grateful king.

The queen of King Aejang (r. 800-809) became ill with a tumor. The king asked Master Sunung and Master Ichong to help her. They tied one end of a piece of string to the tumor, the other to a tree and chanted special verses. Miraculously, as the tumor withered, the tree died. Out of gratitude for the monks' services, the king built Haein-sa Temple. Later the temple was greatly enlarged.

There are many stories associated with Haein-sa. One of these stories happened during the Korean War. At that time, many guerrillas hid in Haein-sa and so the order was given for the temple to be bombed. The pilot flew over the buildings, trying to judge where best to drop his bomb. As he gazed down at the beautiful pattern created by the juxtaposition of the magnificent halls, he could not bring himself to destroy such a lovely place. He was court-marshaled and imprisoned. After the war, however, he became a national hero.

After passing through the three gates, there is a large courtyard. On the left is a new building, built for teaching and sheltering some of the many people who come to ceremonies and festivals. On the right is the large Bell Pavilion.

Continuing on up the next flight of stairs, you arrive in a courtyard in front of the Main Hall. The Main Hall was constructed in 1818 on the foundations of the one built by Master Sunung and Master Ichong. Inside, there are seven statues, from the left they are: 1) an iron Avalokitesvara, 2) a wooden Manjusri, 3) a wooden Vairocana which was formerly the principal statue before the present main statue was installed, 4) Vairocana, the principal statue made in 1769, 5) a wooden Ksitigarbha, 6) a wooden Samantabhadra, and 7) an iron Popgi Bodhisattva (an unusual Bodhisattva known as "Born of Truth" in English). The wooden Vairocana, the Manjusri and the Samantabhadra statues were all carved from a big ginkgo tree during the Koryo Dynasty. There are many paintings in the hall. Ich'adon with the white blood spurting out of his neck, Wonhyo and Uisang as well as other great masters are to be seen. The elaborate carvings are typical of the Choson Dynasty.

Another special feature is the paintings of the Buddha's life. These are found behind the main statues, to the left, and are highly detailed and rather unusual.

Behind the main shrine, up a steep flight of granite stairs, are two long buildings, National Treasure No. 52, which house the wood blocks of the Tripitaka Koreana, the Buddhist texts. Constructed in 1488, the buildings escaped the fires which burnt down the rest of the temple in 1817.

The Tripitaka Koreana, National Treasure No. 32, was originally carved in the 11th century in a temple on Kanghwa Island. It was believed that the possession of these wood blocks would protect the country against invasion — ironically, the blocks themselves were later burnt by invaders, the Mongols! In the 13th century a new set was undertaken at the orders of King Kojong (r. 1213-1259) and these were transported from Kanghwa Island on the heads of nuns to Haein-sa for safe-keeping.

The manufacturing process usually accepted is:

- the wood used is white birch;
- for three years it is submerged in sea-water;
- for three years it is boiled in sea-water;
- for three years it is dried in the shade.

It took about 16 years to carve the 52,330,152 characters on the 81,258 blocks and, because of the uniformity of the carving, it is believed that the work was done by one man. When printed, there are about 6,791 large, Chinese-style volumes.

At present an average 220 monks and novices live within the temple compound. During the meditation seasons, three months in winter and three months in summer, the number increases. Around Haein-sa there are 15 hermitages where about 200 women live. There are also a few men's hermitages. In all, as the monk who gave the information put it, there are about 500 "mountain men" living in and around Haein-sa. The temple is the largest in Korea in terms of residents and it has the largest monks' university.

Surrounded by magnificent mountains, Haein-sa Temple draws thousands of visitors from all over the world every year.

THE TEMPLE OF THE (SANGHA) FOLLOWERS: SONGGWANG-SA

Songgwang-sa, "Spreading Pine Temple," on Mount Chogye-san, is the third of the Three Jewels Temples, representing the Buddha's followers: monks and laity. Many famous monks have lived here. Therefore there is a formidable collection of stele and pagodas containing the ashes of some of these masters. The most famous resident monk was Master Chinul (1158-1210). He was responsible for building up the temple.

In 1190, Master Chinul realized his life-long wish to create a situation in which like-minded people could live and practice Buddhism together. His group was called the "Concentration and Wisdom Community." For seven years they lived in a small temple but, as the community grew, Master Chinul looked for the ideal place to move to. In order to find the right place, he carved a crane out of wood and it flew away and finally landed in the place where Songgwang-sa is today. There he built a small hermitage on Mount Chogye-san which he expanded to accommodate his growing community and it became known as Kilsang-sa and eventually Songgwang-sa. The Masters' Portrait Hall was built where the bird actually landed and the temple came to represent the Sangha, the followers of the Buddha. Chinul exhorted his fellow meditators in the true spirit of the community he had founded in the following way:

"... we will renounce fame and profit and stay in seclusion in the mountain forests. There, we will form a community designed to foster constant training in concentration and wisdom. Through worship of the Buddha, recitation of texts, and even through common work, we will each discharge the duties which we are assigned and nourish the self-nature in all situations. We vow to pass our whole lives free from entanglements and to follow the higher pursuits of accomplished and true men. Wouldn't this be wonderful?"

Master Chinul was the Korean source of part of a great and ancient Buddhist debate which is still going on. He believed and taught that enlightenment is quite easily reached but that practice must continue afterwards in order that the person gets rid of the habit energies. This was called Sudden Awakening and Gradual Cultivation as opposed to Sudden Awakening and Sudden Cultivation, in which, after the struggle to reach the difficult stage of enlightenment, cultivation is no longer necessary.

Songgwang-sa Temple was destroyed during the Hideyoshi Invasion and rebuilt sometime in the Choson Dynasty. Before destruction, Songgwang-sa Temple had grown to a large size, with many monks in residence. After the Hideyoshi Invasion, the temple was repaired and rebuilt many times but it never returned to its former glory. In 1988, however, the monk-in-charge worked hard to re-establish the former greatness of the temple by building it up according to the original foundations. Fourteen buildings were reconstructed including the magnificent Main Hall.

The Main Hall was built in 1988. Usually the Main Hall is the highest building but in Songgwang-sa that is not so. The Teaching Hall, the Masters' Portrait Hall and the residence of the Spiritual Leader are in the highest positions in Songgwang-sa because this is one of the Three Jewels Temples, making it different from other temples. In the Main Hall, the three main statues are the past Buddha, Dipankara, the present day Buddha, Sakyamuni, and the Future Buddha, Maitreya. Along with the Buddhas, there are four Bodhisattvas: Manjusri, the Bodhisattva of Wisdom, Samantabhadra, the Bodhisattva of Practice, Avalokitesvara, the Bodhisattva of Compassion, and Ksitigarbha, the Bodhisattva who helps the suffering.

Just near the residence of the Spiritual Leader of Songgwang-sa is his assistant's living place. This little house dates from the 15th century and has a traditional chimney. It is one of the oldest living quarters still in use in Korea. National Treasure No. 42 is kept at Songgwang-sa Temple. It is a wooden Buddha-triad casket, which seems to have been created using techniques foreign to Korea. Another National Treasure is No. 302: the building housing the Medicine Buddha, the Universal Healer, which was constructed without girders or beams. There is also one 800 year-old stump of an aromatic tree.

Two bridges span a picturesque stream that flows in front of the temple entrance; the arch-covered one is considered architecturally unusual. In front of the main bridge entrance into the temple, there are two small houses completely separate from the rest of the temple. Opinions vary on their purpose. Some say they were for keeping the name and remains of the dead who had specially asked to be kept near the temple for a period of regret after their death. Others say they were the place in which, after a bath, members of the royal family donned their wedding clothes just before marriage. These houses are unique to Songgwang-sa.

The late Master Kusan (1901-1983) set up an International Zen Center at Songgwang-sa Temple. Many foreigners who wished to experience life in a Zen Temple were attracted to this beautiful place; today, people still come from all over the world to live and practice here. Sonam-sa, a temple on the other side of Chogye-san Mountain, is well worth a visit, too.

THE TEMPLE OF BEAUTIFUL GATES: POMO-SA

Other Famous Temples

The Temple of Beautiful Gates: Pomo-sa

Pomo-sa stands on Kumjong-san, a mountain at the end of the T'aebaek Range which forms the backbone of the Korean peninsula. The mountain is carefully described in a Choson Dynasty geography book as having a huge rock at the summit on top of which there is a golden well which never, ever dries up.

Legend tells that the water of this well has very special magical properties. One day a golden fish came from heaven and has lived there ever since. Thus the name of the temple came to be "Heavenly Fish." Elsewhere it is said that the fish came from Nirvana, the Buddhist state of non-suffering. So the temples name became "Where fish from Nirvana Play."

It is recorded that Pomo-sa Temple was established by Master Uisang (625-702) in 678 during the reign of King Munmu (r. 661-681), one of the greatest Shilla kings, the first to unite the peninsula in 668. During one of the Japanese invasions of the peninsula, the king had a dream in which he was told to get Master Uisang to chant for seven days and then establish a temple on Kumjong-san Mountain. So the king organized the meeting and, at the end, the earth opened up and all the Buddhas and Bodhisattvas appeared and helped to drive away the Japanese.

Destroyed during the Hideyoshi Invasion, Pomo-sa Temple was reconstructed in 1602 and renovated in 1613. However, Shilla pagodas and lanterns still remain.

Pomo-sa is very famous for its gates. The temple is laid out in an unusual manner. The compound, composed of three levels, is clearly divided. The upper level is around the Main Hall. The second level is around the Poje-ru, the "Save all Beings" Hall and the lower part includes the three gates. The first gate is called the One-pillar Gate. It was built in 1614 and is Provincial Treasure No. 12. One reason for the strange name is that, when you look from one side, the two pillars appear as one! Another is that all who enter are urged to search for the truth of the oneness of mind. The second gate is the Four Guardians' Gate where the four awesome protectors of the temple greet you. The Four Guardians all bear a fierce countenance and trample the opponents of Buddhism under their feet. Of Hindu origin these protectors are said to have helped Siddhartha Gautama, the Buddha-to-be, to leave his father's house on the night of his renunciation by each taking hold of one hoof of Siddhartha's horse and lifting him over the palace walls.

The third gate, Gate of Non-duality represents the fact that, though the visitor is passing from the secular world into the spiritual world of the temple, these two worlds are not different from one another, they are not-two, non-dual.

The third level of the compound centers around the very beautiful Main Hall. It is Treasure No. 434 and was rebuilt by Master Myojun in 1614. The interior wooden carvings show a very refined level of Choson Dynasty craftsmanship. On the ceiling, there are many flowers which have been carved because of the legend that, whenever the Buddha teaches, flowers always fall from the heavens.

Pomo-sa has two main stupas. The three-storey stupa is from the Shilla Period about

830. It is four meters in height and is Treasure No. 250. The seven-storey stupa is new. Relics of the Buddha, brought to Korea by a Indian monk, have been enshrined within it. Just nearby there is the only stone lantern in Pomo-sa, Pusan Cultural Asset No. 16 which dates from the 9th century.

There is a famous painting of Vairocana in Pomo-sa. It used to hang behind the statue but now it is in a separate building. The harmony of colors gives the viewer a lovely feeling when looking at the painting.

In the mountains near Pomo-sa Temple, there are 11 different hermitages.

Each one is very individual and delightful to visit. Pomo-sa is a wonderful temple to go to because, as you climb up above sprawling Pusan, you can enjoy the famous forest of wisteria trees.

A TEMPLE OF EMOTIONS: CHONDUNG-SA

This is a temple which tells the story of sweet revenge. What has revenge got to do with a Buddhist temple? One would think little as people who know anything about Buddhism, think of compassion and Buddhism in one breath. Chondung-sa is a temple on Kanghwa Island to the west of Seoul, at the mouth of the Han River. Well known as the sanctuary to which Korean kings with their courts fled to take refuge from the numerous Mongol and Manchurian invasions which took place during the Koryo and Choson dynasties, King Kojong (r. 1213-1259) moved the capital to the island in 1232 in order to be safe from invaders.

The main fortress, Samnang-song, which houses the temple, Chondung-sa, dates from the time of the 25th Koryo king, Ch'ungyol (r. 1204-1308). The king had two wives. The first wife was Chinese, a daughter of Kublai Khan. The second was Korean Queen Chonghwa. Queen Chonghwa was jealous of the favor shown to her Chinese counterpart and so obtained a potion from a soothsayer. The rumor of her actions passed around the court and she was imprisoned. In her loneliness she was drawn to the temple, then known as Chinjong-sa. She offered a beautiful jade lamp to the temple in 1282 from which the name "Temple of the Donated or Inherited Lamp" or Chondung-sa came.

The site of present-day Chondung-sa is ancient. The first temple was built in 381 CE by a Buddhist monk. The site must have been considered auspicious and important as the first buildings went up only nine years after the introduction of Buddhism to the Koguryo Kingdom in 372. After that the temple was burnt down and reconstructed many times.

Chondung-sa's present-day Main Hall dates back to 1855 and is a reconstruction of a hall which was completed in 1621 following the destruction of an earlier one by fire in 1614. It is a shrine to Sakyamuni Buddha who is depicted in the style of Sokkur-am — the famous grotto in Kyongju. The Buddha is flanked on the left by Manjusri, the Bodhisattva of Perfect Wisdom, and on the right by Samantabhadra, the Bodhisattva of

Perfect Compassionate Action.

As you approach the hall, look carefully way up in the eaves at the corners of the rafters of the hipped-and-gabled roof, there you can just see a tiny human figure, one at each corner. The story goes something like this:

When the hall was being built, a special carpenter was hired. He stayed in the nearby village next to the liquor shop. There he fell in love with the daughter of the owner of the shop but, as he was poor, he could only promise to marry the girl when the hall was completed. Eventually the carpenter was paid and he set off to claim his bride. The girl had other plans. She took the money and ran away with her other love. And so the forsaken carpenter carved his two-timing girl up in the rafters eternally bearing the burden of her deceitfulness.

Revenge at Chondung-sa does not stop there. Just near the entrance, there's a huge ginkgo tree. The tree was famous for the great yield which it gave every year and so sometime during the Japanese Colonial Period (1910-1945), the oppressors demanded more ginkgo nuts than ever before. At this Master Chusong, a monk renowned for his special powers, became annoyed. For three days he chanted under the tree and from that day to this not a single nut has fallen.

After the Main Hall, the next most important object to see is the iron bell, Treasure No. 393, which is housed in a small building near the entrance. The inscription engraved on it says that it was cast at a Chinese temple, Chungming-su, in Hwaichow, China in 1097, during the Northern Sung Period; it is the only Chinese bell designated a Korean treasure.

Another of Chondung-sa's claims to fame is the fact that it was here that the 81,258 wooden printing blocks that make up the famous Tripitaka Koreana (now preserved in Haein-sa Temple) were carved and stored; there are still 104 wood-blocks kept at Chondung-sa, one was lost during the war. They are kept in the Main Hall to the right of the Buddha.

There are three more important shrines at Chondung-sa. A Medicine Buddha Hall next to the Main Hall; a small building housing some of the traditional gods; and a shrine to the Bodhisattva who helps people who are in trouble.

In order to reach Chondung-sa, you have to pass through the entrance to Samnang-song Fortress. The fortress is said to have been built in a single day by the three sons of the mythical founder of Korea, T'angun, who was born in 2333 BCE. He was the son of a bear woman and Hwanung, a heavenly god.

THE TEMPLE OF FILIAL PIETY: YONGJU-SA

Yongju-sa is the result of a son's longing for his dead father and a tribute to filial piety. The father of King Chongjo (r. 1776-1800) died and he could not rid his mind of the image of the death scene. Some time passed and then, one day, he heard a lecture on the Parental Benevolence Sutra, a text which explains the debt that children have to their parents. He decided to rebuild Kilyang-sa in memory of his father and move his father's tomb there. Throughout his life, he visited the temple often.

One day when the king was there, he noticed that the pine trees near his father's tomb were dying from being eaten by a kind of caterpillar. He was so upset that the pine trees near the tomb should die that he took one of the caterpillars and killed it by biting into it with his teeth. After that there were no more caterpillars eating the trees.

Originally the temple had been constructed by Master Yomgu in 854 and then greatly enlarged in 952. Even though the temple is not in the mountains, far away from the bustle of the world, it bestows a sense of peace and well-being on those who enter its gates.

The name of the temple, as is so often the case, comes from a legend. On the night before the day of the completion of the building activities, King Chongjo dreamt of a dragon soaring up into the sky and there receiving the Pearl of Truth, the Wish-fulfilling Gem. (This is the ball-like structure that most dragons carry in their mouth.) Therefore the temple came to be called "Dragon's Pearl of Truth Temple."

Dragons are auspicious animals with divine properties. Considered a symbol of regal authority, the dragon was also thought to dispel evil spirits.

Dragons are usually related to heaven and water and are used in rain rituals. Considered protectors, they have always been seen as important in preserving Korea from invasion and so there are many legends about sea dragons who defend the peninsula. King Munmu wished to be reborn as a great dragon to protect his country and so he was buried under a large rock in the sea off the east coast. The kings of the family who founded the Koryo Dynasty were all reputed to be descendants of the Divine Sea Dragon and each one of the family had a dragon scale in his or her armpit.

The temple soon became a major one and in 1911 was made one of the 24 main temples of the Korean Buddhist Chogye Order; it has 48 smaller temples under it in that area. The monks' training school was established in 1955. The meditation center was built in 1969 and has become the main one of Kangwon Province.

Yongju-sa is unusual in many respects. The gates are patterned after the royal ancestors' shrine or even a palace and not after a normal temple. Thus Sammungak, Three Gates, stands where the Four Guardians' Gate should stand as in the Pulmyo, one of the famous royal shrines. Next there is a five-storey stupa in front of a pavilion and not in front of a Main Hall; this is another example of the temple being like a palace. Again as in a palace, the pillars are made of stone not of wood and some of the buildings are in palace style.

The Main Hall enshrines three Buddhas. Sakyamuni, the Historical Buddha, is in the center, the Medicine Buddha is to the east and Amitabha, the Buddha of the Western Paradise, is to the west. Behind the statues is the only western-style picture in a temple in

Korea. It is painted in perspective which is very unusual. The canopy over the statues is very delicately and finely carved. Below it are five dragons in the clouds with the sun and a phoenix. On either side there are celestial beings as well.

The copper bell of Yongju-sa, National Treasure No. 120, is very special. It is presumed to have been cast in the early 10th century, during the Koryo Dynasty, because of the style of the dragon. Shilla bells have a dragon holding the bell with two legs. In Yongju-sa, the dragon is holding the bell up with just one leg, important in the study of bells.

There are some other important artifacts at the temple. Apart from a golden incense burner and a copper incense burner donated to the temple by King Chongjo, there are two books written by the king which show his deep feeling for Buddhism and his strong devotion to his father. There is an unusual five-storey stupa behind the hall dedicated to Ksitigarbha, the Bodhisattva who helps those in trouble. It has a small wooden sign with the names of the donors on it. This stupa was also built for King Chongjo's father.

A TEMPLE OVERLOOKING A RIVER: SHILLUK-SA

The temple overlooks the wide Southern Han River. Sitting in the little traditional pavilion on the banks of the river, one can easily imagine terror provoked by the dragon-horse...

On either side of the Southern Han River the people were being tyrannized by a dragon-horse who lived on an island in the middle of the river. Master Naong (1320-1376) put a magical bridle over it and tamed the wild animal. Therefore the temple came to be called "Divine Bridle."

Apart from this legend, the founding of the temple seems shrouded in mystery. One thing is certain, Master Naong definitely had a lot to do with this temple. He was a remarkable man and his story is woven into almost every aspect of Shilluk-sa.

Master Naong was ordained at the age of 20 and spent ten years in China. He then became a celebrated Zen master who formed his own school of thought using very dynamic teaching methods and was also appointed "King's Teacher," a special position of great importance. He integrated chanting — for him a state of mind in which there is no thinking — into the dominant Meditation School and advocated never forgetting the name of Amitabha, the Buddha of the Western Paradise.

Master Naong lived most of his life at Shilluk-sa. At his death, clouds of five colors covered the mountain and there was rain from a cloudless sky falling on the temple. When the body was cremated, it yielded innumerable relics, these were enshrined in a special bell-shaped stupa — reminiscent of Indian ones — which is Treasure No. 228. Some time later, the temple was greatly enlarged.

The tomb of King Sejong (r. 1418-1450) was moved to Yoju in 1469 and it was decided that Shilluk-sa would become the royal memorial temple for the king and the royal family. The temple was greatly rebuilt in 1472 when about 200 rooms were repaired or newly made. The name was changed a number of times, eventually becoming Shilluk-sa. After that many Confucian scholars passed time at the temple — in spite of the persecution of Buddhism — until the 16th century Japanese and 17th century Mongolian invasions which left most of the temple in ruins. The final rebuilding was in 1928.

The Main Hall is Provincial Asset No. 132. It is a Paradise Hall enshrining Amitabha Buddha, Samantabhadra, the Bodhisattva of Practice, and Avalokitesvara, the Bodhisattva of Compassion. The calligraphy board which hangs there is the writing of Master Naong and it says "Hundreds of Millions of Years." The hall is beautifully decorated. On the left wall there is a painting of Ksitigarbha with entourage and on the back wall is an altar for death and memorial ceremonies. Above the table there is a picture of Ch'ilsong, the Seven Buddhas. One more picture shows the guardian of the Buddha's teachings, Tongjin. He is accompanied by gods, ministers and officials.

Originally, in the late 14th century, to the south of the Paradise Hall, there was a Tripitaka Hall, a place for housing the Buddhist texts in the form of wood-blocks. The monument there, Treasure No. 230, was written by a famous scholar. It records various facts about the shape and style of the building and the fact that the texts were carried to Haein-sa. Especially beautiful is the Judgement Hall with Ksitigarbha and the Ten Judges. Attending the kings are various servants and behind them are the pictures of the various hells, with their tortures. From the Buddhist viewpoint, hell is not necessarily somewhere else, it is here and now, often created in our own minds.

In the compound of the house where the head monk lives, there is a special trestle garden which dates from 1468. Also in the same compound there is a statue of Master Naong. Behind the statue there is a picture of the master with masters Muhak (1321-1405) and Chi-gong (?-1363). Muhak was advisor of Yi Tae-jo who founded of the Choson Dynasty and moved the capital to Seoul according to advice from Master Muhak who was a famous geomancer. (The name "Seoul" is derived from the place near which the Buddha spent much time, Sravasti. In Chinese, Sravasti became Sarbol and in Korean, Seoul.) Master Chi-gong was an Indian monk whose Sanskrit name was Dhyanabhadra. Tibetan monks believe that he is an incarnation of a Tibetan lama. He came to Korea in 1328. After his death in China, his remains were brought back to Korea. Other remembrances of Master Naong include a marvelous ginkgo tree planted by the master at the foot of the hill. Also the master's meditation place by the Southern Han River is marked by a pavilion next to a little pagoda. To the east of the monastery is a hill on which is a seven-storey, brick pagoda which is 9.4 meters high and is the only existing Koryo brick pagoda. It was erected in honor of the famous monk Wonhyo who visited Shilluk-sa. The base is granite and the rest is brick with various impressed floral decorations.

THE HOME OF MANJUSRI BODHISATTVA: WOLJONG-SA

Shilla Master Chajang founded this temple, Calm Moon, on Odae-san, a famous mountain in Korea. It was destined to become a famous place for spreading Buddhism. The story of the origin of the temple goes something like this...

Master Chajang went to China in about 636 because he had a great wish to see Manjusri Bodhisattva on Wutai-shan, the name of a mountain which, when pronounced in Korean, becomes Odae-san. Following the Chinese system there are five plateaux on Odae-san Mountain, part of the T'aebaek Mountain Range on which the principle Bodhisattvas live. Each abode is marked with a hermitage. In the middle there is Saja-am, to the east is Kwanum-am, to the west is Sujong-am, to the south is Chijang-am, and to the north is Miruk-am. There is a story that the two sons of King Chongshin, Poch'on and Hyomyong, each met 50,000 Bodhisattvas on the five peaks. Therefore this place is considered very special.

It is said that on this mountain, Master Chajang chanted before a stone statue of the Bodhisattva beside a pond, hoping to fulfill his long-cherished wish. On the seventh night of his religious practice he had a dream in which the Buddha gave him a poem of four lines. After waking up, he couldn't understand the words because they were in Sanskrit. Next day, a monk came and gave him a robe of the Buddha's, one of the Buddha's bowls and one piece of the Buddha's skull. The monk then remarked that the master looked pale and troubled. Master Chajang explained that he had received a verse he could not understand. The monk explained the verse thus,

"Thoroughly to understand all teachings of the Buddha; Selfhood possesses nothing;

Understand the teachings in this way;

Then you can see Rochana Buddha."

The mysterious monk then told the master to go to Odae-san in Shilla and that there he would find 10,000 Manjusris.

After seven more days of chanting, a dragon appeared who told him that the old monk had been Manjusri and that now he must go and build a temple to the Bodhisattva. So he set off for Shilla.

In 643, Chajang reached Odae-san but the mountain was so veiled in fog that he couldn't see anything. During the three days that he waited he stayed in a thatched hut — this hut became Woljong-sa much later. The master left and went to Wonyung-sa where he finally met Manjusri and recognized the Bodhisattva.

Various masters stayed here for different lengths of time until finally a temple was built. Burnt down and rebuilt a number of times, the last disaster was during the Korean War when about ten buildings were burnt down by the Korean army — many temples had become refuges for the rebel forces and so they were destroyed.

The Main Hall, according to its name, should enshrine a Vairocana Buddha. Instead there is a statue of Sakyamuni but the more important statue is of an unusual Bodhisattva, 1.8 meters high, probably a Medicine Bodhisattva, National Treasure No. 139. Said to have been found in the Diamond Pond to the south of the temple, the statue is offering something. The story of this Bodhisattva originates from the Lotus Sutra. The head is covered with a hat, the face is long and the ears are slightly hidden by long hair. Around the neck there are three lines which are so beautifully carved that they look like necklaces. The elbow is resting on the head of a young boy. Because of its unusual style, the statue is thought to have been carved in the 11th century by craftsmen belonging to a special sect; it is therefore important to the history of carving.

The octagonal nine-storey pagoda is National Treasure No. 48. It stands 15.2 meters high and because of its harmony and the skill of the carving, it is representative of many-angled, many-storied stupas of the Koryo Period.

One of the more recent masters, Han-am (1876-1951), lived here. When he was a 22, while on a journey to the Diamond Mountains (traditionally very important to Buddhists, now in North Korea), he suddenly got the strong impression that he should become a monk. So he ordained immediately and lived most of his life at Woljong-sa.

During the Korean war, when the Korean army was sent, he saved part of the temple. As the soldiers came to execute their orders to destroy the temple, the master put on his ceremonial monk's robes and went into one of the halls. The soldiers ordered him to come out but he replied, "You are soldiers, you have to follow orders, it is your duty. I am a monk, so my duty is to keep this hall, so please burn it and go." The soldiers couldn't bring themselves to destroy it, so they only burnt one door. The master then returned to the hermitage where he stayed. On his way there he stuck his stick in the ground and it has since grown into a fine tree, a maple.

THE TEMPLE OF COMPASSION: NAKSAN-SA

Naksan is Korea's Potalaka Mountain, the place where Avalokitesvara Bodhisattva lives. Since ancient times the subject of much respect, the Bodhisattva embodies the idea of perfect compassion. Many miraculous stories are told and many special ceremonies and art works relating to Avalokitesvara have made the Bodhisattva into a very central figure in Mahayana Buddhism. The Bodhisattva is depicted in many different forms. Sometimes with four, six or more hands, there are many statues and paintings in which Avalokitesvara has 1,000 hands, each with an eye, so that the Bodhisattva can see where those in trouble are and help them. Avalokitesvara represents the ultimate in compassion within each one of us and is usually considered to be neither male nor female. The Bodhisattva lives on a sea-bound island. The sea is filled with protecting dragons to whom all but the pure of heart fall prey. In the background of many paintings are waterfalls, rocks and often luscious plants and trees.

It is therefore no surprise to find Korea's Potalaka on Naksan Mountain overlooking the Eastern Sea. The temple built there is called Naksan-sa. It was founded by Master Uisang in 676 CE, the 16th year of the reign of King Munmu. The temple is dominated by a statue of Avalokitesvara which took six years to create. It recalls the legend of the founding of the temple...

The master, a famous Avatamsa monk, heard that Avalokitesvara was staying in a cave on a mountain overlooking the Eastern Sea. So he went there to meet the Bodhisattva. After seven days of spiritual practice, he received a magical string of Buddhist beads made of pure crystal. Next the dragon of the Eastern Sea gave him a fabulous jewel. The master then practiced for a further seven days and only then met Avalokitesvara and was told, "On the peak above my seat, you will find a pair of bamboo plants growing. Build a Main Hall there." After building the hall the master deposited the beads and the jewel inside.

Soon after, Uisang's friend, Wonhyo, came to visit. On his way he is supposed to have met two different women, both were forms of the Bodhisattva. When he reached the cave, a storm suddenly rose up and he was unable to enter and meet the true Bodhisattva. During Master Wonhyo's visit, the two friends discussed a poem written in the form of a seal. This seal, the Avatamsa Ilsung popkye to — literally "Decorated by flowers, One Vehicle, Reality of Myself in the World Seal" — which is in the shape of the mathematical diagram for infinity, was written by Uisang as a present for his teacher, Chih-yen, in China when he was leaving after studying there for eight years. It is one of the great offerings of the Korean people to the world and its essence is:

In one is all,
In all is one.
One is identical to all,
All is identical to one.

This is the central theme of the Avatamsaka School which Uisang spread throughout Korea on his return from China.

During the Choson Dynasty, the temple was repeatedly rebuilt and destroyed. The present buildings date from 1953.

The Main Hall is a splendid tribute to Avalokitesvara. Exquisitely decorated, the hall is full of statues of the Bodhisattva in various poses. There you can see the many forms that Avalokitesvara takes and appreciate the skill of Korean wood carving.

In spite of the many destructions and reconstructions, a few ancients things remain. The Arched Gate (Provincial Tangible Cultural Property No. 33), built in 1467 during the reign of King Sejo (1455-68), is believed to have been built from 26 stones each of which was contributed by each one of the 26 magistrates governing the 26 towns of the area by order of the king.

The fine seven-storey pagoda, Treasure No. 499, is also believed to have been erected during the reign of King Sejo. It measures 6.2 meters high, including the finial. The body and roof stone of each storey is made of a single stone. It is well preserved, especially in that it has an intact finial which consists of an inverted bowl, a wheel and a bijou on a bronze staff, resembling those of Tibetan style pagodas found in Yuan, China. Another

Provincial Tangible Cultural Property, No. 34, is the adobe wall surrounding the Main Hall. It also dates from the reign of King Sejo and is highly regarded for the designs which have been used in its creation. Only part of it is original, the rest has been recently restored.

The bronze bell is dated 1469 according to an inscription. The Bodhisattvas, the pattern of lotus petals and waves on the body of the bell and the twin dragons on the top have all been beautifully cast.

Naksan-sa has not forgotten Avalokitesvara's home. Potalaka is represented by a lovely two-storied hall. Nearby is a pond full of water-lilies — at the right time of year.

THE TEMPLE OF FREQUENT CHANGE: SHINHUNG-SA

Shinhung-sa is the main temple of the area known as Outer Sorak-san Mountain. The temple is remarkable for its constant changing over the centuries. For not only did it change position and name, but also the school of Buddhism to which it adhered.

Actually Shinhung-sa stood where the New Sorak Hotel stands today. It was founded by Master Chajang in 652 and named Hyangsong-sa. The temple was burned down in 699 and Master Uisang rebuilt the temple three years later on its present site. Once more destroyed in 1645 at the time of the Japanese invasions, all the monks left the temple and only three monks remained. One night the three monks had a dream in which they met a god who told them what to do. He said that if they built the temple behind the original site, then the temple would never be touched by three main disasters: fire, water and wind. The monks built the temple there and called it Shinhung-sa, "Divinely Inspired Temple."

There is a one kilometer path leading up to the One-pillar Gate. The path passes relic containers and memorial tablets of great monks who have lived and died at the temple.

Next comes the main compound. Behind the Gate of the Four Guardians there is a two-storey study hall. On the stone stairway and retaining wall near the Main Hall there are several unusual reliefs. These are guardians, defending Buddhism from those that would harm it. The temple is built on a foundation of natural stone with four large natural stones at the corners of the base. The Main Hall, a Paradise Hall, is built on an east-west axis facing towards the east. On the walls of the outside of the building there are the Ten Oxherding pictures and some pictures of stories about famous Zen masters.

Inside the hall, Amitabha is enshrined accompanied by Avalokitesvara and Mahastramprapta, the Bodhisattva of Power. The statues are said to have been made in the time of Uisang, in the 7th century. They sit under a bright canopy of yellow dragons and behind the statues is a painting showing Sakyamuni with various Bodhisattvas, the guardians at the four corners and some monks including a very aged Kasyapa and a very young-looking Ananda, the Buddha's long term attendant. On the northern wall is a painting of the protector of Dharma, Tongjin, with celestial beings, ministers, Bodhisattvas, and gods. Included in the gods is the Kitchen God who has an unusual beard and holds antlers in his hand. There are also warriors armed with swords, tridents and other weapons.

The Ten Oxherding pictures, dating from 12th century Song China (1126-1279), are very important to the school of Zen. Although the style and actual pictures vary enormously, the message of the pictures remains the same.

To the right of the Main Hall there is the Bell Pavilion which is a very good example of Choson architecture.

The Judgement Hall is dedicated to the benevolent Ksitigarbha, the Bodhisattva who cares for those in trouble. Behind the statue is a painting showing the Bodhisattva and guardians. The walls and ceiling are painted with Taoistic images. Recently, during restoration, some interesting printing plates made of wood were found. They are thought to date from the 17th century and they contain some texts, like the Lotus Sutra, some Buddhist ceremonies and the writings of some Korean masters.

The Sanshin between the Main Hall and the Judgement Hall contains a picture of the Mountain God with his tiger. Usually pictured with a tiger, Sanshin is particularly remembered after any large ceremony. This is because everyone is grateful for being able to have the temple built on the mountain. Toksong, the Lonely Hermit, is actually more Buddhist in origin and represents the sole practitioner. Ch'ilsong, the Big Dipper, controls human life expectancy and women who have just given birth traditionally offered a skein of thread to Ch'ilsong as a symbol of their hope for a long life for their baby. In Shinhung-sa, Ch'ilsong is surrounded by the sun and the moon, seven stars, the master of the South Polar star, and lots of heavenly beings.

Two kilometers from the temple there is a lovely pagoda, Treasure No. 443. In the surrounding mountains and forests there are a number of interesting hermitages, some of which partly date back to the time of Master Chajang.

THE TEMPLE OF THE TWO PAGODAS: PULGUK-SA

Pulguk-sa is the best known and, if we accept the legends, one of the oldest temples in Korea. The name means "Buddha Land" and it is located on the outskirts of Kyongju, the capital of the Unified Shilla Period. The temple, first built in 535 during the reign of King Pophung (r. 514-540), was much smaller than the present structure. King Pophung was the first Shilla king to accept Buddhism. He and his queen eventually renounced the throne and were ordained.

In 751, the temple was built up during the reign of King Kyongdok (r. 742-765) by Kim Tae-song, the chief minister, in honor of his parents. There is a story that Kim Tae-song's birth into the prime minister's family was announced by a mysterious voice. To honor his parents, he designed and had Pulguk-sa Temple built. He recalled the poor parents of his previous birth, too, and built Sokkuram in their memory.

Pulguk-sa Temple epitomizes the spirit of Shilla, bearing witness to the great architectural achievements of that period and showing a highly refined form of aesthetic beauty. Twenty-three times renovated — the most recent was in 1973 — the symmetry, balance and grace of former times is ever preserved. The temple is built on a series of terraces made of gigantic stones fitted together without mortar.

There are six national treasures to be seen. The most important are probably two of the most famous monuments in the whole of Korea. They are the two mortarless stone pagodas which stand complementing each other in the courtyard of the temple. Sakyamuni Pagoda, National Treasure No. 21, symbolizing the Buddha's contemplation and detachment, is representative of the trend in the Unified Shilla Period when pagodas were simplified to consist of three storeys. The ratio of the widths is 4:3:2, the width of the lower base being equal to the height of the main structure above the upper base. The simplicity of this pagoda is enhanced by the complexity of its twin, Pagoda of Many Treasures, National Treasure No. 20. It is actually an enlarged relic holder, one of the types of vessels used to store the remains of the Buddha and, later, other great monks.

Legend tells that they were both created by a mason called Asadal who came from the former kingdom of Paekje. He left his young wife Asanyo promising to return as soon as the pagodas were completed. After years of waiting, Asanyo journeyed to Kyongju but was prohibited from visiting the pagodas as no outsiders were allowed. She was told to wait near a pond and that, when the pagodas were completed, they would be reflected in the pond. She waited long and patiently and eventually, out of desperation, cast herself into the pond; Sakyamuni Pagoda is sometimes called "Pagoda without Refection."

Pulguk-sa Temple is particularly famous for the graceful staircases, actually bridges, leading up to the temple complex. They are the oldest stone bridges in Korea and are called bridges because they lead from the secular world to the Land of the Buddha. In addition, originally there was a lake in front of the temple and boats used to float visitors to these staircases. The one to the east is called Blue and White Cloud Bridge (National Treasure No. 23). The second bridge-stairway, to the west, is called the Lotus Flower and the Seven Gems (National Treasure No. 22).

There are two, 8th century, bronze statues, one of Amitabha, the Buddha of Light (National Treasure No. 27), the other of Vairocana, the Buddha of Cosmic Power, (National Treasure No. 26). Both are believed to have been cast in the 8th century. The Amitabha statue is in the Paradise Hall which is connected to the Vairocana Hall by a covered corridor. The statue in the Vairocana Hall is considered to be the oldest bronze Buddha in Korea. Both statues are exceptionally fine examples of early Unified Shilla art and greatly prized for their exquisite charm.

Kyongju is one of the world's greatest out door museums. Nam-san, a mountain not far from Pulguk-sa Temple, is rich in Buddha statues and pagodas carved there during the Unified Shilla Period. The museum, too, is excellent.

Sokkuram

Kim Tae-song's other creation, Sokkuram, "Cave of the Buddha," was made at the same time as Pulguk-sa Temple — about 751. The man-made cave houses one of the most beautiful Buddha statues in the world. High up on Mt. Toham-san, behind Pulguk-sa Temple, the cave was constructed in order that the early morning rays of the sun fall on the face of the Buddha. The nine-meter high, domed rotunda also contains an eleven-headed Avalokitesvara statue, which is famous for its exquisite beauty.

Thirty-nine Bodhisattvas, the Buddha Sakyamuni's ten enlightened disciples, gods and guardians are also found in the cave, which was built to represent the Buddhist world.

You enter the grotto from the side and pass into a corridor in which, through a huge glass window, you can see the lovely Buddha statue. Just on the other side of the glass there a chamber in which chanting and bowing is done (Sokkuram is a functioning temple). A short passageway, at the entrance to which there are two guardians, leads into the main chamber.

The colossal Buddha statue sits surrounded by 39 Bodhisattvas, ten disciples, gods and other guardians. All are carved from white granite and show a skill and artistry rarely seen elsewhere. This is the perfection to which the Golden Period of the United Shilla reached.

The Buddha is in the "Bearing Witness Pose." When the Buddha had attained enlightenment in Bodhgaya in northern India over 2,500 years ago, he was challenged as to his right to sit on the earth. He touched the ground and the earth bore witness to his many good deeds, granting him that right. The whole pose of the Buddha portrays the peace, tolerance and uprightness which Buddhism is famous for.

During the Choson Dynasty, when Buddhism was persecuted, this national masterpiece was forgotten. Then one cloudy day, in 1909, a lone postman suddenly had to take shelter from a thunderstorm. He dashed into the only place available: a cave. There, as his eyes grew accustomed to the dim light, he saw the magnificent statue.

In 1913, the Japanese occupation government spent two years repairing the grotto. As cement was used, repairs had to be made again in 1920, and UNESCO further aided the government from 1961 to 1964 in further restoring the precious cave. It is now on the UNESCO Heritage list as one of the wonders of the world.

The Buddha has sat here for over 1,000 years. Unfortunately, in modern times, it has become necessary to protect the statue from vandals and from temperature changes. Therefore visitors can no longer enter the grotto itself. In spite of this, a visit to Sokkur-am Grotto is well worth the trip because the gaze of the Buddha will stay with you forever.

THE SOLDIER-MONK'S TEMPLE: CHIKJI-SA

The Chikji-sa of today is very different from the temple of days gone by. One of oldest temples in Korea, Chikji-sa was built in the foothills of Mt. Hwangak-san and originally consisted of 40 buildings. After almost total destruction during the Hideyoshi Invasion, only 20 buildings were rebuilt in 1602. It is believed to have been originally established in 418 during the reign of King Nulchi (r. 417-458) by Master Ado who first brought Buddhism to Shilla however, Buddhism was only fully accepted in about 527. Chikji-sa Temple was rebuilt by Master Chajang in 645, during the reign of Queen Sondok (r. 632-647). Destruction and reconstruction succeeded each other with major renovations in the 10th century and again from 1966 to 1981.

The name of the temple is very unusual, "Direct Pointing Temple." There are three theories concerning the origin. Master Ado is reputed to have pointed to Mt. Hwangak-san and said, "There is a good place for a great temple to be built." Elsewhere it is recorded that Master Nungyo of the late Koryo Dynasty measured the site with his hand instead of a ruler. Finally, the name reflects the core of Korean Buddhism, the teaching that describes Zen as "direct pointing to the human heart, not relying on words and letters."

The most famous monk associated with this temple is Master Samyong (1544-1610). Born in 1544, he was orphaned at an early age and ordained at Chikji-sa Temple at the age of sixteen. He then studied under Master Sosan (1520-1604) in the Diamond Mountains and both of them led an army of some 5,000 trained soldier-monks to fight off the Japanese invaders of the sixteenth century. At the beginning of the invasion, King Sonjo (1567-1608) fled the capital, leaving a poorly-trained, weak army to defend the country. In desperation he called Master Sosan who was 73 years of age who, in spite of his advanced age, managed to recruit an army of 5,000 monk-soldiers. Master Samyong, one of Sosan's main disciples, was put in charge of the main part of the operation.

After the invaders were routed, Master Samyong was sent as an envoy to the Japanese court in 1604 and, after completing a peace treaty, he returned home with 3,000 prisoners. Due to his merit the temple was restored. Master Samyong died in 1610 at Haein-sa and there is a memorial shrine to him at Chikji-sa Temple.

After the One-pillar Gate there is the huge Four Guardians' Gate. On entering the compound you can see two, three-storey pagodas which date from the Unified Shilla Period; one in front of the Main Hall (Treasure No. 606) and one in front of the 1,000 Buddhas Hall (Treasure No. 607). In the Main Hall, a building representative of Choson architecture, there are the Three Jewels, a name for the triad of Sakyamuni, Amitabha and the Medicine Buddha. The painting behind the statues is Treasure No. 608. To the west there is a second big monastery compound which contains monks' living quarters, the head monk's house, the meditation hall and various other buildings.

There are other shrines as well. Attached to the Avalokitesvara Hall is a memorial shrine for Master Samyong. Inside the 1,000 Buddhas Hall there are small white Buddhas made of Kyongju jade dating from the Choson Period; the main statues date from 1852. They form a triad of Vairocana, the Medicine Buddha and Sakyamuni. Among the little statues there is one of a naked baby and it is believed that if you see it first, then you will have a son. The pictures of the guardians date from 1886.

To the right is the Judgement Hall in which the Ten Judges are set in two rows of five. Each judge is accompanied by three servants and two guardians ward off evil by the door. There is a Disciples' Hall which contains some lovely images of the Buddha's enlightened followers.

The most valuable object in Chikji-sa is a statue of the Medicine Buddha, Treasure No. 319. It dates from the Unified Shilla Period and, guessing from the form of the statue, scholars place it at the end of the 9th century. It is 1.61 meters high and both statue and halo are made of granite. The right hand is on the right knee and the fingers are in a position known as "making evil surrender." In the left hand there is a vessel for medicine.

Chikji-sa also has a famous bell. It is 1.44 meters high and the diameter of the mouth of the bell is 1.13 meters. According to the inscription on the bell it was cast in 1713. On the upper part of the bell the mantras for breaking the hells and "Om Mani Padme Hum" are inscribed. The top and the decorative strip are characteristic of Chinese bells and commonly found on Choson bells.

Only just over three hours from Seoul, Chikji-sa Temple is a wonderful day's outing.

A TREASURE TROVE OF A TEMPLE: PUSOK-SA

Master Uisang was eagerly studying in China when a piece of secret information was revealed to him. T'ang warlords were planning to attack, conquer and annex Shilla, Uisang's beloved home land. The information came to the young monk through the lovelorn daughter of a high ranking T'ang official at whose home Uisang was staying. Uisang lost no time. He immediately set out to warn his country men. Finding the master gone, the daughter rushed after him, but was too late for the ship had already weighed anchor and was disappearing over the horizon. In desperation the girl flung herself into the sea and drowned. This supreme act of sacrifice transformed her into a dragon which guarded over the ship all the way back to Shilla. The attack averted, Uisang set himself to the task of searching for the ideal temple site.

He found it on Mt. Ponhwang-san but the villagers refused to vacate the chosen spot. Once again, the dragon appeared. Threatening to hurl a massive rock on the village, the people fled and the dragon came crashing to the earth and exhaled its last breath. This is the site of the Main Hall of Pusok-sa today. To the west you can see a piece of rock, a small portion of the one hurled by the dragon. Therefore Pusok-sa is called "Temple of the Floating Stone." Uisang averted another Chinese invasion by performing a special ceremony some years later.

From a geomancy point of view, Pusok-sa is very auspicious. In Korean, as in Chinese, geomancy is called the study of "wind and water." The ideal site should be encircled by mountains with specially high ridges on the northern side extending to the east. These ridges are known as the Blue Dragon. On the western side there should be some more ridges and these are know as the White Tiger. In addition, Pusok-sa, constructed in 676 at the orders of King Munmu, is a temple which shows the transition period between those originally built in the plains during the period of the Three Kingdoms and those built in the mountains during the Koryo and Choson periods. The original temples were centered around a single pagoda—single Main Hall pattern. The later temples consisted of a Main Hall and two pagodas.

From the beginning Uisang made the temple the headquarters of his Avatamsaka sect. However, Korean Buddhism is never quite so clear-cut. The temple also has all the trappings of one dedicated to Pure Land, to the philosophy of the Western Paradise presided over by Amitabha Buddha. Therefore the Main Hall, National Treasure No. 18, enshrines Amitabha. Originally built in 676, the present structure dates from 1358, one of the oldest wooden buildings in Korea. The architectural style is worth looking at closely. The foundation is of granite. The columns supporting the roof are fitted with brackets which seem complicated at first but which are actually amazingly simple. The hipped-and-gabled roof is in perfect proportion to the body of the building, giving the hall a unique feeling. Inside, the statue sits in the west facing east because it is an Amitabha, Buddha of the Western Paradise. It is the oldest clay statue in Korea, National Treasure No. 45, and, although it is a Koryo statue, it reflects faithfully the style of Shilla statues.

To the left of the Main Hall, at the bottom of a steep bluff, lies the legendary floating stone. To the right of the stone is a three-storey pagoda behind which is a pavilion dedicated to the Chinese girl who, in the form of a dragon, helped Master Uisang. The portrait in the pavilion is of the same girl.

Chosadang, National Treasure No. 19, a hall for keeping the portraits of great masters, lies 100 meters to the northeast of the Main Hall. It was built 150 years after the Main Hall. Originally, the building was decorated with wall paintings but these have been moved to a protected place. The six frescoes, four of guardians and two of Bodhisattvas, are National Treasure No. 46 and they are the best existing examples of Koryo Period wall painting.

Just under the eaves of Chosadang, there is a tree. It sprang from a stick which Uisang put there on his way to India. He is reputed to have foretold that if a tree grew it would never die. And so it is, ever green and blooming after 1,300 years!

Pusok-sa has many treasures. The flagpole supports are Treasure No. 255; the Koryo wood-blocks are Treasure No. 735; the pudo, conical stone objects in which the remains of famous monks are kept; the two stone pagodas; and the monument to Master Wonyung, a National Teacher of the Koryo Period, are only some of the wonderful objects which have survived Korea's turbulent history. In particular, the stone lantern, National Treasure No. 17 which dates from the Unified Shilla Period, should be carefully looked at. A masterpiece of proportion and design, the fine reliefs of lotus petals and Bodhisattvas make it a precious gem.

THE TEMPLE OF THE FUTURE BUDDHA: KUMSAN-SA

Kumsan-sa or Gold Mountain Temple is located on Mt. Moak-san near Chonju.Originally built in 600 CE, according to the temple records 38 monks were ordained at the temple in that same year. After numerous destructions and rebuildings, the present buildings were erected in 1635 after the others were destroyed in the Hideyoshi Invasion of the 16th century. There are many treasures which pre-date the present buildings. The temple is now one of the principle centers of the region and one of the biggest in Korea.

Master Chinp'yo (known around 742-780) was responsible for the construction of the temple from 762 to 766 when he enlarged the existing number of buildings. According to a legend, Master Chinp'yo, after returning from China, had a vision of Maitreya Buddha and he received a book on divination in two rolls and 189 divination sticks from Maitreya. This book on divination then became the principal authority on the subject in Korea. And due to this, King Kyongdok invited the master to his palace in order to receive instruction and predictions.

Master Chinp'yo decided to build a temple to Maitreya and call it Kumsan-sa. On his way, he met a dragon king who presented the master with a robe of jade and guided him to Kum-san forest. There, miraculously, men and women from everywhere came to help. The temple was built in a few days and when it was completed, Maitreya came to give Chinp'yo his final ordination.

In memory of this event, Chinp'yo created a Maitreya Buddha Hall, the focal point of Kumsan-sa. After that, the master set up a platform and taught the people well.

This Maitreya Buddha Hall (National Treasure No. 62) is over 20 meters high. It is the only ancient, wooden, three-storey hall in Korea, each storey has a different name and so a different name board. The first floor is "Great Compassion Hall." The second is "Dragon Flower Meeting" and the third is "Maitreya Hall." In order to support the immense roof, special corner eave pillars were created.

Enshrined is a statue of the future Buddha, Maitreya. This gilded, standing statue is 11.82 meters high and is flanked by two attendants, each 8.79 meters high. The Maitreya statue is modeled after a Shilla statue although it actually dates from the early 20th century. The hand position is one of "have no fear." The assistants date from the Choson Period. On the southern wall is a painting of Maitreya giving the monks' rules to Chinp'yo. Because of this strong connection with Maitreya, Kumsan-sa followed the Dharmalaksana, or Dharma Aspect School.

In Korea, the traditional buildings of palaces and temples are painted with amazingly bright colored geometrical patterns. These designs are called "tanch'ong," meaning "red and blue," the principle colors used. Tanch'ong was introduced to the peninsula through the Koguryo Kingdom probably somewhere about the time that Buddhism was accepted, in 372 CE. The main aim of tanch'ong is protection of the wood. The wood is carefully treated before applying the base or background pigment in order to protect it from humidity and decay. Then the design to be painted on is outlined using chalk powder over pinholes made in the paper of the design. Now the wood is ready to receive the bright colors of the mineral paints used. Finally a coating of oil is applied and the paintings are gone over with a hot iron.

In this way the wood is protected from the elements as well as from mold and bugs.

In front of the Maitreya Hall is a strange hexagonal stone pagoda, Treasure No. 27. Dating from the Koryo Period, probably late 10th century, this kind of hexagonal, sometimes octagonal, pagoda was popular at the time. It stands 2.18 meters high and the 11 remaining storeys are well balanced. Originally it probably had 13 storeys.

Kumsan-sa Temple has many other treasures. Among them, the five-storey pagoda is thought to date from the Koryo period. It is Treasure No. 25 and is rather different from other pagodas of the period. Possibly this difference is the result of some foreign influence. Next to the five-storey pagoda is a stone bell, a pagoda shaped like a bell, Treasure No. 26, similar to the one at T'ongdo-sa and the one which holds Master Naong's ashes at Shilluk-sa. It probably dates from early Koryo and the technique used in carving it is very refined. This form of pagoda is thought to have been imported from India. There are Buddhas and guardians carved on the face of the stone. The stone lotus support or pedestal is Treasure No. 23 and thought to date from the 10th century. It is to the southeast of the Main Hall and shows a very refined level of carving. The upper lotus is open, the lower lotus is finely balanced with the upper one. There is also a stone lamp, Treasure No. 828; an incense burner stand; a Dew Pillar, Treasure No. 22, of undetermined use; and a flagpole, Treasure No. 28.

THE TEMPLE NAMED AFTER A PHILOSOPHY: HWAOM-SA

Hwaom-sa Temple's name is taken directly from that of one of the most influential texts in the history of Korean Buddhism: the Avatamsaka Sutra.

The underlying theme of the text is the universal oneness of all things.

Built on the slopes of striking Mt. Chiri-san, Hwaom-sa Temple is one of Korea's most beautiful places. Records state that the site was between the kingdoms of Shilla and Paekje and that it was first selected by Master Yon-gi in 554 in the reign of King Chinhung (r. 540-576). Master Uisang expanded the temple in 634 when he introduced the Avatamsa philosophy. The temple was destroyed by the Hideyoshi Invasion and rebuilt by Master Pyogam in 1630 under King Injo (r. 1623-1649).

The temple follows the one Main Hall-twin pagoda pattern on a north-south axis of the Unified Shilla Period. In this plan, two pagodas were built in front of one Main Hall in the main courtyard. In Hwaom-sa, the eastern pagoda, Treasure No. 132, is an unadorned five-storey pagoda and the western, Treasure No. 133 is a richly decorated double-pedestaled pagoda which is ornamented with the eight divine generals, four guardians and the zodiac animals. The pagodas are respectively Treasures 132 and 133.

The Main Hall was built in 1630 and is an important example of middle Choson period architecture; it is Treasure No. 299. The central statue is of Vairocana, the Cosmic Buddha on the right of which is Sakyamuni and on the left is Rochana.

Let us take a look at Rochana Buddha. In Buddhism, depending on the period and the ™fashion?(sometimes one Buddha or Bodhisattva is more popular than another), Rochana can be a form of Amitabha, the Nirmanakaya or the mind-made, emanation body. In a triad with Vairocana, the Dharmakaya, or uncontaminated body, Rochana Buddha is the Sambhogakaya or physical form, the enjoyment body, of the Buddha. Then Sakyamuni is the Nirmanakaya or emanation body. There seem to be no hard and fast rules to these identification and they changed constantly.

To the east of the Main Hall is the Judgement Hall in which graphic paintings of the hells can be seen. To the west is the hall dedicated to Avalokitesvara, the Bodhisattva of Compassion. The beautiful coffered ceiling shows a traditional lotus flower decor.

Behind the Main Hall, there is a path which, after about 150 meters, leads to Sambul-am, Hermitage of the Three Buddhas. There in the Thousand Buddhas Hall are statues of Sakyamuni, Amitabha and the Medicine Buddha with Bodhisattvas with cap-like diadems. There are shrines of the Big Dipper and the Mountain God as well.

To the left of the Main Hall is the Hall of the Enlightened Emperor.

(Emperor is a name for the Buddha, the Awakened One who is lord over himself..) Built in 1702 or 1703, the 160 meters high, double-roofed building is one of the most magnificent in Korea. It is National Treasure No. 67. The large high roof is a tribute to the high rank of the Buddha (who came from a royal caste). Dating from the last century, the ceiling is covered with carved and painted lotuses in mandala form and fine cosmic patterns. The statues on the pedestal are, from the left, Avalokitesvara, Amitabha, Samantabhadra, the Bodhisattva of Practice, Sakyamuni, Manjusri, the Bodhisattva of Wisdom, Prabhutaratna, Gnanakara. This rich and rare configuration combines traits of the Avatamsa School and the Zen School with popular devotional Buddhism.

Originally the building was called Changyukjon. Legend tells that 100 monks prayed for 100 days to build the hall. One night, an old monk dreamt that Manjusri told him how to collect enough money. Each monk must wet his palm and then touch flour. The one to whom the flour didn't stick was the right person; this was Master Songnung. Manjusri instructed him to ask help from the first person he met the next day. This person turned out to be a beggar woman who, after vowing to be reborn in a rich family, died.

A few years later, Master Songnung met a princess who was very pleased to see him. One of her hands had never opened and the master managed to open it. On the palm was written Changyukjon. On seeing this, King Sukchong (r. 1674-1720) decided to help. When the hall was renamed, the king called it Kakhwangjon. Originally the entire Avatamsaka Sutra was carved on granite plates on the walls, but most of it was destroyed by the 16th century invaders. Remaining fragments have been deposited below the statues.

In front of this hall there are two important monuments. One is the six-meter high stone lantern, National Treasure No. 12. It is the biggest lantern in Korea. The other is a lion pagoda which is Treasure No. 300.

Four sitting lions support a pagoda and each lion's face seems to express a different emotion. Both of these stone objects date from 670.

Behind the hall, up a steep path, there is another lion pagoda. It also dates from the 7th century and is National Treasure No. 35. Four crouching lions on a relief-adorned pagoda carry an elegant granite reliquary, the roof of which is layered downward in typical Shilla style. Between the lions is the figure of a nun standing facing a stone lantern a few meters away. She is the mother of the temple founder Yon-gi, who himself is said to be crouching under the stone lantern opposite offering a cup of tea. Hwaom-sa Temple, set in beautiful mountainous countryside, is a wonderful place to go.

TEMPLE OF THE LIFE OF THE BUDDHA HALL: POPJU-SA

Two kilometers before the entrance to the temple is a tree many might miss. It is a 600 year-old pine tree near the road. Legend tells that it bowed its branches in front of King Sejo? a story of guilt. King Sejo was the second son of King Sejong; he succeeded the throne by murdering his nephew.

In old age he suffered from a severe skin ailment and tried to find solace from his ailment as well as his bad conscience in the forests of Sogni-san Mountain.

One day he met a young woman whose two boys called him grandfather. The woman was Princess Uisook, Sejo's daughter, who had to flee her father because she had pleaded for the life of the murdered nephew. At this meeting the king begged for forgiveness and invited these members of his family back to the palace. The princess refused saying that she preferred her simple life and she later fled further south.

Located on Songni-san Mountain, Popju-sa, "The Dharma Staying" temple, is believed to have been founded in 553, during the reign of King Chinhung; Master Uisang helped build it up. There is a record which states that, at times, 3,000 monks lived here. Eight times renovated, the last occasion was in 1906. Popju-sa is a Head Temple and has some 27 lesser temples under it.

Behind the entrance gate there are two granite pillars dating from 11th century which were used to support the temple painting for special occasions.

In a pavilion on the right side is the 2.70-meter diameter iron pot dating from 720. There is a record which states that the pot was used in the 12th century to serve monks and pilgrims.

The Main Hall or Hall of Great Light is a shrine to Vairocana, Sakyamuni and Rochana. Behind these three images there are three paintings of the Buddhas accompanied by enlightened disciples, Bodhisattvas as well as by a youthful Ananda and a very elderly Kasyapa. Sakyamuni and Rochana are surrounded by rainbows and Vairocana is surrounded by a huge white halo, symbolizing the absolute.

The five-storey pagoda, the oldest wooden pagoda in Korea, was originally built in 553; it is National Treasure No. 55. A copy of this pagoda was made in Nara 50 years later at Horiuji. (In Japan, the original pagodas are still standing but in Korea they've all been destroyed by the numerous invasions. A copy of the original pagoda is in the Seoul National Museum.) This one was constructed in 1624 and it has been carefully preserved since then. It is a "Life of the Buddha" or "Eight Paintings Hall" with large murals telling the story of the life of Sakyamuni Buddha; the paintings are not in chronological order.

The beautifully carved beams are painted in special designs. Around the central pillar, Buddhists circumnambulate as a practice of remembering the Buddha and the task before them to understand his teachings. There are four statues of Sakyamuni, each one facing one of the four cardinal directions, each one showing a different mudra or hand position. The Buddha facing east has the pose of fearlessness, the one facing west is in the pose of Turning the Wheel of the Dharma (teaching), the one facing south shows the earth touching pose and the Buddha facing the north is lying down, Buddha in the dying pose — very rare in Korea.

The entourage shows Bodhisattvas and disciples brightly clad and bejewelled. There are some women among the followers.

In front of the paintings, there are 340 little white Buddhas representing the innumerable beings in all places in all world systems. These images are often called disciples even though they actually have the marks of Buddhas.

These marks include the long ears, the curled hair and the bump on the head.

Gazing down at the pagoda is a 33-meter high, 160 ton copper Maitreya Buddha. In 1872, King Kojong's father took the Maitreya Buddha statue made by Chinp'yo. In 1939, a new statue was started but couldn't be completed.

So in 1964, President Park donated money for a new statue and this allowed the temple to finish the statue with cement. In 1990, the statue was replaced with this bronze one. Nearby there is a two-meter high statue of a woman carrying a pot in her hands. The statue is reputed to be Sujata who offered food to the Buddha just before he attained enlightenment.

Other treasures include a four-meter stone lantern which is Treasure No. 15. There's also a water basin, National Treasure No. 64, shaped like a half-opened magnolia flower. It used to stand in front of the previous Maitreya Hall and is a symbol of the pond in the paradise of the Future Buddha. The lion lantern, National Treasure No. 5, consists of a rare Shilla lantern about 3.3-meters in height dating from 720, made during the reign of King Sondok (r. 702-737).

Tourists may enjoy the many trails leading up to different hermitages and to the peak of Mt. Songni-san.

THE TEMPLE OF THE ANCIENT MAIN HALL: SUDOK-SA

According to temple records Sudok-sa was founded by Master Sungje in the late Paekje period. It is further recorded that, during the reign of King Uija (r. 641-660), Master Sungje taught the Lotus Sutra in 647 at the temple. There is also another record which states that the temple was founded by one Master Chimyong in 599 during the reign of Paekje King Pop (r. 599-600).

The temple has had many famous masters living and teaching in it. Kyongho (1849-1912), a well-known, present-day master lived here. He ordained quite young and when he was 31, while on his way to Seoul, he saw many dead people from a recent cholera epidemic. This changed his life and he practiced hard and attained true understanding. He was the teacher of many great monks, one of the best known was Master Mangong (1872-1946) who also lived at Sudok-sa and where, it is recorded, he gave a special teaching in 1898. Another personality connected with the history of the temple was a nun called Iryop (1869-1971) who lived in Kyongsong-am hermitages. She was a famous writer. One of the main temples of Korea where there is a comprehensive training center comprised of a meditation hall, a monks' college and a center for studying monks' rules, Sudok-sa also has a Panjang, a Spiritual Master. There are five of these specially selected masters in Korea at any one time. In addition to Sudok-sa, there is one at Haein-sa, one at T'ongdo-sa, one at Songgwang-sa, and one at Paekyang-sa. The Chogye Order has a Secular Leader who is elected for four years of office and a Spiritual Leader who holds office for ten years. At present (1998) the master of T'ongdo-sa holds that position.

When visiting Sudok-sa, you pass through the dragon- ornamented granite One-pillar Gate in order to reach the main monastery compound. The compound is terraced and one interesting feature of the arrangement of the buildings is the fact that the old meeting hall is out of line of the main axis of the temple buildings. In front of it is a three-storey Shilla pagoda which was erected in the second half of the 7th century.

Inside the main courtyard area, there is a second, older seven-storey granite pagoda dating from the early 7th century, or from the Paekje Kingdom. It has the typical curved-up edges to the roofs on each of its storeys. The nearby lantern is modern, copied from an ancient one.

The Main Hall, National Treasure No. 49, is a shrine to an important triad. It was built in 1308 and is the oldest wooden building in Korea of which there is a definite record of the year of construction. It is nothing short of a miracle that the building has stood through successive invasions in which everything of any value seems to have been destroyed almost everywhere else in the country. Its recorded history and the beauty of the design make it extremely important to Korean culture.

Inside there are three Buddhas and two Bodhisattvas. The three Buddhas represent some of the main features of Buddhism. Sakyamuni is the Historical Buddha, the original teacher. Amitabha is the Buddha of Infinite Light and Bhaisagyaguru is the Medicine Buddha, the Universal Healer. In addition there are two Bodhisattvas: Manjusri, Perfect Wisdom, and Samantabhadra, Perfect Practice. There is a legend which tells that the original paintings on the ceiling and pillars were done by a Koguryo master. On the back wall of the hall is a painting of Ksitigarbha and the Ten Judges and to the right there is another painting of the gods who are indigenous to Korea. Unfortunately, the wall paintings, National Treasure No. 48, created during the Koryo Period, have not been so lucky. Most of them were destroyed in the Korean War and the remaining ones have been moved to the museum. These paintings are famous for their elegant, realistic style and they demonstrate the magnificence of Koryo art.

In front of the Main Hall there is a beautifully balanced Unified Shilla Period stupa, Provincial Tangible Cultural Asset No. 103. The stupas of that period capture some loveliness which was lost in the succeeding generations of art. The proportions of the storeys, the curve of the corners, the size of the stands for each successive layer, all go to make a work of art which cannot fail to please the eye.

On the way to Chonghye-sa, a small temple above Sudok-sa, about 15 minutes walk up the mountain there is a ten-meter granite statue of Maitreya, the Future Buddha. It has a double Korean cylindrical hat, a coat reaching down to the ankles and an imposing attitude in the expression carved on its face. The statue was erected by Mangong.

Nearby is the stupa erected by the disciples of Mangong in memory of their master. It is considered unusual because it has a large spherical stone on the top. There is an inscription on the stupa which reads "The whole world is a single flower."

UNMUN-SA TEMPLE

Unmun-sa Temple is one of Korea's major temples and it is situated on Tiger mountain. A Shilla monk built a hermitage on this mountain and, after three years of intensive meditation, he attained enlightenment.

Originally called Taejakgap-sa "Great Magpie Hillside" Temple, in 937 the king who founded the Koryo Dynasty changed the name to Unmun-sa, meaning "Cloud Gate" Temple.

The temple has a famous tree. Said to be 500 years old, legend tells that it grew up from a branch planted by a passing monk. In 1950, Unmun-sa Temple became the largest bhikkuni training center in Korea. About 250 students regularly follow a three to four year course in Buddhism.

SOKNAM-SA

"Southern Rock Temple" was built by Toui-kuksa in the 9th century. One of the great monks in the history of Korean Buddhism, Master Toui chose this beautiful spot on Mt. Kaji-san.

At first the temple was small but then it was taken over by bhikkunis in the early part of this century and greatly enlarged. In-hong Sunim was mainly responsible for the development and the creation of three separate meditation halls — one for beginners and experienced practitioners, one for more advanced practitioners and one for three year retreats.

Today the temple has up to 100 ordained women in the meditation season living and practicing together. Ordained women of all ages live here and the traditional style of practice and lifestyle are rigorously followed. There are two very fine pagodas to visit at this temple as well as enjoying the lovely mountain stream.

TEMPLES IN SEOUL

As many visitors to Korea have little time to visit the temples in the mountains, we thought that it would be good to offer a short description and directions to some of the more famous Seoul temples. Please do take the time to visit some of them, you may be very surprised at the experience!

THE CENTER OF THE LARGEST SECT OF KOREAN BUDDHISM: CHOGYE-SA

Chogye-sa Temple is the only major temple within the old city walls of Seoul. Built in 1910, the temple was first called Kakwang-sa. The name was changed to T'aego-sa during the time of the Japanese Occupation and in 1936, the temple became the headquarters of Korean Buddhism's Chogye Order. It is extremely important to all Korean Buddhists.

In 1954, after the great clean-up movement to rid the country of any vestiges of the Japanese occupation, the temple came to be called Chogye-sa. This is the name of the mountain on which the Sixth Patriarch of Chinese Chan Buddhism, Huineng (638-713), lived. He is highly revered by Korean Buddhists and his life and teachings are constantly studied and remem-bered.

Born poor and illiterate, Master Huineng attained enlightenment on hearing the Diamond Sutra being chanted while he was selling wood. Eventually he was recognized by the Fifth Patriarch and became his successor. His teachings are simple. One of the most beautiful sayings ascribed to him is a true example of Buddhism. "In all conditions we should be humble and polite." Today, Chogye-sa is the main temple of Korean Buddhism and its major sect, Chogye, which is a Zen sect.

The Main Hall was built in 1 year and 7 months, from March 1937 until October 1938. It is an impressive, wooden structure which is decorated on the outside with paintings of the Buddha's life and teachings, and huge, wooden latticework doors — well worth taking a careful look at. Inside, the comparatively small Buddha statue is of unknown origin. There is a story told, however, that it came from Tokab-sa in Cholla Province. Behind the statue is a traditional painting. The central figure is Sakyamuni, the Historical Buddha, and on either side of him, from the bottom up, are guardians, Bodhisattvas, and, at the top, there are some of the Buddha's disciples. On either side of the glass case containing the Buddha, on the inside, there are cases containing sutras carved on wooden blocks. The central shrine is flanked by paintings of hundreds of Buddhas. They are symbolic of the many Buddhas in the universe and the fact that we are all Buddhas without knowing it!

This temple hall is a major center of Buddhist events. Nearly every night of the year there is some kind of religious activity going on: a lecture, chanting and bowing classes, special ceremonies and celebrations. Behind the Main Hall of Chogye-sa, is the headquarters of the Chogye Order. All kinds of activities also take place there: visiting monks and dignitaries host meetings; there are exhibitions; and a weekly newspaper is printed.

In front of the Main Hall is a seven-storey pagoda containing a relic of the Buddha which was brought to Korea by a Sri Lankan monk in 1914. People bow as they pass and make offerings of candles and incense in memory of the Buddha. There are traditional stone lanterns on either side of the pagoda. In front of the Main Hall to the left, there is Bell Pavilion. There hang the drum, the bell, the gong and the fish, instruments used to regulate temple life and call all willing sentient beings to listen to the liberating words of the Buddha which are chanted at every ceremony. First the drum is rhythmically beaten calling the animals. Then the large bell calls those who suffer and live in the realms of torment — in the morning it is struck 33 times for the different heavenly states and 28 times in the morning. And then the cloud-shaped gong calls the beings of the air. The log carved into the shape of a fish calls all that live in the water. At 4 a.m. and at 6 p.m. in winter and 7 p.m. in summer, every day of every year a monk is in charge of sounding these instruments at Chogye-sa — it is a wonderful sight to see.

Beside the Bell Pavilion, there is a newly constructed traditional building. It houses the offices of the temple in the basement, a meeting hall on the ground floor and the offices of training monks and teaching Buddhism on the floor above.

Behind the Main Hall there is a newly constructed hall, called the "Hall of the Virtuous Kings" and it is dedicated to Amitabha, the Buddha of Universal Light. Beside the principle Buddha, there are Ksitigarbha, the helper of those in trouble and Avalokitesvara, the Bodhisattva of Compassion.

In the Chogye-sa compound, there is also a 500-year-old white pine tree supposed to have been brought from China; it is Natural Monument No. 7. The tall, zelkova tree beside the pagoda is draped with lanterns on the Buddha's Birthday in May of every year. At that time the entire courtyard is filled with lanterns and, standing on the platform of the Main Hall, you can gaze down on the sea of shimmering lotuses.

There are many Buddhist shops just outside Chogye-sa where you can buy books, bells, mokt'aks, statues, and other souvenirs and mementoes.

CHIN-GWAN-SA

Chin-gwan-sa was originally built in 1101 CE. Then in 1403, Sooryuk-sa was built on the ruins of the original temple in memory of the nation's founders. Burnt down during the Korean War, it was rebuilt in 1964 by a bhikkhuni, Chin-gwan Sunim. Now it is a women's temple where between ten and twenty bhikkhunis live.

When you enter the main compound, passing under the building used for the thriving children's meeting on Sunday and other events, the Main Hall is directly in front of you. To the left are the living quarters for the nuns. To the right of the Main Hall are smaller shrines. The first hall, recently rebuilt, contains Ksitigarbha with all the judges, the second is the abode of the Mountain God and the Recluse, the third is where people light lamps to remember the departed, and the last is Amitabha's shrine with all the enlightened disciples. The Mountain God's shrine and the one with many small lamps both pre-date the rest of the present temple buildings.

Down to the left there is a path running to the toilets and to the two-storey, new eating hall/kitchen complex. Upstairs there are rooms for senior nuns.

HWAGYE-SA

Hwagye-sa, "Flower Stream Temple" is on Samgag-san Mountain. It was built in 1552 by Master Sinwol during the reign of King Chung-jong (r. 1506-1544) the 11th king of the Choson Dynasty, destroyed in 1618, during the reign of King Kwanghaegun (r. 1608-1623) and then rebuilt the following year by Master Dowol.

After 240 years, the temple became so dilapidated that two monks, Yongsun and Pamyun had it repaired in 1865. The statues of Bodhisattva Ksitigarbha and the Ten Judges in the Judgment Hall are especially famous. Beautifully carved by Master Nawong in the late Koryo Dynasty, the figures were brought to Hwagye-sa in 1877 by Queen Mother Chodaebe. After that the temple served the royal family.

There are two famous urns on either side of the Main Hall. These were donated by Queen Hongdaebe, wife of King Hunjong (r. 1834-1849).

Hwagye-sa is the home of the Kwan-um International Zen Center which was started by Seung-san Sunim. Foreign monks and lay people live here practicing the traditional way of life of Korean temples.

KURYONG-SA

Kuryong-sa, "Nine Dragons" Temple, is the Seoul branch of T'ongdo-sa, the temple of the Buddha in Pusan. A modern temple with a very modern outlook, the temple is proud of its varied facilities: there is something for everyone.

The spacious 10,000 Buddhas Hall is not only used for chanting but also for lectures. In addition there is a meditation room, a kindergarten, a center for the young, and lots of accommodation for the many foreign visitors. Then there is an exhibition room in which Buddhist objects and traditional culture are shown, a vegetarian restaurant, a small theater and a reading room. As the temple is also interested in traditional culture, there is a tea room where the Korean tea ceremony is taught.

PONGUK-SA

Ponguk-sa was built in 1395 by Muhak Desa (1327-1405), a monk who was famous for geomancy and the person who chose the site of Seoul for the capital city of the, then, new Choson Dynasty. At first it was called Yaksa-sa because the main Buddha statue was of the Medicine Buddha or Universal Healer. Muhak Desa hoped that the temple would bring blessings to the new Choson Dynasty so that it would flourish forever. As a result there are all the shrines necessary for bringing good luck in the temple compound. There is a shrine for the Mountain God, one for the Recluse and one for the Seven Stars (the Big Dipper), all traditional shrines of ancient Korea. These are in addition to the more common Hall of Judgment and the Main Hall. There are also living quarters for the monks. The lay-out of the temple is especially pleasing.

PONGUN-SA

Pongun-sa was first built during the reign of King Wansong (r. 785-798) by the National Master Yonhoe. In 1551 it became the main temple of the Zen Order. Then, after 1945, it came under the direct control of the Headquarters of the Chogye Order.

The main concern of the temple is in education. To this end, there are many programs organized in order to accommodate anyone and everyone. There are different activities for each age group of children and university students, there are discussion and study groups; the temple supports the main Monastic University.

The temple compound is an example of a traditional temple. There are the gates, shrines, and living quarters. A visit to this temple gives the impression of a mountain temple.

PULGWANG-SA

Pulgwang-sa, "Buddha's Light" Temple, is one of Korea's most fascinating temples. The buildings themselves are not so special, it is the orientation of the work being done which is particular. Opened on October 16, 1975, the temple is totally dedicated to social work and aims at helping all members of society. A major activity is the creation of small groups in which anyone can have the opportunity to study the Buddha's teachings and awaken to a clear view of reality.

Understanding the many problems facing people, the temple has organized many support groups. There is a special group that helps members through crises and another aimed at compassionate social work among less fortunate people. Then there is a thriving kindergarten, a publishing company, and various educational programs.

PONG-WON-SA

Pong-won-sa was originally built on the site of today's Yonsei University in 889 by Master Toson (827-898). In 1748 it was moved to its present site by Master Chanjup. King Yongju wrote an inscription and the temple became known as "New Temple." The present buildings were erected in 1911, but the Main Hall was destroyed during the Korean War. The 3,000 Buddhas' Hall is the largest wooden structure in Korea. Pong-won-sa is the home of the T'aego Order, an order of married monks and the second largest in Korea. It is especially famous for traditional ceremonies, chanting, religious dancing and art. At present three national treasures live there: Buddhist Art, Ritual Song and Ritual Ornamentation.

TAEGAK-SA

Taegak-sa, "Great Enlightenment" Temple, was established in 1894 by Baek, Yong-song Sunim, one of the leaders of the independence movement against the Japanese. He was a monk who became a hero to Buddhists and non-Buddhists alike. When the government-in-exile returned to Korea from Japan after the Japanese Occupation, they were welcomed at Taegak-sa because of the fame of the founder.

The temple is the place chosen for the translation of the Tripitaka Koreana from Chinese into Korean. This project was started by Yong-song Sunim who wanted to make the Buddha's teachings available to everyone. About 50 of the 6,791 volumes have been translated so far.

In 1987, the temple was largely rebuilt and it continues to be an important place to Korean Buddhists.

TOSON-SA

Toson-sa was founded by Master Toson (826-912) who, after traveling far and wide, decided that Samgak-san was the best mountain on which to build a temple because he felt that Buddhism would flourish there. This prophesy was to come true over 1000 years after his death for this is where the famous monk, Master Chungdam (1902-1971) lived.

Master Toson was a very learned monk. He had studied astronomy and geography as well as Buddhism. When he came to Samgak-san he recognized its special features and there, using his magical power, he cut a huge boulder in two and carved a Medicine Buddha on the surface. Today, that 20 foot-high stone Buddha is the source of much wonder and reverence. Many go to visit it and there are stories of people being cured of serious ailments because they had the faith to do their religious practice in this place. Up, up you go to the temple, perched in the crags on the very top of Samgak-san.

CHANTS

THE HEART SUTRA

Chanting takes place at every Buddhist ceremony in almost every Buddhist group all over the world. The aim of chanting is to remind ourselves of the Buddha's teachings and share them with others. The main problem with human life is that we forget the lessons we have learned, we forget that desire gets us nowhere, we forget that we are going to die. In addition, the vibrations emanating from the sounds of the voices are considered beneficial to the body and soothing to the mind. In Korea, chanting is usually accompanied by the mokt'ak, a wooden percussion instrument, and, sometimes, a hand bell.

The thrice daily, temple chanting always includes the following two chants: the Heart Sutra and Homage to the Buddhas. The Heart Sutra is one of the most important teachings in Mahayana Buddhism in general, and in Korean Buddhism in particular. Although difficult to understand for those unfamiliar with Buddhism, the reader can catch a glimpse of the transcendental through its lines.

HOMAGE TO THE BUDDHAS

May the sweet scent of our keeping the precepts, of our meditations, of our wisdom, of our liberation and of the knowledge of our liberation — may all this form a shining cloud-like pavilion and pervade the whole universe. May it do homage to all the countless Buddhas, Dharma and Sanghas in all the ten directions.

Mantra of Incense Offering: Om-ba-a-ra-to-bi-ya-hum. (3 times)

We most devoutly pay homage to the teacher of all the three worlds, the great teacher of all beings, to our guide, Sakyamuni Buddha.

We devoutly pay homage to the eternally existent assembly of all the Buddhas, in all the ten directions, of the past, present and future as countless as the lands and seas in Lord Indra's net.

We devoutly pay homage to all the Teachings, eternally existent, in all the ten directions, in the past, present, and future as countless as the lands and seas in Lord Indra's net.

We devoutly pay homage to all Bodhisattvas and Mahasattvas, and most especially do we commemorate the Bodhisattvas Manjusri, Sariputra, Samantabhadra, the most compassionate and loving Avalokitesvara, and he, the Lord of many vows, Ksitigarbha.

We devoutly pay homage to the countless compassionate and love-filled Communities, and most especially do we commemorate those who have received personally the Buddha's teachings on Mount Gridhakuta — the ten major disciples, the sixteen holy ones, the five hundred holy ones, and all of the one thousand five hundred great Attained Ones.

We devoutly pay homage to those great patriarchs and teachers who have come from the West to the East, those who have come to Korean shores, and who have transmitted the Light of the Teaching down through all generations. Likewise we pay homage to masters of all traditions, recognized throughout the ages, and to our various numberless spiritual teachers and friends.

We devoutly pay homage to all Sanghas, eternally existent, in all the ten directions, of the past, present, and future as countless as the lands and seas in Lord Indra's net.

We earnestly desire that the inexhaustible Three Precious Ones will most lovingly and compassionately receive our devotions, and that they will empower us spiritually; we further most earnestly desire that together with all creatures in the universe, we may attain Buddhahood at one and the same time.

TEACHINGS

THE PRECEPTS

A Buddhist is a person who takes refuge in the Buddha, the Teachings and the Community of Buddhists and who takes five training rules, precepts, by which he lives his life. Although the same in all schools of Buddhism, in Korea they are expressed as follows:

The First Precept: I take the training rule of abstaining from killing and henceforth practice loving-kindness.

Killing roots out the seeds of love and compassion. To kill another is to feast on our friends and relatives from previous lives. It leads to rebirth in painful states and does not give us rebirth in the human body necessary for attaining enlightenment.

The Second Precept: I take the training rule of not taking things which have not been given and of practicing generosity. Takings things which have not been given to us roots out virtue and wisdom. By desiring things belonging to someone else, we allow greed to grow and we behave like animals.

The Third Precept: I take the training rule of controlling sensual and sexual desire and of practicing awareness.

Lack of control of the senses destroys the seeds of purity and simplicity. It leads to a life of no peace and stability and a future in the lower realms.

The Fourth Precept: I take the training rule of not lying, gossiping or speaking harshly and of practicing wholesome speech.

The tongue is sharper than the sword, wrong speech destroys the seeds of truth and cuts off the flowers of goodwill. The only future for one who is careless of speech is suffering.

The Fifth Precept: I take the training rule of refraining from intoxicants which cloud the mind and of practicing clear mindedness.

Alcohol and drugs destroy wisdom and cause behavior which creates piles of regrets. Practice awareness and live a life free from regret!

GREEDLESS HARMONY

A talk given by a modern Korean master,

Ven. Songch'ol (1912-1993)

The sons and daughters of Buddha are free on the eternal path of liberation, and the sons and daughters of Confucius sing of the Great Age of Sages. The sons and daughters of Jesus are replete in their infinite glory, and the sons and daughters of Mohammed have hearts bursting with joy and happiness.

The world is a single home, and all of mankind is one. So let's forget such useless discrimination as "self" and "others," and forget national, racial and other barriers. Let's treat those of other religions as members of our own, and those of other nations as our compatriots.

To harm others is to harm yourself, and to help others is to help yourself. Treat the sick as if they were yourself, and serve the anguished in every way that you can.

It is awful to disguise personal profit and greed as patriotism and fraternity, so let's rid ourselves of this completely. With a pure heart, let's all help one another and let's all trust one another. Let's respect one another and love one another, and let's all harmonize as one. As I sit leisurely without thoughts of "self" and "others," plum blossoms begin to cast their fragrance into falling snow.

INSPIRING YOURSELF TO PRACTICE

Inspiring Yourself to Practice was written by the Shilla Monk Wonhyo (617-686). It consists of 706 characters, contained in one roll. In Korea, the text is one of the most important in the curriculum of the temple training, during the period of study. The text stresses the need to eliminate one's karmic bond with the world and to begin immediately to practice. The original Chinese text is kept at Haein-sa Temple, near Taegu, and the annotated version is kept at Songgwang-sa Temple, in Sunchon.

- Numbers in the text refer to explanatory notes at the end.

All the Buddhas
Who reside within the splendid realm of Nirvana
Have, throughout countless eons,
Discarded their desires and undergone arduous training.
Sentient beings
That transmigrate within the burning house of desire
Have, for countless generations,
Failed to discard their greed and desire.

The gates to heaven (the Pure Land)
Are not blocked;
Yet, few are those who enter them.
This is because most people make their home
Among the three poisons.

The evil realms have no real power to seduce us,
Yet many enter them.
The deluded mind values
The four elements that make up the body
And the five desires
As if they were jewels.

This being so,
Is there anyone who does not long
To retire to the seclusion of the mountains
In order to practice the Way?

Yet people do not go there;
They remain caught up in desire.
Although you do not
Retire to the mountains
To cultivate your mind,

You should strive with all your energy
To perform good deeds.

If you can renounce your own pleasure,
You will become as trusted and respected
As the sages.
If you can undergo
That which is difficult,
You will become as respected
As the Buddha.

Those who greedily seek after things
Join the ranks of demons.
Those who give with compassion
Are the disciples of the Dharma King.

High mountains and lofty peaks
Are where the wise reside.
Green pines and deep mountain valleys
Are home to those who practice.
When hungry, such people pick fruit from trees
To calm their empty stomach.
When thirsty, they quench their thirst
With water from a stream.

Although we eat fine foods
In an attempt to carefully preserve this body,
Our bodies will definitely face destruction;
Even though we cover this body
With soft cloth,
Our lives are sure to come to an end.

Make a small mountain cave where echoes resound
Into a hall to chant the Buddha's name.
Let the sad cry of a wild goose
Be the heart-warming call of a friend.

While bowing, your knees may become
As cold as ice,
But you must not long for a warm fire.
Your stomach may writhe with hunger,
But you must not give in to your thoughts of food.

One hundred years pass like the blinking of an eye,
So why don't you practice?
How long is a lifetime?
Can you afford to neglect practice,
Wasting your time on leisure?

It is only he who renounces
All of the desires in his heart
That is rightfully called a practicing monk.
Only he who no longer yearns for the ways of the world

Is called "a monk who has renounced the house-holder's life."
A practitioner who is caught
Within the net of worldly desires
Is like a dog who wears
Elephant's hide.
A man who practices the Way
Yet remains attached to worldly desire
Is like a hedgehog
Who tries to enter a rat hole.

Some people, in spite of their outstanding ability and wisdom,
Choose to live in the busy atmosphere of the city.
All the Buddhas feel pity and concern for such people.
Other people, although they have not yet developed
A deep practice,
Still choose to stay in the contemplative atmosphere of the mountains.
The sages feel a great joy
When they see such people.
There are those who are skilled and learned,
But do not follow the precepts.
They are like men who are told of a cache of jewels
But do not get up and go to it.
There are those who practice steadfastly
But lack wisdom.
They are like men who want to go east
But mistakenly walk towards the west.

The actions of a wise man
Are like steaming grains of rice
In order to make a bowl of rice.
The actions of a man who lacks wisdom
Are like steaming grains of sand
In order to make a bowl of rice.
Everyone knows how to eat and drink
In order to satiate their hunger;
But no one seems to understand
The method of training –
The way to transform the ignorant mind.

Practice and wisdom must exist side by side.
For they are like the two wheels of a cart.

Likewise, helping oneself and helping others
Are like the two wings of a bird.
If you absent-mindedly chant for your donors
Over the morning offering of porridge
Without understanding the meaning,
You should feel ashamed
To face those who give alms.

If you chant
During the lunch-time ceremony
Without attaining the essence of the words you utter,
Won't you be ashamed to face
Great people and sages?

Everyone hates squirming insects
And those who can't distinguish between the dirty and the clean.
Likewise, the sages feel disgust with those monks
Who cannot distinguish between the defiled and the pure.
If you wish to be through with this world's conflict,
Good conduct is the ladder
That ascends to heaven.

Therefore, one who violates the precepts
And yet wishes to help others
Is like a bird with broken wings
That puts a turtle on its back and tries to fly.

If you're still not free from your own faults,
You will not be able to free others of their faults.
So why do you, who violate the precepts
Receive that which is provided by others?

It does not benefit you in the least
To merely maintain your physical body

If you neglect to practice.
And all your concern for this transient, fleeting life
Will not preserve it.

If you've set your sights
On the virtue of the great masters,
You must endure even the longest hardships.
Once you've set out for the Tiger Throne,
You must forever leave all your desires behind you.

When the cultivator's mind is pure,
All the devas bow in praise of him.
When a follower of the Way loves lasciviousness,
The good spirits leave him.

At death, when the four elements of the body scatter,
You cannot preserve the body and remain in it any longer.
Today, evening has already arrived;
Tomorrow morning will soon be here.
So, practice now before it is too late.

Worldly pleasures are unsatisfactory;
Why do you greedily cling to them?
Enduring joy can be won through a single effort in patience;
Why won't you practice?

Those who practice feel shame
To see a seeker of the Way who remains attached to greed.
The virtuous man laughs
At the seeker who forsakes the householder's life
But is still wealthy.

Words, such as these written here, go on and on,
Yet clinging attachment does not come to an end.

"I'll do it next time" — such words go on and on,
Yet you fail to put an end to clinging.
Clinging goes on and on,
Yet you fail to renounce worldly matters.
Your mind is filled with endless devious plans,
Yet you do not make up your mind to put an end to them.
"Today will be different," you say,
Yet you continue to perform evil actions every day.
"Tomorrow, tomorrow," you say,
Yet few are the days when you really do something good.
"This year will be different," you say,
Yet your defilements are without end.
"Next year I'll do it," you say,
Yet you don't grow in wisdom.

The hours pass,
And too soon a day and night are over.
The days pass,
And soon it's the last day of the month.
The months pass,
And suddenly another new year has come.
The years pass,
And in the blinking of an eye,
We find ourselves at death's door.

A broken cart
Cannot be driven.
When you're an old man,
You cannot begin to practice.
When you lie down,
You will succumb to laziness.
And when you sit,

Your mind will be overwhelmed
With stray thoughts.

For many lifetimes, you have failed to practice,
Passing your days and nights in vain.
Having lived many lifetimes in vain,
Will you again fail to practice during this lifetime?

This body will inevitably come to an end;
Who knows what body you will have next time?

Isn't this an urgent matter?
Isn't this an urgent matter?

Chapter - 6

Buddhism in Mongolia

The indigenous religion of Mongolia prior to Buddhism was shamanism, which focused specifically on rituals and nature deities. There are still elements of modern Mongolian Buddhism that display the early amalgam between Buddhism and local shamanistic practices, such as the Mongolian Buddhist dance, the tsam. In addition to this dimension, Tibetan Buddhist monasticism made an important impact on the early development of Mongolian Buddhism. The Buddhist monkhood always have played significant political roles in Central and Southeast Asia, and the Buddhist sangha in Mongolia was no exception. Church and state supported each other, and the doctrine of reincarnation made it possible for the reincarnations of living Buddhas to be discovered conveniently in the families of powerful Mongol nobles, until this practice was outlawed by the Qianlong Emperor.

By the beginning of the twentieth century, Outer Mongolia had 583 monasteries and temple complexes, which controlled an estimated 20 percent of the country's wealth. Almost all Mongolian cities have grown up on the sites of monasteries. Yihe Huree, as Ulaanbaatar was then known, was the seat of the preeminent living Buddha of Mongolia (the Jebtsundamba Khutuktu, also known as the Bogdo Gegen and later as Bogd Khan), who ranked third in the ecclesiastical hierarchy, after the Dalai Lama and the Panchen Lama. Two monasteries there contained approximately 13,000 and 7,000 monks, and the prerevolutionary Mongol name of the settlement known to outsiders as Urga, Yihe Huree, means "big monastery".

Over the centuries, the monasteries acquired riches and secular dependents; they gradually increased their wealth and power as those of the Mongol nobility declined. Some nobles donated a portion of their dependent families — people, rather than land, were the foundation of wealth and power in old Mongolia — to the monasteries; some herders dedicated themselves and their families to serve the monasteries either from piety or from the desire to escape the arbitrary exactions of the nobility. In some areas, the monasteries and their living buddhas (of whom there were a total of 140 in 1924) also were the secular authorities. In the 1920s, there were about 110,000 monks, including children, who made up about one-third of the male population, although many of these lived outside the monasteries and did not observe their vows. About 250,000 people, more than a third of the total population, either lived in territories administered by monasteries and living Buddhas or were hereditary dependents of the monasteries. With the end of Manchu rule in 1911, the Buddhist church and its clergy provided the only political structure available, and the autonomous state thus took the form of a weakly centralized theocracy, headed by the Jebtsundamba Khutukhtu in Yehe Kuriye.

By the twentieth century, Buddhism had penetrated deeply into Mongolian culture, and the populace willingly supported the lamas and the monasteries. Foreign observers usually had a negative opinion of Mongolian monks, condemning them as lazy, ignorant, corrupt, and debauched, but the Mongolian people did not concur. Ordinary Mongolians apparently combined a cynical and realistic anticlericalism, sensitive to the faults and the human fallibility of individual monks or groups of monks, with a deep and unwavering concern for the transcendent values of the church.

Early Mongolian contacts with Buddhism are dated to the fourth century, when the activities of Chinese monks among the population of this border area are reported in contemporary Chinese sources. Buddhist influences spread as far as the Yenisei region by the seventh century, as evidenced by Buddhist temple bells with Chinese inscriptions found there. Another factor in the spread of Buddhism into Mongolia was the flourishing of Buddhist communities in the predominantly Uighur oasis states along the Silk Route. Furthermore, the palace that was built by Ogedei Khan (1229-1241) in Karakorum, the Mongol capital, was constructed on the foundations of a former Buddhist temple; some of the murals from this temple have been preserved, Sources for this early Buddhist activity are rather scarce. Reports in Mongolian sources on the early spread of Buddhism shroud these missionary activities in a cloak of mysterious events that testify to the superiority of Tantric Buddhism over other religions during the reign of Khublai Khan (1260-1294). Contacts with the Sa-skya pandita Kun-dga'rgyal-mtshan (1182-1251) were established during Ogedei's reign, but Buddhism only gained influence with the Mongols after their expeditions into Tibet, which resulted in the sojourn of Tibetan monks as hostages at the Mongol court. The activities there of the lama (Tib., bla ma) 'Phags pa (1235-1280) resulted in an increase in conversions to Buddhism, his invention, in 1269, of a block script led to the translation into Mongolian of great numbers of Buddhist religious literature, the translations often based on already existing Uighur translations. The legend that Chinggis Khan had previously invited the Sa-skya abbot Kun-dga'-snin-po (1092-1158) lacks proof.

In spite of the extensive translation and printing of Buddhist tracts, conversion seems to have been limited to the nobility and the ruling families. Judging from the Mongols' history of religious tolerance, it is rather doubtful that Buddhism spread among the general population on a large scale. Syncretic influences resulted in the transformation of popular gods into Buddhist deities and the acceptance of notions from other religions during this period.

After Mongol rule over China ended in 1368 the practice of Buddhism diminished among the Mongols, deteriorating into mere superstition or giving way once again to the indigenous religious conceptions of the Mongols and to shamanism. It was not until the sixteenth century that a second wave of Buddhist conversion began, brought about by the military expeditions of Allan Khan of the Tumet (1507-1583) into the eastern border districts of Tibet, which resulted in contacts with lamaist clerics. Within the short period of fifty years, beginning with the visit of the third Dalai Lama to Allan Khan's newly built residence, Koke Khota, in 1578, practically all of the Mongolian nobility was converted to Buddhism by the missionary work of many devoted lamaist priests. The most famous of these were Neyici Toyin (1557-1653), who converted the eastern Mongols, and Zaya Pandita, who converted the western and northern Mongols. Sustained by princes and overlords who acted according to the maxim "huius regio, eius religio," inducing the adoption of the new faith by donations of horses, dairy animals, and money, the population willingly or forcedly took to Lamaism. Shamanism was outlawed, idols sought out and burned. The establishment of many new monasteries opened to a greater part of the population the opportunity to become monks, resulting in a drain on Mongolian manpower. The monasteries, however, became similar to those of early medieval Europe; they were the cradles of literature and science, particularly of Buddhist philosophy. By 1629 many other lamaist works were translated into Mongolian, including the 1,161 volumes of the lamaist canon, the Bka'-'gyur (Kanjur). Tibetan became the lingua franca of the clerics, as Latin was in medieval Europe, with hundreds of religious works written in this language.

During the Ch'ing dynasty in China, particularly during the K'ang-hsi, Yung-cheng, and Ch'ien-lung reign periods, the printing of Buddhist works in Mongolian was furthered by the Manchu emperors as well as by the Mongolian nobility. Donating money for copying scripture, cutting printing blocks, and printing Buddhist works were thought of as meritorious deeds. Works on medicine, philosophy, and history were also published and distributed. The spiritual life of Mongolia became strongly influenced by religious and semi-religious thoughts and ethics. Sponsored by the K'ang hsi emperor, a revised edition of the Mongolian Bka'-'gyur was printed from 1718 to 1720; translation of the Bstan-'gyur (Tanjur) was begun under the Ch'ien-lung emperor in 1741 and was completed in 1749. Copies of the completed edition (in 108 and 223 volumes, respectively, for the Bka'-'gyur and Bstan'-'gyur) were given as imperial gifts to many monasteries throughout Mongolia.

In the eighteenth century elements of indigenous Mongolian mythology were incorporated into a national liturgy composed entirely in Mongolian. A century later there were about twelve hundred lamaist temples and monasteries in Inner Mongolia and more than seven hundred in the territory of the present-day Mongolian People's Republic. More than a third of the entire male population of Mongolia belonged to the clergy. The monasteries, possessing their own economic system and property, formed a separate administrative and political organization. In the twentieth century the decline of monasteries and Lamaism was brought about by inner strife and a changing moral climate as well as by political movements and new ideologies. Recently have some monasteries been reopened in the Mongolian parts of China, in the Mongolian People's Republic, and in Buriat-Mongolia in the former U.S.S.R., but the question of whether the younger members of the population will embrace the faith again remains open.

Traditional Mongols worshipped heaven (the "clear blue sky") and their ancestors, and they followed ancient northern Asian practices of shamanism, in which human intermediaries went into trance and spoke to and for some of the numberless infinities of spirits responsible for human luck or misfortune. In 1578 Altan Khan, a Mongol military leader with ambitions to unite the Mongols and to emulate the career of Chinggis, invited the head of the rising Yellow Sect of Tibetan Buddhism to a summit. They formed an alliance that gave Altan legitimacy and religious sanction for his imperial pretensions and that provided the Buddhist sect with protection and patronage.

Altan gave the Tibetan leader the title of Dalai Lama (Ocean Lama), which his successors still hold. Altan died soon after, but in the next century the Yellow Sect spread throughout Mongolia, aided in part by the efforts of contending Mongol aristocrats to win religious sanction and mass support for their ultimately unsuccessful efforts to unite all Mongols in a single state. Monasteries were built across Mongolia, often sited at the juncture of trade and migration routes or at summer pastures, where large numbers of herders would congregate for shamanistic rituals and sacrifices. Buddhist monks carried out a protracted struggle with the indigenous shamans and succeeded, to some extent, in taking over their functions and fees as healers and diviners, and in pushing the shamans to the religious and cultural fringes of Mongolian culture.

Tibetan Buddhism, which combines elements of the Mahayana and the Tantric schools of Buddhism with traditional Tibetan rituals of curing and exorcism, shares the common Buddhist goal of individual release from suffering and the cycles of rebirth. The religion holds that salvation, in the sense of release from the cycle of rebirth, can be achieved through the intercession of compassionate buddhas (enlightened ones) who have delayed their own entry to the state of selfless bliss (nirvana) to save others. Such buddhas, who are many, are in practice treated more as deities than as enlightened humans and occupy the center of a richly polytheistic universe of subordinate deities, opposing demons, converted and reformed demons, wandering ghosts, and saintly humans that reflects the folk religions of the regions into which Buddhism expanded. Tantrism contributed esoteric techniques of meditation and a repertoire of sacred icons, phrases, and gestures that easily lent themselves to pragmatic (rather than transcendental) and magical interpretation.

The religion posits progressive stages of enlightenment and comprehension of the reality underlying the illusions that hamper the understanding and perceptions of those not trained in meditation or Buddhist doctrine, with sacred symbols interpreted in increasingly abstract terms. Thus, a ritual that appears to a common yak herder as a straightforward exorcism of disease demons will be interpreted by a senior monk as a representation of conflicting tendencies in the mind of a meditating ascetic.

In Tibet Buddhism thus became an amalgam, combining colorful popular ceremonies and curing rituals for the masses with the study of esoteric doctrine for the monastic elite. The Yellow Sect, in contrast to competing sects, stressed monastic discipline and the use of logic and formal debates as aids to enlightenment. The basic Buddhist tenet of reincarnation was combined with the Tantric idea that buddhahood could be achieved within a person's lifetime to produce a category of leaders who were considered to have achieved buddhahood and to be the reincarnations of previous leaders. These leaders, referred to as incarnate or living buddhas, held secular power and supervised a body of ordinary monks, or lamas (from a Tibetan title *bla-ma,* meaning "the revered one)". The monks were supported by the laity, who thereby gained merit and who received from the monks instructions in the rudiments of the faith and monastic services in healing, divination, and funerals.

Buddhism and the Buddhist monkhood always have played significant political roles in Central and Southeast Asia, and the Buddhist church in Mongolia was no exception. Church and state supported each other, and the doctrine of reincarnation made it possible for the reincarnations of living buddhas to be discovered conveniently in the families of powerful Mongol nobles.

Tibetan Buddhism is monastic. By the beginning of the twentieth century, Outer Mongolia had 583 monasteries and temple complexes, which controlled an estimated 20 percent of the country's wealth. Almost all Mongolian cities have grown up on the sites of monasteries. Yihe Huree, as Ulaanbaatar was then known, was the seat of the preeminent living buddha of Mongolia (the Jebtsundamba Khutuktu, also known as the Bogdo Gegen and later as Bogdo Khan), who ranked third in the ecclesiastical hierarchy, after the Dalai Lama and the Panchen Lama. Two monasteries there contained approximately 13,000 and 7,000 monks, and the prerevolutionary Mongol name of the settlement known to outsiders as Urga, Yihe Huree, means big monastery.

Over the centuries, the monasteries acquired riches and secular dependents; they gradually increased their wealth and power as those of the Mongol nobility declined. Some nobles donated a portion of their dependent families—people, rather than land, were the foundation of wealth and power in old Mongolia—to the monasteries; some herders dedicated themselves and their families to serve the monasteries either from piety or from the desire to escape the arbitrary exactions of the nobility. In some areas, the monasteries and their living buddhas (of whom there were a total of 140 in 1924) also were the secular authorities. In the 1920s, there were about 110,000 monks, including children, who made up about one-third of the male population, although many of these lived outside the monasteries and did not observe their vows. About 250,000 people, more than a third of the total population, either lived in territories administered by monasteries and living buddhas or were hereditary dependents of the monasteries. With the end of Chinese rule in 1911, the Buddhist church and its clergy provided the only political structure available, and the autonomous state thus took the form of a weakly centralized theocracy, headed by the Jebtsundamba khutuktu in Yihe Huree.

By the twentieth century, Buddhism had penetrated deeply into Mongolian culture, and the populace willingly supported the lamas and the monasteries. Foreign observers had a uniformly negative opinion of Mongolian monks, condemning them as lazy, ignorant, corrupt, and debauched, but the Mongolian people did not concur. Ordinary Mongolians apparently combined a cynical and realistic anticlericalism, sensitive to the faults and the human fallibility of individual monks or groups of monks, with a deep and unwavering concern for the transcendent values of the church.

THE SUPPRESSION OF BUDDHISM

When the revolutionaries—determined to modernize their country and to reform its society—took power, they confronted a massive ecclesiastical structure that enrolled a larger part of the population, monopolized education and medical services, administered justice in a large part of the country, and controlled a great deal of the national wealth. The Buddhist church, moreover, had no interest in reforming itself or in modernizing the country. The result was a protracted political struggle that absorbed the energies and attention of the party and its Soviet advisers for nearly twenty years. As late as 1934, the party counted 843 major Buddhist centers, about 3,000 temples of various sizes, and nearly 6,000 associated buildings, which usually were the only fixed structures in a world of felt tents. The annual income of the church was 31 million tugriks, while that of the state was 37.5 million tugriks. A party source claimed that, in 1935, monks constituted 48 percent of the adult male population. In a campaign marked by shifts of tactics, alternating between conciliation and persecution, and armed uprisings led by monks and abbots, the Buddhist church was removed progressively from public administration, was subjected to confiscatory taxes, was forbidden to teach children, and was prohibited from recruiting new monks or replacing living buddhas. The campaign's timing matched the phases of Josef Stalin's persecution of the Russian Orthodox Church. In 1938—amid official fears that the church and monasteries were likely to cooperate with the Japanese, who were promoting a pan-Mongol puppet state—the remaining monasteries were dissolved, their property was seized, and their monks were secularized. The monastic buildings were taken over to serve as local government offices or schools. Only then was the ruling party, which since 1921 gradually had built a cadre of politically reliable and secularly educated administrators, able to destroy the church and to mobilize the country's wealth and population for its program of modernization and social change.

USES OF BUDDHISM

Since at least the early 1970s, one monastery, the Gandan Monastery, with a community of 100 monks, was open in Ulaanbaatar. It was the country's sole functioning monastery. A few of the old monasteries survived as museums, and the Gandan Monastery served as a living museum and a tourist attraction. Its monks included a few young men who had undergone a five-year training period, but whose motives and mode of selection were unknown to Western observers. The party apparently thought that Buddhism no longer posed a challenge to its dominance and that— because Buddhism had played so large a part in the country's history, traditional arts, and culture, total extirpation of knowledge about the religion and its practices would cut modern Mongols off from much of their past, to the detriment of their national identity. A few aged former monks were employed to translate Tibetan-language handbooks on herbs and traditional medicine. Government spokesmen described the monks of the Gandan Monastery as doing useful work. Buddhism, furthermore played a role in Mongolia's foreign policy by linking Mongolia with the communist and the noncommunist states of East and Southeast Asia. Ulaanbaatar was the headquarters of the Asian Buddhist Conference for Peace, which has held conferences for Buddhists from such countries as Japan, Vietnam, Cambodia, Sri Lanka, and Bhutan; published a journal for international circulation; and maintained contacts with such groups as the Christian Peace Conference, the Afro-Asian People's Solidarity Organization, and the Russian Orthodox Church. It sponsored the visits of the Dalai Lama to Mongolia in 1979 and 1982. The organization, headed by the abbot of the Gandan Monastery, advances the foreign policy goals of the Mongolian government, which are in accord with those of the Soviet Union.

RELIGIOUS SURVIVALS

Buddhism survives among the elderly, who pray and attend services at the Gandan Monastery; in the speech of the people, which is rich in Buddhist expressions and proverbs; and in the common practice of including statues or images of the Buddha on families' special shelves with photographs of relatives and other domestic memorabilia. Mongolian Buddhism, which restricted full participation in the ritual to monks and kept Tibetan as the language of ritual and sacred texts, was more vulnerable to persecution than a religion more widely dispersed among the populace would have been. Studies done among the Buryat Mongols of Siberia by Soviet ethnographers in the 1960s and the 1970s found that elimination of the complex and conceptually sophisticated culture of Tibetan Buddhism had led to a growth of the decentralized and flexible folk practice of shamanism. Similar survival or adaptation of folk religion in Mongolia would be possible, although Mongolians have published no comparable studies of religion at the local level. Approximately 4 percent of Mongolians, primarily those living in the southwest, are Muslims, as are many of their kin across the border in China. Freedom of religion is guaranteed by the 1960 Constitution.

BUDDHISM IN MONGOLIA AFTER 1900

In 1990 Mongolia turned from a communist country highly dependent, economically as well as ideologically, on the Soviet Union, into a democratic country. Free elections took place for the first time ever, and the country managed the transition to a democracy patterned after the Western model comparatively well. In 1992 the Mongols confirmed this historic turn by giving themselves a democratic constitution. The shaking off of communist rulership brought about a resurgence of Mongolian religious traditions, Buddhism and the *autochthonous* Mongolian religion alike. In northern Mongolia, the revival of the indigenous religious traditions of the Mongols, including *owô*-worship, the mountain-cult and, of course, shamanism, seem to be predominant. But in the rest of Mongolia, Buddhism has experienced a massive renaissance. "Buddhism" in the Mongolian context denotes Tibetan Buddhism in its Mongolian form.

Tibetan Buddhism underwent distinctive changes and adaptations in the Mongolian cultural context, from the late sixteenth century on. In the early twentieth century Mongolia belonged to a Tibetan Buddhist world which stretched from Ladakh to the lower Wolga regions. Up to 600 monasteries and temples spread over the country, with up to one third of the male population leading a monastic life. In 1990, however, there existed but one functioning Buddhist monastery, Gandantegchinlin in Ulânbâtar, the capital of Mongolia. This monastery was more or less a state-dependent establishment, with only a few carefully chosen monks deemed "trustworthy" by the communist government. Choibalsan, the "Mongolian Stalin," ensured that these monks and lamas were puppets under communist rulership. The establishment of Gandanthegchinlin as the only functioning monastery in the country and the state protection of the monasteries of Kharkhorin and Erdeni dzuu was initially forced upon Choibalsan by Stalin himself, who was pressured by a delegation sent to the Soviet Union by President Roosevelt in 1944.

In 1990 approximately one hundred lamas studied at Gandanthegchinlin, forty of whom were destined to teach in the few functioning monasteries of the Soviet Union. A traditional Buddhist education, however, was not possible, as it was forbidden to study Buddhist philosophy and dialectics, the core subjects of higher Tibetan Buddhist education. Today nearly 200 monasteries and temples have been restored throughout the country. More than 3000 monks are registered (the number of nuns is not ascertained), and there is ongoing teaching activity, mostly carried out by Tibetan teachers from the Tibetan exile community in India. Here we will concentrate on the situation after 1990, without however, referring any more than necessary to the history of Buddhism in Mongolia.

THE REVIVAL OF BUDDHISM

When communist rule in Mongolia broke down, the country looked back at the ultimately fruitless attempt to erase all religion from the Mongolian landscape, the indigenous religion as well as Buddhism. During the 1930s nearly all the monasteries and temples were destroyed or secularized; the monks were either killed or forced to marry. Laymen and monks succeeded in hiding some of the religious books and cult objects from the government and its catchpole, but most of the Buddhist literature and religious objects were destroyed during the years of the communist purges.

The sudden revival of Buddhism in Mongolia after 1990 is only astonishing at first glance. Religion never ceased to exist in Mongolia. Even in the communist era many Mongolians found a way to practice religion secretly. Today even former party leaders admit to having practiced Buddhist rites or to consulting astrologers during the time when the practice of religion was officially forbidden. Since 1992 freedom of religion has been guaranteed in the constitution, and the separation of religious and secular institutions has been established. This new freedom of religion is observable everywhere in the country. People flock to the monasteries, making circumambulations, giving offering to the Buddhas and Bodhisattvas whose statues are either being restored or built anew. In 1996 a huge statue of the Bodhisattva Nidüger üjegci (Avalokiteshvara) in the Maitreya temple in Ulânbâtar was installed. The yearly Mayidari festival, first introduced in 1657 at the Erdeni dzuu monastery by the first Jebtsundampa Khutukhtu Zanabazar, was held again at Ulânbâtar, in May of 2000 at the Gandanthegchinlin monastery. This monastery recently opened new colleges, structuring the monastic institution after the Tibetan dGe-lugs-pa model. In order to also make Buddhist teachings available for smaller monasteries in the countryside, lamas are sent to these establishments. In 1998 the number of monks at the Gandanthegchinlin monastery was over 300 and is still growing. The abbot of the monastery is considered by other clerics to be the head abbot of all of Mongolia's monastic establishments. His prominent position could, at least theoretically, be threatened by the Ninth Khalkha Jebtsundampa Khutukhtu, who has already visited Mongolia one time. The Jebtsundampa Khutukhtu, also called Bogdo Gegen or Bogdo Khan, was the highest Buddhist dignitary in Khalkha Mongolia up to 1924, when the eighth Jebtsundampa died. Upon the death of this Buddhist incarnation, who from the time of the third Jebtsundampa was always an ethnic Tibetan, the communist government decided *per decree* against his further incarnation. Even so, his reincarnation was recognized in 1932 in a boy of four by the Reting Rinpoche in Tibet, but due to the political circumstances his existence remained hidden but for a few insiders. He later fled to India with the Dalai Lama and lived quietly at Darjeeling and Mysore with his family.

In 1991 Mongolian lamas requested the Dalai Lama's information regarding the Ninth Jebtsundampa Khutukhtu, and only then was he officially acknowledged as the ninth incarnation of this Buddhist lineage that goes back to the famous Taranatha, a Tibetan Buddhist historian of the sixteenth century. In the same year the Jebtsundampa Khutukhtu moved to Dharamsala where he was officially enthroned. In 1999 he visited Mongolia, where he was acknowledged as the head of Mongolian Buddhism. The visit, however, met with political obstacles due to the Jebtsundampa's strong ties to the Tibetan exile government and the Dalai Lama. The Chinese government was opposed to his visit, and therefore the ties between this most important Mongolian Buddhist incarnation and his spiritual homeland were not further strengthened by it.

THE RENAISSANCE OF MONASTICISM

The revival of Buddhism in Mongolia brought about a strong interest in monastic life, for women as well as men. Whereas in the early 1990s the majority of monks were old, today the young monks outnumber the old ones. It is not only religious devotion that leads to the rapid increase of clerics among the population. Being a monk or nun is considered a job, and the clergy receive a small income. This may well be strong motivation to join a monastery, in view of the bleak prospect of unemployment for a large part of the population.

The demographic factor, however, causes problems concerning the education of the monks and nuns. Knowledge of the holy scriptures, the liturgy, and the offering of ceremonies and rituals in general, is scarce. The old generation of monks is rapidly dying out. Thus, well educated Buddhist teachers are rarely to be found among the Mongolian clergy. Under these circumstances it is not surprising that from the beginning of the period of religious freedom in Mongolia, the Tibetan exile community and the Dalai Lama took a keen interest in the renaissance of Mongolian Buddhism. Throughout the last seven centuries, Tibet and Mongolia have maintained strong cultural, political, and religious ties, and from the late sixteenth century onward, lamas of the dGe-lugs-pa school of Tibetan Buddhism managed to convert the entire population of Mongolia (with the exception of the Buryat Mongols) to Buddhism in less than fifty years.

Since the early seventeenth century, Tibet and Mongolia have shared a common religious identity within the broader religio-cultural context of the Asian countries dominated by Mahayana Buddhism. Thus, in the early 1990s Tibetan lamas started to come to Mongolia in order to instruct the Mongolian clergy and to develop a programme of higher education for them. The former Indian ambassador to Mongolia (from 1989 to 2000), Bakula Rinpoche, a native of Ladakh, played a central role in this influx of Tibetan Buddhist knowledge. He tried to reestablish Mongolian Buddhism on the basis of dGe-lugs-pa monasticism. This aim implied the enforcement of celibacy among Mongolian monks and nuns.

Bakula Rinpoche himself ordained quite a number of young monks and nuns. Bakula Rinpoche's modelling of Mongolian Buddhism on the dGe-lugs-pa tradition was, however, contested. Mongolians consider the fact that the majority of monks turn their backs on their monastery and live life as pastoral herdsmen to be a distinctively Mongolian Buddhist way of life. Today the pattern of leading a religious *cum* secular life in Mongolia is forming. Young people, after having performed their work and/or domestic duties, during the afternoon drop by the monastery with which they are affiliated and carry out their religious obligations, either by reciting texts or by performing religious ceremonies. Half of their day is thus spent in pursuit of a spiritual life although they are not properly ordained.

Due to a lack of knowledge of the philosophical and ritual differences of the various schools of Tibetan Buddhism, the monks and nuns often cannot determine with certainty the order of Tibetan Buddhism to which they belong. Since the late sixteenth century the dGe-lugs-pa has been dominant, but schools like the bKa'-brgyud-pa, the Sa-skya-pa, and the rNying-ma-pa have also been active in Mongolia.

WHO PAYS FOR IT ALL?

The rebuilding of monasteries destroyed in the communist era and the erection of new ones costs money. Who pays for these buildings? On one hand, Mongolian Buddhism, since the beginning of the twentieth century, has been connected in many ways to the international Buddhist world. It is not only Tibetan Buddhist institutions that are providing a knowledge transfer to Mongolia, which has suffered such a severe loss of its traditional Buddhist culture. International Buddhist institutions have also helped establish the necessary financial support to revive the Buddhist traditions. On the other hand, the Mongolian people constantly donate money to restore old monasteries, temples, and stupas, and to establish new ones. "All things here are donated by local people. And even the building was erected with their help," says a twenty-three year-old monk of the Shankh monastery, which was built in the seventeenth century by Zanabazar. Sometimes only a *ger*, a felt tent, is erected, which serves as the temple where monks and lamas perform religious services. In view of the economic difficulties the country is facing after the breakdown of the Soviet Union, and the transition to a free market economy, it is noteworthy that Mongolians still find the means to finance the building of Buddhist temples and monasteries. Once established, the monasteries depend on the continuous financial support of lay people, as is customary in Buddhist societies throughout Asia.

CREATING A NEW MONGOLIAN CULTURAL IDENTITY: THE ROLE OF BUDDHISM — AND OF CHINGGIS QAN

The fact that the Mongolian government also financially supports the restoration of Buddhist monuments brings me to an intriguing question to be asked in the context of the revival of Buddhism in Mongolia: what role does Buddhism play in the process of creating a new collective cultural identity for the Mongols?

Considering the fact that the whole of the rather lengthy article twelve of the Mongolian Constitution deals solely with the emblems of national identity, and that these national emblems, which consist of the State Emblem, the Banner, the Flag, and the Seal, are described in terms that refer both to the traditional religion and to Buddhism, it is obvious that Buddhism is considered of prime importance in the constitution of Mongolian identity. The State Emblem, the *sülde*, an *autochthonous* religious symbol into which the vital energy of the ruler is incorporated and which is deeply grounded in Mongolian indigenous ideas of the soul, is rooted in the white lotus, one of the most important symbols of Buddhism, which serves as its base. Furthermore, here the *keyimori* (the "wind-horse"), the *cindamani* (the "precious jewel"), and the *ghurban cagh* (the "three times" of past, present, and future), all of which play such a prominent part in Buddhist mythology and philosophy, are pointed out as vital parts of the "symbols of the independence and sovereignty of Mongolia." Since the early seventeenth century Buddhism has played a vital role for the construction of Mongolian religious and cultural identity. Since the conversion of the Altan Qaghan of the Tumed Mongols and other Mongol rulers and nobles, the dGe-lugs-pa tradition of Tibetan Buddhism has become dominant in the whole of Mongolia (including Outer and Inner Mongolia).

The unique conversion technique of Buddhism, used as early as the seventh century, during the first introduction of Buddhism into Tibet, was also employed in the Mongolian context: the indigenous deities were incorporated into the Tibetan Buddhist pantheon as "guardian deities," all of them, of course, operating on the level of "conventional truth." Toward the end of the seventeenth century, Cinggis Qan, who was worshipped throughout Mongolia as a powerful ancestral deity, was already incorporated into the Tibetan pantheon as the Bodhisattva Vajrapani. The Mongols were thus integrated into the Tibetan-Buddhist universe, which in the symbolic representation of the three Bodhisattvas Avalokiteshvara, Manjushri and Vajrapani, included Tibet, China and Mongolia as the three poles of the Tibetan-Buddhist world. Since the seventeenth century, Mongolian religious and cultural identity has been constituted by two separate factors, indigenous religion and Tibetan Buddhism. Thus the cultural identity of the Mongols is founded in religious syncretism, defined from the point of view of the religious actor.

Since the seventeenth century, the growing number of the Buddhist clergy led to an increasing asymmetry between the indigenous religion and the Buddhist foundation of Mongolian religio-cultural identity. At the turn of the twenty-first century we can detect a reverse motion. Whereas since the eighteenth century the religious language of the Mongols was Tibetan, today the language problem is an open question, which in the long term seems to have been decided in favor of the Mongolian language. Buddhist treatises and prayers for everyday use are increasingly being translated into Modern Khalkh Mongolian, abandoning Classical Tibetan as the language of the religious.The increasing self-consciousness of the Mongols is obvious in the symbolic meaning they attach to the use of the language. The translation of Buddhist texts into the Mongolian language may be interpreted as an indication that Mongolian Buddhism in the twentieth century is determined to adapt to the challenges of a modern, secularized society, seeking its own way apart from the pressure of the traditional, conservative Tibetan dGe-lugs-pa clergy.

FROM MUSEUM MONASTERIES TO PLACES OF WORSHIP

'In 1990, all barriers to religion broke down, and opportunities to practice Buddhism were allowed throughout Mongolia. Numerous religious centres in rural areas opened and the number of practising Buddhists increased dramatically.'

Lay people have been returning to worship in the monasteries and nunneries since religious freedom was allowed in 1990. Whether in the larger monasteries such as Gandan or the smaller ones, the scenes are the same: monks and nuns chanting prayers and the lay people coming to pray and ask for blessings from the monks. Gandan, for so long a museum monastery, has now become a vibrant place of worship once again serving not only inhabitants in Ulaanbaatar but visitors from all over Mongolia and from other countries. Outside people waft incense at the 'Boiphor' before entering the temple. Inside they queue to circle the temples clockwise, prayers are requested and paid for and blessings received then, as they exit, they turn the prayer drums sometimes prostrating themselves on bed-like couches. Regardless of the weather the temples performing prayers are usually full.

Buddhism is spreading after the demise of the Communist regime, a continuity with the old traditions. The same scenes can be observed amongst the lay people that can also be seen amongst the monks where the young learn by copying the older members of their community. A large part of the revival - the building of new temples, the training of monks is being achieved through the donations from these people.

BUILDING AND RESTORATION

'The Mongols have an innate aversion from fixed buildings, and in many places in Mongolia - in the principality of Dondurgun for example - it is still forbidden to all, including the Chinese traders, to erect permanent masonry. The free steppe is not to be "bound" by heavy buildings, and the nomads are never to forget their first duty, that of following the herds of cattle on their eternal wanderings to new grazing-grounds and new watering-places. But to monastery and temple these rules do not apply, for these form the dwellings of gods and their servants the lamas, and for such human considerations do not come into question.'

During the time of the Stalinist purges over 800 temples and monasteries were destroyed. Since 1990, building work on a small and grander scale has been developing all over Mongolia.

Erdene Zuu Monastery at Kharakhorin in Ovorhangai province has received a grant of Tg 32 million from Unesco and Tg 19 million from the Mongolian Government, altogether about £60,000. Erdene Zuu is one of the oldest Buddhist monasteries built in 1586 on the remains of the 13th century capital 'Khar-Khorum'. Recently the United Nations has given special protection to a phallic symbol located within its walls.

Gandan Monastery, Mongolia's largest monastery, has been busy with restoration work to its temples, building new temples and a hostel to sleep young monks and the restoration of the Magjid Janraiseg Buddha, the original of which was destroyed and melted down and used for bullets during the Communist purges.

Dashchoilin Monastery was originally founded in 1764. It is now flourishing and the second largest monastery in Mongolia. Like Gandan it attracts funding not only from the lay people who visit but also from major organisations from outside Mongolia. Dambajav, the head Lama is Vice President of the World Buddhist Federation and represents the North Asian Region.

Pethub Monastery was initiated by the Indian Ambassador to Mongolia, Kushok Bakula who is also a Buddhist monk. Unlike at other monasteries in Mongolia, monks at this new monastery are celibate. Mongolian Buddhist art also benefited from this project as Phurbat, head of the art department, at Gandan Monastery was commissioned to decorate the temple within the monastery.

The building of small monasteries and nunneries can been seen throughout Mongolia; examples of nunneries in Ulaanbaatar are Tugs Bayasgalant and Narkhajid. Their funding mainly comes from people who form the congregation.

EDUCATION

"While faith is very important and basic," says Bakula Rimpoche, the Indian Ambassador to Mongolia, "it is not enough; people must have knowledge."

Schools for novice monks and nuns are an integral part of Buddhist religious establishments. Tibetan language, Philosophy and Logic are on the curriculum as well as religious ceremonial (including music and dance) education. In some cases where numbers are very small and there may be only one or two monks or nuns, they may attach themselves to a larger establishment for the purposes of education.Two examples of this were one nun who was at a small Ger temple with her mother but went to Pethub Monastery for her teaching and a second nun who was at a nunnery on the outskirts of Ulaanbaatar but went to Lamrim Monaster

Dashchoilin Monastery has one monk doing an MA at the University of Hawaii, has brought a Ladake monk from India to teach Tibetan and Logic. Similarly in the nunneries, Tibetan is being taught to the nuns and in the Tugs Bayasgalant centre, Gantamur is teaching novice nuns the religious 'Luugin' ceremony. Often knowledge is passed on by a younger student being attached to an older person experienced in the subject.

MONGOLIAN RELIGIOUS ART

'Throughout most of the 13th and 14th centuries, the Mongols, a nomadic and warlike people, ruled much of China and Central Asia. "I had read about the migration of artists under Genghis Khan and his successors, said Mrs. Wardwell. " They would capture whole cities, kill most of the people, and save the craftsmen, shipping weavers from Iran to Central Asia and Mongolia in some cases and those from China as far west as Samarkand in others."

Phurbat, the Head of the Art Department at the Gandan Monastery in Ulaanbaatar studied Buddhist art at Dharamasala in Himachal Pradesh, North India, where he trained with Tibetan master painters in exile. It was here that he also met his Korean wife Kim who had trained in Western art in Korea and was then studying Buddhist art. On his return to Mongolia he started the Buddhist art school at Gandan where they are now reviving the art of Mongolian Buddhist painting, Mongolian religious appliqued 'thangkas' and sculpture and decorative art.

ART SCHOOL

Each morning, before the day's work begins, prayers are said. In 1998 there were twenty students training for six years; some are monks, others lay students. The students start their training by doing 300 paintings to develop their creativity. They then follow all the stages of 'thangka' painting step by step, after which they learn icon painting. They also learn to make canvases using traditional methods which involves using cotton and jessel made by glue and chalk.

PAINTING

Mongolian painting is noted for its fluid lines and contrasting colours also for its use of dotted brush strokes. Because of their nomadic lifestyle, Mongolians are very good at painting animals. As well as Tibetan Deities, Mongolian deities are often included in their work indicating a Shamanistic influence on Mongolian Buddhism.

APPLIQUED 'THANGKAS'

These are pieced together using silk thread with different types of silk and brocade but are like paintings. Semi-precious gems are sometimes added to the work, a practice only found in Mongolia.

SCULPTURE

The most famous Buddhist sculptor was Zanabazar (1635-1723) who trained in Tibet and it is in his tradition that sculpture in the department is developing.

MONGOLIAN BUDDHIST MEDICINE

'Historical data shows that Mongolian doctors mastered pulse taking more than two thousand years ago. In 634, the Khan Soronzongombo of Tibet was gravely ill and summoned the best healers from many countries, including India and China. After all had failed to diagnose the illness, a Mongolian healer arrived in khan's court and accurately discovered the cause of the problem using the pulse. In 789, Khan Tesrondevzun of Tibet arranged a competition among medics from India, China, Pakistan, Nepal, Persia, Khotan, and Mongolia. The winner was a Mongolian healer. As a result the khan issued an edict ordering the translation of the Mongolian medical treatises, Jadva zaril (An Analysis of the Pulse) and Sotvo shashdag jug (A Special Method Used by Mongolian Healers) into Tibetan.'

The Manba Datsan clinic and training centre for Mongolian traditional medicine was originally set up in Mongolia in 1760 and is now reviving training for treatment by traditional medicine which was prohibited between 1937 and 1990. As part of the State policy to promote Mongolian national religion, culture, customs and historic tradition, the Manba Clinic has been licensed by the Government and is undertaking the following activities:

1. Religious services
2. Clinical and medical treatment
3. Small medicine producing factory

4. Training and research activities
5. Traditional Medical Institute

RELIGIOUS SERVICES

The monks are mostly trained at the Buddhist University before going to the Centre. Further training in the practice of specific rituals and prayers relating to the medicine Buddha are then undertaken. This enables the monks to bestow blessings and perform meditation. They also make astrological calculations.

CLINICAL AND MEDICAL TREATMENT

Diagnoses using traditional methods are made and patients are treated with medicinal herbs, powder, pills, precious healing ointment. Treatments can involve non-medicinal therapy such as acupuncture, moxibustion, manipulation, massage, bloodletting, scarifying treatment, exorcism, mantra and meditation.

SMALL MEDICINE PRODUCING FACTORY

On the site of the Centre is a small medicine factory where over 100 traditional products are produced. These are made from imported and local ingredients, both animal and plant. Photography was not permitted in the factory because of the sterile conditions in which the work is undertaken.

TRAINING AND RESEARCH

The Centre is presently translating treatises on traditional medicine from Tibetan into Mongolian. It is also compiling data, for publication, of indigenous Mongolian herbs. Future plans involve training doctors to run MA and PhD courses in traditional medicine.

TRADITIONAL MEDICAL INSTITUTE

The Institute's aim is to restore training in traditional medicine by training doctors, over a five year period, in 70% traditional and 30% Western medicine. The teaching staff are medical doctors, scientists and Buddhist monks. Entry is competitive for students aged 18 -24 who take entrance examinations in Mathematics, Chemistry and Physics. The Institute has international links with India, China, Japan, USA, Switzerland, Austria and Russia.

Between 1990 and 1997, 44,000 people attended the Centre for medical checks and treatment. 120,000 were prescribed either Mongolian or European medicines available from the hospital's pharmacy.

ASTROLOGY AND FORTUNE TELLING

"Then I followed my guide in through the tent door and set foot in the dim temple of the 'tantra' cult. The air was thick with incense, and the dark mysticism of Central Asia closed in

about me. In the restless light from the fire and the oil lamps I caught glimpses, through misty veils of smoke and incense, of the room's astounding colours. In the middle of the tent, behind the crackling fire, sat Seng Chen between the two lama astrologers, and I was conducted to the place opposite to him, so that the circle was completed."

"Mongolia adheres to the lunar calendar and their New Year is called 'Tsagaan Sar' or 'White Month' which symbolises happiness and holiness. The date for New Year varies as it depends on the phase of the moon; in 2000, the Year of the Dragon fell on 6 February. Tsagaan Sar is an occasion for giving gifts, visiting families, the presentation of Khadag (silk ribbons symbolising prosperity and long life) and preparing Mongolian food such as 'buuz' (meat dumplings) and when plenty of Airag (fermented mare's milk) and vodka are drunk. In the countryside, in the gers, old customs are maintained: each person starts the day by walking in the direction decreed by the lamas. The environment is honoured by leaving trays of food and other offerings at 'ovoos' - roadside shrines, again showing the Shamanist influence - and songs in praise and gratitude to nearby valleys and mountains are sung.

Originally a monastery for Chinese Buddhism, Geser Sum is now a working monastery, training young monks. It also practices traditional Buddhist medicine but is best known for astrology and fortune telling. From early morning there are queues of people waiting for 'counselling'. One lady, who came with her son, was born in Arhangai province and had lived in Ulaanbaatar for many years. She asked if she should return to Arhangai and the Lama said prayers and chanted. Dates and venues were asked, calculations made, the Lama consulted his scripts. The lady was told she should return to Arhangai; she paid the Lama and left. The next people who were already in the room waiting, sat down and asked their questions. The young woman who came with an older lady asked if she should go to Korea or Germany to study. After performing the same ritual as he had done with the previous people, the Lama told her to go to Korea. She then asked if her uncle should stay in America, again the calculations and scripts advised her that he should.

HISTORY OF MONGOLIAN BUDDHIST ART

Buddhism, the teachings of the Buddha, are often referred to as the Dharma - the truth or wheel of the law. The execution of a craft is not just an economic compulsion but a sacred duty. It is believed that every individual is born to do his/her ordained work through which alone they can progress spiritually, and through the fulfillment of this Dharma to final Moksha or liberation.

The word "buddhism" comes from the Sanskrit word "buddha," which means "the awakened one".Buddhism, or buddhadharma, is the proclamation of, and journey toward, an awakening of human potential. In the mysticism of Buddhism, Tara represents the mother goddess and the female personification of compassion. - In Buddhist thought, the "God Realm", literally, the universe where the gods dwell, is a symbol of the nearness of heaven state of mind. Buddhism does not try to explain whether there is an ultimate God or not. Instead, the Buddha taught that we must strive through our own efforts to achieve liberation from anguish and suffering. - Buddha spoke of an Eightfold Path to Enlightenment which is traditionally represented as an eight-spoked wheel. The path is a guide to living life compassionately and non-violently.

LAMAISM

Tibetan Buddhism, a highly ritualistic religion with a huge pantheon of gods and goddesses, inspired the religious art of Mongolia. As in most religions, there is a need to create cult images in painting and sculpture, as well as ritual objects and other paraphernalia associated with worship of the deities. There was a great deal of cultural exchange and travel between Tibet and Mongolia. Tibetan lamas proselytized in Mongolia, and Mongolians went on pilgrimages to Tibet. There was even a fusion of the art styles of the neighboring countries India, Nepal, and China. The local crafstmen in turn copied these religious objects, often of a high artistic caliber. Mongolian artists, like their Tibetan counterparts, followed the prescriptions of religious texts in order to create a sacred image.

The sculptor or painter fashioning the image of a god had to comply with the iconography and proportions of that particular deity set down in the religious texts. - Buddhism is a philosophy espoused by Siddhartha Gautama approximately 563BC, which focused on understanding the path to salvation in a world of constant suffering. Buddha was the name given to Siddhartha by his followers and means "enlightened one". Buddha is sometimes given the title Sakyamuni meaning "sage of the Sakka people", after the people into whom he was born. The Manchus were also followers of Tibetan Buddhism, and they, too, produced paintings, sculptures, and ritual objects made in the Tibetan style, not only for the emperors' personal use but also as gifts for the high lamas of Tibet and Mongolia. Many of these Chinese art objects of Tibetan inspiration are known as "Sino-Tibetan" or "Tibeto-Chinese" art.

SCULPTURES

Although a bronze seated Buddha from Tibet may share similar iconography with examples made in Mongolia or China, certain characteristics distinguish the images. Buddhist sculptures have in their statuary hand gestures and they have specific meanings (Hand Gestures - Mudras - Symbols of Deeper Meaning).

In the late seventeenth and early eighteenth centuries, the sculptor par excellence among the Buddhist countries of Asia was Bogd Gegeen Zanabazar (1635-1723), the first Juvchindamba Khutagt, or Bogd Geegen, and the greatest sculptor of Mongolia. His artistic talent was already apparent when he was a young boy, when he was observed to be fond of drawing and building houses and temples with his little friends. At the age of fourteen he went to Tibet, where he was ordained by the Panchen Lama and proclaimed

Jebtsundamba Khutuktu by the Fifth Dalai Lama. At that time the Potala Palace was being reconstructed, and Zanabazar must have come in contact with the many artistans and craftsmen at work in Lhasa. Upon his return to Mongolia in 1651, he was accompanied by hundreds of Tibetan lamas and many artists and craftsmen, sent by the Fifth Dalai Lama to propagate the faith and to build monasteries.

The most outstanding sculptor of Mongolia was the First Bogdo Gegen, Zanabazar. His statues are far more alive in expression and body, and more broad shouldered than Tibetan ones. The postures are canonical, but give an impression of great stateliness. His female statues, such as of the twenty-one Taras, are more sensuous than Tibetan counterparts. Mongolian sculpture follows his style.

THE ZANABAZAR SCHOOL OF SCULPTURE OF OUTER MONGOLIA

The sculptures of the Zanabazar school are generally made in two pieces; the body and the pedestal are made separately and then soldered together. The smaller sculptures are made in one piece, and sometimes a mold was used to produce multiple wax models. Most of the sculptures are gilded, and the mercury gilding is especially beautiful. Following Tibetan tradition, the lotus pedestals of the sculptures by Zanabazar and his school are distinctive. Instead of the oval and rectangular throne types common in Tibet, they show a preference for circular or drum-shaped pedestals and semioval pedestals with tall bases.

Some sculptures of Outer Mongolia are amalgams of gathered pieces from various places and combined together to form a single sculpture. The base, halo, and even attributes that appear together may not have been intended to do so. It is difficult to say whether this is a Mongolian custom, or one caused by necessity. This is certainly true in Chinese art, as in porcelains and lacquers from the Ming dynasty. - Higlights of the works of Mongolian art displayed in the Zanabazar Fine Arts Museum, the Choijin Lama Temple Museum and the Bogd Khan Palace Museum in Ulaanbaatar.

DOLONNOR OR DOLON-NOR

Inner Mongolian Style formerly a large monastic complex and crafts centre in Inner Mongolia and Mongolia's most famous bronze workshops.Most of the works known from Mongolian temples were not made in situ (in the Gobi region of southern Mongolia, Oyu Tolgoi contains in-situ metal "copper-gold") but originated in China or Tibet. Actually, some of the so-called Chinese sculptures were made in Inner Mongolia, or by Dolonnor craftsmen residing in Urga (today's Ulaanbaatar). Dolonnor, about two hundred miles northeast of Beijing, is located near the ox-bow section of the Luan River in the old province of Khahar, now the southeastern section of Inner Mongolia.This part of Inner Mongolia is one of the largest producers of iron and coal in China, and Dolonnor, at least through the first quarter of the twentieth century, was famous for its manufacture of Buddhist images in bronze.

Many sculptures from the Qianlong period, whether of wood or metal, are similar in style to these Dolonnor pieces. Some of these lamas must have been trained artists. They were a mixed bunch; besides Chinese from the various provinces, there were Jesuit missionaries from Europe and their Chinese students, Nepalese, and, last but not least, Tibetans.

There were great schools of Tibetan painting and statue making at Dolonor Monastery in Inner Mongolia and at the various Tibetan monasteries in Beijing. The artists at both places were mostly Chinese. Tibetan thangkas and statues were mass-produced starting in the early nineteenth century in Beijing, and during the second half of the nineteenth century at Dolonnor. They were distributed throughout Mongolia and Buryatia, as well as northern China and Tibet.

PAINTING

The Buddhist paintings of Mongolia are directly related to the painting tradition of central Tibet. They can be painted on white, red, or black backgrounds. They are executed on cotton stretched on a frame. The cloth is first sized with a solution of chalk, glue, and arkhi (milk vodka), and then polished with a smooth stone when dry. The image is then drawn in charcoal according to the proportions in the shastras, or sometimes the artist may use a pounce. The pigments consist of mineral and vegetable colors, mixed with yak-skin glue. The finished piece is framed with silk brocades from China, and a thin stick and a wooden roller are inserted at top and bottom for hanging.

Mongolian paintings are noted for their fluid line work, contrasting colors, and the intricate designs in gold. Characteristic Mongolian elements can be detected, such as the lotus pedestal in thangkas. There are also present the five principal animals (camel, horse, yak, sheep, and goat), soft peaks, and colorful clouds. The appliqué (*zeegt naamal*) of Mongolia is like a giant thangka or painting. The embroidery needle and thread take the place of brush and ink, while pieces of silk and brocade are transformed into areas of color. Where one finds gold highlights in Buddhist paintings, in appliqués one finds gold threads, carefully couched along the edges, and golden brocades are cut into jewellry shapes. Appliqué thangkas came into Mongolia together with Vajrayana Buddhism. Mongolians are familiar with this technique for the excavated felt carpet of the Huns from the Noyon Uul burials already showed a combination of embroidery and appliqué. The Urga (today's Ulaanbaatar) area is especially renowned for its appliqués used for decorating temples and palaces.

Appliqués are called "silk paintings" in Mongolia because silk and brocades were used for garments and accessories such as belts, hats, and purses. In the monasteries, silk is utilized in many ways; to clothe lamas and deities alike; for cushions and throne backs; for canopies; and for framing thangkas. Appliqué are further ornamented with tiny coral beads, such as coral, pearls, and turquoise is a purely Mongolian practice.

Chinese style Tibetan statues, for instance of forceful protector figures, tended to be more muscular and asymmetrical than their Tibetan counterparts. They usually had slight free-style adaptations not in accordance with canonical measurements. There were used different alloys from those made in Tibet, so that the color of the statues was often lighter. Many Chinese artists were in Mongolia as well, and sometimes their influence can be seen.

- **Blockprints**; pressed from wood blocks onto paper or cloth.
- **Tsagali**; initiation cards, small painted cards used during Tantric initiation ceremonies.
- **Charts**; astrological, medical, and protection talismans.
- **Murals** - wall paintings: the principal art form of Buddhist and Bon religion.

RITUAL OBJECTS

- ritual bell in brass with low-grade silver or quality silver with embedded coral and turquoise - ritual bell in bronze base with brass top and silver carved - dorje in silver with embedded coral and turquoise - carved dorje in brass, bronze, copper or silver

The bell and dorjie represents the image that wisdom and method are an undivided unity so the dorjie and the bell are never parted or employed separately.

- prayer wheel with silk covering
- phurpa ritual dagger - painted wooden ritual staff - bon phurpa in wood - manuscript (sutra book) - carved and painted sutra cover - Tibetan trumpet made of brass and copper with fine details

MANDALA

Mandala; geometric models of a pure universe and the archetypal deities. The symbolism of meditation Mandalas has a rich tradition. The outer form of these so-called holy circles is a geometrical diagram, a Yantra, and each detail of its construction has symbolic meaning. The essence or purpose of the Mandala is concerned with the process of invocation, the calling in and realization of the spiritual force within the contemplator himself. All these different picture-tools have essentially the same inner meaning and purpose, but there are Mandalas to suit all levels of consciousness: for the spiritually, for highly developed people, for average people and for people not yet developed.

SUTRA COVER - BOOK DECORATION – CARVED AND PAINTED

Mongolians realized early that books were essential in disseminating of Buddhism. Although Tibetan was the liturgical language of Mongolia, rulers, both Mongol and Chinese, made sure that the Kanjur and Tanjur were translated into Mongolian and published. Sutra-printing took place in many monasteries of Mongolia, on paper purchased from China and Tibet. The same technique used in painting is applied to book decoration. Texts are outstanding for their lavish ornamentations, with the text embossed on sheets of silver and gilded. Gold, silver, coral, pearls, lapis lazuli, turquoise, steel, copper, and mother-of-pearl, were ground up for use as pigments, and the sutra was written in the nine colors on black paper in a fine calligraphic hand. In general, wood is scarce in Mongolia. Mongol scribes illustrated the title page on paper and then framed it with softwood, which was then embellished with Chinese brocades.

THANGKAS

The Mongolian style of Tibetan painting maintained the iconography but adapted the details of the background. In Tibetan thangkas (scroll paintings framed in brocade), the backgrounds typically have stylized snow-capped mountains and lakes. In Mongolia, the rolling grasslands and hills of Mongolia are more frequent. The small human figures in the background tend to look more like Mongolians than like Tibetans, and eventually the facial features of the main deities also acquired Mongolian traits. Thus, the faces tend to be larger and rounder than Tibetan ones. The Mongolians also tend to use more shading than the Tibetans to depict body musculature, although this is occasionally found in Tibetan thangkas as well.

The Buryats follow the Mongolian style, with some minor variations in details. The Chinese style of Tibetan thangkas had typically bright, garish Chinese colors, in contrast to the more subdued colors of the Tibetans. They had a great amount of gold leaf work, more than the already considerable amount found on Tibetan thangkas.

– **Mongolian thangkas** are colored painted on black, red, or gold background. - **Gau;** thangkas in brass, silver and copper. - **Parma**; painted prints; pressed from wood block onto cotton, then painted and framed as thangkas

The Qianlong emperor of China was known to have remounted Tibetan thangkas in the Chinese style.

SAKHUIS

Fine Art of Mongolia, which includes the Buddhist bronze sculptures and painting thangkas. The deities depicted in the sakhuis have a vigor and vitality typical of the people of the Steppes. They are thought of as sacred objects and used as amulets. The deities of the pantheon are divided so as to represent the dual nature of all things in the Universe. There are the strong and vengeful manifestations of deities who maintain order through authority and fear, such as Mahäkäla, as well as the nurturing deities such as Tara and Bodhisattva Avalokitesvara.

TEMPLE ARCHITECTURE

The temple architecture of Mongolia has strong Chinese as well as Amdo-Tibetan influences. Temples often have green tile roofs, not found in Central Tibet. At one monastery, for instance Erdene Zuu, there would be some buildings in pure Tibetan style, with massive walls sloping outwards and windows with black trapezoidal-shaped fringes around them, and next to them buildings in Chinese influenced Mongolian style.

In Buryatia, the temples and monasteries were built mostly of logs, in Siberian fashion. This was not found in Mongolia or Tibet, where buildings were made mostly of stone or clay. The early Buryat temples were built by Russian workers and were influenced by the style of Russian Orthodox churches. Some early ones even had a central dome with four smaller domes over the four corners. In Tuva, some temples were also built of logs, but in a more simple, square style than in Buryatia.

Although the external style of the temples was influenced by local customs and tastes, the internal decoration and arrangement of the main prayer halls were standardly Tibetan. There were rows of columns covered with multicolored brocades and thangkas, walls with elaborate frescoes and a wild array of bright colors. The front wall had elaborate, painted cases for scriptures and statues, an enormous statue, usually of Buddha, in the center, and a throne for the Dalai Lama before the main statue. Thangkas were hung wherever possible. Everything was ornate and elaborately decorated.

As in Tibet, the monks sat in parallel rows, facing each other, perpendicular to the front of the temple. The chanting was in the Gelug style, using deep bass voices, with monks producing overtones so that each person sings a chord. The long brass horns, oboes, conchshells, cymbals, bells, and drums that accompany Tibetan chanting are found throughout. Copious amounts of salted butter tea is drunk everywhere in Buddhist Central Asia, as in Tibet.

Stupe – Suvraga (in the Mongolian language) - a structure of building – the house of holy relics – "Spiritual Monument".

Ovoo Heap or cairn, is the Lamaist equivalent of a shamanists' shrines. This is a heap of bones formed on the stone altar by the remains of sacrificed animals at the *tailgan*. They would be inhabited by local spirits.

Chapter - 7

Buddhism in Taiwan and Hong Kong

BUDDHISM IN TAIWAN

Religion in Taiwan is very complex. Most people should probably be defined as followers of traditional Chinese folk religion, rather than as Buddhists. However, Buddhism still plays a very important role in Taiwan.

STATISTICS

Government statistics claimed that in 1990 there were 4.8 million Buddhists (about 20% of the population) and around 2000 priests in Taiwan. In 2004 the Government gave a figure of 5.5 million Buddhists compared with 0.6 million for Protestant Christianity. Buddhism has been growing in popularity but it is hard to say how many Buddhists there really are in Taiwan because these numbers include many people who regularly contribute funds to organizations without any real interest in their Buddhist teaching. For example, in 1998 Tsu Chi claimed around 4 million members of which only 7000 participated in its activities.

Buddhist associations are found on most university campus, there are eight Buddhist universities and colleges, three main Buddhist hospitals. and cable TV has a few channels devoted to Buddhist teaching. There are also 28 registered Buddhist publishing houses and over 4000 registered Buddhist temples (compared to around 3500 registered protestant churches). These are all signs that Buddhism is impacting Taiwanese society.

BUDDHISM'S ARRIVAL IN CHINA

When Buddhism reached China in the 1st Century AD it mixed with other Chinese philosophies such as Confucianism and Taoism. The aesthetic teachings of the Buddha and the emphasis on separation from the world and monastic living clashed significantly with the pragmatism of the Chinese and the duties of sons to produce heirs. Buddhism in China needed to evolve to fit in with Chinese culture. The result of this 'evolution' were many new schools of Buddhist thought, the most popular being Pure Land Buddhism and Chan Buddhism (more popularly known in the West by its Japanese name 'Zen')

Pure Land Buddhism

Pure Land Buddhism ties in with popular Taoist interest in magic and spiritual forces and so mixes quite well with Chinese folk religions. The help of Buddha may be gained through reciting Buddhist chants. This form of Buddhism believes in the idea of a Pure Land, a Western paradise comparable to the idea of heaven, which can be entered through faith in Buddha. There is no idea here of the extinction of Nirvana as in more traditional Buddhism. Its stress on the equality of all people makes this form of Buddhism more appealing to the grass roots Chinese. Pure Land Buddhism has a strong emphasis on moral teaching and basic social virtues, which overlaps with Confucianism.

Chan (Zen) Buddhism

Chan focuses on meditation that is able to generate instant enlightenment. Chan Buddhism has no emphasis on a concept of heaven, chanting the name of the Buddha or on moral teaching. Aspects of this type of Buddhism known in the West include the development of physical skills and meditation on paradoxes. Chan has encouraged practitioners to become highly skilled at physical tasks. The idea is that when one masters a physical task to the point that it may be done without thinking, then a deeper awareness of surrounding reality may be achieved. This is the background to the famous Kung Fu skills of China's Shaolin Monks and the book, "Zen and the art of Motorcycle Maintenance". Meditation on paradoxes such as the famous "what is the sound of one hand clapping?" is used to jar the mind loose from the bondage of language and enable deep mystical insights into the meaning of meaning.

TAIWAN BUDDHISM

Orthodox Buddhism has grown in Taiwan, however, when there is a clash between traditional Chinese values and Buddhism, Taiwanese usually choose to interpret Buddhism in terms of Chinese culture, not the other way around. Taiwanese organizations have built more Buddhist temples per capita than anyone else in the world but Taiwanese have much understanding of core Buddhist beliefs such as the Four Noble Truths and reincarnation only plays a minor part in their thinking of life after death.

In recent decades, Buddhism in Taiwan has come to focus to external charitable acts and involvement in society. Emerging Buddhist leaders call for building a "Pure Land" in this world. They place a strong emphasis on involvement in humanitarian works in society such as relief and medical work.

This has changed the image of Buddhism and resulted in many becoming regular donors to Buddhist funds despite having little interest in or understanding of Buddhist teaching. Buddhist teaching is actively promoted through the establishment of Buddhist universities, teaching conferences attracting international speakers, and small group studies at a local level. Buddhist groups have extended their teaching strategy to involve the popular media including free magazines and newsletters, radio and cable TV. Buddhist groups employ top professionals in management roles and through careful image management in the media have achieved recognition and approval by the Taiwanese public.

Without doubt Buddhism is growing in Taiwan and Taiwan Buddhist organizations are playing a significant role in the promotion of Buddhism worldwide. Fifty years ago as most people in Taiwan looked to the West as the source of all progress Buddhism had the low image of the poor uneducated monk with nothing to offer a society looking to modernize. Today Buddhist organizations are affluent and are sending priests to gain doctorates at prestigious universities in the west. They are making impressive use of media and information technology and have even adapted such traditional Christian activities as weekend retreats for lay people, children's camps and cell groups for their own use. Taiwan is the only Asian country where ordination of women as Buddhist nuns is fully accepted and as a result women play a prominent role in Taiwan's Buddhism.

Three of the most notable organizations in Taiwan are: Fo Guang Shan (Buddha Mountain of Light School)

Founded by Master Hsin Yun with the aim of spreading Buddhism worldwide, they now have 100 chapters in 60 countries. This has been described as 'humanistic' Buddhism where followers are directed towards the suffering of people in the world and participation in concrete social welfare activities to relieve suffering.

Tsu Chi Foundation

Founded by the Buddhist Nun Master Cheng Yen who in 1996 was nominated for a Nobel peace prize. Tsu Chi is involved in charity work in Nepal, Thailand and North Korea. They are noted for their response to disasters all over the world and very prominent in Taiwan. Tzu Chi runs a 750-bed hospital in Hualien, the largest hospital in Eastern Taiwan. Tsu Chi is a global organization with 78 offices in the US and over 4 million supporters worldwide.

Dharma Drum Mountain (DDM)

This organization was founded for the spread of Chan Buddhism. They are in the process of building a Buddhist global education complex which will include a research center, a university, a monastery, a museum and international conference hall. The organization is also known for its emphasis on environmental protection and reduction of waste in daily life.

BUDDHISM AND FOLK RELIGION[

The majority of Taiwan's grassroots people believe in Chinese folk religions. These believe in a host of gods arranged in a heavenly hierarchy similar in structure to the ancient Chinese court. Folk religion, which mixes ancestor worship in the home, offerings to ghosts, temple worship and the use of spirit mediums, is behind most of the significant festivals in Taiwan. Many adherents mix Buddhist ideas with a folk religion worldview seemingly unconcerned by the contradictions. Many in Taiwan will call themselves Buddhist when in fact their real belief is in folk religion. One of the roots of this confusion may lie in the Japanese attempt to suppress Chinese religions during the 50 years that they governed Taiwan. At this time to prevent closure many folk temples installed Buddhist statues and called themselves Buddhist temples. In many homes today it is common to see a Buddhist statue alongside the ancestor tablets with pictures of folk gods in the background. This syncretism makes it hard to define who is a true Buddhist in Taiwan.

THE SUCCESS OF BUDDHISM

The growth in popularity of Buddhism is due to a number of factors including: aggressive "evangelism"; social and political involvement; a non-religious approach promoting meditation as a key to general health and well-being. Retreats involving a few days of teaching on meditation are being held by a number of Buddhist organizations throughout Taiwan. Attending such retreats is perhaps the major Buddhist activity in which the average person would be likely to consider participation.This has strong resemblances to New Age teaching in the West, allowing individuals to select religious beliefs and activities that bring personal benefit without the need to make long term commitments to a religious organization's, activities or codes of moral behavior.

At the present time Buddhism has a done much to popularize and modernize its image and has large amounts of funds available which it is spending on medical and social work and education.

It is not surprising then that Taiwan has become a significant center for Buddhist world mission. Many grassroots people in Taiwan, may have little understanding or interest in Buddhism's philosophical teachings. However, they consider it to be "local" even if they don't understand it or give it a prominent role in their lives. In comparison they consider Christianity to be "foreign". Thus Buddhism, and people's identification of themselves as "Buddhist" remains a significant challenge to Christian evangelism in Taiwan.

BUDDHISM - GROWING POPULARITY

In Taiwan, Buddhism is attracting more and more people towards it with every passing year. Buddhism has become an integral part of the life of the people of Taiwan. A large number of people in Taiwan accept to become nuns and monks. Further proof of the growing popularity is the marked increase in the attendance of the school children, teenagers, college students and teachers in the Buddhist camps organised. There are more than 100 Buddhist camps that are backed by local temples and education authorities all through Taiwan each summer. Additionally, a number of periodicals and other media efforts contribute to increase the popularity of Buddhism in the country.

BUDDHISM IN HONG KONG

Buddhism, an Indian Religion and Taoism, a traditional Chinese religion, have a considerable number of adherents in Hong Kong (90% claim to be Buddhist), although the numbers of true Buddhists who have taken the Refuge are only 700 thousand. and there are more than 600 temples in the HKSAR. The history of some of these temples can be traced back to more than 700 years ago, while some others have been built in recent years. Notable temples include the Wong Tai Sin Temple located in the Wong Tai Sin District in Kowloon. This popular temple is dedicated to the Taoist deity, Wong Tai Sin. Besides that, the Chi Nin Nunnery in Diamond Hill is a group of temple structures in Tang Dynasty's architectural style. It is now open to the public following the completion of its redevelopment in 2000.

The Po Lin Monastery on Lantau Island is famous for the outdoor bronze statue, Tian Tan Buddha, which attracts a large number of visitors during the weekends and holidays. It is now linked to the city's latest tourist attraction Ngong Ping 360 Skyrail. The cable car and park complex is built around a Buddhism theme, featuring sites of the Wisdom Path and the Po Lin Monastery.

Besides, buddhists' organizations and temples in Hong Kong have long been involved in social welfare and education in the city. The Buddhist's Association of Hong Kong operates a dozen primary and secondary schools, hospices and elderly homes as well as centres for youth and children in Hong Kong.

The leadership of mainstream buddhists organizations have aligned themselves with the establishment in Hong Kong. For example, high-ranking Buddhist Association's executives have openly endorsed the re-election of the city's Chief Executive Donald Tsang. Several of the association's members were on the drafting committee of the Basic Law - Hong Kong's mini constitution.

Under the leadership of the former Chief Executive Tung Chee Hwa, the SAR government formally recognized the influence of Buddhism in Hong Kong. In 1997 the SAR government designated one public holiday in May or June to mark Buddha's birthday, which replaced the Queen's birthday. This year Buddha's birthday is on May 24th. Tung himself is a Buddhist and participated in major, widely publicised Buddhist activities in Hong Kong and China.

Academic studies and research of Buddhism in Hong Kong have thrived over the past 10 years. The University of Hong Kong has a Centre of Buddhist Studies. The Chinese University of Hong Kong also has a Centre for the Study of Humanistic Buddhism.

Chapter - 8

Buddhism in Central Asia and Russia

Although Buddhism never developed a missionary movement, Buddha's teachings nevertheless spread far and wide on the Indian subcontinent and from there throughout Asia. In each new culture it reached, the Buddhist methods and styles were modified to fit the local mentality, without compromising the essential points of wisdom and compassion. Buddhism, however, never developed an overall hierarchy of religious authority with a supreme head. Each country to which it spread developed its own forms, its own religious structure and its own spiritual head. The most well-known and internationally respected of these authorities at present is His Holiness the *Dalai Lama* of Tibet.

There are two major divisions of Buddhism. The Hinayana, or Modest Vehicle, emphasizes personal liberation, while the Mahayana, or Vast Vehicle, stresses working to become a fuliy enlightened Buddha in order to be best able to help others. Each has many sub-divisions. At present, however, three major forms survive: one Hinayana, known as Theravada, in South East Asia, and two Mahayana, namely the Chinese and Tibetan traditions.

The Theravada tradition spread from India to Sri Lanka and Burma in the third century B.C.E., and from there to Yunnan in southwest China, Thailand, Laos, Cambodia, South Vietnam and Indonesia. Pockets of Indian merchants practicing Buddhism were soon found on the coast of the Arabian Peninsula and even as far as Alexandria, Egypt. Other forms of Hinayana spread from that time to modern-day Pakistan, Kashmir, Afghanistan, eastern and coastal Iran, Uzbekistan, Turkmenistan and Tajikistan. These were the ancient states of Gandhara, Bactria, Parthia and Sogdia. From this base in Central Asia, they spread further in the second century C.E. to East Turkistan (Xinjiang) and further into China, and in the late seventh century to Kyrgyzstan and Kazakhstan. These forms of Hinayana were later combined with Mahayana aspects that also came from India so that Mahayana eventually became the dominant form of Buddhism in most of Central Asia.

The Chinese form of Mahayana later spread to Korea, Japan and North Vietnam. Another early wave of Mahayana, mixed with Shaivite forms of Hinduism, spread from India to Nepal, Indonesia, Malaysia and parts of South East Asia starting in about the fifth century. The Tibetan Mahayana tradition, which, starting in the seventh century, inherited the full historical development of Indian Buddhism, *spread throughout the Himalayan regions and to Mongolia, East Turkistan, Kyrgyzstan, Kazakhstan, northern Inner China, Manchuria, Siberia and the Kalmyk Mongol region near the Caspian Sea in European Russia.*

THE MANNER IN WHICH BUDDHISM SPREAD

The expansion of Buddhism throughout most of Asia was peaceful and occurred in several ways. Shakyamuni Buddha set the precedent. Being primarily a teacher, he traveled to nearby kingdoms to share his insights with those who were receptive and interested. Likewise, he instructed his monks to go forth in the world and expound his teachings. He did not ask others to denounce and give up their own religion and convert to a new one, for he was not seeking to establish his own religion. He was merely trying to help others overcome the unhappiness and suffering that they were creating for themselves because of their lack of understanding. Later generations of followers were inspired by Buddha's example and shared with others his methods that they found useful in their lives. This is how what is now called "Buddhism" spread far and wide.

Sometimes the process evolved organically. For example, when Buddhist merchants visited and settled in different lands, some members of the local populations naturally developed interest in these foreigners' beliefs, as with the introduction of Islam to Indonesia and Malaysia. Such a process occurred with Buddhism in the oasis states along the ***Silk Road*** in Central Asia during the two centuries before and after the common era. As local rulers and their people learned more about this Indian religion, they invited monks from the merchants' native regions as advisors or teachers and, in this manner, eventually adopted the Buddhist faith. Another organic method was through the slow cultural assimilation of a conquering people, such as the Greeks into the Buddhist society of Gandhara in present-day central Pakistan during the centuries following the second century B.C.E.

Often, however, the dissemination was due primarily to the influence of a powerful monarch who had adopted and supported Buddhism himself. In the mid-third century B.C.E, for example, Buddhism spread throughout northern India as the result of the personal endorsement of King Ashoka. This great empire-builder did not force his subjects to adopt the Buddhist faith. But by posting edicts engraved on iron pillars throughout his realm exhorting his people to lead an ethical life and by following these principles himself, he inspired others to adopt Buddha's teachings.

King Ashoka also actively proselytized outside his kingdom by sending missions to distant lands. On some occasions, he acted upon the invitation of foreign rulers, such as

King Tishya of Sri Lanka. On others, he sent monks as envoys at his own initiative. These visiting monastics, however, did not forcefully pressure others to convert, but simply made Buddha's teachings available, allowing people to choose for themselves. This is evidenced by the fact that in such places as South India and southern Burma, Buddhism soon took root, while in others, such as the Greek state and West Asia, there is no record of any immediate impact.

Other religious kings, such as the sixteenth century Mongol potentate Altan Khan, invited Buddhist teachers to their realm and proclaimed Buddhism the official creed of the land in order to help unify their people and consolidate their rule. In the process they may have prohibited certain practices of non-Buddhist, indigenous religions and even persecuted those who followed them, but these heavy-handed moves were primarily politically motivated. Such ambitious rulers never forced their subjects to adopt Buddhist forms of belief or worship. This is not part of the religious creed.

If Shakyamuni Buddha told people not to follow his teachings out of blind faith, but to examine them carefully themselves before accepting them, how much less so should people accept Buddha's teachings out of coercion from zealous missionaries or royal decree. Thus, for instance, when Toyin Neiji in the early sixteenth century tried to bribe Eastern Mongol nomads into following Buddhism by offering them livestock for each verse they memorized, people complained to the highest authorities. In the end, this overbearing teacher was punished and exiled.

BUDDHIST PERCENTAGE BY COUNTRY

Here is the percentages of Buddhists in some nowaday Central Asia countries from many different sources:

Buddhism by country in the Central Asia

Country	Population(2007E)	% of Buddhists	Buddhist total
Afghanistan	31,889,923	0.3% (approx)	95,670
Kazakhstan	15,422,000	0.53%	81,843
Kyrgyzstan	5,317,000	0.35%	18,610
Mongolia	2,874,127	94%	2,701,679
Tajikistan	7,076,598	0.1%	7,076
Turkmenistan	5,097,028	0.1%	5,097
Uzbekistan	27,780,059	0.2%	55,560

BUDDHISM IN AFGHANISTAN

The Buddhist stupas and monasteries and the massive statues carved out of a sand rock at Bamiyan in the heart of Afghanistan were the wonder of tourists, scholars and connoisseurs of art and culture and scholars are no more, devastated by the Islamic Fundamentalists' Taliban terrorist regime of Afghanistan, not-withstanding the international plea against this iconoclasm, unleashed on the cultural heritage of the ancestors of the present day people of Afghanistan.

Afghanistan, situated in the mid-point of Asia and the cross-roads between the north and south, east and west and in the famous "Chinese Silk Route" due to its geographical position became in bygone times the rendezvous of different peoples and various civilisations, namely Aryan, (Bactrian or Rigvedic), Achaemenian, Greek, Kushan and Buddhist. The cumulative effect of this cross-cultural fertilisation found its expression in different schools of art, embodying techniques borrowed from different lands and climes, but modified and remoulded according to the ethos of the Afghan people. The Greek culture found its paths into Bactrian art in the fourth century BC, when the country became a part of the vast Macedonian Empire and came to be totally influenced by the Greek culture and philosophy. In mid-third century BC during the reign of Emperor Asoka of India, Buddhism found its way into Afghanistan.

It was in Afghanistan that Greek realism and surrealism intermingled with Indian mysticism, giving birth to a new school of art now accepted by the world as the Gandhara School of art, which had its epicentre at Hadda, six miles south of modern Jalaalabada (Nangahara of Buddhist era) in Afghanistan. In the second century AD with the ascension of Kanishka to the throne, Afghanistan became a great seat of Buddhist learning and the arts. It was from this pivotal centre that Buddhism reached Sinkiang, China and Mongolia. Kanishka, being intellectually convinced of the realism and pragmatism of Buddhism became a Buddhist and later became a very liberal, generous and steadfast promoter of Buddhism and Buddhist art and culture. During his long and epoch-making rulership (120 to 160 AD), Buddhism and Buddhist art and culture became the life-blood of his far-flung empire. Consequently, the famous Gandhara or Graeco- Buddhist school of sculpture progressed by leaps and bounds.

This new school on Afghan spill defied the Buddha, the founder of Buddhism, and his images became the cynosures of worship and veneration to the exclusion of primitive modes of worship. In Afghanistan, Buddhism compromised with many elements of foreign culture and gave them a Buddhist outlook. The old schools of art never "idolized" Buddha but was represented by an empty seat, a footprint, an umbrella, riderless horse or even a vacant throne. According to the new techniques of art that bred on Afghan soil, Buddha came to be portrayed in human form, with aesthetically rich serenity and compassion on the face and the entire body, inspiring the worshipper to take the path of the Four Sublime States of Buddhism: Loving-kindness (Metta), Compassion (Karuna), Blissful Joy (Mudita) and Equanimity (Upekkha). Kanishka had two capitals: Capsie (modern Bagram, 35 miles north of Kabul), has summer residence, and Purushapura (modern Peshawar), his winter palace. He being the indefatigable promoter of Buddhism built stupas and monasteries very specially in these two locations, and elsewhere in his vast empire. In Peshawar, Kanishka built a beautiful Sangharama (monastery like the Mahavihara of Anuradhapura) with a lofty stupa of about 150 feet in height, a most breath-taking construction of the time.

Capisa was dotted with viharas and statues. One of these, Shalokia, was built by his Chinese princess who was taken as a hostage and kept in Kanishka's court. This monastery was in a state of preservation. The famous Chinese pilgrim monk, Xuan Zang, visited Afghanistan in the seventh century AD, as attested by the pilgrim's travel notes. He describes that great many monasteries were ubiquitous in Bamiyan, and the smaller statue at Bamiyan (35 metres in height) and the stupa at its feet (no longer in existence) which were to become the cynosure of the Buddhist past of Afghanistan. Bamiyan valley in those far-off days was a great seat of culture, comparable to Nalanda, Ajantha, Ellora, Odanpura, Wikremashila of India and Mahavihara, Abhayagiri Vihara, Jetawana Vihara of Anruadhapura of Sri Lanka and also to Cittalapabbata of Mahagama of Rohana, in the southern province of Sri Lanka. Bamiyan, lying on the trade route linking India with Balkh, through which trade in spices, pearls, ivory and cotton raw material were traded and it was also on the famous Chinese Silk Route, that linked Mid-west Asia with the Chinese Empire and other East Asian empires.

History has it that the pearls, gems, cotton ivory and spices were from Sri Lanka being transited through South Indian ports from the great port of Sri Lanka, Mahatittha (Mannar) on the west coast of Sri Lanka, now a buried port city. This trade rendezvous of Bamiyan continued until the invasion of Genghis Khan in the early part of the thirteenth century and as very correctly said by Jawaharlal Nehru in his book, Discovery of India, "The dagger of Islamic invasion went through the heart of India" and this was fate of Afghanistan too.

Bamiyan is only 145 miles north of Kabul and a motor-road, now occupied by the Taliban demons, leads to it through the picturesque valleys of Kohdanan and Ghoraband. At a distance of about 110 miles from Kabul there is a deep ascent, named Shibar Pass, which is snow-capped in winter. About 19 miles ahead of this Pass, the road branches off; one to the right leads to Mazar-Sharif and Katghan, while the other to the left leads to Bamiyan. The road to Bamiyan runs parallel to the river of Bamiyan and girdles the range of hills. After six miles and old mud fort on a steep rock is called the city of Zahak-I*Msran. From thenceforth, the valley widens and the city of caves, where once reclusive Buddhist monks would have lived in meditation, appears. This is the historic city of Bamiyan, lying at the foot of a reddish hills, some 9,000 ft above mean sea level, which also forms the dividing line between the gigantic mountain ranges - the Hindu Kush and the Koh-i-Baba.

The valley of Bamiyan, sunk deep in the pleateau, is between 8,000 and 9,000 ft above mean sea level. To the south is the snow-capped range of Kh-i-Baba range running to 16,000 to 17,000 feet. The passes, the hilly ranges, valleys and the girdling river give Bamiyan the ideal backdrop to a Buddhist centre of learning and orectic and it was undoubtedly a glorious centre of Buddhism, that enveloped the entire Afghanistan, until Islamic invasions took over Afghanistan. Little is left of the ancient city, being victimised by barbaric fundamentalists and still the capital exists, known now as Shahr-i-Ghulghols (City of Uproars). Gigantic statues of Buddha (53 and 35 metres in height) with smaller ones in different directions are carved out of the sedimentary rock on the sides of the Bamiyan gorge.

These statues once coated with reinforcements to withstands the rigours of climatic changes in this hilly terrain, were a source of inspiration and religious fervour for the sore-footed weary pilgrim who, trotted over the land with just a sack tied to a walking stick and held on the shoulder, for there were no vehicles to travel but just a donkey to be their pack animal and companion through the desolate human unfriendly terrain and weather gods. Xuan Zang, who saw these stupendous monasteries and statues and other Buddhist artifacts in 630 AD said very laconically and implicitly, "The Golden Line Sparks on Every Side". The two masdove statues (175 ft and 125 ft in height) were begun in the second century AD under the patronage of Emperor Kanishka and the several others, probably in the fourth or fifth centuries AD. The niches of the Buddha statues carry, now marred, beautiful frescoes, giving the archaeologist a pointer as to the path arts of India found its way to Afghanistan and percolated it with Greek, Roman and Sassanian elements prior to it being conveyed to China and Japan through Sinkiang. The early Moslem writers (prior to the thirteenth century AD) speak in glorious terms.

One writer, Yaquibi, describes it in detail and mention the frescoes that adorned the niches of the caves where statues of the Buddha were depoited. He says, the inhabitants called the big statue the "Red Buddha" and the smaller one the "Grey Buddha". Early in the thirteenth century, the city of Bamiyan and all its inhabitants were swept off the face of the valley by Genghis Khan, the Mongol. The legend has it that his grandson, Mutugen, son of Jaghati, was killed in action during the siege of Bamiyan. When the town surrendered after a long and arduous battle, Genghis, the revengeful fiend of fundamentalism in its early dressing ordered that no living being, man or animal, was to be spared. The ruined town was named Mao - Baligh (The Bad Town). How true are the words of the savant Jawaharlal Nehru, today it is not the dagger but gun powder and mortars that destroy the Buddhist cultural heritage of their own ancestors by the barbaric Taliban. It is time that the all governments of the world take cognisance of this "Cultural Cleansing" and action similar to those in Kosovo - "Serbia Ethnic Cleansing" be taken against the Taliban, as the freedom of religion and cultural heritage of the human race are in jeopardy and other similar organisations would take a leaf off the book of Taliban demons.

BUDDHISM IN RUSSIA

Historically, Buddhism was incorporated into Russian lands as early as the late 16th century, when Russian explorers travelled to and settled in Siberia and what is now the Russian Far East. It is also believed that Indian King Ashoka had sent monks to spread Buddhism all over the world including Siberia. Mongolian and Tibetan lamas first appeared on the eastern shores of Lake Baikal in the middle of the 17th century and quickly spread Buddhism in the area. Later in that century Buddhism emerged as the dominant religion in Tuva. The Kalmyks who migrated from China to the lower reaches of the Volga River in the later half of the 17th century also professed Buddhism. Tzarist authorities were fairly tolerant with respect to Buddhists.

Buddhist monasteries, or datsans - appeared in other areas of Buryatia, too. Within a short time most of the Buryats living east of Lake Baikal were converted to Buddhism. In 1764, Zayaagiyn Damba Darjaa, the high priest of the Tsongol datsan - the oldest in the Baikal region - became head of the entire Buddhist clergy with the title Bandida Khamba Lama. In the late sixteenth century the Kalmyks were converted to Buddhism by Mongolian lamas in Dzungaria (China). In the seventeenth century, they moved to the lower reaches of the Volga River, retaining their religion. At that time the Kalmyks gained access to the first works of Buddhist literature translated from the Tibetan language.

The main form of Buddhism in Russia is the Gelukpa school of Tibetan Buddhism. Although Tibetan Buddhism is most often associated with the peoples of Tibet, in the north the school spread into southwestern and northern China, Mongolia, and finally Russia. In the south, it took hold in Bhutan and parts of northern India and Nepal.

Afterwards, it began to spread into the geographically and culturally adjacent Russian constituent regions known today as: Amur Oblast, Buryatia, Chita Oblast, Tuva Republic, and Khabarovsk Krai. There is also Kalmykia, another constituent republic of Russia that is in fact the only Buddhist region in Europe, perhaps paradoxically located to the north of the Caucasus. Buddhism has been in Russia for four centuries.

In the second half of the XVIIth century Buryats were incorporated into Russia. Beginning from 1727 when the treaty determining the borders between Russia and Manchu-Chinese empires was signed the Buryats started the official development within the Russian state. In Czarist Russia, where Orthodoxy was the predominant state religion, Buddhists were subjected to certain restrictions. Buddhist monks (lamas) were made dependent on the local police and were subordinated to the chief provincial board. The regulations for the lamaist clergy, introduced in 1853, established the almost despotic reign of officials under the czar. The latter made the most important assignments concerning even the clerical posts; in official documents the Buddhists like all non-Orthodox Christians were called "otherbelievers", or "the followers of the alien belief" (Russian: *inovertsi*) and the religious problems of the Buddhist were the concern of a special department for foreign religions. Nevertheless, Buddhism began spreading among the Buryats in the 17th century and became an essential and significant element of social, spiritual and material life of most Buryat ethnic groups, and has played a great role in their political and spiritual consolidation. This process of consolidation was stimulated by the formation of a centralized system of the Buryat Buddhist religious administrative structure.

The spread of the Shambhala myth and the Kalachakra Tantra in the West has a history of its own. It does definitely not first begin with the expulsion of the lamas from

Tibet (in 1959) and their diaspora across the whole world, but rather commences at the beginning of the twentieth century in Russia with the religious political activity of an ethnic Buryat by the name of Agvan Dorjiev. He was convinced that the union of Tibet with Russia would provide the Highlands with an extremely favorable future, and was likewise able to convince the hierarchy upon the Lion Throne of the merits of his political vision for a number of years. He thus advanced to the post of Tibetan envoy in St. Petersburg and at the Russian court. His work in the capital was extremely active and varied. Since the end of the 19th century Buddhism had become fashionable among the Russian high society.

Tibetan medical doctor Peter Badmayev was head of the most famous private hospital in St. Petersburg. There the cabinet lists for the respective members of government were put together under his direction. R. Fülöp-Miller has vividly described the doctor's power-political activities: "In the course of time medicine and politics, ministerial appointments and 'lotus essences' became more and more mingled, and a fantastic political magic character arose, which emanated from Badmajev's sanatorium and determined the fate of all Russia. The miracle-working doctor owed this influence especially to his successful medical-political treatment of the Tsar. Badmajev's mixtures, potions, and powders brewed from mysterious herbs from the steppes served not just to remedy patient's metabolic disturbances; anyone who took these medicaments ensured himself an important office in the state at the same time" (Fülöp-Miller, 1927,).

For this "wise and crafty Asian" too, the guiding idea was the establishment of an Asian empire with the "White Tsar" at its helm. Buryats had received initiations into the Time Tantra from the Ninth Panchen Lama which were supposed to have been of central significance for Russias future vision. At the center of Agvan Dorjiev 's activities in Russia stood the construction of the Buddhist temple in St. Petersburg. The shrine was dedicated to the Kalachakra deity. A painter by the name of Nicholas Roerich, who later became a fanatic propagandist for Kalachakra doctrine, produced the designs for the stained-glass windows. Work commenced in 1909. In the central hall various main gods from the Tibetan pantheon were represented with statues and pictures, including among others Dorjiev's wrathful initiation deity, Vajrabhairava. Regarding the décor, it is perhaps also of interest that there was a swastika motif which the Bolsheviks knocked out during the Second World War.

Stalinist secret police agents tried to oppress all religious groups, leading to a decline in Buddhism. Tibetan Buddhism is primarily practiced by the indigenous peoples in various regions of central and eastern Russia, except for a few Russian converts based mainly in the larger cities such as St. Petersburg or Moscow, where there is greater access to urban Buddhist centers or similar facilities.

The other major form of Buddhism found in Russia is the more commonly known Mahayana Buddhism, primarily practiced by the Vietnamese or Chinese immigrant communities based mainly in the large cities.

The Russian Federation and Austria are the only two European states today that recognize Buddhism as an "official", though not necessarily "state religion" in their respective countries. On top of that, Russia also recognizes it, along with Islam, Judaism, and of course Orthodox Christianity, as native to Russian soil in the 1993 Constitution of the Russian Federation. All other religious groups are unrecognized, and must officially register and be subject to rejection by the state.

There are a few dozen Buddhist university-monasteries throughout Russia, but concentrated in the Russian Far East and Siberia, known in Russian as Datsans. Adherents to Buddhism account for approximately 700,000 in the Russian Federation, about 0.5% of the total population.

Organizations: The highest authority for Russian Buddhists is the Central Buddhist Board based in the Ivolga Datsan in the Buryat. (A permanent office in Moscow is concerned with external relations). The congress of clergy and laity convenes once in four years and elects the members of the Board. Head of the Central Buddhist Board is Bandida Khambo-lama.

Russian Buddhism is representative of the Gelugpa school ("the School of Virtue"), which is a branch of Tibetan Buddhism in the Mahayana tradition, that is, "the broad path" of salvation from endless rebirth in the world of suffering. Russian Buddhism has a number of specific ritual peculiarities that have taken shape over the course of history. Historically it has been marked by the prevalence of rural lamas living outside datsans because of the nomadic way of life. To some extent, this tradition has survived to this day. In keeping with tradition, six major holidays, khurals, are celebrated annually and are attended by a large number of people who bring various gifts to datsans as well as money and food for lamas.

Tsagaalgan is a holiday celebrated on the eve of the lunar new year, which usually falls in February. This khural is devoted to the twelve miracles of Buddha during his dispute with six preachers of heresy. Services and a series of religious rites are conducted to mark the occasion. Buddhists, dressed in their best clothes, come to pray together for well-being and more happiness. On the eve of the new year, a solemn evening ritual is performed during which food is served to the doksheetsi, the protectors of the faith. This involves the ritual burning of Dugzhub, a magic pyramid of paper and wood; according to a Buddhist belief, a ritual fire consumes all evil thoughts.

A long note from a big white conch proclaims the first day of the lunar new year. A traditional service is held to celebrate the Sagaan Sar ("white month") holiday.

In the main temple lamas, replacing one another, pray for fifteen days for peace and goodness. The khural Duyn-khor, a second major holiday, lasts three days in April. It is dedicated to the preaching of the sacred teaching of Kalachakra.

The third major holiday is Gandun-Shunserme, devoted to the birth and enlightenment of Buddha and his attainment of nirvana. It is celebrated in early summer.

The fourth holiday Maidari is dedicated to Maidari, the Buddha of the future (Maitreia). It is always celebrated for two days in midsummer. People spend the first day in many hours of devout prayer. On the second day the gilded statue of Maidari is solemnly carried out of the temple and placed on a chariot twined with silk ribbons. It is surrounded by lamas in ceremonial dress. A green horse of plaster is harnessed to the chariot, and the procession sets off around the datsan. This ceremony symbolizes Maidari's tour of the universe and the spread of his grace throughout it. Several thousand people gather in the datsan for the procession. Akharang, a big copper shield, is struck with a mallet, and its sounds can be heard far away. There is a fanfare, the drums roll, and conchs are blown. The procession stops at every turn of the monastery walls for a reading of sacred Scriptures. Many Buddhists attending the procession try to approach the chariot, to hold onto its beam and harness, and to throw money at the feet of the statue of Maidari.

The last two khurals are celebrated with less splendor, but they also attract large crowd of believers. Lhabab Düisen, marked in autumn, is devoted to the Buddha's return from the thirty-third heaven. The holiday Zula is dedicated to the passing away of the father of Lamaism,Bogdo Tsongkhapa. A thousand candles are lit during the service.

During the khurals prayers are said in honor of the protectors of the faith and for well-being and peace on earth.

Lamas who live in monasteries observe the Dulva, a traditional moral and ethical code. Depending on the level of ordination, they participate in services and philosophical discussions and perform special religious rites at the people's request.

Recently, in addition to Buryats, Kalmyks, and Tuvinians, more and more Russians, Ukrainians have been attending Buddhist services. Previously, they all went to pray at the Ivolga datsan, but today, with the 1991 reopening of the temple in Leningrad, followers of Buddhism from the European part of the country will travel there, too.

BUDDHISM IN SCIENCE

In Russia, academic Buddhist studies began from the middle of the 19th century. By the end of the century, the Russian Buddhological School had won international prestige. With the discovery of Buddhist manuscripts in Central Asia at the beginning of the 20th Century, a new stage in the study of Buddhism began. The Central Asian, Sak and Uyghur Buddhist texts with their Chinese and Tibetan translations have been published. The international series *Bibliotheca Buddnica,* founded in Russia by S.F. Oldendurg and F.I. Tsherbatsky became the center of Buddhist studies; attracting the greatest scholars of the world: L. de La Vallee Poussen, Max Walleser, Sylvan Levi and others.

From 1897 to 1937, the most important Buddhist texts in Sanskrit, Tibetan and Uyghur on Buddhist philosophy, logic, etc. were printed in a 30-volume series. In 1960, V.N. Toporov published a translation of *Dhammapada,* becoming the 31st volume, and A.I. Vostrikov's book *The Tibetan Historical Literature* became the 32nd. Many of the works published, particularly on Buddhist logic, have been regarded as unsurpassed. In the enormous volume of buddhological works, the quantitative contribution of Russian scientists has been rather modest, but their qualificative aspect is of high value.

In 1985 with the publication of the *Monuments of the Indian Texts from Central Asia* by G.M. Bongard-Levin and M.I. Vorobyova-Desyatovskaya the edition of this series was continued. Later on a few other publications appeared. Among them one can mention the study and the translation from Sanskrit of the first part of the *Abhidharmakosa* done by V.I. Rudoi (BB, vol. 35), the translation from the Pali of the *The Questions of Milinda* (Milindapanhi) carried out by A.V. Paribok (BB, vol. 36) and also the publication of the work by the Chinese author Huei Tsyao: *Biographies of the Distinguished Monks*(Gao Sen Chuan) carried out by M.E.Ermakov.

At present Buddhism is studied at research centers in Moscow, St. Petersburg, as well as in Ulan-Ude, Elista and Kyzyl. The buddhologists in Moscow concentrate their efforts on the role of the Buddhist cult as well as the place and role of Buddhism in social and political life of Asian countries, and its influence on the culture and traditions of oriental peoples. In St. Petersburg, scholars are mainly engaged in deciphering ancient Indian inscriptions and textological research in the field of Buddhist art and old Uyghur, Tibetan, Mongolian and Chinese texts and treatises. In buddhological studies —mainly pursuing the fields of sinology and indology— notable achievements have been made; whereas in the fields of Tibetan and Mongolian studies, the scope of research has not been so broad. Nevertheless, all the buddhological studies are closely interrelated. A great many texts in the Tibetan language, translated from Sanskrit, are accessible now; though their original texts in Sanskrit have been lost. Therefore the value of these Tibetan texts becomes all the more significant. The fact that in Russia, there is a living tradition of Tibetan Buddhism, spread among Buryats, Kalmycks and Tyvanians, greatly contributed to the development of Tibetan and Mongolian studies, and within their frame to the buddhological studies.

Buddhism in Buryatia, a region in Central Asia and Southern Siberia, which was the northern-most point of the spread of Buddhism. The Buryats were, and are still are the largest Buddhist population in Russia. The Buryats, Kalmycks and the Tyvanians are the three Buddhist nationalities in Russia, historically belonging to the common Mongolian spiritual realm and to the Tibetan and Mongolian cultural and religious tradition of the great Central Asian civilization. Tibetan religious and cultural influence has been playing, up to now, an important role in the culture and history of these peoples.

In the beginning, Buddhist monasteries were the centers, not only of culture and learning, but in fact they became moral and ethical regulators of everyday life of Buryat families. Buddhism stimulated the formation of the nation's intellectual potential. There appeared different monastic educational faculties with many learned monks and scholars. Among them we can mention Agvan Dorjiev (1857-1930), one of the tutors of the 13th Dalai Lama, who was his representative in the Russian court and played a great role in

Tibet's international political life, establishing various relations between Tibet and Russia. By the beginning of the century, Buddhism had become quite strong and this caused the anxiety on the part of the Christian church.

In order to adapt the Buddhist teaching and church to the rapidly developing and changing world, Agvan Dorjiev and some prominent Buryat scholars initiated a modernization movement among Buddhist clergy and intellectuals, proclaiming the necessity of combining the Buddhist philosophy with the best achievements of Western culture and civilization. The movement has gained a wide scope in Buryatia. It was due to the fact of mutual interest of both: the Buddhist clergy wanted to preserve somehow the church, by means of modification, whereas local intelligentsia regarded Buddhist ideas as a cultural and social basis for further national development after being freed from pagan elements.

Though "modernists" played an important role in the national liberation movement of Buryats and promoted national and cultural autonomy of Buryats within the Russian Federation and establishing of the Buryat-Mongolian Autonomous Republic after the revolution, still the movement was doomed to failure because it was unrealistic to expect gaining self-administration for Buryat people by means of religious reforms and revival of national culture neither before the revolution nor after it. The attempt of these "modernists" to emphasize similarity of ideas in Marxism and early Buddhism also failed. This movement is all the more noteworthy because no comparable developments took place in Tibetan Buddhism until after the confrontation with Chinese communism in 1949. By 1935 there were about 45 or 46 Buddhist temples and monasteries in Buryatia.

BIBLIOGRAPHY

Adikaram, E.W. (1953) *Early History of Buddhism in Ceylon,* (2nd ed.) Colombo: Gunasena.

Anisaki Masaharu (1916) *Nichiren: The Buddhist Prophet,* reprint Gloucester, Massachussets (1966).

Aris, Michael (1978) *Bhutan, the Early History of a Himalayan Kingdom,* Warminster, UK: Aris & Phillips.

________________ (1994) Raven *Crown: The Origins of Buddhist Monarchy in Bhutan,* London: Serindia.

Banerjee, A.C. (1957) *Sarvastivada Literature,* Calcutta.

Basham, A. L. (1954) *The Wonder That Was India,* London.

Beyer, Stephan V. (1973) *The Cult of Tara: Magic and Ritual in Tibet,* Berkeley: University of California Press.

Chakravarti, Uma (1987) *The Social Dimensions of Early Buddhism,* New Delhi: Oxford University Press.

Ch'en Kenneth (1964) *Buddhism in China: A Historical Survey,* Princeton.

Cozort, Daniel (1986) Highest *Yoga Tantra: An Introduction to Esoteric Buddhism of Tibet,* Ithaca, NY: Snow Lion.

Dasgupta, Shashi Bhusan (1974) An *Introduction to Tantric Buddhism.* 3rd ed. Calcutta: University of Calcutta.

Dutt, Nalinaksha (1970) *Buddhist Sects in India,* Calcutta.

Dutt, Sukumar (1957) *The Buddha and Five After-Centuries,* London.

________________ (1962) *Buddhist Monks and Monasteries of India,* London: G. Allen and Unwin.

Gombrich, Richard F. (1996) *How Buddhism Began: The Conditioned Genesis of the Early Teachings,* London: Athlone.

________________ (1988) *Theravada Buddhism: A Social History from Ancient Benares to Modern Colombo,* London: Routledge and Kegan Paul.

Grousset, Rene (1931) *The Civilizations of the East, vol.* 2, India, London.

Hanayama Shinsho (1960) *A History of Japanese Buddhism,* Tokyo.

Hazra, Kanai Lal (1982) *History of Theravada Buddhism in South-East Asia: With Special Reference to India and Ceylon,* New Delhi: Munshiram Manoharlal.

Hirakawa, Akira (1974-1979) Indo bukkyoshi, 2 vols., Tokyo.

Hirakawa, Akira (1990) A *History of Indian Buddhism: From Sakyamuni to Early Mahayana,* Honolulu: University of Hawaii Press.

Holt, John Clifford (1996) *The Religious World of Kirti Sri: Buddhism, Art, and Politics in Late Medieval Sri Lanka,* New York: Oxford University Press.

Hopkins, Jeffrey (1985) *The Kalacakara Tantra,* trans. London.

Horner, I.B. (1936) *Early Buddhist Theory of Man Perfected,* London.

Jayatilleke, K.N. (1963) *Early Buddhist Theory of Knowledge,* London.

Joshi, Lal Mani (1967) *Studies in the Buddhistic Culture of India, During the 7th and 8th Centuries A.D.* Delhi: Motilal Banarsidass.

——————— (1967) *Studies in the Buddhistic Culture of India,* Delhi.

King, Winston Lee (1980) *Theravada Meditation: The Buddhist Transformation of Yoga,* University Park: Pennsylvania State University Press.

Kitagawa, Joseph M. (1966) *Religion in Japanese History,* New York.

Law, B.C. (ed.) (1931) *Buddhistic Studies,* Calcutta.

Legge, James (1886) *A Record of Buddhist Kingdoms,* Oxford.

Lester Robert C (1973) *Theravada Buddhism in Southeast Asia,* Ann Arbor.

Malalgoda, K. (1976) *Buddhism in Sinhalese Society, 1750-1900.* Berkeley: University of California Press.

Masuda Jiryo, (1925) 'Origins and Doctrines of Early Indian Buddhist Schools', *Asia Major, vol. 2, pp.1-78.*

Matsunaga, Alicia (1969) The *Buddhist Philosophy of Assimilation,* Tokyo.

McGovern W.M. (1922) *An Introduction to Mahayana Buddhism,* New York.

Miler, Robert J. (1959) *Monasteries and Culture Change in Mongolia,* Wiesbaden.

Mitra, Rajendaralala (1971) *The Sanskrit Buddhist Literature of Nepal,* Calcutta.

Mullin, Glenn H. (1986) *Death and Dying: The Tibetan Tradition,* East Grinstead, W. Sussex: New Knowledge Books.

Nakamura Hajime (1980) *Indian Buddhism: A Survey with Bibliographical Notes,* Tokyo.

Narain, A.K. (1980) *Studies in History of Buddhism,* Delhi: B.R. Pub. Corp.

Radhakrishnan, Sarvepalli (1927) Indian Philosophy, vol.1 (2nd ed.), London.

Rahula, Walpola (1956) *History of Buddhism in Ceylon,* Colombo: Gunasena.

——————— (1974) *What the Buddha Taught* (Rev. ed.) New York: Grove.

Rao, S. K. Ramachandra (1979) *Tibetan Meditation: Theory and Practice,* New Delhi: Arnold-Heinemann.

Ray, Reginald A. (1994) *Buddhist Saints in India: A Study in Buddhist Values and Orientations,* New York: Oxford University Press.

Reynolds, Frank E (1981) *Guide to Buddhist Religion,* Boston.

Rhys Davids, T.W. (1903) *Buddhist India,* London.

Robinson, Richard H., and Willard Johnson (1982) *The Buddhist Religion: A Historical Introduction* (3rd ed.) Belmont, CA: Wadsworth.

Ruegg, David S. (1967) *The Study of Indian and Tibetan Thought,* Leiden.

_______________ (1981) *The Literature of the Madhyamaka School of Philosophy in India,* Wiesbaden.

Sarao, K.T.S., (ed.) (1995) A *Textbook of the History of Theravada Buddhism,* Delhi: University of Delhi.

Saunders, E. Dale (1964) *Buddhism in Japan,* Philadelphia.

Seneviratne, H. L. (1978) *Rituals of the Kandyan State,* Cambridge: Cambridge University Press.

Skilton, Andrew (1994) *A Concise History of Buddhism.* Birmingham: Windhorse.

Snellgrove, David L. (ed.) (1957) *Buddhist Himalaya,* Oxford.

_______________ (1984) Indo-*Tibetan Buddhism: Indian Buddhists and their Tibetan Successors,* Boston: Shambhala.

Snellgrove, David, and Hugh Richardson (1968) *A Cultural History of Tibet,* New York: F.A. Praeger.

Streng, Frederick J. (1967) *Emptiness: A Study in Religious Meaning,* Nashville.

Suzuki, B.L. (1938) *Mahayana Buddhism* (3rd ed.), NewYork.

Thomsen Harry (1963) *The New Religions of Japan: Rutland,* Vt.

Tucci, Giuseppe (1949) *Tibetan Painted Scrolls, 2 vols.* translated by Virginia Vacca, Rome.

Varma, V.P. (1973) *Early Buddhism and Its Origins,* New Delhi.

Warder, Anthony Kennedy (1980) *Indian Buddhism* (2nd ed.) Delhi: Motilal Banarsidass.

Watters, Thomas (1904-1905) *On Yuan Chwang's Travel in India, 2 vols.* London.

Wayman, Alex (1973) *The Buddhist Tantras: Light on Indo-Tibetan Esotericism,* New York.

INDEX